EXPERIMENTAL & PROTOTYPE
U.S. Air Force Jet Fighters

Dennis R. Jenkins and Tony R. Landis

ISBN-13   978-1-58007-111-6

Item Number SP111

specialtypress
PUBLISHERS AND WHOLESALERS

39966 Grand Avenue
North Branch, MN 55056 USA
(651) 277-1400 or (800) 895-4585
www.specialtypress.com

Printed in China

Distributed in the UK and Europe by:

Midland Publishing
4 Watling Drive
Hinckley LE10 3EY, England
Tel: 01455 233 747 Fax: 01455 233 737
www.midlandcountiessuperstore.com

Library of Congress Cataloging-in-Publication Data

Jenkins, Dennis R.
  Experimental and prototype U.S. Air Force jet fighters / Dennis R. Jenkins and Tony R. Landis.
    p. cm.
  Includes bibliographical references.
  ISBN 978-1-58007-111-6
 1. Fighter planes--United States--History. 2. Research aircraft--United States--History. 3. Jet planes, Military--United States--History. I. Landis, Tony. II. Title.

UG1242.F5J4598 2008
623.74'640973--dc22
                    2007051838

On the Front Cover: *The Convair XF-92A (46-682) on the seaplane ramp at the Convair facility in San Diego, California.* (San Diego Air & Space Museum via Robert E. Bradley)

On the Front Dust Jacket Flap: *The first four production Century Series designs. Of the aircraft pictured, only the first XF-104A (53-7786) is a prototype.* (AFFTC History Office Collection)

On the Front Endsheet: *Inboard profile of the proposed Convair XP-92 ducted-rocket-powered interceptor. This design never progressed past the mockup stage, although the XF-92A aerodynamic demonstrator was flight-tested.* (National Records Center, St. Louis)

On the Front Page: *The "fighter circle" showing most of the fighters tested at Edwards during the 1950s. Clockwise from the top: F-86D, F-89, F-94C, F-100, F-101A, F-102A, F-104A, YF-105, F-106A, F-80C, F-84F, and F-86F.* (AFFTC History Office Collection)

On the Title Page: *The first YF-12A (60-6934) in its natural titanium and black paint scheme. Photos have recently surfaced showing the aircraft did not have the black fuselage chines for at least its initial flight.* (Lockheed Martin)

On the Last Page: *One of the Northrop YF-17s at sunset.* (National Archives)

On the Back Endsheet: *Inboard profiles of the Convair XP-81 and Republic XF-103. Both aircraft used unusual powerplant combinations, and neither made it into production.* (National Records Center, St. Louis)

On the Back Cover:
Top: *The second General Dynamics YF-16 (72-1568) showing its innovative "broken sky" camouflage scheme that, unfortunately, did not seem to work all that well in the desert sky over Edwards.* (National Archives)

Bottom Right: *An early artist rendering of the F-108 shows a delta canard and three vertical stabilizers. This concept was continually refined into the design that was shown at the mockup inspection.* (Boeing Historical Archives)

TABLE OF CONTENTS

AUTHORS' PREFACE – A LONG, HARD ROAD VII

INTRODUCTION – ENTER, THE JET FIGHTER VIII
    Gas Turbine Engines x
    Designation Systems xiii
    Naming Conventions xv

CHAPTER 1 – INNOVATIVE DEAD ENDS 1
    Vultee XP-54 "Swoose Goose" 1
    Curtiss XP-55 Ascender 6
    Northrop XP-56 10
    McDonnell XP-67 "Bat" 14
    Vultee XP-68 17

CHAPTER 2 – THE FIRST JETS 19
    Bell XP-59A Airacomet 24
    Northrop XP-79B 32
    Lockheed XP-80 Shooting Star 42
    Convair XP-81 52
    Bell XP-83 60
    Republic XP-84 Thunderjet / YF-84F Thunderstreak 64
    McDonnell XP-85 Goblin 80
    North American XP-86 Sabre 86

CHAPTER 3 – ALL-WEATHER FIGHTERS 95
    Curtiss XP-87 Blackhawk 96
    Northrop XF-89 Scorpion 102
    Lockheed YF-94 108
    North American YF-95A (YF-86D) Sabre 113
    Lockheed YF-97A (YF-94C) Starfire 113

CHAPTER 4 – POINT-DEFENSE INTERCEPTORS 115
    Republic XP-91 "Thunderceptor" 115
    Convair XF-92A 122

CHAPTER 5 – PENETRATION FIGHTERS 131
    McDonnell XF-88 132
    Lockheed XP-90 138
    North American YF-93A (F-86C) 144
    Republic XF-96A (XF-84F) Thunderstreak 147

CHAPTER 6 – MISSILES? 149
    Hughes XF-98 Falcon 149
    Boeing / MARC XF-99 Bomarc 153

CHAPTER 7 – CENTURY SERIES FIGHTERS **157**
Development Lament 158
The Cook-Craigie Plan 158
North American YF-100 Super Sabre 160
McDonnell F-101 Voodoo 164
Lockheed XF-104 Starfighter 166
Republic YF-105 Thunderchief 172
North American F-107A (F-100B) "Ultra Sabre" 176
XF-109 180

CHAPTER 8 – CENTURY SERIES INTERCEPTORS **183**
SAGE   (Semi-Automatic Ground Environment) 184
Convair YF-102 Delta Dagger 185
Republic XF-103 192
Convair F-106 Delta Dart 197

CHAPTER 9 – LONG-RANGE INTERCEPTORS **199**
North American XF-108 Rapier 200
Lockheed YF-12A 204

CHAPTER 10 – THE END OF AN ERA **209**
McDonnell F-110 Spectre 210
General Dynamics F-111 Aardvark 214
Northrop F-5 Freedom Fighter / F-20 Tigershark 215

CHAPTER 11 – ANOTHER REVOLUTION **221**
McDonnell F-15 Eagle 223
General Dynamics YF-16 Fighting Falcon 224
Northrop YF-17 Cobra 228

CHAPTER 12 – THE STEALTH GENERATION **231**
Lockheed Stealth Fighter 232
HAVE BLUE Demonstrators 232
F-117A 233
Advanced Tactical Fighter 233
Lockheed Martin YF-22 235
Northrop YF-23 237
Joint Strike Fighter 240
Boeing X-32 240
Lockheed X-35 242

APPENDIX A – COMPANY HISTORIES **245**

APPENDIX B – NOTES AND CITATIONS **251**

APPENDIX C – INDEX **257**

Authors' Preface

A LONG, HARD ROAD

The title of the book says it covers "Experimental and Prototype U.S. Air Force Jet Fighters," and this is mostly true. A few of the final piston-engine prototypes are also covered, partly as an introduction to the jets that followed, but mostly because we think they are interesting and had a good selection of photographs to show. In any case, the selection of aircraft was somewhat arbitrary. Although the first criteria was that the aircraft should have an "XF" or "YF" (or "XP/YP") designation, a few aircraft are included that did not carry the desired designation, but should have. There are also probably a few aircraft that are missing – particularly prototype production variants (an example would include the YF-94C – we included that one, but probably missed others). The process became a little harder for later designs, since the Air Force frequently did not label the first aircraft as "XF" or "YF" (for example, there was no XF-15 or YF-15) for political reasons. We included some that interested us; we skipped others that have been well covered elsewhere.

This is not intended to be the ultimate or final history of experimental and prototype Air Force jet fighters. The project actually began as a photo scrapbook, intended to show seldom-seen photographs of these aircraft. While searching for photos in various archives, new data was uncovered about many of the designs, so we decided to expand the project and provide a limited narrative on each type, as well as some explanation about why the Air Force believed it needed the aircraft to begin with, and the ultimate outcome of each program. In some cases, we are able to correct discrepancies in previous published reports (for instance, the XP-79 was never intended to ram enemy aircraft, and the XRF-87A would not have been powered by four J47 engines). Other times, we may have erred, since our research was not exhaustive. We therefore caution the reader to use this book as a source, not necessarily the source.

The reader will also notice that the individual sections are somewhat uneven in their level of detail. In cases that we believed we had new information, we wrote a lot; in areas where we used already published sources, we were less verbose since we had nothing new to add to the discussion. Despite its limitations, we hope you enjoy the book.

Dennis R. Jenkins
Cape Canaveral, Florida

Tony R. Landis
Tehachapi, California

Contrary to many published reports, there is no evidence in the documentation indicating that the rocket-powered Northrop XP-79 (or the jet-powered XP-79B shown here) was ever intended to ram enemy aircraft. (Gerald H. Balzer Collection)

ENTER, THE JET FIGHTER

The progress made in developing jet fighters was truly amazing, at least up through the early 1960s. The XP-59A was, by all accounts, a truly marginal machine, in no way better than the piston-powered P-51. The F-80 was much better. The F-86 better still. The Century Series of fighters was the ultimate expression of turbojet engines, mechanical flight controls, and discrete function electronics. The next revolution, begun by the F-111 but embodied by the F-15 and F-16, introduced turbofan engines, composite materials, and integrated electronics. The F-22 added stealth, vectored thrust, and even more sophisticated electronics. The progress was amazing, but it took a lot of work.

Despite the United States claiming the first controlled powered flight – courtesy of the Wright Brothers – the Europeans soon gained the preeminent position in aeronautical technology. Indeed, U.S. aircraft manufacturers fell so far behind the Europeans that no American fighter design saw combat during World War I. The few U.S. squadrons that deployed to Europe flew foreign fighters, such as the French Spad and Nieuport 17. In fact, the only American aircraft that received widespread use during World War I was the Curtiss Jenny trainer.

Toward the end of the war, American companies began planning to produce French and British fighter designs under license, but the industry soon abandoned these efforts at the urging of the War Department, which favored indigenous designs. In an unusually farsighted decision, in 1915, Congress further encouraged the domestic industry by creating the National Advisory Committee for Aeronautics (NACA) to help regain aeronautical technology leadership. Despite significant assistance from the NACA, the U.S. aircraft industry continued to draw many aerodynamic and structural concepts from the Europeans. Nevertheless, the NACA developed several important breakthroughs, particularly streamlined engine cowlings and variable-pitch propellers. American companies also contributed significant innovations, such as multi-spar wings that found widespread use around the world by the late 1930s.

Despite the advance of technology, the basic open-cockpit, single-seat, single-engine, biplane fighter design changed little during the two decades following the end of World War I. This can be explained, at least partly, by the extremely small number of fighters procured by the United States. Out of roughly 1,400 aircraft in service with the U.S. Army Air Service in 1924, fewer than 80 were fighters. Throughout the early 1930s, the Army and Navy together fielded only five permanent fighter squadrons.

Because of the small production runs of any single type, few companies chose to specialize in fighters or even in military aircraft in general. Nonetheless, Curtiss emerged as the most successful developer of fighter aircraft, and versions of the Hawk series served as first-line fighters for the Army and Navy throughout the 1920s and 1930s. Boeing also became a leading fighter company with the P-12/F4B and P-26 "Pea Shooter."

During the mid-1930s, several technological innovations dramatically increased the performance of fighters for the first time since World War I. These new, all metal, monocoque, low-wing monoplane airplanes featured retractable landing gear, enclosed cockpits, and guns in the wings, quickly making the biplane fighters that preceded them obsolete. Interestingly, these rapid changes reduced the relative importance of the experienced industry leaders and opened the field to others. At the same time, the winds of war enveloping Europe spurred major rearmament programs that greatly expanded the number of companies that could be profitably supported.

Almost overnight, entirely new companies became major contenders. For instance, the company founded by Alexander P. de Seversky in February 1931, won an important fighter competition in 1936 by beating a Curtiss entry. The resulting P-35, designed largely by Alexander Kartveli, was the first U.S. Army Air Corps monoplane fighter with retractable landing gear and an enclosed cockpit. Lockheed, a struggling developer of commercial transports, won a 1937 Air Corps fighter competition with the radical twin-boom P-38 Lightning. At the same time, Lawrence Bell founded his company in

The first military aircraft built by the Bell Aircraft Company was the unusual YFM-1 Airacuda bomber-destroyer. (NMUSAF Archives)

July 1935, and developed the unorthodox twin-engine YFM-1 Airacuda using company funds. Only 13 Airacudas were produced, but Bell went on to build thousands of the mid-engine P-39 Airacobra and P-63 Kingcobra, mainly for foreign air forces.

Nevertheless, the former industry leaders did not just fade from sight. While Boeing committed most of its corporate resources to developing the B-17 Flying Fortress long-range bomber, Curtiss continued development of its Hawk series, leading to the P-40 that found fame in the Pacific during the early part of World War II.

The late 1930s also saw the emergence of some of the later legends among U.S. fighter manufacturers. North American Aviation, established in 1935 when the Air Mail Act forced a reorganization of the aviation industry, began modifying its NA-16 trainer into simple lightweight fighters. On the other side of the continent, James McDonnell resigned as chief engineer at the Glenn L. Martin Company and established his own operation in St. Louis during 1939. Over the next year, his small team of engineers submitted a dozen proposals to the Army and four to the Navy, most of which were for novel new fighter designs. All were rejected, but McDonnell persevered.

On the eve of Pearl Harbor, it remained unclear what companies would survive, but by the end of World War II, Lockheed, North American, and Republic (as Seversky had become) had risen as the most successful fighter manufacturers. The Lockheed P-38 played a critical role during the early stages of the war and remained in production throughout the conflict. However, the majority of observers agree that the most successful Army fighters were the Republic P-47 and the North American P-51. With a total production run of 15,683, the P-47 was the U.S. fighter produced in the greatest number. Although it enjoyed a slightly smaller production run of 14,855, the P-51 is generally considered the best mass produced fighter of the war.[1]

World War II also radically changed the essence of the American aircraft industry. The huge production runs transformed small-scale cottage companies into the largest mass-production industry in the world. Before 1940, typical production contracts were several dozen aircraft, whereas war production runs numbered in the thousands or tens of thousands. Prior to the war, the companies had frequently been run single-handedly by their founders, perhaps assisted by the chief engineer. This soon became impossible, and legions of young managers in complex organizational structures were supported by extensive engineering and technical staffs. Written procedures and detailed drawings replaced word-of-mouth communication and hands-on engineering supervision. Thus, the mobilization for World War II largely created the basic infrastructure used during the Cold War that came later.

The United States won World War II in large part by massively out producing both Germany and Japan, not by developing cutting-edge aeronautical technologies. By 1943, the United States had standardized on a small number of satisfactory military aircraft and emphasized maximizing production instead of designing the revolutionary aircraft frequently pursued by Germany. Ironically, although the United States produced some of the best operational fighters of the war, it had again fallen behind in advanced aeronautical technology.

Acknowledgements

Like any project of this magnitude, it would not have been possible without assistance from many friends and colleagues, plus several large organizations. The authors extend our gratitude to: Dave Arnold and Nicholas A. Veronico at Specialty Press, Gerald H. Balzer, Robert E. Bradley at the San Diego Air & Space Museum, Col. Walter J. Boyne (Air Force, Retired), Joseph D. Caver, Sylvester Jackson, and Archie Difante at the Air Force Historical Research Agency, Tony Chong, Mark Cleary at the 45th Space Wing History Office, Kev Darling, Ed Drumheller II, Mark L. Grills in the NASA Glenn Research Center archives, Erik Hehs, Wes Henry and Brett Stolle at the National Museum of the United States Air Force, Craig Kaston, Denny Lombard and Michael Moore at Lockheed Martin, Mike Lombardi and Tom Lubbesmeyer at the Boeing Archives in Seattle, Scott Lowther, Mike Machat, Pat McGinnis at the Boeing (Douglas) Archives in Long Beach, Jay Miller, Ken Neubeck, William J. Norton, Terry Panopalis, Stan Piet, David Robarge at the CIA, Joshua Stoff at the Cradle of Aviation Museum, Eric Voelz at NARA/St. Louis, Dr. James Young, Freida Johnson, Craig W. Luther, and Ray Puffer at the AFFTC History Office, the NASA Dryden Flight Research Center, and the staff in the Archives II still photo reading room.

Just before the beginning of World War II, the development of the gas turbine engine provided a clear but unrecognized commentary on aircraft design. Previously, airframe development had been limited by the available powerplants; every new operational requirement was keyed to the oft-tortuous development of a more powerful reciprocating engine. Frequently, airframe designers were too optimistic and anticipated greater power than was actually realized, and several otherwise satisfactory airplanes were underpowered and cancelled prior to production. The reason was simple: the design of powerful piston engines was more expensive and time-consuming than the design of airframes.

Despite the difficulties, increasingly more powerful piston engines were brought into production with larger displacement, increased supercharging, and vastly greater complexity. In England, the 24-cylinder Rolls-Royce Eagle ultimately achieved 3,450 horsepower, while in Germany the 28-cylinder BMW 803 radial engine recorded 3,950-hp. The similar 28-cylinder Pratt & Whitney R-4360 ultimately achieved 3,800-hp and became a workhorse engine in the post-war Convair B-36, Boeing B-50/C-97, and Douglas C-124.

The largest piston engine developed in the United States was the Lycoming XR-7755, a 7,755-cubic-inch, liquid-cooled, 36-cylinder, four-row radial engine that was intended to generate 7,000-hp. This huge engine was 10 feet long, 5 feet in diameter, and weighed 6,050 pounds. During testing, the prototype produced 5,000-hp at 2,600 rpm, using 580 gallons of high-octane avgas per-hour. Nine over-

The Lycoming XR-7755 was the largest piston engine developed in the United States, and was almost unthinkably complex. Only a single prototype was produced before the program ended. (NMUSAF Archives)

head camshafts could be shifted axially for maximum power in one position and cruise efficiently at the other. The complexity was almost unthinkable.

Development of the XR-7755 began at Lycoming in Williamsport, Pennsylvania, in the summer of 1943. Not even bench tested until after the war, the XR-7755 was the pinnacle of piston engine development but was never required, for which maintenance crews were undoubtedly grateful. With the end of World War II, the military no longer needed an engine of this size, and the single prototype now resides at the National Air and Space Museum in Washington, D.C.

Gas Turbine Engines

As piston engines increased in power, so to a greater degree did their mechanical complexity, weight, size, maintenance requirements, fuel consumption, and cost. The gas turbine engine arrived on the scene at a horsepower equivalent to the best reciprocating engines. In contrast to the complexity of the piston engine, the jet engine did not require the same investment in heavy manufacturing tools, and it was relatively simple and inexpensive to produce. Perhaps even more important, from the standpoint of absolute speed, the jet engine eliminated the need for a propeller, with its inherent complexity and limitations.

American engineers had been aware of the theoretical potential of gas turbine engines for some time. In fact, during the early 1940s, Hall Hibbard, Willis Hawkins, Clarence "Kelly" Johnson, Phil Coleman, and the forward-thinking Nathan C. Price at Lockheed conducted a preliminary design of what they believed was the next-generation combat aircraft. The outcome was the L-133, a jet fighter that used a rear-mounted straight main wing along with a forward canard. A pair of Lockheed-developed L-1000 axial-flow turbojet engines provided an estimated maximum speed of 600 mph. On 30 March 1942, Lockheed submitted an unsolicited proposal for the L-133 to the

Army. However, the expediencies of war and the need to produce existing combat types left few resources to pursue such a radical concept, and the L-133 became a footnote in history.

Given the urgency of war, it is a tribute to Sir Frank Whittle and Dr. Hans von Ohain that the development of the first jet engines was tolerated in their respective countries. The number of pioneers in the turbine engine field was very small; besides Whittle and von Ohain, the only contributor of comparable stature was Dr. Franz Anselm, who developed the axial-flow Junkers Jumo 004 used in the Messerschmitt Me 262. This, however, ignores Nathan Price at Lockheed, who did not seriously impact engine development, and the development team at Rolls-Royce, which did.

The industrial leadership established by the United States during the war would not be maintained easily in a world of rapidly changing technology. For the most part, U.S. companies were not well positioned to exploit the new technologies, most of which had been developed in Germany and the United Kingdom. However, the organizational structure and sheer size of U.S. industry, coupled with massive spending by the U.S. government, ensured American companies would move to the forefront of aeronautical technology.

After the war, the piston engine was quickly abandoned for fighters and then bombers; it wasn't long before transport and utility aircraft became turbine-powered. Designers were encouraged because, for the first time, engines and airframes could be designed almost in parallel, or so it seemed.

Industry exploited the situation with designs in numbers that probably will never be seen again. Jet engines appeared to be relatively simple to manufacture, and Allison, Curtiss-Wright, General Electric, Lycoming, Marquardt, Pratt & Whitney, and Westinghouse competed in virgin territory. Soon, however, the list began to dwindle as manufacturers found the engineering skill necessary to reach new levels of power and reliability was difficult to master. As had been the case with piston engines, the producers of turbine engines would ultimately shrink to two or three.

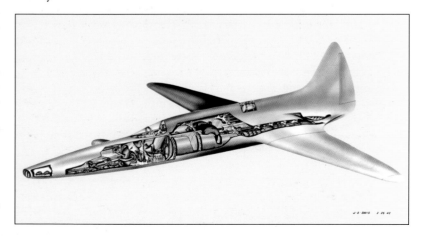

The Lockheed L-133 concept was an interesting blend of the old (straight wings) and the new (axial-flow turbojets), coupled with the unusual (the wing position and canards). (Lockheed Martin)

Lockheed L-100 Gas Turbine Engine

On 30 March 1942, Lockheed submitted preliminary model specifications for the L-133 jet-powered fighter to the Army. Given the pressure of producing combat aircraft, the Army expressed little interest in the L-133 itself, but the L-1000 axial-flow turbojet engines were intriguing. The primary features that interested the Army were the axial-flow compressor and the multi-stage turbine. At a meeting on 21 August 1942, researchers from Wright Field commented that the L-1000 appeared overly complicated, although Lockheed engineers believed them to be relatively simple. At this point, the engine was 24 inches in diameter, 139 inches long, and weighed 1,235 pounds. It was expected that the engine would develop 6,700-pounds-force (lbf) of thrust at takeoff and 2,200-lbf at 50,000 feet. Further investigation by Wright Field engineers revealed several flaws in the L-1000, but the Army felt the engine offered sufficient promise to warrant further development.[2]

Not everybody in the Army was happy about an airframe manufacturer developing an engine, although Northrop was also developing the Turbodyne turboprop around this time. The Power Plant Laboratory at Wright Field "did not believe it is good policy to encourage aircraft manufacturers to enter the field of aircraft engine manufacturing as their facilities are not adequate for engineering and manufacture of power plants, and thus additional facilities will have to be provided by the government." Ultimately, this scenario came to pass and significantly slowed progress on the L-1000 project.[3]

Letter contract W535-ac-40690 was issued on 19 June 1943 for a single L-1000 engine at a cost of $1,275,934 plus a four-percent fixed fee. Oddly, several weeks later Lockheed terminated the contract because it could not reach agreement with the Army on intellectual property rights. These disagreements were worked out and the contract was reinstated on 31 July 1944. At a meeting on 28 May 1945, Lockheed requested that the delivery date be extended from 1 August 1945 to 1 June 1946 and indicated the need for an additional $507,325 to complete the first engine. These changes were largely because the pressures of wartime production had made people and facilities unavailable for the advanced engine project. The Army agreed to the schedule change but declined to provide additional funds.[4]

As predicted by the Power Plant Laboratory, Lockheed did not have the specialized machine tools required to fabricate the L-1000. Consequently, Lockheed subcontracted about 60-percent of the project to the Menasco Manufacturing Company, also located in Burbank. About two-thirds of the parts required for the first engine were complete by September 1945 when Lockheed advised the Army that it intended to subcontract the entire assembly and test of the engine to Menasco. The Army concurred with this decision but warned Lockheed that it remained responsible for the ultimate performance of the contract. Lockheed had ultimate engineering responsibility, although Menasco would be granted non-exclusive license to manufacture the engine under Lockheed patents.[5]

In May 1946 the Army expected that the first L-1000 would be bench-tested in August 1946, and depending on the results of the initial tests, the engine could be sufficiently developed to power an experimental airplane about 18 months later. Some Army engineers, however, advised caution, stating, "any firm planning which is based on the successful realization of this engine should be approached with caution since there are several features incorporated in it which are highly desirable but possibly somewhat difficult to bring through." Nevertheless, on 6 June 1946 the Army provided an additional $1,937,000 to procure sufficient parts to assemble four XJ37 (as the L-1000 had been designated) engines with delivery expected in 12 months. Lockheed added that an initial production run of prototype engines could commence as soon as 1947 with about $5 million in additional funding.[6]

Initially, work at Menasco was delayed since the company was busy supplying high-precision components – mainly landing gear – to many of the Southern California airframe manufacturers. After V-E Day, the U.S. government began canceling many production contracts, freeing up resources at Menasco, but somehow this did not seem to speed up work on the L-1000 project. In February 1946, all Lockheed personnel assigned to the L-1000 project were transferred to Menasco, and a new facility in Burbank was dedicated to the development of the engine. This also seemed to make little difference.

At this point, it becomes difficult to trace the history of the L-1000, although it is widely reported that Menasco never assembled a complete engine; all photos (see the one below) seem to show a full-scale mockup, not an actual engine. In late 1946, the Wright Aeronautical Corporation received Army contract W33-038-ac-16288 to complete the development of the L-1000, but no record of their progress could be located. In any event, the first axial-flow turbojet designed in the United States never materialized as a production engine, and Lockheed quietly abandoned the jet engine business. That did not really matter, since by now the L-1000 had been largely overshadowed by the technologically inferior – but more developed – Whittle W.1 centrifugal-flow turbojet.

This L-1000 mockup shows a clean, modern-looking axial-flow engine compared to the centrifugal-flow turbojets of the era. (NMUSAF Archives)

North American Aviation emerged from World War II as one of the premiere fighter designers in the United States, having produced the P-51 Mustang and the first American swept-wing jet fighter, the F-86 Sabre. The YF-93 was the company's first attempt to capitalize on the lessons-learned from the F-86 to build a larger and higher-performance aircraft. Ultimately the YF-93 was not produced, leading North American to begin development of the F-100 Super Sabre. (Boeing Historical Archives)

The progress of fighter design was marked by a curious set of factors. The rapid development of jet engines caused military requirements to be increased to levels that would have been considered absurd just a few years before. However, two other revolutions in aircraft design, both as important as the development of the jet engine, were also going on, but their effects have been generally overlooked because they were so much slower in coming to maturity and less obvious to most observers.

The first was the almost painful development of an effective air-to-air missile. Expectations had been high for rocket-powered projectiles ever since the first LePrieur rockets were launched from Nieuport 17s during World War I. Germany spent a considerable amount of its scarce resources trying to develop workable air-to-air missiles during World War II, fortunately without much success. Despite the expenditure of massive effort by several countries, missiles did not see widespread use until the protracted conflict over Southeast Asia, but even then, their utility was limited by their relative unreliability and the rules of engagement imposed by politicians seven thousand miles away. Not until the most recent generation of missiles and fighter tactics did the concept of the missile-equipped jet fighter reach maturity.

The second revolution has been almost completely ignored in popular writings since it is hidden completely under the skin. The ever-increasing sophistication of computers, not only for onboard use but also during the design of the aircraft and its systems, has revolutionized the aircraft industry even more than the jet engine. Modern computer-based design tools have allowed airframes to be optimized for weight and performance in ways not previously imagined, and computers can manufacture jet engines with tolerances almost inconceivable to humans. Digital fly-by-wire control systems allow the latest generation of fighters to be dynamically unstable in all three axes, permitting phenomenal maneuverability. It has been a long, hard road, but modern combat aircraft are incapable of functioning without their electronic masters.

Ironically, the technology revolutions have had a detrimental effect on the length of time required for development and also on the quantity of aircraft ultimately procured. The development cycle for the P-51 had been measured in days, and the P-80 in months. Even as late as the F-15 and F-16, the development and flight-test periods were measured in years; with the F-22 and F-35 they will be measured in decades. This meant that not only would older fighters have a much longer service life than their predecessors, but newer fighters would be procured in far smaller numbers, almost returning to pre-World War II levels.

Designation Systems

The U.S. Army accepted its first aircraft in 1909, but a formal designation system was not established until 1919. Given the small number of airplanes involved, this was not an immediate problem. In many ways, this first system established the designations we have all become familiar with, but this is not obvious at first glance. In this initial system, there were 15 basic mission types, such as "PA" for Pursuit-Air-Cooled and "PW" for Pursuit-Water-Cooled, followed by a sequential number indicating how many different designs of that type had been ordered.

This system proved somewhat complicated, however, and in 1924, a simplified version was adopted that reduced the basic mission types to only 10. Perhaps the most significant change came in the pursuit category, which replaced the previous five designations with a simple "P" for Pursuit. Over the next 20 years an additional 22 basic mission types would be introduced, and this was the system used by the Army during World War II. Not surprisingly, the U.S. Navy pursued a completely different route than the Army, but that is beyond the scope of this book.

The National Security Act of 18 September 1947 created the U.S. Air Force as an independent entity. The new service adopted a revised designation system that set the standard for the joint-service system currently in use. In general, this system was not significantly different from what the Army Air Forces had been using at the end of World War II, although "F" for Fighter replaced "P" for Pursuit. One unusual aspect of this system was that a few unmanned missiles were allocated numbers in the normal Fighter (F-98 Falcon, etc.) and Bomber (B-61 Matador, etc.) sequences; these were later changed to dedicated missile designations (GAR-1/AIM-4 Falcon and SM-61 Matador in these examples). [7]

The Joint System

On 18 September 1962, the Department of Defense adopted a universal designation system that applied to all of the U.S. military services. In essence, the Air Force had been using this system since 1947, although there were a few tweaks and all numbering was restarted at one. This system is described in DOD Directive 4120.15, "Designating and Naming Defense Military Aerospace Vehicles." Although generally referred to as Air Force Instruction 16401, this system is also contained in Army Regulation 70-50 and Navy Air Instruction 13100.6. The U.S. Coast Guard generally complies with this regulation, requesting designations through the Naval Air Warfare Center, while NASA and NOAA comply when it is convenient (and are under no obligation to do so).

The official designation for aerospace vehicles is called a Mission Design Series (MDS). For the purposes of this book, the important parts of the designation are that experimental models have an "X" prefix, and prototype models have a "Y" before the "F" for Fighter. Some vehicles have an "R" for Reconnaissance before the "F," then an "X" or "Y" before that.

Most, but not all, vehicles also have a popular name assigned to them (usually by the manufacturer) and this goes through the same approval process as the designation. Names that appear initially in quotes, such as "Thunderceptor," were never officially approved by the government.

The engine system was initially documented in Air Force/Navy Aeronautical (ANA) Bulletin 306 during 1946. In May 1968, a revised system was defined by MIL-STD-879, which was later absorbed into the current MIL-HDBK-1812 in February 1991. There are six types

McDonnell Aircraft Company had not been a player during World War II, and its first fighter design, the exotic XP-67 "Bat," had failed to attract any production orders. The company's second major foray into Air Force fighters, the XF-88 (shown here without its later afterburners) also failed to enter production, despite winning the penetration fighter competition. Finally, the company scored a base hit with the F-101 Voodoo, followed by a grand slam home run with the hugely-successful F-4 Phantom II. (National Archives)

of turbine engines defined: "J" for Turbojet, "T" for Turboprop or Turboshaft, "PJ" for Pulsejet, "RJ" for Ramjet, "TF" for Turbofan (added in 1959), and now "F" for High-Bypass Turbofan (added in 1970). The Army and Air Force use odd numbers from 31 up, while the Navy uses even numbers from 30 up; don't ask why they started at 30, since nobody seems to remember. The numbers are assigned in numerical sequence separately by each service, so the J52 was, in fact, a later engine than the J65 since the Navy developed fewer engines than the Air Force. Note that there is no dash between the engine type letter and the model number (i.e., it is J79, not J-79) – this is particularly important with later turbofans since the F-15 is powered by the F100 engine, which is decidedly different from the F-100 fighter.

Piston engines are designated based on their total displacement. The general scheme is a configuration prefix, the displacement rounded to the nearest 5 cubic inches, and then various model and modification codes. This system is also defined in MIL-HDBK-1812. There are four current configuration designators; "O" for Opposed, "R" for Radial, "C" for Rotating Combustion, and "V" for Vee (previously, "I" for Inverted and "H" for Horizontally-Opposed were also used). In theory, this designation system could lead to the same designation for two different engines. For instance, the Liberty 12 engine of the 1920s and the Merlin engine of World War II were both known as V-1650. However, it is doubtful this would happen for two engines in service at the same time, and if it had come up, one or the other engine would likely just "fudge" its displacement to a higher or lower number to avoid confusion. In reality, today, most piston engines use their manufacturer designations since there are very few military-only engines.

Rocket engines generally follow the example of turbine engines. The designation system for rocket engines was originally defined in ANA Bulletin 352 in 1948, later included in MIL-STD-815, and finally absorbed into the current MIL-HDBK-1812. The only difference in the original system was that odd model numbers were reserved for the Air Force and Army, while the Navy used even model numbers. This is similar to early jet engine designations, except that for rockets the sequence started at 1 instead of 30. Also similar to the turbine engine system, there is no dash between the engine type letter and model number (i.e., LR99, not LR-99). There are three current types; "LR" for Liquid Rocket, "SR" for Solid Rocket, "LSR" for Liquid/Solid Hybrid Rocket. It appears that only the Air Force continues to use this system; Navy rocket motors are usually designated in the MARK/MOD numbering system, while the Army uses its Ordnance Number nomenclature.[8]

Project Designations

In early 1941, the Experimental Engineering Section of the U.S. Army Air Corps Materiel Division (soon reorganized as a part of the new Army Air Forces Materiel Command,) began to assign "MX" designators (for Materiel, Experimental) to many of its research and development (R&D) projects. Issued by the security organization at

Wright Field, Ohio, these designators provided a non-descript means of identifying new R&D programs in engineering orders, correspondence, and procurement contracts. At first MX designations were largely limited to aircraft, engines, major components, and ordnance, but as the war effort broadened they soon reflected a continually expanding range of military aviation R&D topics, and that trend accelerated even more in the immediate post-war period. In fact, twice as many MX numbers were issued between 1946 and 1950 as had been issued during World War II. MX designations were generally assigned very early in a project's evolution, and thus many MX numbers were subsequently cancelled or completed without producing anything more than a research report.[9]

Weapons Systems Designations

About the same time that the project designations were abandoned in the 1950s, the Air Force implemented a series of Weapons Systems (WS) designations. Of importance to this book, the 100-series numbers were reserved for "strategic systems" (usually bombers, but also nuclear strike fighters), 200-series for "air-defense systems" (interceptors), and 300-series for "tactical systems" (fighters). Other types of systems had higher numbers. An alpha suffix was frequently added, initially consisting of an "A" for weapons systems and "L" for reconnaissance systems. Later the "A" was incremented to "B" or "C" for improved versions of the systems.

Naming Conventions

We are not even going to attempt to keep names correct for each date mentioned in the text. For the Army Air Corps and Army Air Forces, we will use Army, and switch to Air Force in late 1947. However, for those interested, here are the dates:

Aeronautical Division, U.S. Signal Corps	1 August 1907
Aviation Section, U.S. Signal Corps	18 July 1914
Division of Military Aeronautics	20 May 1918
U.S. Army Air Service	24 May 1918
U.S. Army Air Corps	2 July 1926
U.S. Army Air Forces	20 June 1941[10]
United States Air Force	18 September 1947

For the major test location, we will standardize on Muroc up through the end of 1949 and Edwards thereafter. These are the dates of the various name changes of the High Desert facility:[11]

March Field Bombing & Gunnery Range	September 1933
Muroc Bombing & Gunnery Range	21 June 1940
Muroc Army Air Base	23 July 1942
Muroc Army Air Field	8 November 1943
Muroc Air Force Base	12 February 1948
Edwards Air Force Base	27 January 1950

Lockheed also emerged from World War II with an excellent reputation for the P-38 Lightning and the first operational jet fighter, the P-80 Shooting Star. Lockheed post-war fighters had brilliant successes, such as the F-104 Starfighter, offset by dismal failures, like the XF-90 penetration fighter. Here, the two XF-90 prototypes pose with one of the YF-94s at Edwards on 22 July 1950. (Lockheed Martin)

Chapter 1

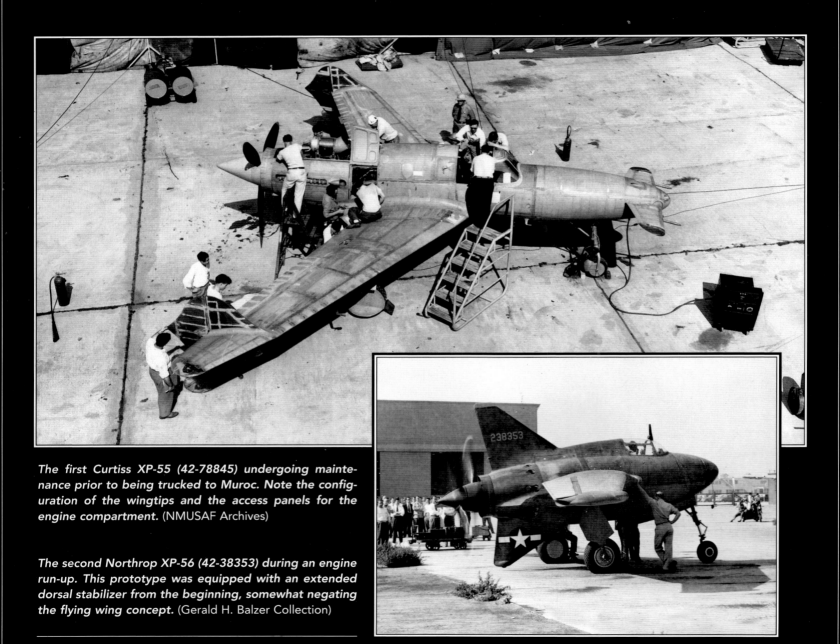

The first Curtiss XP-55 (42-78845) undergoing maintenance prior to being trucked to Muroc. Note the configuration of the wingtips and the access panels for the engine compartment. (NMUSAF Archives)

The second Northrop XP-56 (42-38353) during an engine run-up. This prototype was equipped with an extended dorsal stabilizer from the beginning, somewhat negating the flying wing concept. (Gerald H. Balzer Collection)

INNOVATIVE DEAD ENDS
RADICAL PISTON-POWERED FIGHTERS

In 1939, the Army Air Corps faced a bleak outlook. The most modern fighters in the inventory, the Seversky P-35 and Curtiss P-36A, could barely break 300 mph, comparing poorly with the German Messerschmitt Bf-109 (340 mph) or the British Supermarine Spitfire (360 mph). There were superior American designs under development, such as the 340-mph Curtiss P-40 and 400-mph Lockheed P-38, but neither was in production, and a preliminary review of the 1939 pursuit competition (Army Circular Proposal 39-770) showed little improvement was forthcoming.[1]

Instead of a traditional competition, in 1940 the Army decided to obtain preliminary engineering data from 13 manufacturers through the informal Request for Data R40-C. The goal of R-40C was to encourage innovative designs to leapfrog the foreign competition. The desired characteristics were delineated in Air Corps Type Specification XC-622 on 27 November 1939, which described a single-engine, single-seat pursuit airplane armed with at least four machine guns. The suggested engines included the 1,250-hp Allison V-1710, the 1,700-hp Continental V-1430 (soon to become the I-1430), and the 1,850-hp Pratt & Whitney H-2600.[2]

The Army expected the designs would range from lightweight conventional 425-mph airplanes powered by the V-1710, to unconventional, 500-mph pusher airplanes powered by the H-2600. The Army received 26 design proposals, unfortunately representing only eight basic concepts – the others were variants created by different engine installations. It was a disappointing response to what, in some respects, had been a grand plan. Nevertheless, several contractors played into the Army's hands by proposing innovative aerodynamic designs.[3]

Maj. Gen. Henry H. "Hap" Arnold approved the evaluation report of the reviewing Board of Officers on 31 May 1940, and by the end of 1940, the Army had ordered prototypes of the Bell XP-52, Vultee XP-54, Curtiss XP-55, and Northrop XP-56. Interestingly, all four used pusher propellers. (The XP-53 designation was assigned to an improved V-1430-powered Curtiss Hawk that was cancelled before it flew.)[4]

The Bell airplane would be cancelled prior to a prototype being completed, the Army instead directing the company toward the development of the similar XP-59, which, in turn, would also be cancelled and the designation reused for the first American jet fighter.

The other three designs would make it to prototype form, with varying degrees of success.

Vultee XP-54 "Swoose Goose"

At the beginning of 1940, the only fighter designed by Vultee had been the unsuccessful Model 48 Vanguard, which had not received an Army production contract. Nevertheless, the Vultee proposal was selected as the first winner of the R-40C competition, and letter contract W535-ac-15019 was issued on 11 June 1940. This $39,700 contract was for preliminary engineering information and two wind-tunnel models, including a powered model to collect data on the proposed counter-rotating propellers. The contract included options to perform the wind-tunnel tests, construct a mockup, and manufacture two experimental airplanes.

When the R-40C circular was released in 1940, the Lockheed P-38 Lightning was the fastest fighter in U.S. service. This is one of the thirteen YP-38s on 22 February 1941. (NMUSAF Archives)

The Model 70 was an inverted gull-wing monoplane with twin-booms flanking the counter-rotating pusher propeller powered by a 1,850-hp Pratt & Whitney H-2600 with a two-stage supercharger.[5] A single-seat cockpit was located in the center section of the magnesium fuselage, just behind the machine gun and cannon armament. The center wing section was designed around a newly developed NACA "ducted wing" where airflow was taken in via narrow slots in the leading edge, directed over the radiators and intercoolers, and then fed into the engine via ducts in the trailing edge. Housing the coolant radiators and intercoolers entirely within the wings was expected to provide a significant reduction in total drag and a corresponding increase in speed.[6]

Other innovations included a seat that could be electrically lowered to the ground for entry to the pressurized cockpit or be catapulted downward to eject the pilot clear of the propeller during an emergency. The gross weight was 9,000 pounds, and the maximum speed was 510 mph at 20,000 feet, taking six minutes to reach that altitude.

The preliminary engineering data was well received. On 19 August 1940, the Army issued a $525,000 contract amendment to authorize wind-tunnel tests, construction of the mockup, and manufacture of the first prototype (41-1210), now designated XP-54 as part of project MX-12. However, almost as soon as the contract was signed, Vultee announced delays in the manufacture of the prototype. On 7 September 1940, the Army agreed to eliminate the pressurized cabin from the XP-54, with the caveat that Vultee would design the airplane so that a pressurized cabin could be retrofitted at a later date. A weight increase to 11,500 pounds was authorized for the cockpit changes.[7]

Nine days later, Vultee instead proposed building a second prototype without pressurization, armament, or other equipment not essential for flying. This would be followed by a fully equipped first prototype. The Army and Vultee agreed to this revised plan on 1 October 1940, and a $690,000 supplemental contract was issued to cover manufacturing the second airplane, designated XP-54A. Because this supplemental agreement was not formally signed until 17 March 1942, the second airplane was allocated a Fiscal Year 1942 (FY42) serial number (42-108994).[8]

On 4 October 1940, the Director of War Production allowed Pratt & Whitney to terminate development of the H-2600 engine so the company could devote its full attention to the air-cooled radial engines that were becoming a backbone of the American war effort.

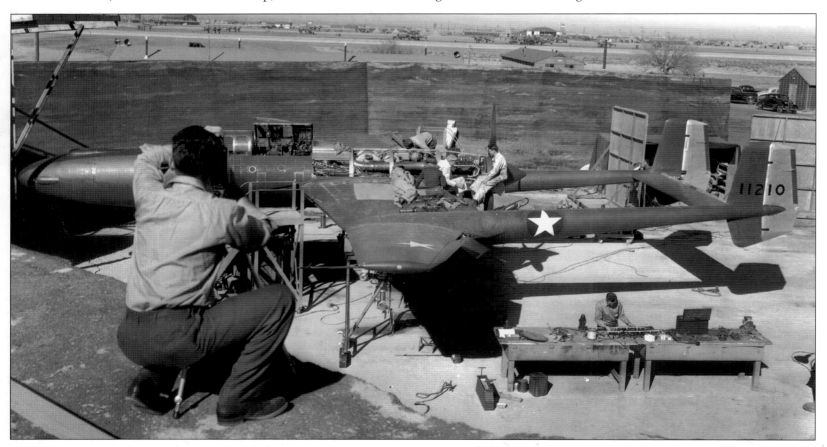

Above and Facing Page: *The first Vultee XP-54 undergoing maintenance at the Vultee facility in Downey, California, before its maiden flight. The top of the engine was easily accessible from the large wing, but access to other areas of the fuselage required maintenance stands due to the height above the ground. Note the silver rudders on the olive drab airplane.* (Gerald H. Balzer Collection)

Two weeks later, the Navy approached the Army about cooperating in the development of the 2,200-hp Lycoming XH-2470 (also called an XI-2470 in some documentation). On 8 October 1940, the Army confirmed its interest in the Lycoming engine to power the XP-54 and Lockheed XP-58. Things apparently happened much faster in the 1940s, since Lycoming provided the Army with installation and performance information for the XP-54 and XP-58 on the same day.[9]

On 10 October 1940, the Army directed Vultee to redesign the XP-54 around the XH-2470 and authorized an increase in gross weight to 16,145 pounds. Vultee estimated the Lycoming engine would provide a maximum speed of 480 mph at 27,000 feet. However, it soon became obvious that the pressurized cockpit was still causing numerous development problems, and on 12 February, the Army agreed to accept both prototypes without pressurization.[10]

The Development Engineering Inspection of the mockup was held on 19 May 1941 at the Vultee plant in Downey, California. Reviewers made numerous comments, but the most serious concerned the engine installation. On 23 May 1941, Maj. Gen. Oliver P. Echols, chief of the Materiel Division, with the encouragement of Maj. Gen. George C. Kenny, directed that the XP-54 be equipped with turbochargers

During the 1930s, Lycoming developed the 12-cylinder I-1230 using $500,000 of its own funds. When its output was deemed insufficient, two of the engines were mounted bottom-to-bottom to create the 24-cylinder XH-2470 seen above. (NMUSAF Archives)

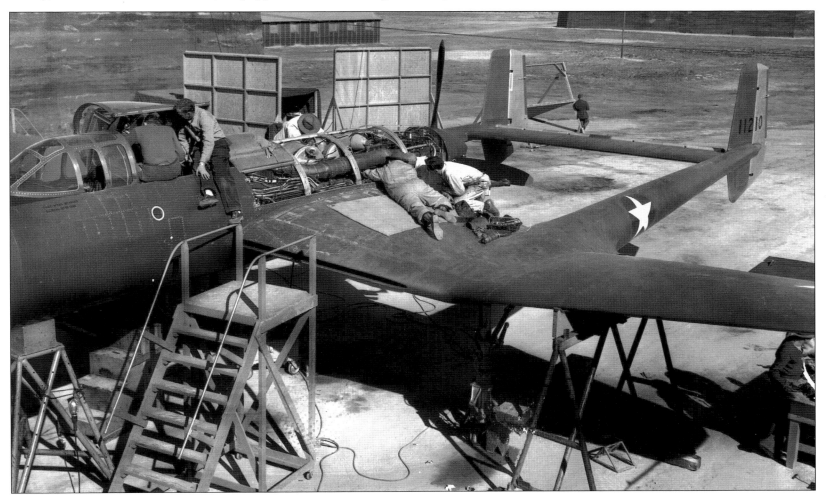

The flight-test facilities used during the 1940s were significantly less sophisticated than those hosted at the modern Edwards AFB in California. Essentially, there was an empty (and hopefully, dry) lakebed, a tent with a generator and radio, and a couple of support vehicles. This is the first prototype XP-54 at Muroc sometime in early 1943. (San Diego Air & Space Museum Collection)

instead of the superchargers-only shown at the inspection. Combined with various other changes suggested by reviewers at the mockup inspection, Vultee was forced to largely redesign the XP-54, again.[11]

Another outcome of the mockup inspection was a desire to re-engine the second XP-54 with the 42-cylinder, 2,350-hp Wright R-2160 Tornado engine driving a set of counter-rotating propellers. This design would have been redesignated XP-68 and progressed, on paper, simultaneously with the XP-54. Largely because of the delays with the R-2160, the XP-68 was terminated on 22 November 1941, and the second prototype was completed as an XP-54 with a Lycoming XH-2470.[12]

The first prototype was completed in late 1942, disassembled, and transported to Muroc for initial testing. On 15 January 1943, Vultee test pilot Frank W. Davis took the first XP-54 on its 31-minute maiden flight. The flight was uneventful except for a malfunction of the Curtiss propeller, which was subsequently replaced by a Hamilton-Standard unit. Davis took the airplane on its second flight on 27 January, and by 11 March, ten flights had made it clear that the 381-mph performance was substantially below the expected 480 mph. Worse, the engine showed metal traces in the oil, so the aircraft was returned to Downey for an engine change. After the engine was replaced, Vultee continued Phase I flight tests at nearby Ontario Army Air Field, and on 28 October, the XP-54 was flown to Wright Field for Phase II performance tests. While at Wright Field the airplane carried "*Swoose Goose*" nose art, a name reportedly coined by Vultee employees in Downey. By late 1943, the continual troubles with the H-2470 led the Navy to cancel the engine program, sealing

the fate of the XP-54 as well. The first prototype was formally accepted by the Army on 11 November 1943. The airplane logged 63.1 hours during 86 flights before it was grounded and eventually tested to destruction in the Structural Test Laboratory at Wright Field.[13]

The second XP-54 was largely similar to the first except that it was fitted with armament and a single experimental General Electric XCM turbocharger instead of the earlier pair of Wright TSBB units. The airplane made its maiden flight on 24 May 1944 from Downey to Ontario. Oddly, photographs of the second XP-54 on this flight show it wearing tail number 1211, implying serial 41-1211. This would give both aircraft consecutive serial numbers, even though they were ordered more than a year apart. Moreover, 41-1211 was allocated to a BT-13A Valiant basic trainer. It is assumed this was a mistake on the part of the Vultee paint shop.[14]

Despite reports that the second XP-54 only made a single flight, Frank Davis' flight log lists 10 flights in the airplane, with the last taking place on 2 April 1945. After the third flight on 3 June 1944, Vultee advised the Army that the engine and turbocharger were not entirely compatible in their present form and were causing mutual damage. They were returned to their respective manufacturers, and new units were installed in the XP-54 on 16 October 1944. The flight log shows Davis flew the aircraft with the new installation on 3 December 1944 and completed six more flights before the project was cancelled. The airplane was salvaged at the San Bernardino Air Depot, and the entire nose section was sent to Elgin AFB, Florida, for armament tests (the guns were never fired in the air). The XP-54 was the last project that Vultee carried out for the Army under its own name.[15]

The second prototype XP-54 (42-108994) initially flew with an incorrect serial number – 41-1211 – painted on the vertical stabilizers. Since the airplanes had been ordered a year apart, it was unlikely they could carry sequential serial numbers. (NMUSAF Archives)

A nice walkaround of the first XP-54 at Wright Field prior to it being tested to destruction in the Structural Test Laboratory. A Vultee "V" with a "Swoose Goose" is painted on each side of the fuselage. Note how high the fuselage sits off the ground. (Gerald H. Balzer Collection)

The XP-54 was the first American fighter to carry an "ejection seat," although it was a simple mechanical device that swung the seat from the bottom of the airplane and clear of the propeller arc. The seat was also used on the ground to enter the cockpit. (NMUSAF Archives)

Curtiss XP-55 Ascender

The Curtiss-Wright response to R-40C was perhaps the most unconventional of the four finalists. It was also one of the last projects led by Donovan Berlin before he left to work on the Fisher P-75. The Curtiss design used an aft-mounted swept-wing with a forward canard for pitch control, an arrangement similar to the later Lockheed L-133. A single pilot sat behind the armament and ahead of the engine that drove a pusher propeller. Vertical stabilizers were mounted about two-thirds of the way outboard on each wing. A Continental I-1430 provided an estimated maximum speed of 507 mph.[16]

On 22 June 1940, the Army issued letter contract W535-ac-15020 for preliminary engineering data and a powered wind-tunnel model as part of project MX-13. The total cost of the contract was $44,000, with $41,000 of this allocated for wind-tunnel work. The wind-tunnel tests showed various undesirable characteristics, the most worrisome of which was a tendency to enter an inverted flat spin after a stall, a typically fatal flaw. Since the Army was not completely satisfied with the results of the wind-tunnel tests, project engineer Edward M. "Bud" Flesh convinced Curtiss management to build a "flying mockup" powered by a 275-hp Menasco C68-5 engine. This testbed was designated CW24-B by the company and had a fabric-covered, welded steel-tube fuselage, wooden wing, and fixed undercarriage. When the flying mockup was almost complete, on 28 November 1941, the Army awarded Curtiss contract W535-ac-22239 to cover the costs of the CW24-B (which was assigned serial number 42-39347) as part of project MX-150.[17]

The CW24-B made its maiden flight at Muroc on 2 December 1941, with Curtiss test pilot J. Harvey Gray at the controls. Although the maximum speed was only 180 mph, the CW24-B proved the basic aerodynamic concepts, but showed a disconcerting lack of directional instability. The first attempt to cure the stability issues resulted in the vertical stabilizers being made larger and moved four feet farther outboard on the wings. Subsequently, vertical stabilizers were also added to the top and the bottom of the engine cowling. Ultimately, the CW24-B made 169 flights at Muroc between December 1941 and May 1942 while flown by 12 different pilots from the Army, Navy, RAF, and Vultee. The airplane was subsequently transferred to the NACA Langley Memorial Aeronautical Laboratory for testing in the 20x40-foot wind tunnel.[18]

Although less than ideal, the CW24-B tests had been encouraging, and on 10 July 1942, the Army issued contract W535-ac-29013 for three XP-55 prototypes (42-78845/78847). Since the Continental I-1430 was experiencing serious delays (and was eventually cancelled), Curtiss switched to the 1,275-hp Allison V-1710 driving a single three-blade propeller instead of the counter-rotating propellers originally proposed. Armament was to be two 20mm cannon and two 0.50-caliber M2 machine guns, but during the mockup inspection in December 1942, the 20mm cannon were replaced by additional 0.50-caliber machine guns.[19]

By 7 July 1943, the first XP-55 had been disassembled and moved via truck from St. Louis to Scott Field, Illinois, where it was reassembled, and various ground tests conducted. Harvey Gray took the airplane on its maiden flight on 13 July 1943 and quickly

The CW24-B prototype was 27 feet, 4 inches long and spanned 36 feet, 7 inches. It was powered by a single 275-hp Menasco C68-5 engine driving a two-blade propeller. Despite its limited performance, it demonstrated that the basic concept would work. (Gerald H. Balzer Collection)

After its flight test program ended, the CW24-B was transferred to NACA Langley for testing in the full-scale wind-tunnel. Although the resulting data did little to help the XP-55 project, it provided valuable data for future canard-equipped aircraft. (NASA Langley)

The first XP-55 (42-78845) seen at the Curtiss-Wright plant in St. Louis prior to its first flight. Note how the canopy folds to allow access to the cockpit. The top of the forward fuselage that normally covers the armament is missing in this photo. (Ray Wagner Collection via Bill Norton)

discovered that the nose-mounted elevator was not effective at low speeds. Curtiss subsequently increased the area of the nose elevator and connected the aileron up-trim to operate when the flaps were lowered, largely correcting the problem. On 15 November 1943, Gray was flying the first XP-55 through a series of stall tests when the airplane suddenly pitched forward 180 degrees onto its back and fell into the same inverted descent predicted in the original wind-tunnel tests. The engine quit, and after a perfectly stable 16,000-foot fall, Gray bailed out safely. The XP-55 was destroyed when it hit the ground. The aircraft had made 27 flights.[20]

At the time of the crash, construction of the second XP-55 was too far advanced to incorporate any changes resulting from the accident. As a result, the second airplane was generally similar to the first except for a slightly larger nose elevator, a modified elevator tab system, and a change from balance tabs to spring tabs on the ailerons. The second prototype made its maiden flight on 9 January 1944, but all flight tests were restricted to avoid the stall zone that had claimed the first airplane.[21]

The third XP-55 incorporated lessons learned from the loss of the first airplane and from extensive wind-tunnel tests at NACA Langley. These revealed that stall characteristics could be improved by adding four-foot wingtip extensions with "trailerons" and increasing the nose elevator travel. However, the maiden flight on 25 April 1944 revealed that the increased elevator limits allowed the pilot to stall the elevator during takeoff.[22]

Army Phase II performance tests were conducted at St. Louis between 16 September and 2 October 1944 by 2nd Lt. Frank G. Morris, Jr. and Maj. Everett W. Leach. The tests included 25 flights totaling approximately 27 hours in the second XP-55, which had been modified to match the configuration of the third airplane. The Army pilots discovered the airplane had satisfactory handling characteristics during level and climbing flight, but at low speeds and during landings there was a tendency for the pilot to over control the elevators because of a lack of any useful feel. Performance with the Allison V-1710 was mediocre at best, and the maximum speed was only 377 mph instead of the hoped-for 507 mph. Engine cooling was also a problem.[23]

Lingering problems, including generally poor stability, remained unsolved when the third XP-55 arrived at Wright Field for further tests. On 27 May 1945, during an air show with more than 100,000 spectators, Capt. William C. Glascow led five other fighters across Wright Field in formation. Glascow made one roll in the XP-55, began another, and suddenly dove into the ground while inverted. The pilot and an unfortunate nearby motorist were killed, and the third XP-55 destroyed.[24]

After the crash, the second XP-55 was flown to Warner Robins Field, Georgia, and subsequently taken to Freeman Field, Indiana, to await transfer to the National Air Museum in Washington. The airplane spent several decades at the Paul Garber restoration facility at Silver Hill, Maryland, before being loaned to the Air Zoo in Kalamazoo, Michigan, (formerly the Kalamazoo Aviation History Museum) in December 2001. After nearly five years of restoration, the second XP-55 was put on display at the Air Zoo on 26 May 2006.[25]

The name Ascender originated as a joke on the part of Bud Flesh, and although the government is normally careful about aircraft names and disapproves comical monikers, somehow this one slipped through. Ascender sounds suitable if pronounced "a-scend-er," however, the true intention is evident if the name is pronounced "ass-end-er." Humorously appropriate.[26]

The third XP-55 (42-78847) shows the all-moving canard at the extreme nose with the armament mounted behind it. (Gerald H. Balzer Collection)

The second XP-55 (42-78846) differed little from the first prototype since it was too far advanced in construction to incorporate lessons-learned from the accident on 15 November 1943 that destroyed the first airplane. (Gerald H. Balzer Collection)

The third XP-55 included all of the lessons-learned from the crash of the first airplane. The stall characteristics were improved by adding four-foot wingtip extensions with "trailerons" and increasing the nose elevator travel. Note the drop tank under the wing. (NMUSAF Archives)

Each airplane carried an Ascender insignia under the cockpit. Here, J. Harvey Gray (on ladder) talks to Robert W. Fausel in the cockpit prior to a flight. Note the USAAF data-block under the rear window identifies the airplane as an XP-55-CS (CS for Curtiss). (NMUSAF Archives)

The first airplane showing its original markings with the serial number on the nose and the USAAC-style national insignia without bars. Note the smooth nose missing the gun fairings used on the other airplanes and the relatively short wing-tips. (Gerald H. Balzer Collection)

On 15 November 1943, Harvey Gray was flying stall tests in the first XP-55 when the airplane suddenly pitched forward 180 degrees onto its back and fell into the inverted descent predicted in wind-tunnel tests. Fortunately, Gray bailed out safely. (Gerald H. Balzer Collection)

The third XP-55 crashed on 27 May 1945, during an air show at Wright Field. Capt. William C. Glascow made one roll in the XP-55, began another, and suddenly dove into the ground while inverted. Glascow and an unfortunate motorist were killed. (NMUSAF Archives)

Northrop XP-56

The Northrop response to Request for Data R-40C was a flying-wing interceptor using the Pratt & Whitney H-2600 driving a counter-rotating pusher propeller. The Northrop entry was the last design approved for procurement as a result of the competition. Contract W535-ac-15021 was signed on 22 June 1940, calling for engineering data and wind-tunnel models as project MX-14. After reviewing the engineering data, the Army exercised its option for a single XP-56 (41-786) and a full-scale mockup. Procuring the airplane and mockup added $393,380 to the original $1.1 million contract.[27]

When the H-2600 engine program was cancelled on 4 October 1940, the Army and Northrop agreed that the Pratt & Whitney R-2800 was the best available replacement. Although the R-2800 was more powerful (2,000-hp versus 1,850-hp), its larger diameter required a wider fuselage and resulted in a five-month delay in the construction of the prototype, as well as a 2,000-pound weight increase and a 14-mph decrease in maximum speed. Since a usable ejection seat had not yet been developed, Pratt & Whitney proposed wrapping explosive cord around the gearbox to blow the propellers away from the airplane should the pilot need to escape.[28]

During the spring of 1941, the Army realized the program would encounter considerable delays if the only prototype were lost or damaged during flight-testing. After determining it would not overwhelm the production capacity at Northrop, the Army ordered a second prototype (42-38353) under contract W535-ac-25060. The $240,365 cost-plus-fixed-fee contract was approved on 5 September 1941, but a modification on 5 April 1943 added $206,056 to cover overruns.[29]

The mockup was inspected on 15 July 1941, with Northrop admitting that the latest type of radio equipment could not be installed without a major redesign of the airplane due to space limitations within the small fuselage. The inspection board decided to allow the program to continue, given its experimental nature. However, the board did order Northrop to redesign the forward fuselage to change the shape from circular to elliptical to improve the armament installation. The canopy was redesigned to provide greater visibility, and various other minor changes were incorporated.[30]

Northrop selected magnesium alloy for the airframe and skin, mostly because national aluminum reserves were thought too small to meet current and future demands, particularly in light of the call by President Franklin D. Roosevelt to build 50,000 airplanes a year. However, there was little experience using magnesium, and fabrication techniques had to be developed while the airplane was being built. Since magnesium did not respond well to conventional welding, Northrop hired Vladimir Pavlecka to develop the heliarc welding system. Northrop later discovered that General Electric had already patented a similar process in the 1920s, but nevertheless was granted a patent on a new type of heliarc welding torch.[31]

Progress following the mockup inspection was slow due to the high demands on Northrop engineering and shop personnel from the higher-priority XB-35 bomber project. Late delivery of the engine and gearbox also hindered progress, as did continued difficulties in perfecting the heliarc welding technique. Northrop finally completed the first prototype in March 1943, and the airplane subsequently underwent various ground tests at the Hawthorne, California, factory.[32]

The first engine runs were accomplished in late March 1943, but Northrop was informed that a propeller blade had recently separated during R-2800 tests at Pratt & Whitney. This necessitated more extensive engine, gearbox, and vibration testing prior to first flight. During these tests, an engine failed because the gearbox mount allowed the propeller shaft to flex excessively. Due to a heavy workload, Pratt & Whitney was unable to furnish a new engine until August, by which time Northrop had installed more rigid engine and gearbox mounts.[33]

Preliminary taxi tests took place at Hawthorne on 6 April 1943, and the airplane tended to yaw sharply at high speeds. Northrop believed this was caused by faulty wheel brakes, and trials were halted until the

The XP-56 full-scale mockup shows the original armament layout with 0.50-caliber machine guns in the extreme nose and further aft on the lower fuselage. Note the single three-blade propeller. (Gerald H. Balzer Collection)

The first XP-56 (41-786) on a trailer on its way to Muroc in early May 1943. Interestingly, Northrop used a commercial trucking company, Lyon Van & Storage. This airplane was faithful to the mockup, with only minor changes. (Gerald H. Balzer Collection)

On 8 October, John Myers was conducting a series of taxi tests and short hops in the first XP-56 when the left tire disintegrated and the airplane went out of control. Fortunately, Myers suffered only minor injuries, but the airplane was destroyed. (National Records Center, St. Louis)

brake system was modified. The airplane was trucked to Muroc in early May, but additional minor changes occupied the next three months.[34]

The maiden flight took place on 6 September 1943, with Northrop test pilot John Myers at the controls. Better described as a "hop," this flight reached an altitude of about 4 feet, a speed of 140 mph, and was approximately 1 mile long. The second flight was made later the same day, reaching an altitude of 50 feet and a speed of 170 mph. After this 2-mile flight, Myers indicated there was a tendency for the right wing to drop and the nose to swing left with an accompanying diving moment. It also seemed difficult to raise the wing with the ailerons, and Myers was not sure if this was caused by high aileron forces or aileron ineffectiveness.[35]

After evaluating the data from this flight, engineers agreed that the airplane suffered inherently poor directional stability. Northrop believed that additional vertical stabilizer area would correct the problem, so the upper vertical surface was enlarged from a mere stub into a surface larger than the ventral fin.[36] The modifications were completed and additional taxi tests performed on 8 October. After successfully taxiing twice across Muroc dry lake at high speed, Myers made a straight flight at an altitude of 15 feet with no apparent difficulty. This was followed by a high-speed taxi run on the return trip across the lake and a second straight flight at an altitude of 15 feet.[37]

On the return taxi run following this flight, the left main tire blew while the airplane was traveling 130 mph. The XP-56 started to yaw to the left, and the tracks of the main wheels crossed about 750 feet later, indicating the airplane had rotated 90 degrees and was skidding sideways and slightly backwards. Just after this point, the tailskid hit the ground, and 30 feet later, the propeller tips hit, followed by the right wingtip. The airplane tumbled backwards and came to rest upside down. John Myers, still strapped in the seat, was thrown clear at the end of the first complete turn and was found about 10 feet ahead

of the main wreckage. There was no fire, and Myers suffered only minor injuries, but the airplane was destroyed. Since the contract specified that all risks were with the government, the Army accepted the first airplane after the crash. Northrop credited the government with $2,355 for items salvaged from the wreck.[38]

After the loss of the first XP-56, Northrop investigated changing the geometry of the landing gear to reduce the possibility the airplane could tumble backwards. Because of the major structural issues associated with this change, it was decided instead to reballast the airplane to move the center of gravity forward and to replace the tail bumper with a small tail wheel to prevent it from digging into the ground.[39]

The first XP-56 at the Hawthorne plant prior to being trucked to Muroc. Note the USAAC-style national insignia. This was replaced by a version with bars when the airplane was stripped of its camouflage prior to the beginning of taxi tests at Muroc. The counter-rotating propellers show up well in this photo. (Gerald H. Balzer Collection)

To improve the rudder action, the control linkage on the second airplane was disconnected from the air brakes that provided rudder control and connected to air valves located in ducts on the wingtips. When the rudder pedal was deflected, the valves moved to prevent air from flowing through the duct in the appropriate wingtip and directed it to a bellows that opened the corresponding air brake, causing the airplane to turn. These modifications delayed the completion of the second XP-56 until early January 1944.[40]

Following the satisfactory completion of ground engine runs, taxi tests of the second airplane took place at Hawthorne to check the effectiveness of the new rudder-control mechanism, including one run at 110 mph. Prior to conducting these high-speed tests, special 10-ply nylon chord virgin rubber tires were installed as insurance against further blow-outs. Subsequently, the airplane was taken to Muroc for flight-tests since the Army believed it was too hazardous to conduct the flights over the densely populated area around Hawthorne. However, the local desert lakebeds were flooded by the winter rains, delaying any action to move the airplane.[41]

In early March 1944, Northrop arranged to install shop facilities and a radio station at Roach Lake, which was the first lake to become dry. After more taxi tests, on 23 March Northrop test pilot Harry Crosby took the second airplane on its 7-minute maiden flight, reaching a maximum altitude of 2,500 feet. Crosby reported the airplane exhibited extreme rudder sensitivity and was nose heavy to the extent of not being controllable by the trim tab alone. Otherwise, the XP-56 performed satisfactorily. On 31 March 1944, the airplane made its second flight, reaching 250 mph and 7,800 feet. This was the first flight during which any maneuvers had been attempted, and the airplane appeared to handle satisfactorily.[42]

Following the fifth flight, a summary report was sent to Wright Field. The reaction to the airplane was unusually favorable, considering that it was a radical configuration and that the first prototype had been lost in a major accident. The chief difficulty experienced during the first five flights of the second airplane was longitudinal and directional instability that made landing with flaps impossible since the diving moment induced when lowering the flaps could not be overcome by the trim tab. Considerable wing heaviness was also experienced on several occasions but could be trimmed out. Northrop believed re-rigging the airplane could cure these problems.[43]

By this time, both Muroc and Harpers Lake were dry. Since maintenance, equipment, and communications facilities were much better at the established sites than at Roach Lake, Northrop ferried the XP-56 to Harpers on its seventh flight. The pilot reported considerable wing heaviness throughout the flight, and the airplane exhibited instability and control reversal at low speeds. No reason for these conditions was immediately apparent, and the airplane was grounded while engineers investigated the issues.[44]

At this point, the Army and Northrop approached the NACA Ames Aeronautical Laboratory in northern California to see if they could assist with the instrumentation and data reduction for further flight tests. However, NACA researchers believed the desired data could be more readily obtained by testing the XP-56 in the 40x80-foot wind tunnel with no risk to pilot or airplane. Unfortunately, a lack of priority delayed the tests, and in January 1946, the plans were cancelled since the XP-56 was no longer considered of tactical value. The Army formally accepted the second airplane on 14 January 1946.[45]

On 20 December 1946, the Army shipped the second XP-56 to Freeman Field to join other World War II aircraft held there for the National Air Museum. The Smithsonian moved this collection to Silver Hill during 1950-51. In 1982, the XP-56 was transferred to Northrop for restoration. Eventually, the airplane ended up at the Western Museum of Flight, but the project was beyond the capabilities of the museum, and the unrestored airplane was returned to the Smithsonian in 1989, where it still languishes.[46]

One of the XP-56s under construction in the shadow of the XB-35 flying wing bomber. Note the installation details of the R-2800 radial engine behind the cockpit. (Gerald H. Balzer Collection)

The second XP-56 (42-38353) was trucked to Roach Lake since Muroc was still wet from the winter rains. Note the top of the dorsal stabilizer differs from the first prototype. (Gerald H. Balzer Collection)

Taxi-tests revealed the need for more vertical stabilizer, so Northrop grafted a large dorsal fin over the original stub unit on the first XP-56. The shape differed from that used on the second airplane (see below and the right photo on the facing page). (Gerald H. Balzer Collection)

The second XP-56 being weighed. The first airplane had initially been painted olive drab and grey, but was stripped to bare metal before flight; the second airplane remained in camouflage for all of its short career. (NMUSAF Archives)

The second XP-56 poses for a portrait. The blackened areas on the aft fuselage are the exhaust stacks for the R-2800. (Gerald H. Balzer Collection)

McDonnell XP-67 "Bat"

James S. McDonnell founded the McDonnell Aircraft Corporation in St Louis, Missouri, on 6 July 1939 and quickly approached the Army with several concepts for new fighter aircraft. Although the Army did not pursue any of these ideas, McDonnell was included on the list of approved manufacturers to receive Request for Data R-40C on 8 March 1940. McDonnell submitted its proposal to the Army on 11 April 1940.[47]

The McDonnell Model 1 – the company's first formal design – was possibly the most radical concept submitted in response to R-40C. Externally it featured virtually unprecedented streamlining by using large fillets at the wing-fuselage juncture that mimicked the blended fuselage used by the much-later Lockheed F-16 and Boeing B-1. A fuselage-mounted engine transmitted power to a pair of wing-mounted two-speed pusher propellers via geared right-angle drive shafts. McDonnell submitted four versions of the Model 1, differing only in engine installations: the 2,500-hp Allison V-3420, 2,650-hp Pratt & Whitney H-3130, 1,850-hp Pratt & Whitney H-2600, and 2,350-hp Wright R-2160 Tornado. The Army eliminated the last two from further assessment based on inadequate performance estimates.[48]

While ranking 21st and 22nd out of 26 entries, the Model 1 nevertheless generated a great deal of interest within the Army, leading to a $3,000 contract for engineering data and a wind-tunnel model on 6 June 1940. Ultimately, the Board of Officers rejected the design because of excessive weight, poor performance compared to the other submittals, and the estimated 42-month powerplant development schedule.[49]

The XP-67 (42-11677) was the first aircraft of its own design built by the McDonnell Aircraft Company and showed the innovative thinking that would allow the company to dominate the fighter market. Note the modern appearance given by the streamlining. (NMUSAF Archives)

Historian Gerald H. Balzer notes that the Model 1 was generally similar to a model made by Lyle Farver in 1938 at the Glenn L. Martin Company. James McDonnell had been the Chief Engineer of the Martin Landplane Division at the time. The configuration of the two concepts is similar except for the use of tractor propellers and a fully faired cockpit in the Martin design. The Martin nacelles are obviously too small for a suitable powerplant, suggesting a fuselage-mounted engine and driveshaft similar to the Model 1 pusher configuration.[50]

On 30 June 1940, McDonnell submitted an evolved Model 2 concept, which the Army rejected a month later. Nevertheless, McDonnell continued to refine the design and submitted the Model 2A on 24 April 1941. This time the Army was more receptive and provided several comments that McDonnell used to tweak the design, which was resubmitted on 15 May 1941. This airplane used a pair of Continental XI-1430-1 engines with General Electric D-2 turbochargers in nacelles on the wings driving conventional tractor propellers. The pilot sat in a pressurized cabin, and armament consisted of six 0.50-caliber machine guns and four 20mm cannon mounted in the nose. The guaranteed maximum speed was 472 mph at a gross weight of 18,600 pounds with 760 gallons of internal fuel.[51]

The Army was sufficiently impressed to assign the effort to project MX-16 on 22 May and designate the airplane XP-67 on 23 July 1941. At some point, the aircraft was apparently reassigned to project MX-127, although no specific reason could be ascertained for the change. Maj. Gen. Oliver P. Echols, the chief of the Materiel Division, approved the purchase of two XP-67s (42-11677/678), a full-scale mockup, one free-spinning wind-tunnel model, one full-scale nacelle test fixture, and a set of engineering reports and data on 14 August 1941. The definitive contract, W535-ac-21218, was approved on 29 October 1941 and authorized an expenditure of $1,508,596 plus a fixed fee of $86,315. As with so many of the early wartime projects, the development cost was severely underestimated, and on 15 February 1943 an additional $2,006,250 was allocated to cover the overruns. Change orders and other adjustments eventually brought the total contract value to $4,624,927, with a fee of $108,549.[52]

By this time, the Model 2A had evolved considerably based on comments received from the Army. For instance, a conference at Wright Field on 29 July 1941 resulted in the armament changing to six 37mm cannon based on an ongoing Army evaluation of the relative effectiveness of 0.50-caliber machine guns, 20mm cannon, 37mm cannon, and 75mm cannon. Two weeks later, the Army requested a series of detail changes that brought the estimated gross weight up to 20,000 pounds.[53]

The Development Engineering Inspection of the mockup took place on 15-17 April 1942 in St. Louis. The most noticeable change was modifying the landing gear to comply with new Army regulations (Revision 5 of the Handbook of Instructions for Airplane Designers) so that the gear retracted into the nacelles instead of the wings. The Army recommended changing the type of turbochargers (to D-23 units) and switching the engines to XI-1430-17 and XI-1430-19 models rated at 1,350-hp for takeoff and 1,600-hp at 25,000 feet. A 15-inch extension was added to the fuselage to improve vision, and the proposed push-pull rod control system was changed to a cable system.[54]

The obligatory overhead view of the XP-67. The innovative streamlining is obvious from this angle, but in reality had little effect on performance since it drastically increased the wetted area, and hence, the parasitic drag of the airframe. (National Records Center, St. Louis)

The shape of the aft nacelle begged for the installation of a turbojet engine, and indeed, McDonnell investigated replacing the I-1430 engines with a V-1710 driving a propeller and an I-20 (XJ39) turbojet in the rear of each nacelle, but this never came to pass. (NMUSAF Archives)

A week of ground-firing tests of the three right-side 37mm cannon was conducted at Wright Field beginning on 26 May 1942 and revealed the need for several changes. The armament was retested in September 1942 with generally satisfactory results, but on 6 October 1942 McDonnell proposed major revisions to allow each cannon to be easily removed from the airplane separately. The Army approved this change on 28 October 1942, resulting in a new series of test firings in February 1943. For unexplained reasons these tests took an extraordinary length of time, finally being completed in March 1944 with generally acceptable results.[55]

In its initial proposal, McDonnell had specified a Lockheed-built pressurization pack for the cabin, and the Army indicated that it would procure the equipment and provide it to McDonnell. However, since the goal for the first airplane was simply to demonstrate the aerodynamic features of the design, the airplane was completed without the pressurization equipment, which, as it turned out, was never installed.[56]

In October 1943, the Army requested McDonnell "hold construction of the second airplane in abeyance" due to changing requirements and various anomalies being uncovered by wind-tunnel tests. The elaborately faired streamlining was ahead of its time, but the wind tunnel testing indicated the expected drag reduction was lost to the added frictional drag from the large wetted area. The idea was that solutions would be tested during the early flights of the first airplane, and the second would be completed with all modifications installed. As it ended up, the second airplane never progressed past 15-percent complete.[57]

The first airplane was substantially complete, except for armament and cabin-pressurization equipment, in time for the safety-of-flight inspection held 1-3 December 1943. The recommendations from the inspection were many and varied, but none involved major modifications. Taxi tests in St. Louis began immediately and continued until 8 December 1943, when fires broke out in both engine nacelles during a ground run-up. The exhaust manifolds had collapsed and caused the adjacent self-sealing rubber oil tanks to ignite. The oil tanks were replaced with metal units, and the airplane was trucked to Scott Field for its first flight.[58]

McDonnell test pilot Everett E. Elliott took the XP-67 on its maiden flight on 6 January 1944. The flight only lasted six minutes and a single circle of Scott Field before Elliott had to make an emergency landing due to "powerplant difficulties." The airplane suffered no major damage. Subsequent examination showed that the turbo compartments had experienced higher-than-expected temperatures, causing the wastegate controls to fail. Exhaust gases from the turbos reversed direction and entered the turbo compartment because of low pressures created in the compartment by the open main wheel doors. The Army suggested installing stainless steel bulkheads to seal the turbo compartments from the rest of the nacelle, improving circulation of cooling air in the turbo compartments and shortening the cowl around the turbo hood.[59]

During the months preceding the first flight, there had been discussions regarding possible revisions to the second airplane and the production design. The most attractive possibility was changing to Allison V-1710 or Rolls-Royce/Packard V-1650 engines with two-stage superchargers in the forward portion of the nacelle and (stillborn) 2,000-lbf General Electric I-20 (XJ39) jet engines in the rear portion, replacing the turbos. McDonnell submitted numerous proposals during 1944, but no particular agreement was reached pending the results of initial flight tests. Since Phase II performance tests were never completed, the various concepts suggested by McDonnell never passed the proposal stage.[60]

Everett Elliott accomplished the second and third flights at Scott Field without incident, but during the fourth flight on 1 February

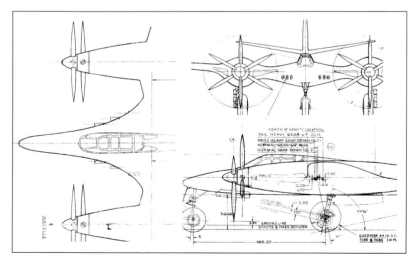

There were proposals to modify the XP-67 with counter-rotating propellers in an attempt to improve performance. Like the jet-powered concepts, these never came to pass, although at least some engineering was accomplished. (National Records Center, St. Louis)

1944, the engines were unintentionally overspeeded and the bearings destroyed. Since replacement engines were not immediately available, the airplane was returned to St. Louis to rework the engine ducts and raise the horizontal stabilizer 12 inches.[61]

The fifth flight was made from Lambert Field in St. Louis on 23 March 1944, and the improved stability and cooling due to the modifications were immediately apparent. Elliott continued to fly the airplane between 5 May and 11 May 1944 when Col. Marcus F. Cooper made the first flight by an Army pilot. Three Materiel Command pilots made five flights in the airplane over the next two days, but came away unimpressed. Comments included that the cockpit layout was "only fair," the take-offs were overly long, the rate of climb was poor, and that comparative flights with a North American P-51B showed the Mustang had a much smaller turn radius. The aircraft was clearly underpowered with the Continental engines, which failed to develop their design rating of 1,350-hp, barely reaching 1,060-hp.[62]

On 20 March 1944, the Army confirmed that McDonnell should continue delaying the construction of the second airplane, although engineering efforts continued. These concentrated on the installation of improved 2,000-hp water-injected I-1430 engines and counter-rotating propellers. On 30 May 1944, the Army authorized McDonnell to install Curtiss counter-rotating propellers on the first airplane as soon as the airplane completed its Phase II performance tests with the normal propellers.

Almost everything was in readiness for the official performance tests when, on 6 September 1944, the first prototype was damaged by a fire that began during a test flight with Everett Elliott at the controls. Elliott landed successfully and was not injured, but unfortunately, the airplane came to rest in such a position that the wind blew flames from the right nacelle over the fuselage, causing extensive damage. Subsequent examination of the right engine revealed that the fire resulted from the failure of a rocker arm on the No. 1 cylinder that allowed hot exhaust gases to enter the intake manifold, causing a backfire that started the fire. At the time of the accident, the first airplane had accumulated 43 flight hours. With the exception of the first four flights at Scott Field, all of the flights had been at Lambert Field.[63]

In view of the lengthy time to either repair the first XP-67 or complete the second airplane, coupled with the seemingly endless series of problems with the temperamental Continental engines and the superior performance possible with the jet-powered fighters under development, the Army decided to terminate the XP-67 contract on 13 September 1944. The War Department approved the termination on 18 September, and McDonnell was officially notified on 27 October 1944. The damaged first prototype and the material for the uncompleted second airplane were subsequently scrapped.[64]

Vultee XP-68

A 17 April 1943 Memorandum Report prepared by Paul B. Smith at the Materiel Command Engineering Division confirms the XP-68 designation was "… reserved for the contemplated Tornado engine version of the XP-54 airplane."[65]

A fire on 6 September 1944 ended the flying career of the XP-67. Initially, the fire was contained to the right engine nacelle, but after landing, the wind blew the flames across the fuselage, causing considerable damage. (National Archives via Kim McCutcheon)

During the XP-54 mockup inspection on 23 May 1941, the Army directed Vultee to include provisions that would allow use of the 2,350-hp 42-cylinder Wright R-2160 Tornado engine driving a set of counter-rotating propellers in the second prototype. This design was redesignated XP-68 and progressed, on paper at least, simultaneously with the design of the XP-54.[66]

The Wright R-2160 was one of the most intriguing engines of World War II since it was a liquid-cooled radial. Wright engineers arranged the 42 cylinders in six radial banks to allow a small overall diameter comparable to early centrifugal-flow jet engines. The engine consisted of three independent 14-cylinder modules using three two-throw crankshafts geared together by six lay-shafts that ultimately drove the propeller reduction gearing. Unfortunately, the engine required a heavy and complicated cooling system that probably negated any aerodynamic advantage it might have otherwise had. Work was never completed, and none of the seven prototype engines manufactured ever flew. The single remaining R-2160 is on display at the Aviation Hall of Fame and Museum of New Jersey in Teterboro.[67]

Ultimately, the XP-68 was cancelled due mostly to poor performance estimates using the R-2160, which needed a 4-to-1 propeller reduction gear instead of the 2-to-1 reduction gear with counter-rotating propellers Vultee envisioned. During September 1941, the Army determined it would be "practically impossible" to use the Tornado engine because the gear ratio required a propeller of larger diameter than could be mounted between the XP-54 fuselage booms. As a result, the Army decided that both XP-54s would use H-2470 engines, and the Army terminated the XP-68 project on 22 November 1941.[68]

Chapter 2

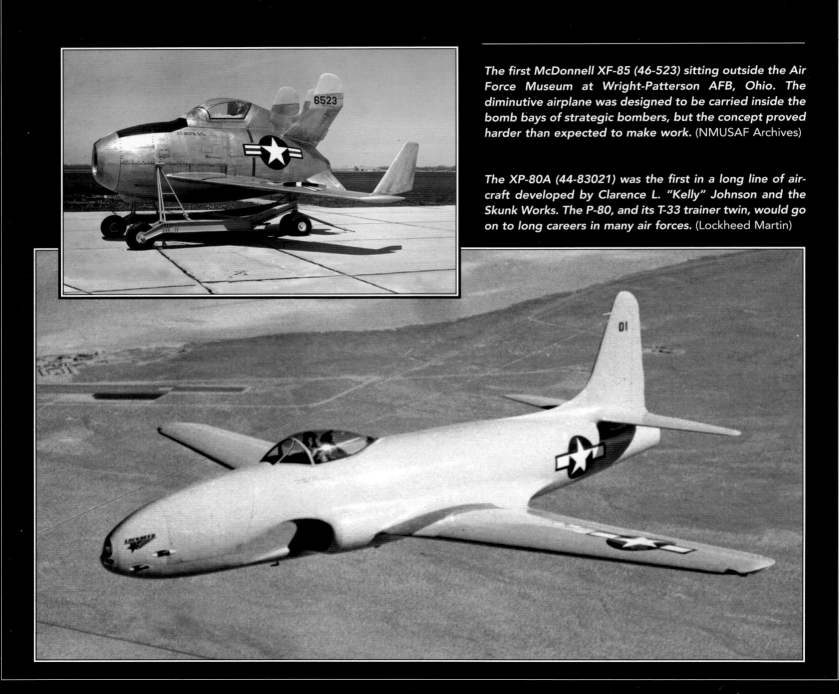

The first McDonnell XF-85 (46-523) sitting outside the Air Force Museum at Wright-Patterson AFB, Ohio. The diminutive airplane was designed to be carried inside the bomb bays of strategic bombers, but the concept proved harder than expected to make work. (NMUSAF Archives)

The XP-80A (44-83021) was the first in a long line of aircraft developed by Clarence L. "Kelly" Johnson and the Skunk Works. The P-80, and its T-33 trainer twin, would go on to long careers in many air forces. (Lockheed Martin)

THE FIRST JETS
AN INAUSPICIOUS BEGINNING

In the late nineteenth century, Englishman Charles Parsons invented a practical steam turbine that soon found widespread use in commercial power plants. By the turn of the century, the Royal Navy had begun building destroyers powered by steam turbines, and within a decade the steam turbine had become the preferred powerplant for fast ships.

Engineers, particularly Sanford Moss at General Electric, soon began experimenting with gas turbines. These early devices were large and consumed about four times as much fuel as an equivalent piston engine. Gas turbines had several major technical hurdles in front of them, including the development of lightweight, heat-resistant materials, and designing an efficient compressor. The development of aviation gas turbines languished for decades, although much of the basic research found application in the turbochargers developed for use on piston engines.

In the United Kingdom, research on aviation gas turbines began in earnest during the 1920s and continued into the 1930s on a small scale. As early as 1926, Alan Griffith, a scientist at the Royal Aircraft Establishment at Farnborough, developed a concept for a gas turbine that used an axial-flow compressor. Griffith envisioned the engine being used to rotate a propeller, and although some basic research was accomplished, nothing approaching flight hardware was built.

The first practical design for an aviation gas turbine is generally credited to Flying Officer Frank Whittle of the Royal Air Force (RAF). One of the more visionary aspects of Whittle's concept was that the engine would use jet thrust to propel the aircraft rather than rotate a propeller. Whittle filed a patent for a centrifugal-flow turbojet in 1930, but neither the government nor the aviation industry showed any particular interest in the concept. In fact, the year Whittle filed his patent, the British government discontinued funding of aviation gas-turbine projects.

Whittle turned to private investors to start a company to develop his engine. In March 1936, Power Jets Ltd. is formally incorporated in England. Whittle, still an RAF officer, is a partner and the chief engineer. The Air Ministry is certain the Whittle engine will never have military application, but allows him to spend six hours per week working for the new company. In October, a Power Jet request for a research grant from the Air Ministry is turned down, but additional private funding was found.[1]

Whittle based his concept on a centrifugal-flow compressor similar to those used in turbochargers, rather than on the axial-flow concept put forward by Griffith. This made it possible to actually build the device with existing technology, and Whittle began assembling his first engine in 1935. This engine used a single-stage centrifugal com-

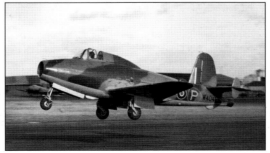

Two Gloster E28/39s were manufactured to test the Whittle engine. Flight Lieutenant P. E. G. Sayer took the first E28/39 on its maiden flight at RAF Cranwell on 15 May 1941. The airplane survived its test program and is currently displayed in the British Science Museum in London. (Left: Kev Darling Collection; Right: Terry Panopalis Collection)

Luftwaffe Flight Captain Erich Warsitz made the world's first jet-powered flight in the Heinkel He-178 on 27 August 1939. (NMUSAF via the Bill Norton Collection)

The Jumo 004 axial-flow turbojet that powered the Messerschmitt Me 262 was significantly more advanced than the Whittle or General Electric centrifugal-flow engines, but was hampered by poor workmanship and the lack of heat-resistant materials. (NMUSAF Archives)

pressor coupled to a single-stage turbine, and it was successfully bench tested in April 1937, although it only produced a disappointing 550-lbf. Nevertheless, after witnessing some of the early tests, the RAF agreed to fund further development of the engine. Power Jets finally receives a contract for the W.1 engine on 7 July 1939, and the initial version of the 623-pound engine delivers 850-lbf. The RAF selects Gloster to develop the E28/39 aircraft to test the engine, and Flight Lieutenant P. E. G. Sayer makes its maiden flight at RAF Cranwell on 15 May 1941.

Separately, Hans von Ohain was granted a German patent for a centrifugal-flow gas turbine engine in 1935, apparently unaware of Whittle's earlier work. Von Ohain had obtained his doctorate in physics at the University of Göttingen before becoming the junior assistant to Hugo Von Pohl, director of the Physical Institute at the university. When Ernst Heinkel asked for assistance in developing a new type of powerplant, Pohl recommended his star pupil. Von Ohain joined Heinkel in 1936 and conducted a successful bench test of his engine in September 1937, only five months after Whittle. The Luftwaffe soon awarded Heinkel a contract for the He-178 test aircraft, and Flight Captain Erich Warsitz made the world's first jet-powered flight in the He-178 on 27 August 1939, beating the British into the air by 18 months. Ohain's He S-3b engine delivered 1,100-lbf, but the engine weighed almost 800 pounds, resulting in a thrust-to-weight ratio roughly equal to the Whittle engine.

These developments were largely unknown in the United States when Maj. Gen. Henry H. "Hap" Arnold, commander of the Army Air Corps, visited England in mid-1941 to discuss providing support to the British war effort. While in England, Arnold was briefed on the Whittle engine and witnessed several flights of the Gloster E28/39. Suitably impressed, Arnold arranged for the British to send several engines and engineering data to the United States. Since they were unaware of German progress toward developing jet-powered combat aircraft, the Allies – especially the United States – viewed the gas tur-

The Messerschmitt Me 262 was the only jet fighter to see widespread service in World War II. Although fast by contemporary standards, the airplane had several fatal flaws and suffered from the same poor workmanship and lack of materials as its Jumo 004 engines. (NMUSAF Archives)

General Electric I-A Turbojet Engine

During the first four decades of the 20th Century, the engine division of General Electric Corporation concentrated primarily on developing and building turbochargers for use on piston enginess. These turbos captured the exhaust gases produced by a piston engine and used them to compress air and deliver it to the engine. This boosted the engine's power and is particularly useful at higher altitudes where the air is thinner.

Sanford A. Moss, who had come to General Electric early in the century as a new Ph.D., had developed the technology for the Army. In 1940, Moss became the first General Electric engineer to receive the prestigious Collier Trophy for "... outstanding success in high altitude flying by the development of the turbosupercharger."

Moss also led the early General Electric development effort on the gas turbine engine. By the late 1930s, these efforts were still experimental and confined to the laboratory. Across the Atlantic, Whittle and von Ohain had already developed workable engines that were powering small experimental aircraft. Finally, in 1941, General Electric received its first contract from the U.S. Army to build a gas turbine engine based on Frank Whittle's design. Six months later, on 18 April 1942, the General Electric I-A engine became the first jet engine to operate in the United States. Even so, the 1,250-lbf engine was a direct copy of the Whittle W.1X. Even more worrisome, although there was little doubt the I-A worked, it guzzled fuel, vibrated badly, and contained parts that wore out quickly — most engines needed overhauled after 10-20 hours of operation. The engine was 72 inches long, 41.5 inches in diameter, and weighed 865 pounds. The I-A designation was an attempt to portray the engine as a new turbosupercharger for security reasons.

Although the I-A powered the initial test flights of the Bell XP-59A Airacomet, the more powerful J31 was adopted for use in production aircraft. Design of the J31 began in January 1943, and General Electric delivered a total of 241 J31s to the Army before production ended in 1945.

(All photos from the NMUSAF Collection)

An improved General Electric I-16 (J31) on a test stand at Wright Field in August 1945. This engine generated 1,610-lbf of thrust from a package the same size and weight as the original I-A. (NMUSAF Archives)

bine engine more as an engineering curiosity than a future weapon. In the meantime, the United States was developing several piston-engine fighters that would ultimately prove very satisfactory.

Having gained the cooperation of the British, Arnold sought an American manufacturer to produce the gas turbine engine. Arnold was reluctant to give the work to any of the established aircraft engine manufacturers – Allison, Pratt & Whitney, or Wright – because their engineering and production capacity was already being taxed by the

pre-war buildup of the U.S. military and by supporting the British and Chinese. Arnold was also worried that these companies would perceive the gas turbine as a threat to their booming piston-engine business. The logical choice appeared to be General Electric, which had experience with much of the technology needed for a turbojet engine through its development and manufacture of aircraft turbochargers. When Arnold contacted General Electric about the Whittle engine, he counseled them, "Consult all you wish and arrive at any decision you please – just as long as General Electric accepts a contract to build fifteen of them."[2]

A similar problem existed when it came to selecting an airframe manufacturer. All of the major companies, and many small ones, were already operating under a large backlog of orders for combat aircraft. One exception was Bell Aircraft in Buffalo, New York. Headed by the well-respected Lawrence D. Bell, with the innovative Robert J. Woods as chief engineer, Bell had a well-deserved reputation for unconventional designs, evidenced by the YFM-1 Airacuda and P-39 Airacobra. Conveniently, the company was also located in close proximity to the General Electric facility in Schenectady, New York, where the engine was being developed. Larry Bell and Hap Arnold quickly came to an agreement.

The jet program was formally launched on 4 September 1941 during a meeting in Arnold's office with representatives from Bell and General Electric. Verbal agreements were reached the following day to build three experimental airplanes and 15 experimental engines. The Army final report noted, "Bell and General Electric were to work in very close collaboration, taking such steps as would be necessary to enjoin secrecy throughout the whole project." Belatedly, the United States finally entered the jet age.[3]

The British Air Commission reported on 22 September 1941 that His Majesty's government had authorized the release of all available

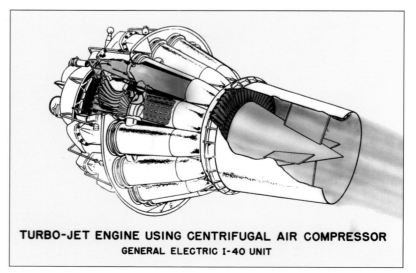

In a centrifugal-flow turbojet, the compressor is driven via the turbine stage and throws the air outwards, requiring it to be redirected parallel to the thrust axis. This is similar to how turbochargers worked on piston engines and was a good starting point for General Electric. Some engines used water-alcohol injection to cool the air before it was combusted, significantly improving thrust for short periods of time. (NMUSAF Archives)

information on jet propulsion to the United States. Just over a week later, on 1 October 1941, the first Whittle W.1X engine arrived in New York, accompanied by a variety of Power Jets personnel. It would be the first of many visits by Power Jets personnel, including Frank Whittle. Over the next few years, General Electric continued to improve the Whittle design. What began as the 1,250-lbf I-A soon became the 1,610-lbf I-16 (formally designated J31), and then the essentially all-new 4,000-lbf I-40 (J33).[4]

From the beginning, there were two competing jet-engine configurations. The initial patents from Whittle and von Ohain used centrifugal-flow compressors. Later German patents, and the engines developed by deHavilland in England used axial-flow compressors, as did the Lockheed L-1000 and most Westinghouse engines in the United States.

The centrifugal-flow compressors on the Whittle and von Ohain engines were a well-understood technology, being conceptually similar to the turbochargers used on many piston engines. However, it forced the use of combustion chambers arranged around the perimeter of the engine, resulting in a large diameter that was difficult to package into an airframe and a duplication of many components such as fuel injectors and igniters. However, centrifugal compressors were easier and cheaper to produce than the competing axial-flow compressor, and Whittle believed the design was robust and more tolerant of the varying intake conditions and throttle changes encountered by a flight engine.

The axial-flow compressor could achieve, in theory, a higher efficiency under ideal conditions since it provided a straight-through path from intake to exhaust. The engine had a smaller diameter, lower blade-tip speeds, and the opportunity for an annular combustion chamber. The designers worried, however, that it would be mechanically less robust and aerodynamically more sensitive to both intake conditions and downstream pressure changes, such as those induced

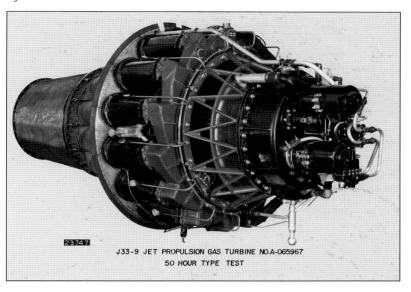

23747

J33-9 JET PROPULSION GAS TURBINE NO.A-065967
50 HOUR TYPE TEST

The 4,000-lbf General Electric I-40 (J33) was the ultimate development of the Whittle design in the United States. It was 103 inches long, 51 inches in diameter, and weighed 1,775 pounds. (NMUSAF Archives)

by rapid throttle movements. It was also, at least initially, more expensive to produce since it required more heat-resistant materials and precise machining tolerances.

Nevertheless, as thrust levels increased and aircraft speeds climbed, the axial-flow compressor became the norm for all turbojet and turbofan engines. However, even today, many small engines (under 2,000-lbf) continue to use centrifugal-flow compressors very similar to the ones initially patented by Frank Whittle and Hans von Ohain.

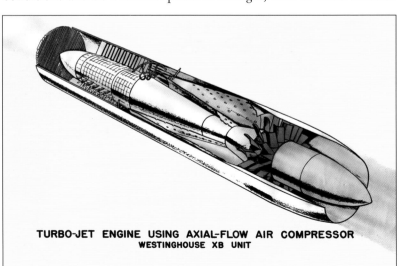

TURBO-JET ENGINE USING AXIAL-FLOW AIR COMPRESSOR
WESTINGHOUSE XB UNIT

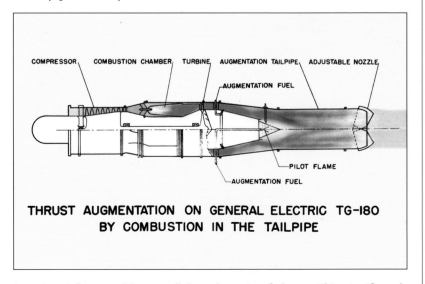

COMPRESSOR | COMBUSTION CHAMBER | TURBINE | AUGMENTATION TAILPIPE | ADJUSTABLE NOZZLE

AUGMENTATION FUEL

PILOT FLAME

AUGMENTATION FUEL

THRUST AUGMENTATION ON GENERAL ELECTRIC TG-180 BY COMBUSTION IN THE TAILPIPE

In an axial-flow turbojet, the compressor is again driven by the turbine, but the airflow remains parallel to the axis of thrust. This significantly improves the efficiency of the compressor and allows a much smaller diameter engine. By comparison, the centrifugal-flow General Electric J31 was 41 inches in diameter, while the similarly powerful axial-flow Westinghouse J30 was only 19 inches in diameter. (NMUSAF Archives)

Bell XP-59A Airacomet

The road to the Airacomet is long and oft misunderstood. It begins, in a convoluted manner, with the Bell XP-52 as part of project MX-3, which was a result of the Request for Data R-40C issued in 1940. Bell had a reputation for submitting unconventional designs, and the XP-52 was no exception. It had a barrel-shaped fuselage with the pilot seated in the nose followed by a 1,700-hp Continental XI-1430 driving a counter-rotating pusher propeller. The wing was swept approximately 20 degrees and twin booms were mounted about one-third of the way along the wings outboard of the fuselage. A horizontal stabilizer connected the two booms. Three 0.50-caliber machine guns were mounted in the front of each boom and two 20mm cannon were located in the lower fuselage. The Army was pursuing the airplane under a Foreign Release Agreement intended primarily for Britain and Russia.[5]

The development of the upright Continental Hyper V-12 liquid-cooled engine began in 1932 as the V-1430, but eventually emerged as the inverted XI-1430 (or, in some literature, IV-1430) engine intended for pursuit planes. Continental successfully tested the engine in 1939, but only 23 were ultimately built, mostly for testing in the Lockheed XP-49 and McDonnell XP-67.[6]

Estimated performance of the 8,750-pound XP-52 included a maximum speed of 425 mph at 19,500 feet, a climb to 20,000 feet in 6.3 minutes, and a service ceiling of 40,000 feet. The airplane was 34 feet long, spanned 35 feet, and stood 9.25 feet high. However, by September 1940, it was apparent the XI-1430 was encountering significant delays, so Bell proposed a modified airplane using a 2,000-hp Pratt & Whitney R-2800 Double Wasp air-cooled radial engine. The Army was preparing to authorize Bell to use the engine in a single prototype XP-52 when the War Department cancelled the XP-52 entirely on 28 October 1940.[7]

In between the XP-52 (Model 16) and XP-59 (Model 20), Bell proposed this Model 19 to the Navy. Note the counter-rotating propellers and the cannon muzzles on the front of each boom. (NMUSAF Archives)

Despite the cancellation, the Army was interested in the revised design, and a $350,000 fixed-price contract (W535-ac-17506) was approved on 26 February 1941 for two similar R-2800-powered XP-59s as part of project MX-45. The XP-59 was little changed from the XP-52 except for the engine and a new 9.5-foot diameter Hamilton Standard counter-rotating propeller. The aft-facing R-2800

Wind tunnel model of the original XP-59 design shows its similarity to the Navy proposal shown at right. The XP-52 was generally similar but used a different engine. (NMUSAF Archives)

The mockup of the XP-59 was never completed, but the Navy had better luck with the Model 19. This is the full-scale mockup showing the armament in the forward fuselage and booms. (NMUSAF Archives)

installation required Pratt & Whitney to develop an engine with reverse flow cooling, dual-rotation gearbox, and a cooling fan, something that sounds easier than it actually was. Bell promised to deliver a 10,463-pound gross-weight airplane with a maximum speed of 450 mph at 22,000 feet. Armament included four 0.50-caliber machine guns and two 20mm cannon.[8]

The contract required Bell to construct a full-scale mockup during the summer of 1941, but in a letter dated 24 September 1941, Bell admitted that a labor shortage and other priorities had prevented it from doing so. On 15 November 1941, the Army requested permission from the War Department to cancel the XP-59, ostensibly due to a lack of progress and the urgent need for Bell to concentrate on the development of the XP-63. This was approved on 25 November 1941, and a week later Bell was ordered to stop work on the XP-59, although it took until 21 November 1942 to officially terminate the contract. Very little detailed design had been accomplished, and the mockup was never completed.[9]

This is when the agreement between Larry Bell and Hap Arnold enters the picture. A month before the Army requested permission to cancel the XP-59, Bell and Arnold had agreed to build three prototype jet fighters. Cancelling the XP-59, which no longer interested the Army in any case, freed up manpower and facilities to work on the jet fighter program. As it turned out, it also provided a convenient cover for a new airplane, which was soon designated XP-59A, hoping to confuse anybody who inadvertently noticed the designation in paperwork or conversation. A similar ploy was taken with the new engine, which was assigned the General Electric I-A designation in the hope that it would be mistaken for a new supercharger. Confusingly, the airplane was assigned a new project number, MX-397.

Larry Bell and Robert Woods agreed to complete the first XP-59A in eight months. Cost-plus-fixed-fee contract W535-ac-21931 was

Whether it was done as a joke or to maintain a cloak of secrecy before its maiden flight, the first XP-59A was fitted with a dummy propeller while it was being towed around Muroc. (AFFTC History Office Collection)

approved on 3 October 1941 with an initial expenditure of $1,644,431, including a six percent fee. The contract also covered one wind-tunnel model "… constructed to the nearest mathematical scale that will produce a model with a span of 36 to 40 inches," three sets of shop and working drawings, and 10 copies of the operating and maintenance manuals. The entire project was classified "special secret," the highest of the military classifications until the advent of compartmentalized information on the atomic bomb program.[10]

These security regulations required that the activity be segregated from the normal work at Bell, so a design center was reportedly established on the top floor of the Buffalo Ford dealership. A separate entrance was built, the windows were welded closed and painted

Bell test pilot Robert M. Stanley, shown here in a YP-59A, became the first jet pilot in the United States when he took the XP-59A on its maiden flight on 2 October 1942. (NMUSAF Archives)

The first jet contrails over the High Desert at Muroc. The second XP-59A (42-108785) awaits its turn to fly while the first airplane is high overhead. (AFFTC History Office Collection)

One of the XP-59As (top) and one of the YP-59As. The large wing intended for high-altitude operation is clearly evident from this angle, as is the shallow splitter plate in the air intake to bleed the boundary layer away from the engine. Note the round wingtips on the XP-59A. (Bell Aircraft)

black, and military guards were posted at the entrance. Hardly inconspicuous. Six Bell engineers then spent the next several months designing the first American jet aircraft. Due to its secrecy, the existence of the project was unknown even to the Army resident representative at the Bell plant. In May 1943, the classification was reduced to "regular secret" and the design team was brought back to the main facility and additional people cleared to work on the project.[11]

Since the General Electric engines were being designed in parallel with the XP-59A, Bell engineers had little knowledge of their characteristics and adopted a fairly conservative design based on early data from Whittle and the RAF. All the engineers had were a few outline drawings of the engine, some basic dimensions, and a rough estimate of its anticipated performance. This information suggested that it would produce a limited amount of thrust, necessitating two engines to achieve what was hoped would be adequate performance.

Within two months, Bell engineers had designed a conventional aircraft with a cantilever, laminar flow, mid-mounted wing fitted with

two 1,250-lbf General Electric I-A engines, one mounted on either side of the fuselage under the wing roots. Given the expected high-altitude capability of the jet engines, the aircraft was fitted with a pressurized cockpit, still a rather unusual feature at the time. Although the XP-59A was primarily viewed as a platform to test jet engines, the Army also viewed it as a potential combat aircraft, so it carried a nose-mounted armament of two 37mm cannon with 44 rounds per gun. On 9 January 1942, the Army approved the initial design and authorized the construction of three XP-59A prototypes (42-108784/786). On 18 April 1942, General Electric conducted the initial ground tests of the I-A engine – the first jet engine to operate in the United States.[12]

Because of the extreme secrecy of the project, the Army decided that no wind-tunnel testing would be done prior to first flight except in the 5-foot tunnel at Wright Field, severely limiting the type and amount of data available to the engineers. If the airplane demonstrated undesirable flight characteristics that could not be cured during flight-testing, additional wind-tunnel work could be accomplished at

One of the XP-59As shows how mottled the olive drab camouflage paint became after being mixed with jet fuel and various oils. (Bell Aircraft)

The General Electric I-A engines were mounted low, which made access relatively easy. This was good since the engines required frequent maintenance and replacement. (AFFTC History Office Collection)

Despite not being equipped with afterburners (which had not yet been developed), the I-A engines on the XP-59As could put on quite a show during run-ups at night. (AFFTC History Office Collection)

other facilities. Also because of this secrecy, it was decided that a new test location was necessary since the traditional location at Wright Field was too exposed, and it presented a safety issue because it was surrounded by a large civilian population. In April 1942, the Army selected a location in the High Desert of California, about 100 miles north of Los Angeles. This location, at Rogers Dry Lake, successively became Muroc Army Air Base, Muroc Army Air Field, Muroc Air Force Base, and finally Edwards Air Force Base. Although the Southern California aircraft companies had used the dry lakes around Muroc for several years, this represented the first official Army acknowledgement of the area as a test location, and prompted the installation of a permanent infrastructure to support flight test.[13]

The first XP-59A was completed in the late summer of 1942, disassembled, and shipped via rail from New York to Muroc. The shipment across the country resembled a comedy of errors, fortunately with a happy ending. Various members of the Bell team were unintentionally left behind at railroad stations, one of the railroad cars went missing in a switching yard, and another was nearly hijacked by a small group of armed men – ironically, U.S. Marines assigned to guard several cars of explosives on the same train. Eventually, the XP-59A arrived at Muroc on 12 September 1942.[14]

On 1 October 1942, Bell test pilot Robert M. Stanley was conducting high-speed taxi tests when the XP-59A inadvertently became airborne for a short time, reaching an altitude of 25 feet. A second "taxi test" later that day reached an altitude of 100 feet. Stanley made the official maiden flight the next day, reaching 6,000 feet on the first flight and 10,000 feet on the second. This was remarkably rapid progress; the first flight of the prototype took

place only 13 months after the contract had been awarded (not quite meeting Larry Bell's optimistic eight-month schedule). Engineers wanted to disassemble the Whittle engines after three hours of operation, but 20 minutes before technicians were to remove the engines from the XP-59A, Stanley invited Col. Laurence C. Craigie, the chief of the Aircraft Projects Branch at Wright Field, to fly the airplane. On 20 October 1942, Craigie became the first Army pilot to fly a jet airplane. The second XP-59A flew on 15 February 1943 and the third late in April.[15]

Early flight-testing was not without its problems. Although the airframe proved generally satisfactory, the jet engines were remarkably troublesome. One of the few flaws attributed to the airframe was a tendency to "snake" from side to side at high speeds, making it impossible to hold guns on a target. More significantly, the initial apprehensions of Larry Bell and Robert Woods about the relatively low power of the jet engines turned out to have been well founded.[16]

YP-59A

In March 1942, the Bell contract was amended to add 13 YP-59A service-test airplanes (42-108771/108783) and a static test airframe for an additional $2,670,337. These were to be powered by the improved 1,610-lbf General Electric I-16 (license-built Whittle W.2, later designated XJ31). Interestingly, Bell did not build mockups of either the XP-59A or YP-59A, although armament mockups were constructed and inspected on 21-22 September 1942 and 5 November 1942. As it turned out, the estimated cost for the 16 airplanes was extremely optimistic, since change order No. 5, dated 2 September 1943, added

$3,039,685 due to "overrun; original estimate too low." It was a simple, but truthful, explanation that would never be acceptable today.[17]

By August 1942, engineering for the YP-59A was essentially complete. Although these were supposed to use the higher-thrust I-16 engines, the fact was that the Army, Bell, and General Electric all knew that these engines would likely not be available in time. Therefore, the first six YP-59As contained provisions to use I-A or I-14 (an interim improvement of the I-A that developed 1,400-lbf) engines.[18]

The first YP-59A reached Muroc in June 1943 and made its maiden flight in August 1943. The Phase II performance tests were conducted using the first YP-59A during October 1943, but the engines suffered severe surges that manifested themselves as a series of backfires and loss of power. The surging occurred only when using high-power settings at high altitudes, and retarding the throttles always eliminated the problem. The phenomenon was not considered particularly hazardous, but it limited performance testing to altitudes below 20,000 feet.[19]

In September 1943, the third YP-59A (42-108773) was shipped to England in exchange for the first production Gloster F9/40 Meteor I. Upon arrival, the YP-59A was assigned RAF number RJ362/G, and it made its first flight from the Gloster facility at Moreton Vallance on 28 September 1943. The RAF pilots found the aircraft to be underpowered with an unacceptably long takeoff run, and the YP-59A was seldom flown because of a dearth of spares and a general lack of interest. The exchange Meteor arrived in the United States in March 1944, and was briefly tested at Wright Field and Freeman Field.[20]

Shortly before the first flight of the XP-59A, the Army had placed an order for 100 production P-59As. However, by the fall 1943, the Airacomet was no longer being considered as a potential combat aircraft and the order was halved on 30 October 1943.

The first jet flight by a Naval Aviator had taken place when CAPT Frederick M. Trapnell flew the first XP-59A at Muroc on 21 April 1943. In December 1943, the eighth and ninth YP-59As (42-108778/779) were evaluated by the Navy at NAS Patuxent River, Maryland. After limited testing, the Navy decided that the Airacomet was unsuited for carrier operations because of the poor visibility from the cockpit and its slow acceleration. In addition, the Airacomet suffered a lack of adequate drag during landing approaches, so that there was a lot of "float" before touchdown when the power was cut. This was caused by the large wing intended for high-altitude operations and the absence of dive brakes, which had been deliberately omitted because of the anticipated mediocre performance. Nevertheless, before the end of the war, the Navy had acquired three prototype Airacomets and during the first year after the war acquired two production models. All were assigned to Pax River and allowed the Navy to introduce pilots to jet-powered aircraft prior to receiving the first North American FJ-1s. The Airacomets were used through January 1948 when LT Ralph H. Beatle became the 96th, and last, Naval Aviator to fly a P-59 series aircraft.[21]

On 6 January 1944, the United States and Britain announced to the public that they had developed jet aircraft and that Bell was producing a jet fighter for service with the U.S. Army. Newspapers carried articles about newly-promoted Brig. Gen. Laurence C. Craigie, the first military pilot to fly the airplane, Lt. Col. Ralph P. Swofford Jr., the Wright Field project officer for the XP-59A and Col. Donald J. Keirn, the XJ31 project officer. Confidence in the airplanes grew, and

The eighth YP-59A (42-108778) was sent to the Naval Air Test Center (NATC) at Patuxent River, Maryland, as Bureau Number 63960. Although unsuited for carrier operations, Pax River operated five Airacomets to introduce Naval Aviators to jet-powered aircraft. (Jim Hawkins Collection)

Initially the Navy operated the eighth YP-59A in its Army markings at Muroc prior to taking the airplane to Pax River. Note the "US NAVY" on the back of the mechanic's jackets. (NMUSAF Archives)

With the arrival of the XP-59As, the test site at Muroc became more permanent and gained a lot of infrastructure, such as the runway shown under construction in this photo. (AFFTC History Office Collection)

A far cry from the multimillion-dollar control rooms of today, this was the "ground control station" for the early XP-59A flights at Muroc – a crate, a radio, and a couple of chairs. (AFFTC History Office Collection)

later in January 1944, two YP-59As were demonstrated in front of President Franklin D. Roosevelt in Washington, D.C. It is interesting to note that there were no serious accidents during the first two years of flying, a tribute to the robust design of the airplane.[22]

In April 1944, the Army conducted formal aerial firing tests of the armament installation at Buffalo, proving what most had already suspected – the P-59 was not sufficiently stable to make a good gun platform. The annoying "snaking" made it nearly impossible to accurately aim the guns. Follow-on Phase II performance tests were conducted on 15 April, this time not impacted by the engine surging problems that had occurred earlier. The performance tests, however, were plagued by an unexpected problem. The aircraft exhibited a tendency to automatically pull out of a dive after reaching a certain Mach number, preventing it from reaching the speeds required to pass the tests. After many attempts, including replacing the fabric-covered elevators with metal units, the Army decided it could live without the data given that the airplane would never see combat. Bell continued to work the issue, but never developed a satisfactory solution. The airplanes were placarded to those speeds and accelerations considered safe based on the dive testing that was completed. Ironically, this unintended safety feature probably enhanced the value of the airplane as a trainer.[23]

The results of the performance tests were disappointing, but not unexpected. The maximum speed of the YP-59A was 358 mph at sea level, 409 mph at 35,000 feet, and 389 mph at 40,000 feet. The rate of climb at sea level was 2,920 feet per minute, decreasing to 1,830 fpm at 20,000 feet and only 940 fpm at 36,000 feet. The time to 36,000 feet was 20.4 minutes. Single engine speed at 10,000 feet was 260 mph. Take-off distance over a 50-foot obstacle was 1,885 feet off a gravel-asphalt runway. This was somewhat less performance than the last generation of piston fighters.[24]

The last YP-59A was accepted by the Army on 8 September 1944, a month after the security classification of the project was reduced to "restricted." The production P-59A differed very little from the YP-59A, but only 20 aircraft (44-22609/22628) were completed before production switched to the slightly improved P-59B (44-22629/22658) under project MX-398. These aircraft used uprated J31-GE-5 engines and had 55 gallons more internal fuel, increasing the maximum range to 950 miles. The last P-59B was delivered in May 1945. The final Army report on the P-59A stated that, "… the development [of the P-59A] was very worthwhile since it proved that the principle of jet propulsion for aircraft was sound and practical, and the airplanes themselves will be good training airplanes for pilots who will later fly jet-propelled airplanes into combat."[25]

In August 1944, the commanding officer at Muroc was ordered to store the first XP-59A so that it could be sent to the National Air Museum when security restrictions allowed. The airplane was shipped to the Smithsonian, via Wright Field, on 18 April 1945 and formally accepted by the museum on 16 June 1945.[26]

XP-59B

The P-59B that was built – a simple update to the P-59A – was not what had originally been proposed as the XP-59B. In early 1942, Bell proposed building a lightweight version of the P-59A using a single 1,610-lbf General Electric I-16 engine. The Army was reluctant to pro-

cure the single engine XP-59B because of the low thrust expected from the engine. However, Bell stressed that a lighter airframe, lower wing loading, easier maintenance, and increased thrust promised by General Electric made the airplane appear practical. Accordingly, the Army awarded a $1,248,286 contract (W535-ac-26614) to Bell on 26 March 1942 for three XP-59B prototypes and two wind tunnel models. The XP-59B mockup was inspected on 3-4 July 1942 and was found satisfactory and "unusually complete." Except for poor rearward visibility, nothing was found wrong with the fundamental design.[27]

Unexplainably, during a series of meetings at Wright Field in December 1942, Bell and the Army agreed that the XP-59B should be redesigned. This was accomplished by 18 January 1943, resulting in a 400-pound reduction in weight at an increase of $598,000 in cost. However, by this time, it had become obvious that the I-16 was going to develop considerably less thrust than the Whittle W.2B it was based on, mostly because some of the original engineering data had been incorrectly interpreted by General Electric. As the Army placed increasing emphasis on rate of climb, the concept of a single engine jet fighter began to lose its appeal. On 15 June 1943, Bell and the Army agreed to cease work on the XP-59B for 60 days while the requirements were reevaluated. In July, the Army recommended cancelling the project since the design had been eclipsed by the Lockheed XP-80 in terms of performance. The contract was terminated on 31 August 1943.[28]

The sixth YP-59A (42-108786) was converted into a drone director with an open cockpit installed ahead of the normal windscreen. A pilot in this cockpit could "fly" remote controlled aircraft via radio signals. Several other Airacomets were similarly modified, although a few had canopies installed over the drone pilot to save him from the freezing temperatures at high altitude. (AFFTC History Office Collection)

Northrop XP-79B

During the fall of 1942, Jack Northrop submitted an unsolicited proposal to the Army for a rocket-powered, flying wing interceptor. Ironically, at the time, the company was overwhelmed with work, and engineers could not be spared to work on the project. Nevertheless, the Army agreed that the design "was well worth developing" and decided to accomplish much of the engineering in-house at Wright Field.[29]

Because the design was so radical, the Army asked Northrop to build a series of "flyable mockups" in its wood shop, which was not as busy as the rest of the company. A contract was awarded in September 1942 for a single rocket-powered MX-324 airplane and two unpowered MX-334 gliders. In each case, plywood was used for the majority of the airframe, although the load-carrying center section was manufactured from welded metal tubing. The MX-324 used a 200-lbf Aerojet XCALR-200 rocket engine that burned red fuming nitric acid and monoethylaniline propellants.[30]

The first MX-334 made its maiden flight at Muroc on 2 October 1942 with Northrop test pilot John Myers at the controls. The MX-324 followed with a glide flight on 30 November 1943, also at Muroc. There was a long time between the initial glide flight and the first rocket flight on 5 July 1944, when Northrop test pilot Harry Crosby released the MX-324 from its P-38 tow-plane 8,000 feet above Harper Dry Lake.[31] Crosby ignited the XCALR-200 for a flight that lasted just over four minutes, becoming the first American-built rocket-powered aircraft to fly. Although Jack Northrop envisioned the aircraft as a pure flying wing, flight-tests showed that a vertical stabilizer was needed at higher speeds. Consequently, a wire-braced plywood dorsal fin was added. Details of MX-324 were not released to the public until 12 February 1947, more than 16 months after the project ended.[32]

While the MX-334 effort was underway, the Army was negotiating with Northrop for a full-scale all-metal prototype interceptor with the understanding that all engineering and fabrication would be subcontracted to another firm. The airplane would be powered by a single 2,000-lbf Aerojet XCALR-2000A-1 rocket engine, assisted by a pair of 1,000-lbf RATO boosters that would be dropped after take-off. The Aerojet engine was unique, using a turbopump that was driven by spinning the exhaust nozzle through slightly offset thrust. The aircraft was theoretically capable of reaching an altitude of 40,000 feet and a maximum speed of 538 mph at 20,000 feet.[33]

Like the MX324/334, the interceptor pilot would lay in a prone position to ensure the aerodynamics of the wing were not disturbed and allow him to endure higher g-loadings during maneuvers. Instead of conventional ailerons, the wing had ducted air intakes at the tips for lateral control, much like the second XP-56. Four 0.50-caliber machine guns with 250 rounds per gun were located in the leading edge of the wing, two per side. Originally, the airplane was to have landing skids, two on each side of the center section, but this was subsequently changed to retractable quadracycle landing gear.[34]

In January 1943, the Army awarded Northrop a $1,330,770 contract (W535-ac-36997) for three XP-79 airplanes, a static test airframe, wind-tunnel models, and the associated engineering data as project MX-365. The contract stipulated that Northrop had to subcontract the majority of the work to Avion so that higher-priority projects at Northrop were not adversely impacted. Avion was essentially the remnants of Jack Northrop's first company, now owned by United Aircraft, and maintained an ongoing relationship with Northrop, including building the N-1M and N-9M flying wing demonstrators.[35]

Welded magnesium was used for most of the XP-79 airframe since the metal was not considered a strategic war material and was easier to obtain, the same reasons it was used in other "futuristic" projects

The MX-324 had been designed by Jack Northrop as a true flying wing, but early tests revealed the need for a vertical stabilizer, resulting in a large plywood fin braced by guy wires. (Tony R. Landis Collection)

The Aerojet XCALR-200 rocket engine in the MX-324 used red fuming nitric acid and monoethylaniline hypergolic propellants to produce a modest 200-lbf. (Gerald H. Balzer Collection)

Unlike pure deltas, the MX-324 landed at a reasonable attitude, and the all-glazed nose of the glider gave the pilot excellent visibility despite his prone position. (Tony R. Landis Collection)

One of the MX-334 gliders was tested in the full-scale wind-tunnel at the NACA Langley Memorial Aeronautical Laboratory. This massive wind-tunnel tested many World War II combat types. (NASA Langley)

Army personnel at Wright Field examine the MX-324 with a manikin posed inside in full flying kit. Although the prone pilot position was essential to the streamlining of the smaller Northrop flying wings, the Army had considerable doubt that it would prove satisfactory. Testing revealed that the prone position increased the amount of accelerations the pilot could withstand, but complicated the control tasks. (Gerald H. Balzer Collection)

The rocket-powered XP-79 differed considerably from the jet-powered XP-79B since it lacked the two large intakes and engine nacelles. Like all Northrop flying wings, it also lacked a tail. (Gerald H. Balzer Collection)

These photos of the XP-79 mockup show the clean lines of the rocket-powered airplane, including the streamlined center section that would have housed the pilot and rocket engine. (Gerald H. Balzer Collection)

such as the Northrop XP-56 and Convair B-36. This choice, however, as with the XP-56 and XB-36, led to some difficulties since fabrication techniques were not well developed. It, however, did give Northrop additional experience with the heliarc welding technique used on the XP-56.

The Aerojet rocket engine burned red fuming nitric acid and monoethylaniline that ignited upon contact with each other, meaning that even minor battle damage could cause a serious fire. Therefore, the welded magnesium construction included heavy-gage skins to provide armor protection for the integral propellant tanks. Despite

The XP-79 would have been powered by a single 2,000-lbf Aerojet XCALR-2000 that used a turbopump driven by spinning the exhaust nozzle through slightly offset thrust. (Gerald H. Balzer Collection)

The position of the cockpit should be enough to dispel any thought of using the XP-79 as a "flying ram" since the pilot had no protection except a thin plexiglass windscreen. (Gerald H. Balzer Collection)

repeated popular references to the XP-79 as a "flying ram," neither the Army nor Northrop ever intended the airplane to ram enemy aircraft. This unfounded rumor undoubtedly began when somebody noted the 45-degree angled armor in the leading edge of the wing that was intended to protect the hypergolic propellant tanks on the original rocket-powered XP-79, not to provide a battering ram.[36]

Only two months into the contract, the Army and Northrop decided to modify the third airplane to use a pair of 1,365-lbf Westinghouse 19B (XJ30) axial-flow turbojets instead of the Aerojet rocket engine. The Westinghouse engine was being developed for the Navy and, in April 1943, the Army asked that four engines be diverted to Northrop. Engineers believed the jet engine would allow more endurance, and it was hoped that the higher thrust of the jet engines (2,730-lbf versus 2,000-lbf) would provide a higher top speed.

Given the small size of the airplane, it should be no surprise that the pilot would have been extremely confined. There was a hand-grip on each side and a set of pedals for the feet, plus a few instruments directly in front of the pilot. Visibility to the front was excellent, but essentially non-existent to the rear. Note the glass reticle for the gunsight. (Gerald H. Balzer Collection)

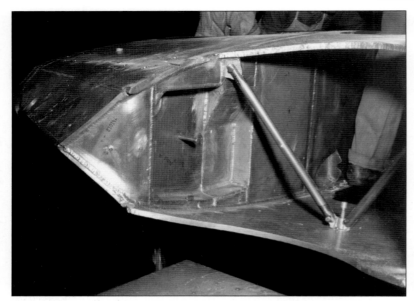
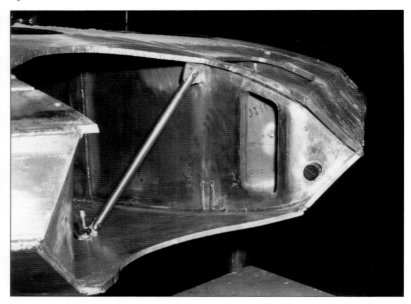

Contrary to many published reports – including at least one by a former Northrop executive – the XP-79 was never intended to ram enemy aircraft. This myth was seemingly begun by a misinterpretation of the armored leading edge shown above, initially designed for the rocket-powered XP-79 to protect the hypergolic propellant tanks and carried over to the jet-powered XP-79B. (Gerald H. Balzer Collection)

The change cost $169,310 and the third airplane was redesignated XP-79B (there appears to have been no XP-79A). The XP-79B was assigned serial number 43-52437, but oddly, no serial numbers seem to have been assigned to the two rocket-powered XP-79s.[37]

In May 1943, Northrop submitted a $3,037,335 proposal to build 13 rocket-powered YP-79s and 13 jet-powered YP-79Bs. However, given that neither design had yet flown, the Army declined pending the results of future flight tests.[38]

Because of the secrecy of the project, a "limited engineering inspection" was held on 3 June 1943 in lieu of the normal mockup inspection. The inspection team concluded that the XP-79 should offer superior speed, rate of climb, and service ceiling performance compared to piston-engine fighters. However, the inspection team concluded that the rocket propulsion system was probably not suitable for an operational airplane. The team was also concerned about the prone pilot position.[39]

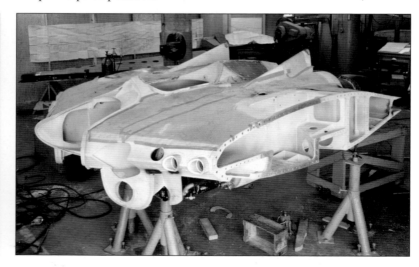

The XP-79B under construction. The all-wing shape of the XP-79 was altered to include an engine nacelle on each side of the pilot. Each nacelle had a short duct from the leading-edge intake to the Westinghouse 19B (XJ30) axial-flow turbojet engine. The photo at left shows the left-hand engine installed during a check-fit. Holes for two 0.50-caliber machine gun nozzles can be seen in the photo at right. (Gerald H. Balzer Collection)

In the XP-79B, small instrument and control panels were located on each side of the pilot. The foot pedals at the back of the cockpit are shown below. (Gerald H. Balzer Collection)

The small size of the XP-79B shows up well in this photo. The hatch on top of the airplane allowed the pilot to enter the cramped cockpit. Note the "danger" warnings on the front of the intakes and the Northrop logos on the side of the engine nacelles. (Gerald H. Balzer Collection)

These photos were taken as the XP-79B was being prepared to be loaded on a trailer for the move to Muroc in early June 1945 – note the ramps in the upper left corner of the top photo. Unlike the original XP-79 mockup, the XP-79B emerged with a pair of large vertical stabilizers and with the wingtip air valves that had been pioneered on the XP-56. (Gerald H. Balzer Collection)

Safely loaded aboard a flatbed truck, the XP-79B was covered with a tarp and driven the 100 miles to Muroc. (Gerald H. Balzer Collection)

The entire trailing edge of the XP-79B wing consisted of various control surfaces. The inner and middle surfaces are deflected in this photo, but the outboard split decelerons are closed. The foot pedals were connected to air valves located in ducts on the wingtips. When a pedal was deflected, the valves moved to prevent air from flowing through the duct in the appropriate wingtip and directed it to a bellows that opened the corresponding deceleron, causing the airplane to turn. (Gerald H. Balzer Collection)

After the inspection, the Materiel Command asked the Aero Medical Laboratory to determine the maximum allowable accelerations for a prone pilot and to assist Northrop in devising the appropriate methods to support the pilot's head in an operational airplane. The Army also contracted with the University of Southern California for similar studies. Eventually, the two organizations devised a method that allowed the pilot to withstand 12-g positive acceleration and still talk and operate the flight controls. A cross-bar control stick was provided for aileron and elevator control, with foot pedals operating the rudders.[40]

During early 1943, Avion indicated that it was having difficulty obtaining data on the rocket engine from Aerojet. The Army soon solved the data transfer issue, but by July 1943 it was becoming obvious that Aerojet was experiencing serious difficulties developing the rocket engine. Because of this, Avion advised Northrop that the first XP-79 would be delayed from 30 September 1943 to 15 December. In September, the date was postponed further to 15 January 1944. Although the aircraft was delayed, apparently Avion and Northrop were good at generating paper – largely reports of only "academic interest" – and in mid-1943 the Army instructed the contractors "to stop all unnecessary work and concentrate on building a flyable airplane." Maybe they were just ahead of their time.[41]

Aerojet continued to have development problems, so in March 1944 the Army decided to give first priority to the jet-powered XP-79B. Westinghouse shipped a mockup engine to Avion on 15 April 1944, and Northrop estimated the XP-79B would be ready for its first flight on 1 August. At the same time, spin-tunnel tests of a model of the XP-79B were conducted at NACA Langley. These indicated that normal spin recovery would be satisfactory and no special problems were foreseen because of the unconventional configuration.[42]

Aerojet finally admitted in June 1944 that the rocket engine for the XP-79 was unlikely to be completed in the near future. Combined with continued manufacturing issues at Avion, this caused the Army to cancel the two XP-79 airplanes and static test airframe. The Avion subcontract was terminated in September 1944 and the two uncompleted XP-79 airframes were scrapped. The material for the XP-79B was moved to Hawthorne on 1 December 1944 where Northrop would complete the airplane.[43]

The first Westinghouse 19B arrived in January 1945, allowing Northrop to begin preflight tests of the XP-79B. The second engine arrived on 26 February. Flutter and vibration tests were completed on 1 May 1945, and a safety-of-flight inspection was conducted on 26-28 May 1945. Overall, the inspection resulted in few comments of consequence. The airplane was shipped to Muroc in early June, and low-speed taxi tests were completed on 11 July 1945. High-speed taxi tests commenced two days later, but several tire failures and a need to redesign the braking system extended the tests into September.[44]

Harry Crosby took the XP-79B on its only flight on 12 September 1945. The airplane initially appeared stable, but 14 minutes after take-off it went into an unintentional roll after Crosby made several steep banks to the right and left. The airplane continued to roll until its wings were vertical, then plunged to the ground from an altitude of 7,000 feet. Crosby managed to bail out of the airplane, but was apparently struck by the wing before opening his parachute; the rip cord had not been pulled when his body was recovered. The Army accepted the airplane as a crash delivery in December 1945, and the contract with Northrop was terminated in January 1946.[45]

No performance tests were conducted prior to the crash, but Northrop estimated a top speed of 547 mph at sea level, decreasing to 508 mph at 25,000 feet. A cruising speed of 480 mph was expected at 25,000 feet. The endurance at 25,000 feet following takeoff and climb was estimated at 147 minutes or 993 miles. It would take 4.72 minutes to climb to 25,000 feet.[46]

The only flight of the XP-79B, on 12 September 1945, ended in a crash after a seemingly uneventful 14 minutes. Northrop test pilot Harry Crosby was killed when he was apparently struck by the wing before he could open his parachute. (Gerald H. Balzer Collection)

Lockheed XP-80 Shooting Star

From the earliest flight-testing of the XP-59A in late 1942, it was obvious that the aircraft lacked the performance the Army was hoping for in a jet fighter. At a 17 May 1943 meeting at Wright Field, the Army briefed Hall Hibbard and Nathan Price from Lockheed on the Bell and General Electric jet programs. At the end of the meeting, the Army invited Lockheed to submit a proposal for a jet interceptor built around the deHavilland Halford H.1B Goblin axial-flow engine. This powerplant was more powerful than the I-A/J31 used in the P-59A and production engines were to be built under license by Allis-Chalmers as the J36. The Army wanted simplicity of design that "would reduce manufacturing and maintenance problems and allow rapid construction of a prototype airplane without the necessity of prolonged research programs." It is what Lockheed would become good at.[47]

The experience gained while investigating the jet-powered L-133 concept put Lockheed in a unique position. As unproductive as the L-133 project had seemed at the time – no real hardware was built and no aircraft were flown – the experience provided the beginnings of Lockheed and Clarence L. "Kelly" Johnson's rise to fame. Johnson had frequently expressed an interest in jet propulsion, so Robert Gross, the president of Lockheed, assigned the young engineer to develop a response to the Army request. Johnson was eager for the opportunity, but wanted to do things his own way. Johnson said in his autobiography, "For some time I had been pestering Gross and Hibbard [the chief engineer] to let me set up an experimental depart-

The first jet fighter proposed by Lockheed was the L-133, which met with a cold reception from the Army. The second attempt, which became the XP-80, would be a great deal more conventional, and much more successful. (Lockheed Martin)

ment where the designers and shop artisans could work together closely in development of airplanes without the delays and complications of intermediate departments to handle administration, purchasing, and all

Lockheed did not build a structural test article for the original XP-80, but did for the larger XP-80A, shown here under construction in the facility Kelly Johnson and Skunk Works used to assemble the second set of prototypes. (Lockheed Martin)

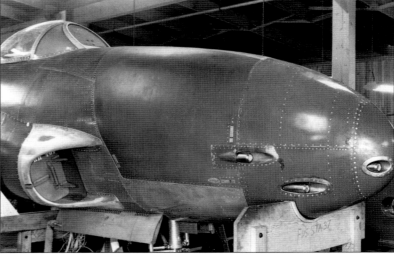

Skunk Works puts the finishing touches on the XP-80 (44-83020) in Burbank. Note the Goblin engine in the lower right photo. (NMUSAF Archives)

the other support functions. I wanted a direct relationship between design engineers and mechanics and manufacturing. I decided to handle this new project just that way." Gross ultimately agreed.[48]

Drawings of the H.1B arrived on 24 May 1943, and Lockheed quickly developed a preliminary design. Johnson and his team placed the heavy engine in the middle and used narrow air intakes on each side of the fuselage. The entire aft section of the fuselage could be removed to allow access for maintenance or replacement of the engine. On 15 June, Kelly Johnson delivered the proposal to Wright Field and two days later, Maj. Gen. Oliver P. Echols, chief of the Materiel Division, and Brig. Gen. Franklin O. Carroll, chief of the Engineering Division, approved contract negotiations with Lockheed. On 24 June, the Army issued a letter contract for $515,018, essentially matching the original $524,920 Lockheed proposal but reducing the fixed fee from six percent to only four percent. The resulting XP-80 airplane (44-83020) was assigned to project MX-409. The final cost of the XP-80, including wind-tunnel models, engineering data, and flight-testing, would be $1,044,335. Almost unbelievably, Johnson agreed to deliver the XP-80 only 150 days later.[49]

To meet this schedule, Johnson, assisted by William P. Ralston and Don Palmer, assembled a small team of engineers and went to a 10-hour

Above and Below: *The original XP-80 (44-83020), named* Lulu-Belle, *at Muroc prior to its maiden flight. The airplane did not carry a visible serial number and Lockheed logos were displayed on the nose and tail. Note the P-38 Lightning chase airplane in the background below.* (Above: Terry Panopalis Collection; Below: Lockheed Martin)

In November 1944, the XP-80 was transferred to the 412th Fighter Group to continue exploring jet aircraft tactics, and *Lulu-Belle* finished its career as a testbed for various configurations of the Goblin engine. On 8 November 1946, the XP-80 was retired and eventually found its way to the Smithsonian National Air Museum. (NMUSAF Archives)

the Drawing Room Manual for the project stated, "Any type of drawing may be used provided it contains sufficient information to build the part or assembly." If the project had been burdened by a complex, traditional drawing system, or any other complicated set of rules, there is no way the aircraft could have been completed in 150 days.

Nevertheless, the hurried and highly secretive nature of the project left some issues unaddressed, such as what to call the whole thing. The original location, during the development of the P-80, was downwind of a malodorous plastics factory. According to Ben Rich's memoir, an engineer showed up to work one day wearing a Civil Defense gas mask as a gag. When fuselage engineer Irving Culver was assigned to answer the group's only telephone one day, he realized that he had no idea how to identify where he worked without giving away the secret of their existence. Like most of the Lockheed engineers of the time, Culver was a fan of the Al Capp comic strip *Li'l Abner*, set in the mountain town of Dogpatch, most famous for its odorous moonshine still. The still was known, in Capp's idiosyncratic spelling, as the "Skonk Works," after the most secret ingredient in the brew. During mid-1943, a Navy official was trying to call Dick Pulver at Lockheed and was mistakenly put through to Culver. When the phone rang, Culver answered it with "Skonk Works, inside man Culver." After an awkward pause, one of the Navy officers asked, "What?" Culver repeated, "Skonk Works." It stuck.[50]

Thus was born the most famous of the secret design bureaus. Culver remembers Johnson was not altogether pleased with the situation, and that when Johnson first heard about the incident "he told me I was fired. Of course, he fired me about twice a day anyway." Johnson hated the nickname but seemed unable to prevent people from using it. As the design bureau became better known, Al Capp

day, 6-day week schedule. They housed themselves in an area of the Burbank Plant B-1 facility that had once been used as a wind-tunnel model construction area, and operated almost completely outside the normal company bureaucracy. The team proceeded with a minimum of paperwork and overhead, and developed rules – or the lack thereof – that were important to the ultimate success of the XP-80. For instance,

Lockheed test pilot Tony LeVier sits atop the first XP-80A (44-83021) while talking to Kelly Johnson. The XP-80As were larger than the XP-80 and more representative of production airplanes. (Lockheed Martin)

The first XP-80A, named *Gray Ghost*, made its maiden flight on 10 June 1944, but crashed after an engine failure only nine months later, on 20 March 1945. LeVier received back injuries in the crash. (Lockheed Martin)

objected to Lockheed's unauthorized use of the name, so Johnson changed the spelling to Skunk Works. In 1973, Lockheed finally trademarked the name and skunk logo.

As the project continued, the Skunk Works quickly grew, and by midsummer, there were 25 engineers and 100 shop mechanics working on the XP-80. The mockup inspection was held in Burbank on 20-22 July 1943. The inspection board was led by newly-promoted Col. Ralph P. Swofford, Jr. – who had been the project officer on the XP-59A – and consisted of five Army officers, supported by seven technical advisors and three observers (one from the U.S. Navy and two from the British Air Commission). Only a few minor changes were recommended, and construction of the XP-80 proceeded rapidly.[51]

On 11 September, the Skunk Works was ready to begin final assembly except for one minor detail: they had never seen a Goblin engine. A non-flyable H.1B finally arrived at Lockheed on 2 November 1943, allowing Johnson to complete the fluid and electrical details in the engine compartment. The completed XP-80 was disassembled and trucked from Burbank to Muroc on 10 November. A week later, the H.1B was ready for ground tests in the XP-80, but during the initial set of engine runs, both inlet ducts collapsed while the Goblin was turning 8,800 rpm. The failure of the ducts was attributed to faulty load cal-

Lockheed completed the second XP-80A (44-83022) on 27 July 1944. This was about two weeks behind the internal Lockheed schedule, mostly because of a decision to install a second seat that could carry an engineering observer. (Lockheed Martin)

The second XP-80A was primarily used as an engine research vehicle. The initial YP-80As experienced a problem with unstable airflow through the intake ducts, so Kelly Johnson rode in the rear seat of the second XP-80A and diagnosed the cause as boundary layer separation along the walls of the duct. A series of boundary layer bleeds along the upper edges of the ducts was added to all subsequent aircraft. (Lockheed Martin)

The first YP-80A made its 45-minute maiden flight on 13 September 1944. The following day the airplane was flown to the NACA Ames Aeronautical Laboratory at Moffett Field, California, for high-speed diving tests. (National Archives)

culations since the ducts were constructed to withstand only 4 psi while the engine had reduced the pressure significantly more than that. Lockheed redesigned the ducts to withstand 12 psi, solving the problem. A subsequent inspection revealed cracks in the engine impeller. Although the cracks and duct failure were not related, both contributed toward delaying the maiden flight of the XP-80. If these problems had not occurred, the XP-80 would have flown 143 days after the contract was signed, slightly beating Johnson's promise.[52]

The British dispatched a replacement flight-rated engine that had been intended for the second deHavilland DH.100 Vampire fighter. The H.1B engine arrived on 28 December and installed in the XP-80 the following day. Various engine runs and taxi tests occupied the next few days without uncovering any significant issues. Lockheed chief test pilot Milo Burcham took the XP-80, now named *Lulu-Belle*, for its maiden flight on 8 January 1944, in front of various army officials and 140 members of the team that had built the airplane.[53]

During two hours of flight-testing during the next two weeks, the airplane was found to have "bad stalling characteristics" since it gave little or no warning of an impending stall and fell off sharply to the right. Lockheed installed a small wing fillet that considerably improved the stall characteristics, although the airplane still fell off to

the right. The original blunt-tipped wing and tail surfaces were replaced with rounded tips after the fifth flight in an attempt to reduce drag. *Lulu-Belle* continued to be used for flight tests and eventually uncovered 137 different issues that Lockheed needed to address. All of these modifications were completed by 7 February 1944.[54]

After 2.94 flight hours, Lockheed turned the airplane over to the Army, which completed an additional 11.32 flight hours between 15 February and 9 March 1944. These tests were limited to 90 percent of the design engine speed, but the airplane nevertheless recorded 486 mph at 5,370 feet and 502 mph at 20,480 feet. This made the XP-80 the first Army aircraft to exceed 500 mph in level flight. The XP-80 flew much better than the XP-59A. By July 1944, just as Allied pilots began to encounter the first Me 262s over Europe, *Lulu-Belle* participated in a series of exercises conducted to develop tactics that American heavy bomber crews could use against attacks by jet fighters. The trials showed that enemy jet fighter pilots would prefer rear-aspect attacks, since during frontal attacks the fighter and bomber merged very rapidly and the enemy pilot had little time to aim and fire. Based on these findings, Army planners moved the formations of American fighters protecting the bombers to higher altitudes to give the defensive fighter crews space to dive and gain speed on the German jets when they attacked the bombers from behind. These tactics proved effective in fending off Me 262 attacks during the last months of the war.[55]

The Army accepted the XP-80 on 15 November 1944, but since the XP-80As were already flying, the usefulness of *Lulu-Belle* quickly declined, and it was retired from testing duties. In November 1944, the XP-80 was transferred to the 412th Fighter Group to continue exploring jet aircraft tactics. Maintenance problems frequently kept the airplane grounded, and *Lulu-Belle* finished its career as a testbed

The XF-14 over the Muroc Maru bombing target on Rogers Dry Lake. From this angle, there is nothing to distinguish the recce version from a YP-80A. In November 1944 this airplane collided with a Lockheed-owned B-25, killing everybody aboard both aircraft. (NMUSAF Archives)

for various configurations of the Goblin engine. On 8 November 1946, the XP-80 was delivered to the Museum Storage Depot at Orchard Park, Illinois. The airplane was later transferred to the Smithsonian Institution and is currently on display in the Jet Aviation Gallery at the National Air and Space Museum.[56]

G-5093 (10-30-44-IMC) XF-14 AIRPLANE SPLIT VERTICAL K-17B 24" CAMERAS (CONFIDENTIAL)

On 1 July 1944, a contract change order converted the second YP-80A (44-83024) into the XF-14 reconnaissance configuration. The six 0.50-caliber machine guns were replaced by a set of cameras shooting through windows in the lower fuselage section in front of the nose wheel. This differed from later RF-80 reconnaissance models that had oblique and vertical camera installations. (NMUSAF Archives)

The twelfth YP-80A was representative of the production P-80As that would follow, including the use of tear-drop-shaped underwing tip-tanks. This was one of three YP-80As (44-83032/33/34) delivered in early 1945 to the 31st Fighter Squadron at Bakersfield Municipal Airport for accelerated service tests prior to production P-80A aircraft being available. (AFFTC History Office Collection)

XP-80A

Both the Army and Lockheed had always realized that they could not import engines from England for production airplanes. Assuming flight tests went well, it was expected that production aircraft would be powered by H.1B engines built under license by Allis-Chalmers as the J36. However, the J36 program ran into difficulties and ultimately failed to produce anything useful. In September 1943, Lockheed proposed a larger and heavier airplane powered by a 4,000-lbf General Electric I-40 (XJ33) centrifugal-flow turbojet. Development on the I-40 had begun in March 1943, and the company ran tests on the first I-40 engine

on 9 January 1944. The Army was sufficiently impressed that it issued a contract for two XP-80As (44-83021/83022) as project MX-409A.[57]

As with the XP-80, Johnson had promised the Army that the two XP-80As would be completed within a short time period, in this case 120 days. He was close – it was 138 days before Lockheed test pilot Anthony W. "Tony" LeVier took the first XP-80A, named *Gray Ghost*, on its maiden flight on 10 June 1944. The first XP-80A crashed after an engine failure on 20 March 1945, but Tony LeVier successfully parachuted from the airplane, suffering back injuries as a result.

Lockheed completed the second XP-80A on 27 July 1944, three days ahead of the official schedule. This was about two weeks behind the internal Lockheed schedule, however, mostly because of a decision to install a second seat that could carry an engineering observer. After its maiden flight on 1 August 1944, the second airplane was primarily used as an engine research vehicle. Early in the test program, the YP-80As experienced a problem with unstable airflow through the intake ducts. Kelly Johnson took a ride in the rear seat of the second XP-80A and diagnosed the cause as boundary layer separation along the walls of the duct. A series of boundary layer bleeds along the upper edges of the ducts was added to all subsequent aircraft.[58]

The second XP-80A was later used as a testbed for the Westinghouse J34 axial-flow turbojet in support of the XF-90 program. As part of these tests, it was fitted with an experimental afterburner developed by the Solar Corporation. Tony LeVier had some harrowing moments testing this experimental combination that resulted in at least one emergency landing. Ultimately, the experiments contributed not only to the XF-90, but also to the F-94 interceptor program.[59]

YP-80A

By February 1944, growing anxiety over the deployment of German Me 262 jet fighters prompted the Army to order 500 production versions of the P-80A. A single, static test airframe and 13 YP-80A service test aircraft (44-83023/035) were ordered as part of project MX-409B on 10 March 1944 at a cost of $4,358,041. These were generally similar to the XP-80As, but, in contrast with the initial prototypes, were manufactured within the mainstream Lockheed organization. The first YP-80A made its 45-minute maiden flight on 13 September 1944. The following day the airplane was flown to the NACA Ames Aeronautical Laboratory for high-speed diving tests.[60]

The performance of the P-80 was significantly better than existing piston-engine types, and the Army wanted a photo-reconnais-

sance aircraft with similar characteristics. On 1 July 1944, a contract change order converted the second YP-80A (44-83024) into the XF-14 reconnaissance configuration. The six 0.50-caliber machine guns were replaced by a set of cameras shooting through a window in the lower fuselage section in front of the nose wheel. This differed from later RF-80 reconnaissance models that had cameras on the side of the nose ahead of the air intakes.[61]

Tragedy struck on 20 October 1944 when the third YP-80A (44-83025) crashed 55 seconds after taking off on its maiden flight, killing Lockheed chief test pilot Milo Burcham. Six weeks later, the XF-14 (44-83024) was destroyed in a midair collision with a Lockheed-owned B-25J (44-29120) near Muroc. Everybody onboard both aircraft perished.[62]

Despite the loss of two airplanes in less than two months, four YP-80As were deployed to Europe to demonstrate their capabilities to combat crews and develop tactics to be used against Luftwaffe Me 262s. This deployment was called Operation EXTRAVERSION. Two YP-80As (44-83026/83027) were shipped to England in mid-December 1944, but the first crashed on its second flight at RAF Burtonwood on 28 January 1945, killing Maj. Frederick Borsodi. The second airplane was bailed to Rolls-Royce, which modified it to test the RB.41 Nene turbojet. The airplane was damaged beyond repair on 14 November 1945 in a crash landing following an engine failure. The other two YP-80As (44-83028/029) were shipped to the 1st Fighter Group at Lesina, Italy, where they flew a small number of operational sorties, but never encountered enemy aircraft. Both survived their tour of duty. One crashed on 2 August 1945 after returning to the United States and the other ended its useful life as a target drone. Three other YP-80As (44-83032/33/34) were delivered in early 1945 to the 31st Fighter Squadron at Bakersfield Municipal Airport for service tests.[63]

XP-80B

Improvements were obviously necessary. A comparison between a captured Me 262 and a YP-80A had shown the German airplane to be superior in top speed at higher altitudes, and in acceleration at all altitudes. The Jumo 004 engine used an axial-flow compressor and a pair of them produced somewhat more thrust (3,960-lbf) than the early J33s (3,750-lbf), although they used about 25-percent more fuel doing so. In addition, the Jumo 004 needed replaced every 10-15 flight-hours, whereas the early J33s could run for 40 hours between overhauls. Researchers believed the Me 262's primary advantages were a thinner wing section, and more direct – and shorter – ducting for the engines.[64]

General Electric continued to improve the J33, and Lockheed proposed fitting a version that used water-alcohol injection to provide additional thrust for short periods. The Army was sufficiently interested to bail the ninth production P-80A (44-85200) for use as the XP-80B prototype. To provide space for the water-alcohol tanks, the internal fuel capacity was reduced from 470 to 425 gallons. A Lockheed-designed ejection seat was fitted, making the P-80B the first operational American fighter so equipped. Contrary

The fourth YP-80A (44-83026) crashed at RAF Burtonwood on 28 January 1945, killing Maj. Frederick Borsodi. This was only the second flight of the airplane after arriving in England. (NMUSAF Archives)

to many reports, the P-80B did not have a thinner wing or a thicker skin, the wing remaining essentially the same all throughout the P-80 series. This rumor may have started by somebody assuming the low-drag wing on the P-80R, which had been the XP-80B prototype, was the production wing.[65]

P-80R

On 7 September 1946, RAF Group Captain E. M. "Teddy" Donaldson set a world speed record of 615.8 mph flying a modified Gloster Meteor F.4. The Army decided that the P-80 provided a possible means to reclaim this record, and Hap Arnold authorized $75,000 for the attempt. In preparation, Skunk Works modified the XP-80B (44-85200) into the P-80R "Racey" using experimental semi-flush intakes and a low-drag canopy.[66]

On its first attempt, the P-80R failed to average over 600 mph over a 3-km course, and the airplane was returned to Burbank for further modifications. The experimental semi-flush intakes were replaced by conventional intakes, the wings modified to reduce drag, and a significantly more powerful Allison J33-A-23 engine was installed that produced 4,600-lbf (dry) and 5,400-lbf with water-alcohol injection. After some initial disappointments, on 19 June 1947 Col. Albert Boyd, chief of the Flight Test Division at Muroc, flew the P-80R to 623.738 mph, giving the United States its first world speed record in almost a quarter-century. The P-80R was subsequently used by the Air Training Command as an advanced trainer and is now on display at the National Museum of the U.S. Air Force.

In June 1948 all P-80s were redesignated F-80 as part of the Air Force-wide redesignation effort. Eventually, 1,732 P-80s were manufactured, consisting of 1 XF-80, 2 XF-80As, 13 YF-80As (including the

On 19 June 1947, Col. Albert Boyd set a new world speed record of 623.738 mph flying the P-80R, named Racey. *Boyd was the chief of the Flight Test Division at Muroc and later went on to command Edwards AFB and the Wright Air Development Center.* (Terry Panopalis Collection)

single XF-14), 525 F-80As, 240 F-80Bs, 670 F-80Cs, 152 RF-80As, and 128 TF-80Cs (redesignated T-33A in 1949, although many more T-33s were subsequently manufactured). The P-80/T-33 also gave birth to the similar F-94 series.[67]

The P-80R (44-85200) in its original configuration with semi-flush intakes and streamlined canopy. The data block on the fuselage identifies the airplane as a "P-80R," not an "XP-80R." (NMUSAF Archives)

After a stint as an high-speed trainer, the P-80R was retired to the old Air Force Museum. Noteworthy here are the revised air intakes, which were larger than normal P-80 inlets. (NMUSAF Archives)

Convair XP-81

Early on, it became apparent that despite their performance advantages, the initial jet fighters would be handicapped by high fuel consumption. The obvious answer, at least for the short-term, was a mixed powerplant that combined a jet engine for performance and another engine for cruising. In the summer of 1943, the Army issued a requirement for a single-place, two-engine, long-range escort fighter with a 1,250-mile operating radius with 20 minutes of combat, a 250-mph cruising speed at 25,000 feet, a maximum speed of 500 mph, and a combat ceiling of 37,500 feet. Other requirements included a "12-degree vision over the nose" and a rate of climb of 2,500 feet per minute at 27,000 feet.[68]

It appears that Consolidated-Vultee was the only company to submit a proposal, doing so in September 1943. While developing the proposal, chief designer Charles R. "Jack" Irvine and chief test pilot Frank W. Davis toyed with many ideas. The high-speed requirement and engine availability immediately led to the selection of a 4,000-lbf General Electric I-40 (XJ33) centrifugal-flow turbojet, but the operating radius and cruise speed dictated the use of a propeller for the second engine, whose selection proved more difficult. Many powerplants were considered, but the choices ultimately narrowed to the Pratt & Whitney R-2800 radial engine, and the General Electric TG-100 (later designated TG-31, then XT31) gas turbine engine driving a propeller – what is today known as a turboprop.[69]

Ultimately, Irvine and Davis concluded that the TG-100 offered a smaller airplane with higher performance. However, this carried certain risks, primarily that the TG-100 was still largely a paper engine

The General Electric TG-100 (XT31) was the first turboprop engine developed in the United States. The engine was to have been tested on a Curtiss XC-113 (a converted C-46), but the experiment was abandoned after the XC-113 was involved in a ground accident. Only 28 T31s were manufactured. (NMUSAF Archives)

with a long, and potentially difficult, development cycle ahead of it. Still, in 1943, everybody realized the end of the piston engine was near, and there seemed little point in developing a new aircraft around soon-to-be obsolete technology. Convair settled on an all-metal, cantilever, low-winged monoplane powered by a TG-100 mounted in the nose with a ventral exhaust and an I-40 in the rear fuselage fed by a pair of dorsal intakes. Nearly all of the power from the TG-100 was delivered via the propeller, and the turbine exhaust contributed only 600-lbf. The turboprop would take the fighter long distances across the Pacific, and the pilot could use the jet engine when needed for takeoff and combat maneuvering.[70]

The first turboprop developed in the United States, the TG-100, dated from a late-1941 Army contract with General Electric in Schenectady, New York, and development progressed at a slow pace because of competing priorities with conventional turbochargers and the new turbojets. The engine first ran without a propeller in May 1943, and an output of 1,650 hp was eventually achieved, but only 28 engines were ultimately produced. The TG-100 was fitted to the Convair XP-81, Ryan XF2R-1, and Ryan XF2R-2.[71]

The Air Force awarded Convair a $4.6 million contract (W33-038-ac-1887) for two XP-81 prototypes (44-91000/001) and a static test airframe on 18 January 1944 as project MX-480. Initially, the Army intended the aircraft strictly as experimental models to test the novel propulsion system, but the contract was subsequently modified to include 13 service-test YP-81s as project MX-796. These would be powered by the lighter and more powerful TG-110 (XT41) turboprop combined with an improved J33 with water-alcohol injection. The wing of the YP-81 would be moved aft seven inches to maintain the center of gravity since the engine weights changed considerably. Convair projected that the maximum speed would increase from 510 mph to 544 mph, and the range, rate of climb, and single-engine performance would also improve "greatly," although no specifics were provided.[72]

Design and construction of the first XP-81 began on 20 January 1944, but in early April, General Electric notified the Army that the TG-100 was running into delays. By September 1944, it became obvious that the TG-100 would not be ready by the time the first airplane was completed. Convair and the Army agreed that installing a Packard-built 1,450-hp Rolls-Royce V-1650 Merlin would allow preliminary flight-testing to proceed. After the nose of the first XP-81 was modified to accept the Merlin, the airplane was partially disassembled and trucked to Muroc. Convair test pilot Frank W. Davis took the airplane on its maiden flight on 7 February 1945, and initial testing concentrated on ironing out the installation issues associated with the I-40 turbojet.[73]

During three months of flight-test using the Merlin, first XP-81 completed 46 flights totaling 47.75 hours. Two major problems presented themselves during these tests: poor directional stability because of the torque effect of the Merlin, and the Aeroproducts propeller throwing oil onto the windshield. Since both of these issues would be eliminated when the Merlin was replaced with the TG-100, neither Consolidated nor the Army was particularly worried. The airplane returned to Vultee Field in Downey, California, on 18 May 1945.[74]

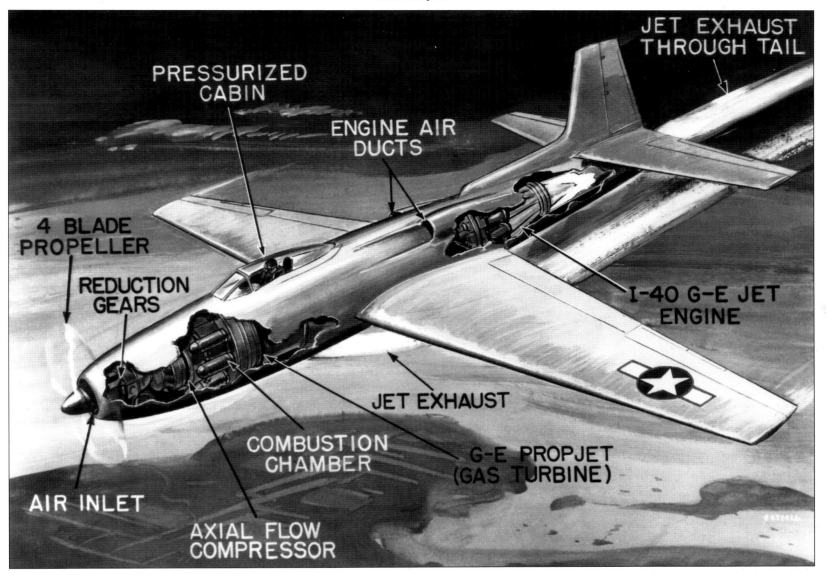

Artist concept showing the location of the major components of the propulsion system. The TG-100 and its reduction gearbox occupied the entire nose of the airplane, with the turboprop exhaust exhausting under the cockpit. The I-40 turbojet engine occupied a fairly traditional location in the rear fuselage and was fed by shoulder-mounted inlets just ahead of the vertical stabilizer. (NMUSAF Archives)

Convair received the first TG-100 on 11 June 1945, and between 23 June and 18 October, the engine was bench-tested for 43 hours and 58 minutes. In the meantime, however, the war against Japan had progressed significantly, and the capture of Guam and Saipan had largely eliminated the need for long-range, high-speed escort fighters. The 13 YP-81s were cancelled shortly before V-J Day, but work continued on the two XP-81s. After the TG-100 was installed, preliminary ground tests were conducted at Vultee Field before the airplane was disassembled and trucked to Muroc.[75]

The TG-100 was run for an additional 36 hours and 41 minutes in the first XP-81 at Muroc as part of the Army acceptance tests. Next came the initial taxi tests, which quickly encountered the control difficulties that were inherent to early turboprops, but which Convair found were greatly affected by the characteristics of the propeller and propeller governor. Contributing to the difficulties, Convair had selected a four-blade, 12-foot-diameter Aeroproducts A542 propeller that demonstrated a reluctance to change pitch and, hence, to develop thrust when the pilot wanted it.[76]

On 21 December 1945, the winter rains were threatening to make the Muroc lakebeds unusable, so Convair decided to make the initial flight despite the known issues with the propeller. Frank Davis took the first XP-81 on a five-minute flight using all turbine power, but as soon as Davis took-off, a heavy vibration was noted coming from the Aeroproducts propeller. This vibration had passed unnoticed during the ground tests because it was masked by the large magnitude buffeting and general vibration always present at high power on the ground. In the air it showed up strongly and, in general, became worse at higher power settings. This vibration was ultimately traced to the characteristics of the Aeroproducts propeller used for the first 21 hours of flight-testing. This propeller was replaced by a 12.5-foot-diameter Hamilton Standard Superhydromatic 4260 with a considerably faster ability to change blade pitch, eliminating much of the vibration since the pilot could effectively change the pitch as he changed power settings.[77]

The directional stability of the first XP-81 was found to be marginal during the initial test flights, so a 15-inch extension was added to the vertical stabilizer along with a short ventral fin. The second XP-81 was fitted at the factory with a longer ventral fin. The proposed armament of six 0.50-caliber machine guns or six 20mm cannon was not fitted to either prototype.[78]

During 15 months of flight-tests, the two turboprop XP-81s only logged 69 flights totaling about 42 hours. The TG-100 was removed every 5-10 hours for inspection, and despite cracks in the turbine wheels and several other anomalies, there were no serious engine fail-

Above and Below: *Initial flights in the first XP-81 (44-91000) were made using a Packard-built V-1650 Merlin piston engine since the TG-100 turboprop was not ready. Note the "fuel pylon" under the wing in the bottom photo.* (San Diego Air & Space Museum via Bob Bradley)

Above and Below: **The radiator for the Merlin was in a fairing just behind the nose gear, with an oil cooler and carburator air intake in the nose just under the propeller spinner. The entire installation was borrowed from a P-51.** (San Diego Air & Space Museum via Bob Bradley)

ures during the test program. The TG-100 was supposed to deliver 2,300 shaft horsepower (shp), but it actually produced only 1,400 shp. Consequently, the performance of the turboprop-powered XP-81 was no better than that of the Merlin-powered version. The power situation was further aggravated by the I-40 producing only 3,750-lbf instead of its advertised 4,000-lbf. Based on the full 2,300-hp output from the turboprop and 4,000-lbf from the turbojet, Convair estimated a maximum speed of 478 mph at sea level and 507 mph at 30,000 feet. Actual speed was a disappointing 400 mph.[79]

The XP-81s handled well in the air, with a good rate of climb and light controls that were well balanced. Unfortunately, the turboprop proved incapable of delivering its planned horsepower, and the two dissimilar engines were never properly harmonized. The airplane also experienced gearbox problems and continued propeller vibration. Test personnel agreed that use of a gas turbine to drive a propeller created several new and serious problems, much different from those encountered using a turbojet or piston engine. Most of these problems concerned the propeller and its governing and control systems. The final report recommended the development of new standards for propeller balancing so that the inherent smoothness of the gas turbine engine could be fully realized. The report also recommended setting requirements for rate-of-pitch-change to guard against excessive torque loads,

Above and Facing Page: *The XP-81 was a large fighter, but was very clean aerodynamically. The large bubble canopy was located ahead of the wing and afforded the pilot good vision in just about all directions, although the turbojet air intakes obscured some of the over-the-shoulder view. Air for the turboprop engine came from an inlet around the propeller spinner.* (National Archives)

using a governor responsive to torque rather than to speed, and developing a propeller capable of automatic emergency feathering.[80]

Coupled with generally lackluster performance, these problems resulted in the program being cancelled on 9 May 1947 at a final cost of $4,578,231, including fee and termination costs. Although the Army had not conducted any official performance flights in either airplane, both were inspected and accepted on 25 June 1947.[81]

At the time the project was cancelled, the Air Materiel Command was engaged in the development of propeller controls for future gas turbine engines. Since wind tunnels for testing the controls under all flight conditions were not available, the Army thought the two XP-81s might find future use as flying testbeds, and the two airframes were placed in caretaker status at Muroc. However, funds were never allocated for the propeller control program and on 29 April 1949, the Air Force ordered the XP-81s be reclaimed. The two airframes were stripped of their usable parts and relegated to the Muroc photo range. There, they languished until August 1994, when Air Force Flight Test Center (AFFTC) Museum curator Doug Nelson salvaged the hulks. The two XP-81s have now been moved to the National Museum of the U.S. Air Force where one or both will eventually be refurbished for public display.[82]

Even after the XP-81 program ended, Convair proposed reviving the design with different powerplants. An unsolicited proposal was sent to the Air Force to modify one of the XP-81 airframes with a 4,000-shp Armstrong-Siddeley Double Mamba turboprop in front and a 6,250-lbf Rolls-Royce RB.41 Nene turbojet in back.[83] The idea was to create a ground-attack aircraft that could be sold on the export market. The Air Force was not impressed, concluding that the "modification does not appear feasible." An engineering evaluation released on 14 September 1950 showed that two-thirds of the fuselage would need to be rebuilt to accommodate the new engines, and the wing would need to be redesigned to carry tip tanks, bomb racks, and rocket rails to support the proposed ground attack role.[84]

The Air Force concluded that the performance of the proposed airplane compared poorly with a similar size and weight airplane designed from the outset for the ground-attack role. Versions of the pure-turboprop Douglas A2D Skyshark would outperform the XP-81 variant in almost all categories. It was also determined that small ground-attack aircraft should not have two engines of different types since that overly complicated maintenance, logistics, and training. No further action was taken on the Convair proposal, and the idea of a mixed-powerplant fighter faded from sight.[85]

The second XP-81 (44-91001) was originally fitted with a 12.5-foot-diameter Hamilton Standard Superhydromatic 4260 propeller in place of the Aeroproducts unit initially used by the first prototype. This propeller was a significant improvement. (Mike Machat Collection)

The second XP-81 was generally similar to the first airplane except for a long ventral fin that ran from under the cockpit to the rear of the fuselage. Both airplanes received 15-inch extensions to the vertical stabilizers to provide additional directional stability (the extension had a round tip instead of the original square tip). Note the D558-1 and XB-46 in the background. (AFFTC History Office Collection)

Both XP-81s were stored for a couple of years after the flight-test program ended because the Air Force thought they might be useful for a propeller controls research program. In 1949 they were excessed and languished on the Edwards range for decades. (Tony R. Landis)

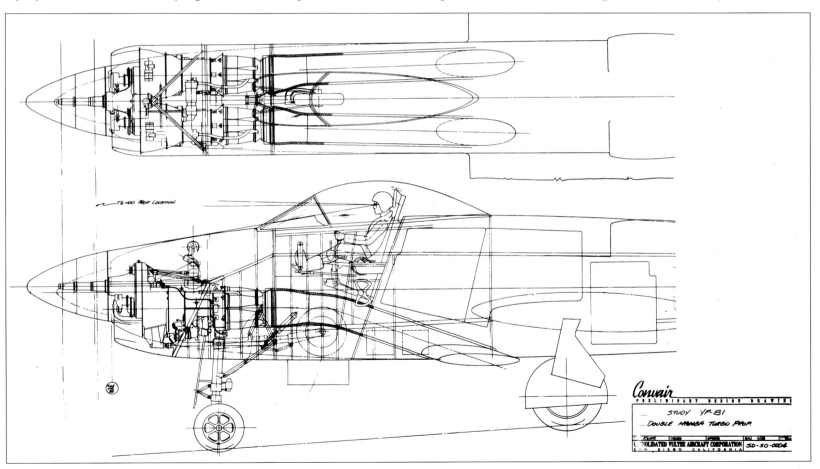

Convair continued to propose variants of the XP-81s for several years after the flight-test program ended. The proposed YP-81 used a 4,000-shp Armstrong-Siddeley Double Mamba turboprop in front and a 6,250-lbf Rolls-Royce RB.41 Nene turbojet in back. In the end, the concept of a mixed-powerplant fighter quietly faded from the scene as turbojet engine technology matured. (National Records Center, St. Louis)

Bell XP-83

One of the primary weaknesses of early jet fighters was their voracious appetite for fuel, resulting in a short range and a limited endurance compared to piston-engine fighters. The idea of mixed powerplants, as demonstrated on the Vultee XP-81, seemed an interim solution at best and was never satisfactorily demonstrated. Seeking better ideas, in March 1943, the Army released a request for proposals for an all-jet, long-range fighter as part of project MX-511.

On 15 October 1943, Bell submitted a proposal for a single-seat, mid-wing, monoplane powered by a pair of 4,000-lbf General Electric I-40 (XJ33) centrifugal-flow turbojets buried on the lower corners of the fuselage much like the P-59. This arrangement had the advantage that no appreciable asymmetric forces were exerted if one engine failed. In addition, no fuselage space was occupied by engines, leaving internal fuselage volume free for fuel and armament. Bell expected the airplane to have a top speed of 540 mph at 32,000 feet and a rate of climb of 2,200 feet per minute at 37,500 feet altitude. The Army was sufficiently interested that it asked bell to submit cost and schedule data for two airplanes and a static test airframe. Bell submitted the requested data on 1 January 1944, calling the airplane the "Bell D-16 Stratosphere Fighter."[86]

At a conference in Washington DC on 4 January 1944, "current items of interest on [the Army} production and development program were discussed." These included the idea of funding an additional project at Bell so that "full advantage could be taken of the two years of experience that Bell had obtained [developing jet fighters]." At the same time, the conferees recommended that jet projects be spread throughout the industry to develop a wider technical knowledge of gas turbine propulsion. On 29 January 1944, the Air Materiel Command recommended ordering 200 aircraft from Bell.[87]

A letter contract (W33-038-ac-2425) was issued on 11 March 1944 for two XP-83 prototypes (44-84990/991) and a static test airframe, plus wind tunnel models, engineering data, and spare parts. The definitive contract was signed on 15 July 1944. The original schedule called for the delivery of the first XP-83 ten months after the letter contract was signed, with the second airplane following 30 days later.[88]

Only seven months later, on 25 February 1945, the first prototype was flown by Bell chief test pilot Jack Woolams, who ultimately logged 25 flights in the XP-83.[89] The airplane was heavier than expected since Bell had used existing parts (such as landing gear struts) to reduce costs and speed the program along. In addition to being overweight, the directional stability of the XP-83, while considered adequate for normal flying, was judged inadequate "for acro-

The first XP-83 (44-84990) at the Bell plant in Niagara. The airplane looked like a scaled-up, and slightly pregnant, XP-59A, but was in fact a completely new design. Note the American and Russian P-63 Kingcobras in the background. (Tony R. Landis Collection)

Like the XP-59A, the XP-83 had a large wing to allow high-altitude operation. The pair of General Electric I-40 (XJ33) engines was mounted on the fuselage corners to leave the entire fuselage free for fuel tanks. (National Archives)

batics or spin recovery." Wind-tunnel tests showed that an 18-inch extension of the vertical stabilizer would cure the stability problems, but it is not certain whether this modification was actually carried out. Increased performance would not be forthcoming given the weight of the airframe and the limited thrust of the engines.[90]

The I-40 engine was an expanded version of the I-16 with a centrifugal compressor. Although the designation credited the engine with 4,000-lbf (hence the "40"), in reality the early engines were lucky to produce 3,750-lbf. Six I-40 engines were allocated to the XP-83 program. The fifth I-40 engine was initially installed in the second Lockheed XP-80A and subsequently returned to General Electric to be modified for installation in the Bell airplane. The first XP-83 was equipped with I-40 engines 5 and 14, while the second airplane was equipped with engines 42 and 43. Two spare engines, 40 and 44, were also furnished to the program.[91]

The first airplane suffered slight damage on 10 June 1945 from a fire caused by a broken fuel line during the 15th flight. Embarrassingly, on 30 July, a pilot started the engines without first activating the hydraulic system, leaving the airplane without brakes. Even idle thrust could push the airplane along fairly well, and it quickly ran into a truck and ambulance parked on the ramp, causing minor damage to the airplane and both vehicles.[92]

The Phase II performance tests took place between 27 July and 31 August 1945 at the Bell facility in Niagara Falls, New York. Capt. Martin L. Smith flew 20 flights that totaled approximately 38 hours while 1st Lt. Frank G. Morris coordinated the tests and analyzed the resulting data. The results showed the airplane was capable of 504.5 mph at 5,540 feet, 522 mph at 15,660 feet, and 493 mph at 35,455 feet. The initial rate of climb was 3,710 feet per minute at sea level, decreasing to only 500 feet per minute at 40,000 feet. Time to climb to the 42,300-foot service ceiling was 29.2 minutes.[93]

Overall, Smith found the ground-handling characteristics of the airplane to be satisfactory, although directional control had to be maintained using the brakes. Initial ground acceleration was slow, but taxiing could be accomplished at idle power. Takeoffs were satisfactory, requiring just less than 3,000 feet. The XP-83 appeared to be dynamically stable longitudinally, but it exhibited a slight pitching tendency due to fuel slosh. There was a marked tendency for the XP-83 to oscillate laterally (snake) just after takeoff and in rough air, and a slight tendency to hunt directionally. Control forces were judged satisfactory, although the XP-83 required a little more effort than equivalent maneuvers in the P-51 or P-80. The roll rate was slightly less than the P-80's, but rolling characteristics were good. Stall characteristics were deemed satisfactory.[94]

To provide additional firepower for new fighters, the Army was developing a new 0.60-caliber heavy machine gun to replace the traditional 0.50-caliber weapon used during World War II. Data on the new guns had been forwarded to Bell in August 1944 with a request to design a six-gun installation for the XP-83. At the time, however, there was not a suitable method for mounting the new weapon and the first XP-83 was built with provisions for 0.50-caliber guns. By the time the second prototype entered production, a mounting method had been devised, although it required a 15-inch nose extension on the XP-83.[95]

The second prototype made its maiden flight on 19 October 1945 with a slightly different bubble canopy and the somewhat longer nose to accommodate six 0.60-caliber heavy machine guns. This aircraft was used in gunnery tests at Wright Field with a new test pilot named Chuck Yeager responsible for the trials.[96]

The performance of the XP-83 was disappointing, and no series production was ordered. Apart from its range, the XP-83 offered no significant advantages over the Lockheed P-80 that was already in production, and further work on the XP-83 project was abandoned. The original cost of the XP-83 had been estimated at $2,322,837, plus $92,913 in fee to Bell, but ultimately, the contract cost the government $4,107,789, plus $101,108 in fee.[97]

The first airplane had been accepted by the Army on 11 October 1945, and was returned to Bell (under contract W33-038-ac-13450) for flight-testing a pair of 20-inch subsonic ramjet engines mounted

When the XP-83 was being designed, the Army was trying to field the 0.60-caliber heavy machine gun. This weapon was delayed, and the first XP-83 was completed with provisions to mount six 0.50-caliber machine guns, although it appears that they were never actually fitted to the airplane. Nevertheless, the muzzle extensions were carried for the entire flight-test program. (National Records Center, St. Louis)

The second XP-83 (44-84991) had a 15-inch longer nose to house the six 0.60-caliber heavy machines guns that would have equipped production airplanes. The contours of the nose did not differ much, making the modification hard to discern. (National Archives)

At the end of its service, the first XP-83 was used as a testbed for ramjet engines under the wings. One of these engines caught fire on 4 September 1946, forcing Slick Goodlin and Charles Fay to abandon the aircraft, which was destroyed. (Lloyd Jones Collection via Bill Norton)

under the wings. During a flight on 4 September 1946, just as the test program was beginning, one of the ramjets caught fire during a test flight, forcing test pilot Chalmers "Slick" Goodlin and engineer Charles Fay to parachute to safety, and the first XP-83 was destroyed in the ensuing crash.[98]

The second XP-83 was accepted by the Army on 27 June 1946 and ferried to Wright Field where the Armament Laboratory used it as a

testbed for the 0.60-caliber heavy machine guns. Unfortunately, the heavier guns did not easily fit into the space available in most fighter aircraft and did not perform particularly well in any case. Maintenance issues with the second airplane reduced it usefulness and the aircraft was declared surplus on 30 January 1947 and subsequently scrapped. The structural test article was tested to destruction at Wright Field during mid 1946.[99]

The first XP-83 (44-84990) in late 1945. At this point it was in storage at Wright Field and was rolled out for various air shows and other displays. The following year it would be made flight worthy and used for airborne ramjet experiments. (NMUSAF Archives)

Republic XP-84 Thunderjet

On 11 September 1944, the Army released a General Operational Requirement (GOR) for a day fighter with a top speed of 600 mph, combat radius of 705 miles, and either six 0.50-caliber or four 0.60-caliber heavy machine guns. In addition, the new aircraft had to use the planned 4,000-lbf General Electric TG-180 (XJ35) axial-flow turbojet engine. Seventeen days later, the Republic Aircraft Corporation submitted a proposal for a single-seat fighter to meet these requirements.[100]

Since the design promised superior performance to the P-80, and Republic had extensive experience in building single-seat fighters, no competition was held for the contract. On 5 December 1944, the Army issued letter contract W33-038-ac-6248 for three experimental airplanes and one static-test airframe. A week earlier the airplane had been designated XP-84 as part of project MX-578, and the name Thunderjet was chosen to continue the Republic "Thunder" tradition that started with the P-47 while emphasizing the new jet engine. On 2 November 1944, the contract was amended to call for a full-scale mockup, static-test airframe, two XP-84s, and an XP-84A that incorporated any changes recommended by the engineering inspection board. The definitive $2,619,132 contract was signed on 12 March 1945.[101]

The clean lines of the XP-84 were evident from almost any angle and somehow the airplane looked "more modern" than the Lockheed P-80. The relative height of the landing gear would allow later models of the F-84 to carry substantial weapon loads. (Cradle of Aviation Museum)

The first XP-84 (45-59475) with the rear fuselage separated to show access to the TG-180 (XJ35) engine. The turbojet was mounted low in the fuselage at the center of gravity and used a long tailpipe to get the exhaust to the rear of the fuselage. The airplane was still in natural metal at this point. Note the simple dolly used to support the aft fuselage. (National Archives)

This photo of the first XP-84 has been described as the first flight, but that has not been confirmed. By now the airplane had received its overall gloss grey paint. Note the large buzz-number under the wing and on the main landing gear door. (AFFTC History Office Collection)

Even before the design was finalized, on 4 January 1945 the Army issued letter contract W33-038-ac-7687 for 25 YP-84 service-test airplanes and 75 production P-84s. On 5 January, the order was changed to 100 P-84As, and eventually the contract stabilized at 15 YP-84As and 85 P-84Bs.[102]

About this same time, Army Headquarters ordered all cost-plus contracts be converted to fixed-price contacts. The Engineering Division decided to take this opportunity to combine the experimental and production airplanes into a single contract (W33-038-ac-6248) that all parties ultimately approved on 5 January 1946.[103]

The XP-84 mockup was inspected 5-11 February 1945, with a multitude of minor changes recommended. Most of these would be deferred to the second or third prototype, and the first airplane looked much like the mockup. Among the changes were the addition of glove-type tip tanks (second and third airplanes only), a pressurized cabin, automatically variable aileron boost, and a variable jet nozzle (all on the third airplane only). Additional changes proposed for production models included armor protection in front of the pilot, an internal radio antenna, an emergency fuel system that ran direct from the tanks to the engine, and the installation of a fire-detection system. In March 1945, a late change directed Republic to make "all efforts" to install an A-1 gunsight and AN/APG-5 range finder into the XP-84A.[104]

Somewhat belatedly, on 7 August 1945, serial numbers were issued for the two XP-84s (45-59475/476) and the XP-84A (45-59477). By late August, the first XP-84 was ready for its engineering inspection, and the Army and Republic decided to replace the double cable-control system with a push-pull rod system to eliminate excessive control forces. Engineers also decided to modify the cockpit to accept an ejection seat similar to one captured in Germany.[105]

On 6 February 1946, the first XP-84 was disassembled, loaded into the Boeing XC-97 transport, and flown to Muroc where it was reassembled. Following ground and taxi tests, on 28 February 1946, Maj. William A. Lien took the XP-84 on its 18-minute maiden flight. It was the first American fighter to have its maiden flight after the end of World War II. Republic conducted 32 hours and 12 minutes of general flight-testing before it released the airplane to the Army for Phase II performance tests. These tests were conducted 2-6 August 1946 using 10 hours and 40 minutes of flight time.[106]

The performance tests were encouraging, especially given the engine produced only 3,750-lbf instead of its advertised 4,000-lbf. A maximum speed of 573 mph was attained at 15,490 feet, and the cruising speed was 478 mph at the same altitude. The airplane could travel 1,160 miles at 35,065 feet using 425 gallons of fuel. The rate of climb

The first XP-84 at Muroc during 1946. The rear fuselage contained the tailpipe, control cables, and little else. Note the sealer applied to various panels around the horizontal stabilizer. (Bill Norton Collection)

The clear canopy used by the XP-84 and early production aircraft was similar to the one used by the competing F-86 and offered excellent visibility. Later models used a reinforced canopy. (National Archives)

at sea level was 5,050 feet per minute, decreasing to 1,320 feet per minute at 35,000 feet. The service ceiling was 44,200 feet. At a gross weight of 13,200 pounds, the airplane needed 3,500 feet to clear a 50-foot obstacle, but only 2,600 feet to land.[107]

The first XP-84 was damaged beyond economical repair on 18 October 1946 at the Shawnee Municipal Airport, Oklahoma, while it was being ferried from Muroc to Wright Field. The airplane was removed by commercial carrier (truck) and taken to Wright Field for gun-firing tests before being scrapped.[108]

The second XP-84 made its maiden flight at Muroc on 15 August 1946 and mostly remained there for testing. On 7 September 1946, this airplane set a short-lived speed record of 611 mph, reclaimed later the same day by a Gloster Meteor that reached 616 mph. The Army formally accepted the first and second airplanes on 14 October 1946.[109]

XP-84A

The third airplane (45-59477) on the original contract was more representative of future production models, and the XP-84A made its maiden flight at Farmingdale on 31 December 1946.[110]

The second XP-84 (45-59476) flying above the high desert of California. Note the white heat shield stretched across the rear of the canopy. (AFFTC History Office Collection)

Despite reports that the second XP-84 remained at Edwards for its entire career, it obviously ventured forth into the real world on occasion, as shown here. This airplane set a short-lived speed record of 611 mph on 7 September 1946, but the British reclaimed the record later the same day with a Gloster Meteor that reached 616 mph. Note the liquid-cooled, Allison-powered Boeing XB-39 in the background. (National Archives)

The YP-84As (45-59483 shown) began to show the airplane's true performance since their J35 engines actually produced 4,000-lbf instead of the 3,750-lbf of earlier engines. (AFFTC History Office Collection)

During 1946, the Army had issued two letter contracts for 412 production P-84s. Despite the relative success of the flight-test program, significant problems began to manifest themselves during 1947. Due to delays with delivery of engines and production of the XP-84A, only limited flight-testing had been completed by the time production P-84Bs began to roll out of the factory in 1947. In particular, the impact of wingtip tanks on aircraft handling was not thoroughly studied and later proved problematic. Republic expressed concerns that production P-84s were in "final stages of completion with little knowledge of certain stability and control characteristics." At the same time, the Army warned Republic that incorporating untested modifications in production models (as had happened in the B-29 and P-80 programs) could "eliminate" the P-84 program.[111]

YP-84A

The 15 YP-84A service test airplanes (45-59482/496) were all delivered by April 1947. These were substantially similar to the XP-84A, except that they were powered by versions of the J35 that actually produced 4,000-lbf. Armament consisted of six 0.50-caliber machine guns,

The second YP-84A provides a stark, modernistic contrast to the old brick buildings of the Republic facility in Farmingdale. The YP-84As remained in natural metal finish, unlike the light grey XP-84s. Note how the anti-glare shield extends all the way to the base of the vertical stabilizer, a feature on many Republic airplanes up through the F-105. (Harry G. Martin via Jim Hawkins Collection)

four in the upper front fuselage and two in the wing roots. The YP-84As were assigned to Muroc and Wright Field for tests and pilot familiarization. On 11 June 1948, the P-84 became the F-84 when the Pursuit designation was replaced with Fighter.[112]

Other than the prototype and 15 service test airplanes, there were no A-model P-84s. The first production version was the P-84B, of which 226 were manufactured, followed by 191 P-84Cs, 154 F-84Ds, and 743 F-84Es delivered to the Air Force and another 100 F-84Es to foreign users. All of these variants looked substantially similar.[113]

When it became obvious to the Air Force that the swept-wing F-84F would not materialize as quickly as planned, an improved F-84E was procured as a stopgap measure. The resulting F-84G was the first fighter capable of in-flight refueling, incorporating a receptacle in the port wing for use with the Boeing-developed flying boom system. Alternately, a probe could be fitted to the left wingtip tank for use with the probe-and-drogue system. The F-84G was also the first single-seat fighter-bomber with nuclear weapons delivery capability. A strengthened multi-framed canopy was introduced, which was later retrofitted to many earlier straight-winged F-84s. Ultimately, the Air Force accepted 789 F-84Gs and another 2,236 were manufactured for foreign customers.[114]

The ninth YF-84A (45-59490) arrived at the NACA Langley Memorial Aeronautical Laboratory in August 1949, but was transferred to the NACA High-Speed Flight Station at Muroc in November. (NASA Langley)

The seventh YP-84A (45-59488) was tested at the NACA Ames Aeronautical Laboratory. The airplane arrived prior to June 1948 since it is still wearing a "PS" buzz number (instead of the later "FS"). Note the air-data boom protruding from one of the left gun ports. (National Archives)

At some point the first YF-84A (45-59482) was modified with a solid nose and NACA-style flush intakes. The exact purpose of this modification is unknown, but it was likely to support various versions of the XF-91 that Republic proposed to the Air Force with solid radar noses and flush intakes. It is uncertain if this airplane flew in this configuration, but the modification appears flight-worthy. (Cradle of Aviation Museum)

The fourth YP-84A at Farmingdale. All 15 prototypes were essentially identical when they left the factory. The main landing gear door shows there is still a large buzz number under the wing. (Harold G. Martin Photo via Jim Hawkins Collection)

YF-84F (YF-96A) Thunderstreak

Republic first proposed a swept-wing F-84F in early 1947 but found little support within the Air Force. The primary reason given by the Air Materiel Command was that "the major changes made it a new development project rather than the modification of an existing type, and because, as a new project, it had little to offer as it presented no new fundamental design features." Alexander Kartveli tried again in February 1948, but an Air Force evaluation showed the airplane "did not compare favorably" with the swept-wing North American F-86.[115]

This did not deter Republic, which continued in-house development on various configurations. On 10 November 1949, Kartveli again proposed a swept-wing F-84, and this time the Air Force was more receptive, assigning the XF-96 designation in December. Part of the enticement was that Republic believed that 55 percent of the F-84E tooling could be used to build the new airplane, minimizing the cost of bringing the high-performance variant into production. A contract change order was issued on 24 February 1950 to cover the construction of a single YF-96A prototype using the fuselage of the last F-84E (49-2430) with a new swept-wing and empennage.[116]

The YF-96A (49-2430) was manufactured using the incomplete fuselage from the last F-84E, along with a new wing and empennage. The airplane retained the slim fuselage of the straight-wing airplanes, as well as the clear bubble canopy. (Mike Machat Collection)

The YF-84F carried an "A" suffix on its buzz number since there was another F-84 with the same last three serial number digits. A long air-data probe protruded from the center splitter in the air intake. By this time, the original vee-shaped front windscreen had been replaced by a more-typical flat-panel of glass. Confusingly, the intake looks like an F-model oval instead of an E-model circle. (AFFTC History Office Collection)

It took 167 days to finish the YF-96A, and when the airplane was rolled out in Farmingdale, it had an unusual windscreen with a V-shaped forward transparency. After initial ground tests in Farmingdale, the airplane was dismantled and transported to Muroc in a Fairchild C-82A and Boeing C-97A. Republic test pilot Otto P. "Bud" Haas took the YF-96A on its maiden flight on 3 June 1950. Republic conducted 30 days of Phase I tests before turning the airplane over to Air Force pilots for Phase II performance tests that ended in November after 64 flights totaling 70 hours. These showed a maximum speed of 693 mph at sea level (Mach 0.93) and a range of 1,716 miles at 514 mph. Although the low-altitude speed was impressive, performance fell off quickly with altitude. The service ceiling was only 38,300 feet, and it took 14.8 minutes to reach 35,000 feet. The Air Force felt the performance improvement over the F-84E was marginal at best, and the project proceeded with a low priority.[117]

Were it not for the Korean conflict, the YF-96A would probably have been cancelled. Although funds to develop new aircraft were still hard to come by, additional funds became available for production of existing types. The Air Force solved this issue on 8 September 1950 by redesignating the swept-wing variant YF-84F to make it appear a variant of an existing type.[118] Nevertheless, a contest among Republic employees resulted in a new "Thunderstreak" name that became official on 2 December 1952. This marks one of the few times that a single aircraft type has had multiple official names.[119]

Late in its life, the first YF-84F was modified with significant anhedral on the horizontal stabilizers and the nose hook and attachment system to be used on the RF-84K FICON (FIghter CONveyor) aircraft. At this point, the airplane was redesignated YRF-84F, although this is somewhat confusing since it had little in common with the prototype YRF-84F reconnaissance variants. The airplane conducted the initial FICON parasite tests with a modified Convair JRB-36F (49-2707) beginning in mid-1953. The tests were generally successful and cleared the way for the modification of 25 RF-84Ks and 10 Convair GRB-36D carrier aircraft. The FICON project was revealed to the public at the National Air Show in Dayton, Ohio, over the 1953 Labor Day weekend. For three days, the YRF-84F and JRB-36F flew a demonstration in which the fighter was launched from the carrier at an altitude of several thousand feet. Maj. Clyde E. Good was at the controls of the YRF-84F, and Ray Fitzgerald piloted the B-36. The YRF-84F was ultimately retired to the Air Force Museum where it is currently on display.[120]

The Air Force believed that more power was needed to improve a relatively sluggish takeoff, climb, and high-altitude performance.

An early photo of the YF-96A shows the vee-shaped windscreen that originally equipped the airplane. This was an attempt to reduce drag, but had a detrimental effect on vision. (Cradle of Aviation Museum)

Despite being a cobbled-together prototype, the YF-96A had a complete set of hardpoints under the wings and conducted at least some weapons trials. (NMUSAF Archives)

Late in its life, the first YF-84F was redesignated YRF-84F and used for the initial FICON tests with a Convair JRB-36F bomber. A non-retractable hook was added to the forward fuselage, and the horizontal stabilizers were canted downward to clear the B-36's bomb bays. During the tests the airplane also received a reinforced canopy from an F-84E. The nose art (seen below left) has "Christine" crossed-out and "George" written below it. (Above: San Diego Air & Space Museum Collection; Below Left: Lockheed Martin; Below Right: AFFTC History Office Collection)

Before beginning full-scale production, in early 1951, the Air Force ordered two YF-84Fs (51-1344/45) powered by 7,200-lbf Armstrong-Siddeley Sapphire axial-flow turbojets. Curtiss-Wright had already acquired the rights to manufacture the Sapphire in the United States as the J65, but production was not expected to begin before September 1951. The Sapphire was considerably larger than the J35 and required a much higher airflow, so Republic redesigned the fuselage, increasing its depth by seven inches and enlarging the nose intake to an elliptical shape. Nobody seemed concerned that a new fuselage, new wings, and a new engine might be a recipe for trouble.[121]

Unlike the first YF-84F prototype that had been modified from a production F-84E, the second and third airplanes were built from scratch. Excepting the deeper fuselage, the second YF-84F looked much like the first prototype. The third YF-84F was completed with wing-root air intakes, leaving a solid nose that could house heavier armament or air-to-air radar, although neither was fitted to the prototype. The airflow through these initial wing-root intakes was not as great as the nose intake, resulting in a substantial thrust loss. The nose intake was retained on production F-84Fs, but Republic continued to refine the wing-root intakes and subsequently used them on the RF-84F, XF-84H, and F-105.[122]

Unfortunately, in December 1950, before testing of the YF-84Fs began, Air Force Headquarters ordered the airplane into large-scale production. Not anticipating significant problems, Republic optimistically signed production contracts for 719 aircraft on 22 March with first delivery scheduled for December 1951. Because of the

The second built-from-scratch YF-84F prototype (51-1345) was completed with wing root intakes that foreshadowed those that would appear on the RF-84F and F-105. The intakes on this airplane were not particularly efficient and restricted engine power, leading to a series of tests in the full-scale wind-tunnel at the NASA Ames Aeronautical Laboratory. (National Archives)

urgent need for improved fighter-bombers in Korea, the Air Force also sought second production sources for both the airframe and engine. The Buick, Oldsmobile, Pontiac Assembly Division of the General Motors Corporation at Kansas City was selected as the second source for the F-84F airframe in January 1951, and the Buick Division was selected as the second source for the Sapphire engine.[123]

The first YF-84F, powered by an imported Sapphire, made its maiden flight at Edwards on 14 February 1951. The second and third YF-84Fs had the deeper fuselage to accommodate the J65, but still used the sliding bubble canopy from the F-84E instead of the faired-in clamshell canopy used on production aircraft.[124]

Despite the original estimate that 55 percent of the tooling used in the production of the F-84E could be adapted to the F-84F, experience proved that only 15 percent could be reused. This problem was quickly compounded by the fact that only three plants in the United States could produce the aluminum wing spar and rib forgings for the airplane, and these were almost fully occupied with satisfying forging requirements for the Boeing B-47, which enjoyed the Brickbat Scheme's priority precedence. The Brickbat Scheme was a high-priority list of critical items designated for specific Air Force procurement programs, and the F-84 was not on it.[125]

To make matters worse, serious delays were encountered in the production of the license-built J65 engines. In July 1951, Republic was forced to admit to the Air Force that the original schedule could not be met. To get the F-84F program back on track, Republic redesigned the wing so that it could be manufactured with different tools and facilities. Although this cured the problem, it added many months to the delivery schedule, forcing the Air Force to purchase the straight-winged F-84G as a stopgap measure. The F-84F and J65 were finally added to the Brickbat Scheme in April 1952, solving many of the supply issues.[126]

The first production F-84F (51-1346) finally made its maiden flight on 22 November 1952, almost a year behind the original schedule. In all, Republic and General Motors built 1,496 F-84Fs for the Air Force, and an additional 852 went to NATO countries under the Mutual Defense Assistance Program (MDAP).[127]

YRF-84F Thunderflash

The third YF-84F prototype had been completed with wing-root air intakes, but these resulted in a substantial loss of thrust and were not adopted for production F-84Fs. However, the Air Force wanted to replace the Lockheed RF-80 with something faster, and concluded that a modified YF-84F with improved wing-root air intakes might make a good photo-reconnaissance aircraft. The Air Force ordered a single YRF-84F prototype (51-1828) and 130 production RF-84Fs on 12 June 1951. This YRF-84F was considerably different from the original YF-84F that had been redesignated YRF-84F during the FICON experiments.[128]

Carl Bellinger took the YRF-84F on its maiden flight on 3 February 1952 at Edwards. This airplane had an F-84E-style sliding bubble canopy and only slightly modified wing-root intakes that still unacceptably limited airflow. The first production RF-84F (51-1829) made its maiden flight on 9 September 1953, and the airplane was soon named Thunderflash. The production airplanes had much larger wing-root intakes to provide adequate airflow, F-84F-style clamshell canopies, and a deeper nose section to house the full complement of cameras.[129]

By December 1957 when production ended, 715 RF-84Fs had been manufactured, with 327 going to foreign air forces as part of the Mutual Defense Assistance Program, and 25 RF-84Fs were converted into RF-84Ks.[130]

The YRF-84F (51-1828) had slightly different wing-root intakes than the second YF-84F and a different nose to house various standard Air Force cameras. These intakes were still not satisfactory and production aircraft used larger ones. (NMUSAF Archives)

The YRF-84F was later tested by the NACA High-Speed Flight Station. The airplane had a standard F-84E-style sliding canopy instead of the F-84F-style clamshell canopy used by production aircraft. Note the pair of large fences on the wing. (NASA Dryden)

The second YF-84F (51-1345) and YRF-84F (51-1828) show the differences between the two airplanes. Externally, the wing-root intakes were similar since most of the changes were to the internal ducting. The noses of the two aircraft were very different. (National Archives)

XF-84H "Thunderscreech"

In the closing days of World War II, Allison began developing a series of turboprop engines for the Navy. The company soon combined ("twinned") two Model 501 (XT38A) gas turbines mounted side by side and connected to a common reduction gearbox to make the 5,850-shp XT40 turboprop. The engine also provided 830-lbf of residual thrust. During cruise, one of the power sections could be shut down to save fuel. This engine was used by the Navy in several developmental aircraft, including the Douglas XA2D, North American XA2J, Lockheed XFV-1, and Convair XFY-1. The only T40-powered aircraft to actually enter service were the Convair P5Y and R3Y flying boats.[131]

In the meantime, the Air Force had been working with Hamilton-Standard and Curtiss-Wright to study supersonic propellers. The performance of conventional propellers falls off dramatically as the tips approach the speed of sound, putting a solid upper limit on the speed of propeller-driven aircraft. A supersonic propeller might allow an airplane to operate in the high transonic – or possibly even the low supersonic – regime.[132]

The XT40 and supersonic propeller appeared to offer a solution to the limited range of early jet fighters, so the Air Force ordered Republic to modify a pair of RF-84Fs (51-17059/60) that were redesignated XF-84H. The turboprop was located in the same position in the aft fuselage as the normal Wright turbojet and drove the gearbox in the nose via a long drive shaft. In addition to modifications to the rear fuselage and nose to accommodate the engine and propeller, a number of changes were made to compensate for the violent torsional flow around the fuselage generated by the stubby three-blade propeller that went supersonic at approximately 3,000 rpm. The left intake was nearly a foot forward of the right, and the horizontal stabilizer was mounted high on the tail to avoid the spi-

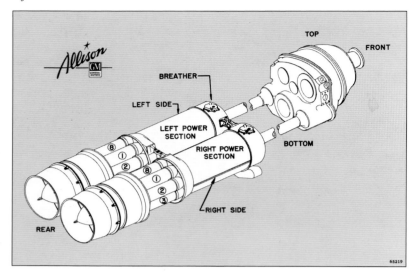

The Allison T40 turboprop engine used two power sections (essentially, jet engines) to drive a single gearbox and propeller. The power sections were located in the center fuselage behind the pilot in the same locations as the normal turbojet engine. (National Records Center, St. Louis)

raling propeller vortices. A triangular fin was placed just behind the cockpit to provide extra yaw control, and Republic incorporated differential control in the wing flaps, creating the first flaperons.[133]

Republic chief test pilot Henry G. "Hank" Beaird, Jr. took the first XF-84H on its maiden flight on 22 July 1955 at Edwards. The usual number of teething problems appeared, but more worrisome was a hideous propeller noise that induced headaches and abrupt nausea in the pilots and ground crews. The incredible noise caused ground crews

The first XF-84H (51-17059) shows that not much of the original RF-84F fuselage remained except for the canopy. The nose, rear fuselage, and empennage was completely new. (National Archives)

The speed brakes around the exhaust pipe would become a feature on the F-105. Note the deployed ram air turbine (RAT) auxiliary power unit just ahead of the vertical stabilizer. (Terry Panopalis Collection)

to dub the XF-84H the "Thunderscreech." Subliminal ultra-low frequency sound waves were later identified as the culprit. By 9 October 1956, Baird had made eight flights in the first XF-84H and four in the second airplane, 11 of which ended in emergency landings. One flight achieved 520 mph of a planned 670 mph, modest by jet standards, but the highest speed achieved by a propeller airplane at the time.[134]

Pure-jet fighters were clearly the way of the future, and neither the Air Force nor the Navy showed any further interest in supersonic propeller research. Although all of the XT-40 programs were eventually cancelled, the lessons learned allowed Allison to build the reliable T56 – basically an enlarged T38 with the power of the T40 still being used on Grumman E-2/C-2 and Lockheed P-3.

Each wingtip sported a large air-data probe in an attempt to keep the instruments out of the propwash. The horizontal stabilizer was mounted atop the vertical for the same reason. A small triangular fin was located just behind the canopy to provide extra yaw control, and Republic incorporated differential control in the wing flaps, creating the first flaperons. (Cradle of Aviation Museum)

The two XH-84F prototypes (51-17059 at left and 51-17060 at right) were essentially identical, differing only in cosmetic items. For instance, the triangular fin behind the cockpit on the first aircraft was painted black, while it was natural metal on the second prototype. Similarly, small black panels along the spine of the first prototype were natural metal on the second. (AFFTC History Office Collection)

The first XF-84H was displayed on a pole at Meadows Field, Bakersfield, California, for several decades. In February 1999, the Air Force Museum removed the aircraft, and volunteers at the 178th Fighter Wing of the Ohio Air National Guard spent more than 3,000 manhours restoring the Thunderscreech. The airplane is currently on display at the National Museum of the United States Air Force. Reportedly, the engine from the second XF-84H was used to support the Douglas A2D Skyshark program and the airframe was scrapped.[135]

YF-84J

In early 1953, Republic proposed modifying the F-84F with an even larger nose intake and deeper fuselage to accommodate an 8,920-lbf General Electric J73 engine. The J73 was developed from the J47 and would form the basis for the later J79 (J47-GE-X24). The Air Force was sufficiently interested to allocate two F-84F airframes (51-1708/1709) as YF-84J prototypes.[136]

Oddly, this photograph of the second prototype while it was still at the Republic factory shows a black triangular fin and panels along the spine, identical to the first airplane. (Cradle of Aviation Museum)

For years, the first XF-84H was displayed on a pole at the Bakersfield airport. In 1999 the Air Force Museum traded a T-38 for the XF-84H, which is now on display at Wright-Patterson AFB. (Tony R. Landis)

The first YF-84J was delivered to Edwards on 24 April 1954 and made its maiden flight on 7 May piloted by Republic test pilot Russell M. "Rusty" Roth. The airplane reached a speed of Mach 1.09 during a 52-minute flight that encountered no major difficulties. Despite a successful, if brief, flight-test program, the Air Force rejected the new engine because it would cost more than $70 million to retrofit the 295 F-84Fs under consideration. The uncompleted second YF-84J was cancelled on 16 June 1954, and the entire program was terminated on 31 August.[137]

There were 7,524 F-84s of all models manufactured. The 4,010 aircraft operated by the U.S. Air Force included 2 XP-84s, 1 XP-84A, 15 YF-84As, 226 F-84Bs, 191 F-84Cs, 154 F-84Ds, 743 F-84Es, 789 F-84Gs, 3 YF-84Fs, 1,496 F-84Fs, 1 YRF-84F, 388 RF-84Fs (including 25 modified into RF-84Ks), and 1 YF-84J. The foreign aircraft consisted of 100 F-84Es, 2,236 F-84Gs, 852 F-84Fs, and 327 RF-84Fs.[138]

Above: *One of the few photographs that could be located of the first YF-84J (51-1708). This aircraft had an even deeper fuselage and larger intake for a J73 engine.* (National Archives)

Below: *The large three-blade propeller generated a hideous noise that induced headaches and abrupt nausea in pilots and ground crews, causing them to dub the XF-84H the "Thunderscreech."* (National Archives)

McDonnell XP-85 Goblin

During the strategic air offensive against Germany, the Army had faced serious opposition from Luftwaffe interceptors, making the development of long-range escort fighters a high priority. The immediate problem was solved by the development of the Republic P-47 and, more especially, the North American P-51 that also escorted the long-range B-29s in the Pacific.

However, the Army was developing the advanced Northrop B-35 flying wing and Convair B-36, whose range far exceeded the capabilities of even the P-51. The first jet fighters introduced near the end of the war had insufficient range to escort the B-17s and B-24s used in Europe, let alone the B-29s used in the Pacific or the future B-35 and B-36 then on the drawing boards.[139]

There were three possible solutions to the problem. The first was to develop a long-range escort fighter. This approach was considered technically feasible, but very expensive. Alternately, the Army could develop aerial refueling techniques for fighters, but this seemed prob-

The U.S. Navy used Curtiss F9C-2 Sparrowhawks as parasite fighters on its two large dirigibles, the USS Akron and USS Macon. Unfortunately, it was a brief experiment. (National Archives)

McDonnell built a full-scale mockup of a Convair B-36 fuselage and bomb bay, along with the mockup of the diminutive XP-85. Oddly, the bomb bay doors shown here do not represent either the original B-36B sliding doors or later B-36D snap-action doors. Nevertheless, the setup allowed McDonnell to demonstrate the concept. (National Records Center, St. Louis)

The XP-85's wings folded vertical to allow the aircraft to be carried completely within the B-36 bomb bay, a feature not used on the B-29 tests. (NMUSAF Archives)

lematic and technically risky. The last possibility was for the Army to revive the parasite fighter concept and have the long-range bombers carry an "internally stowed fighter" with them.[140]

In the early 1930s, Curtiss F9C-2 Sparrowhawk fighters had successfully conducted similar operations on a routine basis, flying from a trapeze slung beneath the U.S. Navy dirigibles *Akron* and *Macon*. First ordered in June 1930, the F9C was less than 20 feet long with a wingspan of only 25.5 feet. A single 420-hp Wright R-975 engine could propel the 2,000-pound fighter to a top speed of 175 mph. When the Navy began building two large airships – *Akron* and *Macon* – it was decided that each airship would be equipped with a small hangar that carried up to five Sparrowhawks. The original XF9C-1 prototype was modified with a hook in front of the canopy, and tests were conducted using the airship *Los Angeles* beginning on 23 October 1931. Six production F9C-2 Sparrowhawks had been ordered a week earlier. By all accounts, the little fighters were quite successful as parasites. Unfortunately, *Akron* was lost on 4 April 1933, followed by *Macon* on 12 February 1935, effectively ending the program. A decade later, the U.S. military would try again.

On 20 January 1944, the Air Technical Service Command (ATSC) began studying the escort fighter problem and by January 1945 had concluded the most viable solution was the parasite fighter concept. At the same time, the Army approached several aircraft companies regarding the feasibility of a parasite fighter. McDonnell was the only company that expressed interest and submitted a proposal in November 1944. The Model 27, designed under the leadership of Herman D. Barkley, would be carried partially inside the bomb bay of a B-29, B-35, or B-36, leaving the lower fuselage and wings exposed to the airstream. The Army rejected this concept in January 1945, concluding that the fighter would have to be carried entirely inside the B-35 or B-36 to minimize drag and reduce the range penalty on the bomber.[141]

The first XP-85 (46-523) was only used for one captive and a single free-flight during the program, mostly because it had been damaged by the NACA and required extensive repairs. (NMUSAF Archives)

On 19 March 1945, McDonnell submitted a revised proposal for an even smaller aircraft with an egg-shaped fuselage, a triple vertical stabilizer, a horizontal stabilizer with pronounced dihedral, and vertically folding swept-back wings. A single 3,000-lbf Westinghouse 24C (XJ34) axial-flow turbojet used a nose intake and a straight-through exhaust. The airplane was only 15 feet long, with a wingspan of 21 feet, an empty weight of 3,984 pounds, and a gross weight of 5,600 pounds, making it, by far, the smallest jet fighter. In fact, the airplane was small-

The second XP-85 (46-524) was the first to fly and was used for most of the flight-test program. The large hook used with the B-29 trapeze was not retractable. Note the emergency landing skid protruding forward of the inlet. (Francis Allen Collection)

The second prototype during an engine test at Edwards; note the fireman holding his ears. The wingtip vertical surfaces had not yet been added to the airplane (see photo at top of page for comparison). (National Archives)

er than the F9C, although it weighed twice as much. The aircraft had a pressurized cockpit, an ejection seat, and the eventual armament was to be four 0.50-caliber machine guns in the sides of the forward fuselage. The top speed was over-optimistically estimated at 648 mph. It would be launched and recovered from a trapeze that extended from its parent aircraft at altitudes up to 48,000 feet. The airplane had an endurance of about 80 minutes and the parasite could be refueled from the bomber fuel system while tucked in the bomb bay.[142]

The Army issued letter contract W33-038-ac-13496 for two prototypes (46-523/524) and a structural test article on 9 October 1945. Oddly, the definitive contract was not signed until 5 February 1947. The airplane was designated XP-85 and assigned to project MX-667. Military characteristics for the little airplane were not issued until 14 March 1947 and were descriptive of the XP-85, rather than requirements for a development program.[143]

At the same time, the Army specified that the 24th and subsequent B-36s would include provisions to carry one P-85 in addition to a reduced bomb load, and it envisioned that some B-36s would be modified to carry three P-85s and no bomb load. Despite later events, it appears that the first few B-36Bs actually had the mounting brackets for the trapeze included in bomb bay No. 1.

Conditional upon the results of flight trials, the Army intended to order an initial batch of 30 production P-85s. However, before the completion of the first prototype, the Army decided on a more cautious approach in which only the two experimental XP-85s would be acquired. If flight tests were favorable, production versions could be ordered later.

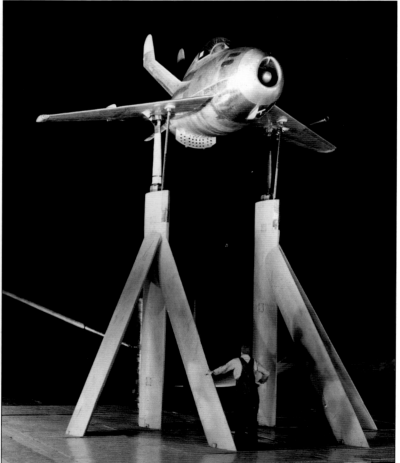

The small size of the airplane limited the amount of space available within the airframe, but most of the equipment was easily reached without the use of workstands. Here a mechanic adjusts the Westinghouse 24C (XJ34) turbojet engine. (National Archives)

The first prototype was tested in the full-scale wind tunnel at the NACA Ames Aeronautical Laboratory, but was extensively damaged when it was dropped while being removed. The NACA repaired the airplane (top), but the second XP-85 was used for most tests. (National Archives)

Since the XP-85 was to be launched and recovered in mid-air, no conventional landing gear was fitted. Instead, a retractable hook was installed on top of the fuselage in front of the cockpit. During recovery, the XP-85 would approach its parent bomber from underneath and the hook would gently engage the trapeze – at least that was the theory. Once securely attached, the aircraft would be pulled up into the bomb bay. If an emergency landing were necessary, the prototypes were provided with a retractable steel skid underneath the fuselage, and the wingtips were protected by steel runners. These would likely have been deleted from any production aircraft.

A mockup of the XP-85 and B-36 bomb bay was constructed at the McDonnell facility in St. Louis. The mockup inspection was held on 10 June 1946 with few significant comments, and McDonnell delivered the first airplane to Muroc in July 1948, but it was then taken to the NACA Ames Aeronautical Laboratory for wind-tunnel testing. Interestingly, the XP-85 was small enough to be transported in a Douglas C-47 to and from Ames. In June 1948, the XP-85 was redesignated XF-85 as part of the Air Force redesignation scheme.[144]

Since a B-36 could not be spared for the project, a Bell-built B-29B (44-84111) was modified with a trapeze for the initial testing. Unlike

A view from the loading pit looking up as the second XF-85 is secured into the B-29 mothership. Note the emergency landing skid under the parasite's fuselage and the multitude of vertical and horizontal tail surfaces. (AFFTC History Office Collection)

Although the XP-85 wings were design to fold when it was inside the B-36 bomb bay, the B-29B (44-84111) was not large enough so the wings were left extended. Here the bomber taxis out for a mission with the second XP-85 tucked into the bomb bay. (National Records Center, St. Louis)

A posed photo taken toward the end of the flight program shows the first XP-85 with its B-29B mothership next to the loading pit at Edwards. Note the long air-data probes and vertical surfaces on the XP-85 wingtips. (National Records Center, St. Louis)

the larger B-36, the XP-85 would not fit completely inside the B-29, leaving it partially exposed, much like the original McDonnell concept. With a wry humor, the B-29 was named *Monstro*, after the whale that swallowed Pinocchio. Unfortunately, the first prototype was dropped while being positioned in the wind tunnel at the NACA Ames Aeronautical Laboratory and sustained considerable damage, so the second XF-85 was used for the initial flight trials.[145]

Several captive flights were made with the XP-85 tucked under the B-29 to verify the mated pair could actually fly, and nothing untold was noted. The first free flight (using 46-524) was on 28 August 1948 at Muroc, but when McDonnell test pilot Edwin F. Schoch attempted to return to the carrier aircraft after a 15-minute flight, trouble began. Following 10 minutes of futile attempts to hook onto the trapeze, the XF-85 smashed into the trapeze, shattering the canopy and forcing Schoch to make an emergency landing on the lakebed using the belly skid.

Following repairs, the airplane made three successful flights on 14-15 October 1948, although each of them was a rather harrowing experience for all concerned. On the fifth flight, the removal of the temporary fairing around the base of the hook resulted in severe turbulence and loss of directional stability, forcing the pilot to make another emergency landing. At the suggestion of Scott Crossfield, who had witnessed the test, vertical surfaces were added to the wingtips to improve directional stability while flying in the turbulent air underneath the EB-29B. Unfortunately, this did not seem to help much, and the sixth flight ended in yet another emergency landing on the lakebed. Only three of the first seven free flights had ended with successful hookups.[146]

The first prototype made its only captive flight on 19 March 1949, and its only free flight, the last of the program, on 8 April 1949. In spite of the problems encountered with recovery, the XF-85 handled quite well in ordinary flight, and Ed Schoch commented favorably on its stability, control, and spin recovery characteristics.[147]

After the 8 April flight, McDonnell recommended that flight tests be temporarily discontinued until a more satisfactory trapeze system could be developed. After a review of the problems encountered so far, the Air Materiel Command recommended continuing the XF-85 program in June 1949. There was $250,000 remaining in FY49 funds and another $150,000 in FY50 funds available, more than enough to cover the development of a new trapeze and the necessary modifications to the two XF-85s. However, the budget climate changed rapidly, and by 1 October 1949, research and development funds had become scarce. The Air Force reluctantly concluded that the recovery operation would probably be beyond the capabilities of the average squadron pilot. In addition, the performance of the XF-85 was inferior to that of foreign interceptors that would soon enter service. Consequently, the Air Force terminated the XF-85 program on 24 October 1949 after 2 hours and 19 minutes of flight time. The program had cost $3,081,612.[148]

The first XF-85 was accepted by the Air Force on 19 June 1950 and was transferred to the Air Force Museum on 20 October 1950. It is currently on display next to a B-36. The second airplane was

An early test (pre-wingtip verticals) of the second XP-85. The hook is engaged, but the trapeze is not closed around the parasite. Releasing proved easy, coming back was troublesome. (NMUSAF Archives)

accepted by the Air Force on 9 August 1950. On 20 October 1950, it was assigned to the Air Force Exhibit Unit at Norton AFB where it was used as a traveling exhibit for many years; it is now at the Strategic Air and Space Museum in Nebraska.[149]

Although the XF-85 was ultimately unsuccessful, it did provide valuable data used when the Republic RF-84F reconnaissance aircraft was adapted for launch and recovery beneath GRB-36Ds as part of the FICON project.

Although unmarked, this is undoubtedly the first XF-85 during a parade celebrating the 250th anniversary of the founding of Detroit, Michigan. (NMUSAF Archives)

North American XP-86 Sabre

As the war in the Pacific marched toward Tokyo, the U.S. Navy was planning to acquire jet-powered carrier-based aircraft that, it hoped, could be pressed into service in time for Operation DOWN-FALL (consisting of Operations OLYMPIC and CORONET), the invasion of Japan planned for May 1946. The Navy initiated the acquisition of four jet fighter types, the Vought XF6U-1, McDonnell XFD-1 (soon redesignated XFH-1), McDonnell XF2D-1 (XF2H-1), and North American XFJ-1 Fury.[150]

Work on the XFJ-1 began in late autumn 1944. The airplane had a straight, thin-section wing set low on a tubby fuselage with a straight-through airflow from the nose intake to the jet exhaust that exited the aircraft under a straight empennage. The laminar-flow wing was borrowed from the P-51 and the single 3,750-lbf General Electric TG-180 (XJ35) axial-flow turbojet was a license-built deHavilland H.1B Goblin. On 1 January 1945, the Navy ordered three XFJ-1 prototypes, and followed this on 28 May 1945 with 100 production FJ-1s.[151]

Based partly on the experience gained from the XFJ-1 effort, North American submitted four different jet fighter designs to the Army between February and April 1945. Of the four designs developed by a team led by Edgar Schmued, one had a configuration generally similar to the P-51 (engine in front of the pilot and a tail wheel), another was identical to the XFJ-1, and two generally resembled the straight-wing Republic P-84.[152]

Ultimately, the Army decided to pursue one of the designs that was quite similar to the XP-84 already under development by Alexander Kartveli at Republic. Headquarters formally approved project MX-673 on 1 May 1945, and North American subsequently received contract W33-038-ac-11114 for three XP-86 prototypes (45-59597/599) and a static test airframe on 18 May. Preliminary design and wind tunnel testing progressed quickly, and the mockup

was inspected on 15-20 June 1945 in Downey, with only minor changes requested. At this point, the projected performance of the XP-86 was underwhelming, being only slightly better than the P-80 and somewhat worse than the P-84. It appeared the North American project would be cancelled even before the first airplane flew.[153]

However, the development effort took a major turn during July 1945, after the Army supplied North American with captured German data on the use of swept-wings to reduce high-speed drag. One German paper dated 1940, in particular, reported that wind-tunnel tests showed significant advantages offered by swept-wings at transonic speeds. A straight-winged aircraft is severely affected by compressibility effects in the transonic regime, but a swept-wing delays these effects, allowing considerably higher speeds. Unfortunately, German research also indicated that the use of wing sweep introduced some undesirable wingtip stall and low-speed stability issues. American researchers had already encountered similar low-speed problems with the swept-wing Curtiss XP-55. It should be noted that this data was derived from extensive wind-tunnel and theoretical studies, and had little to do with the Me 262, which enjoyed a swept-wing mostly to compensate for center-of-gravity issues and not because of any perceived aerodynamic benefit.[154]

North American immediately began a series of design studies using a swept-wing and empennage on a single-seat fighter. The results proved encouraging, and it rapidly became obvious that the straight-wing XFJ-1 and XP-86 were going to quickly become obsolete. In August 1945, project aerodynamicist Laurence P. Greene suggested adopting a swept-wing configuration for the XP-86. North American informally received permission from the Army to discontinue work on the straight-wing XP-86 and devote its efforts to redesigning the airplane to incorporate a swept-wing. The company cautioned, however, that the redesign would delay the delivery of the XP-86 approximately one month.[155]

The full-scale mockup of the swept-wing airplane, complete with a detachable rear fuselage to show maintenance access to the General Electric TG-180 (XJ35) engine. (National Records Center, St. Louis)

The design of the Navy XFJ-1 (BuNo 39053 seen here) had a significant influence on the XP-86, although the swept-wing allowed a considerably streamlined outer mold line. (Jim Hawkins Collection)

On 11 September 1947 the first XP-86 (45-59597) was trucked to Muroc using back roads through the foothills. Note the person resting on top of wingtip. (National Records Center, St. Louis)

The design gross weight of the swept-back design increased from 12,100 pounds to 13,100 pounds, and the wing area increased from 255 square feet to 274.4 square feet. Maximum speed increased from 582 mph at 10,000 feet to 633 mph to 18,500 feet, but the rate of climb decreased (mostly due to the extra weight) from 5,520 feet per minute at sea level to only 4,950 feet per minute. The combat radius at 35,000 feet decreased from 713 miles to 652 miles, again mostly due to the extra weight of the swept-wing.[156]

Unfortunately, engineers discovered that little engineering from the straight-wing airplane was applicable to the new design, so the entire project reverted to the preliminary design stage. This gave engi-

neers even more freedom to make changes. For instance, the engine was moved 28 inches aft to make room for additional fuel and improve the center of gravity. In addition, the cockpit was enlarged to allow another German innovation, the ejection seat, to be fitted, but this necessitated spreading the main top fuselage longerons.[157]

A new mockup inspection took place on 28 February 1946, with the Army requesting a multitude of changes, mostly minor, but a few of consequence. All of this resulted in the XP-86 taking considerably longer to develop than the XFJ-1. The Fury took to the air for the first time on 27 November 1946, but the XP-86 still had almost a year more of work ahead of it before its maiden flight. Nevertheless, on 20 December 1946, the Army issued a letter contract for 33 P-86As, but interestingly, no service test aircraft (YP-86) were ordered.[158]

The first unarmed XP-86 was finally rolled out in Inglewood on 8 August 1947, and a safety-of-flight inspection three days later uncovered little of significance. Flutter and vibration tests revealed nothing unexpected, so the airplane was trucked to Muroc for flight-testing. Tragically, during the afternoon of 16 September 1947, cooling tests were being conducted on the XP-86 when a North American employee walked in front of the airplane and was sucked into the air intake. The employee was killed and the engine severely damaged.[159]

Repairs were accomplished quickly and a new engine installed. On 1 October 1947, North American test pilot George S. "Wheaties" Welch took the XP-86 on its maiden flight, accompanied by a P-80 pace airplane and a P-82 photographic airplane. The flight went well until it came time to lower the landing gear. After several tries, the main gear latched in the down position, but the nose gear remained only partially deployed. All normal and emergency efforts failed to extend the nose gear, so Welch elected to land on the mains and attempt to hold the nose up as long as possible. On final approach, the engine was turned off and Welch made a hard landing on the main gear. The impact was sufficient to extend and lock the nose gear, and

The first prototype sitting in the North American factory waiting to be trucked to Muroc for flight-testing. The XP-86 was in overall natural metal finish with national insignia, serial number, and a P-for-Pursuit buzz number. This airplane was unarmed and did not even have the machine gun muzzle cutouts on the forward fuselage. Nevertheless, it looked like a production aircraft. (National Records Center, St. Louis)

Overhead view of the first XP-86 shows the clean lines of the swept-wing and the wing leading-edge slats that automatically deployed when they were needed. (National Records Center, St. Louis)

The wing markings were typical of the era. The national insignia was painted perpendicular to the fuselage, while the buzz number was swept with the wing. (AFFTC History Office Collection)

the airplane suffered no damage. Subsequent examination showed the rod controlling the sequence valve had broken, probably due to an extremely fast nose-gear retraction sequence. Corrections were made in short order, but not before several flights were made with the wheels locked in the down position.[160]

Official Army Phase II performance testing during December 1947 showed generally good agreement with the initial guarantees made by North American. The maximum speed was 627 mph at 16,000 feet,

close to the 633-mph estimate. Average cruising speed was actually significantly better at 455 mph at 35,000 feet, versus an expected 426 mph. The range suffered a bit, only 1,190 miles at average cruising speed, versus the 1,215 miles North American guaranteed. The service ceiling was lower than expected at 41,200 feet instead of the predicted 43,500 feet, and it took 6.18 minutes to climb to 20,000 feet versus the guaranteed 5.0 minutes. It took 3,116 feet to take off over a 50-foot obstacle, significantly better than the expected 3,540 feet, but the landing

The third XP-86 (45-59599) was fully armed, with six 0.50-caliber machine guns behind retractable muzzle covers. The airplane was also used for rocket trials. (AFFTC History Office Collection)

The first XP-86 shows the original long-range external tanks. These were later changed to use more conventional pylons, spacing the tanks further from the wing. (AFFTC History Office Collection)

A nice family portrait of the three XP-86s (from the back, third, first, and second). At this point, none of the airplanes seems to be equipped with the nose-mounted machine gun armament, although all are using the post-June 1948 "FU" buzz numbers. (National Archives)

roll was 2,855 feet instead of the 2,660 expected. Overall, North American and the Air Force thought this performance was satisfactory given the relative immaturity of the airframe and engine.[161]

The second and third XP-86 prototypes (45-59598/599) joined the test program in early 1948. As is often the case, each prototype was slightly different, and the third prototype was the only one to have fully automatic leading-edge slats, armament, and a gunsight. Flight-testing of the XF-86s was accelerated as much as possible since production F-86As were already rolling down the assembly line. All three prototypes were officially accepted by the Air Force on 30 November 1948, although by that time, their designation had changed to XF-86. The first prototype crashed in September 1952 after logging 241 flight hours, and the other two airplanes were finally retired in April 1953. The total cost of the XP-86 development effort, including the three prototypes, was $4,707,802.[162]

North American received a contract for 33 production P-86As on 20 December 1946, even before the first XP-86 had flown. Some sources claim the first production airplane (47-605) was designated YP-86A, but no official documentation supports this. The P-86A was outwardly similar to the last two XP-86s, but used 4,850-lbf General Electric TG-190 (J47) engines. The First Fighter Group at March AFB, California, was the first operational user. Oddly, when first F-86A was delivered, the airplane still did not have a name. In February 1949, the group held a contest that resulted in Sabre being approved on 4 March 1949. In all, 554 F-86As were built, followed by 393 F-86Es, and 1,959 F-86Fs.[163]

The F-86C was the North American entry in the 1948 penetration fighter competition. By the time the prototypes were built, the airplane had been redesignated YF-93A, and more detail is contained in that section of this book.

YF-86D

On 28 March 1949, North American began work on an interim all-weather interceptor to supplement the Lockheed F-94 until the Northrop F-89 was available. This was the first attempt to build a single-seat all-weather jet interceptor. An afterburning General Electric J47-GE-17 turbojet was selected, along with an electronically controlled fuel-scheduling system. The nose air intake was redesigned to make room above it for the AN/APG-36 search radar antenna, marking one of the most distinctive features of the "Sabre Dog."[164]

Instead of using conventional cannon armament, plans were made for a battery of twenty-four 2.75-inch folding-fin aerial rockets (FFAR), nicknamed Mighty Mouse, mounted in a retractable tray under the fuselage. The FFAR, developed jointly by North American and the Navy, was based on the World War II German R4 rocket. The rocket had a 7.55-pound explosive warhead, a velocity of 2,500 feet per second at burnout, and a range of 4,500 yards. The launcher took only a half-second to extend, and the FFARs could be fired in groups or in salvo.[165]

On 19 July 1949, the Secretary of the Air Force formally endorsed the interceptor project, and a letter contract for two prototypes and 122 production aircraft was issued on 7 October 1949. Since the new aircraft had only 25 percent commonality with the original F-86A, the Air Force assigned a new F-95 designation. The first YF-95A was rolled out of the North American plant in September 1949. Oddly, the two prototypes had serials numbered (50-577/578) at the end of the production run. The definitive contract was approved on 2 June 1950, adding 31 more F-95As.[166]

The first airplane was trucked over the foothills to Muroc on 28 November 1949, and George Welch made the maiden flight on 22 December. The first Hughes E-3 fire-control system arrived at

The first YF-95A (50-577) left no doubts as to its new designation. According to the North American press release, "NAA employee Clem Lawson christens the airplane with a paint brush." (National Archives)

North American on 26 May 1950. The system was installed in the second YF-95A, and after some initial airworthiness flights at Muroc, this aircraft was bailed to Hughes on 17 October 1950 for continued tests of the fire-control system.[167]

For political reasons, the F-95A was redesignated F-86D on 24 July 1950. At the time, separate appropriations had to be made by

The nose markings were removed after the designation was changed to YF-86D on 24 July 1950. Note the unusual "YF" buzz number instead of the correct "FU" prefix, and the larger aft fuselage to house the afterburning J47-GE-17 engine. (National Records Center, St. Louis)

The F-86K was a simplified version of the F-86D intended for NATO countries that did not need the electronics that integrated the Sabre Dog into the Semi-Automatic Ground Environment (SAGE) used in North America. Externally, the airplane was nearly indistinguishable from its American counterpart. This the first YF-86K (52-3630) before it was delivered to Italy. (National Records Center, St. Louis)

Congress for new types of aircraft, but developments of existing types came under a different budget category, making the F-86D much easier to sell to Congress than the F-95A. The same fate met the F-96 (F-84F) and F-97 (F-94C).

In 1952, the first YF-86D was modified with a low-set horizontal stabilizer that was planned for the supersonic F-100. The horizontal stabilizer was moved to a position below the chord plane of the wing to keep it out of the wing wake at high angles of attack and would help to prevent the dangerous tendency of a swept-wing aircraft to pitch up suddenly and violently following a stall. This sometimes-deadly phenomenon had come to be known as the "Sabre dance," and had been the cause of numerous accidents in the F-86.[168]

Eventually, 2,504 F-86Ds were manufactured and the airplane served as one of the main air-defense weapons against Soviet bomber attacks. The F-86L was a conversion of existing F-86D airframes to interface with the Semi-Automatic Ground Environment (SAGE) computerized ground-controlled intercept system.[169]

YF-86K

On 22 January 1953, the Air Force notified North American that Italy wanted to manufacture a two-seat version of the F-86D equipped with a simplified fire-control system and cannon armament. North American replied that a two-seat airplane would be too costly and time-consuming to design, and proposed a simplified version of the F-86D to be supplied under the Mutual Defense Assistance Program (MDAP).[170]

Two government-furnished F-86Ds (52-3630 and 52-3804) were modified into YF-86Ks beginning on 14 May 1953. The first YF-86K made its maiden flight on 15 July 1954, piloted by North American test pilot Raymond Morris. Both YF-86Ks were shipped to Italy after initial tests, and 120 production aircraft were manufactured by North American and 221 more by Fiat.[171]

YF-86H

The development of a fighter-bomber version of the F-86 began on 16 March 1951. To accommodate the new 8,920-lbf General Electric J73 engine, the fuselage was stretched two feet, increased in diameter, and used a larger air intake. Four underwing hard points were added for bombs or drop tanks. The Air Force ordered two YF-86Hs (52-1975/1976) and 150 production aircraft, but by the time the contract was signed on 3 November 1952, this had increased to 175.[172]

The first YF-86H made its maiden flight on 10 April 1953 with North American test pilot J. Robert Baker at the controls. Early flight tests did not uncover any major problems, but by the time the first ten F-86Hs had been delivered at the end of June 1954, several serious accidents had occurred. The Phase II performance tests confirmed "numerous deficiencies" existed in both the airframe and engine, and testing did not resume until October 1954.[173]

Although the F-86H had been ordered as a fighter-bomber, in 1952 the Air Force reclassified it as a day fighter, and in 1954 another reclassification called the aircraft a tactical support fighter. The development effort continued to be fraught with problems, but

This is the F-86H structural test article in its test rig. This sort of testing allows the manufacturer and military to verify the airframe will withstand the expected stresses. (National Records Center, St. Louis)

The first YF-86H (52-1975) shows the extremely long air-data probe extending from the nose. Note the "U.S. Air Force" marking under wing versus the more normal "USAF." (AFFTC History Office Collection)

eventually the F-86H emerged as a satisfactory fighter. Production totaled 475 aircraft, with the last delivered in August 1955.[174]

YF-86J

A single F-86A (49-1069) was loaned to Royal Canadian Air Force in October 1951 and fitted with a 6,600-lbf Avro-Canada Orenda Series 10 axial-flow turbojet under the YF-86J designation (although there is some uncertainty about how official this designa-

tion was). A proposed production run of similar aircraft was cancelled in favor of licensed production (still using the Orenda engine) of the F-86E, and the single YF-86J was returned to the United States in December 1953.[175]

All totaled, North American built 6,297 F-86s, Canadair 1,815, Commonwealth Aircraft Corporation in Australia 112, Fiat 221, and Mitsubishi 300. The U.S. Air Force accepted 3 XP-86s, 554 F-86As, 393 F-86Es, 1,959 F-86Fs, 2 YF-86Hs, 473 F-86Hs, 2 YF-86Ds, and 2,504 F-86Ds (all L-models were converted from F-86Ds).[176]

The first YF-86H with the long air-data probe and no gun muzzle outlets. Compare the markings on the vertical stabilizer with the in-flight photo at the top of the page. (AFFTC History Office Collection)

The first YF-86H with six gun muzzles that appear to have been painted onto the nose. Although designed as a fighter-bomber, the F-86H retained a large bubble canopy. (Jim Hawkins Collection)

The Early Turbojet Engines

General Electric J33 (I-40) assembly line at Allison. This engine was used in the XP-80, XP-81, and XP-83. (NMUSAF Archives)

Two Allison-produced engines, the J35 (hanging) turbojet and T40 turboprop, shown in December 1949. (National Archives)

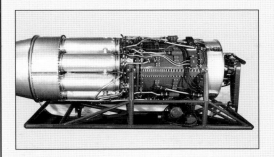

General Electric-designed, Allison-produced J35 (TG-180) axial-flow turbojet, as used in the straight-winged F-84 series and XF-86. (NMUSAF Archives)

Westinghouse J34 (24C) axial-flow turbojet from the XF-85. (NMUSAF Archives)

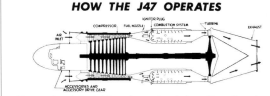

HOW THE J47 OPERATES

Air enters through the air inlet at the front of the engine, and passes into the compressor. Here its pressure is multiplied about five times by the hundreds of blades packing it into smaller and smaller space. Forced into the eight combustion chambers, it is mixed with atomized fuel and burned. Constant burning increases the energy of the compressed air and forces it to expand through the turbine and out through the tail cone. The turbine, operating like a windmill, supplies the power to spin the compressor. The expanding gases, pushing their way out the rear at about 1200 miles per hour, give the plane a forward thrust much as air forcing its way out of an ordinary balloon causes the balloon to fly through the air.

APPARATUS DEPARTMENT, GENERAL ELECTRIC COMPANY, SCHENECTADY, NEW YORK

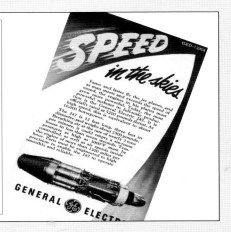

General Electric J47 (TG-190) turbojet, as used in the F-86A. (NMUSAF Archives)

Chapter 3

Above: *The YF-94C (50-955) initially incorporated a larger rear fuselage and new wing, but retained the early-model nose, intakes, and canopy. The tip-tanks were a non-standard configuration, matching neither the earlier models nor the production Starfire design.* (Lockheed Martin)

Left: *The XP-89 (46-678) shows the upswept aft fuselage that inspired the Scorpion name. The aircraft initially flew without the tip tanks that became characteristic of the production models. This Scorpion was overall gloss black with a red serial number.* (Northrop via Tony Chong)

ALL-WEATHER FIGHTERS
NEITHER RAIN NOR DARK OF NIGHT...

During July and August 1945, the Army began issuing tentative characteristics for the fighter and bombardment aircraft expected to be required in the post-war world. Each of these characteristics was reviewed by Generals Carl Spaatz and Curtiss LeMay, as well as a group of senior ground forces officers. One common thread through all of the concepts was that the 0.50-caliber machine gun was inadequate, and all future designs – fighter and bomber – needed heavier armament. This was expected to consist of the tried-and-true M24 (later called the T-31) 20mm cannon, a newly developed 0.60-caliber T-17 heavy machine gun,[1] the T-110 rocket launcher (and its T-131 unguided rockets),[2] 2.75-inch folding-fin aerial rockets (FFAR), and 5-inch high-velocity aircraft rockets (HVAR).

Fighter aircraft were divided into three general categories – an all-weather offensive fighter, a point-defense interceptor, and a long-range penetration fighter. It was expected that the all-weather fighter would be the largest and heaviest of the three fighter types and the point-defense interceptor would be the smallest. Requests for proposals (RFP) for each of these types followed.

On 28 August 1945, the Army released an RFP for an all-weather offensive fighter capable of 525 mph at 35,000 feet, 530 mph at sea level, the ability to climb to 35,000 feet in 12 minutes, and a 600-mile combat radius at 10,000 feet. Power would be provided by at least two engines, and because of the low-altitude and range requirements, piston engines were anticipated instead of the new turbojets. Armament was assumed to be six 0.60-caliber heavy machine guns or six 20mm cannon.[3]

Somewhat unusually, the Army did not issue the final requirements until 23 November 1945 with the release of the "Military Characteristics for an All-Weather Fighter," although a tentative version had been sent to potential contractors on 6 August. This airplane was intended to prevent a recurrence of the "Battle of the Bulge" during which tactical air support for ground troops was lost due to unfavorable weather conditions. The requirements specified an offensive fighter capable of seeking out and destroying enemy aircraft and ground targets in all weather conditions, day or night. Seemingly, the Army was seeking something of a combination of a light attack aircraft (like the Douglas A-26) with a long-range, radar-equipped fighter (like the Northrop P-61). These requirements would eventually morph into an all-weather interceptor instead of an offensive fighter.[4]

Bell, Consolidated, Curtiss-Wright, Douglas, Goodyear, and Northrop ultimately submitted proposals. The Bell, Convair, and Goodyear entries were clearly deficient in their projected performance and were eliminated early in the evaluation. Curtiss offered a large, four-jet derivative of its XA-43 attack aircraft with side-by-side seating for the pilot and radar operator. Douglas submitted an adaptation of the Navy XF3D-1 Skyknight carrier-based, all-weather fighter. Northrop submitted three proposals, one based on the existing P-61, one on the radical XP-79B, and an all-new twin-jet design.

The Army favored the Curtiss design, if for no other reason than Curtiss-Wright would likely go out of business if it did not win the contract. In January 1946, the Army elected to use the remaining

The Douglas F3D Skyknight originated in 1945 with a Navy requirement for a jet-powered, radar-equipped, carrier-based night fighter. The design was briefly considered for Air Force use. (National Archives)

funds from the XA-43 development effort to build a single proto-type of the XP-87. However, the Army was also intrigued by the Northrop two-engine proposal and ordered two XP-89 prototypes in May 1946. (The XP-88 designation had been assigned to a new penetration fighter in the interim.)[5]

Around this time, the Army decided that all future all-weather fighters would use four 20mm M24 (T-31) cannon in a movable nose turret that allowed the angle of fire to be varied from zero to 90 degrees from the centerline. In May 1946, the Army contracted with the Glenn L. Martin Company for the design and manufacture of this turret and its associated fire-control system as project MX-769. The nose turret, aimed by a modified AN/APG-3 radar from the B-36, would be government-furnished equipment for the XP-87 and XP-89.[6]

In the meantime, a Cold War began to develop between the Western Allies and the Soviet Union. During the 1947 Aviation Day display at Tushino, a trio of four-engine Tupolev Tu-4 long-range strategic bombers flew over the reviewing stands. The Tu-4 was a copy of the Boeing B-29 based on examples that had been interned in the Soviet Union after forced landings following raids against Japan. It was expected that the Soviets would soon have atomic bombs and North America might be vulnerable to nuclear attack from the air.

The immediate post-war years had left the Air Force without any modern all-weather fighters to face this new threat. The wartime Northrop P-61 night fighter was forced to soldier on for a few more years, and radar-equipped adaptations of the piston-engine North American P-82 were hastily developed and deployed. Although the Air Force had initiated the development of the XP-87 and XP-89 all-weather fighters, neither would be available quickly since they were all-new designs. In response, the Air Force ordered Lockheed to adapt the TP-80C two-seat trainer into an all-weather fighter, the F-94. Similarly, North American was directed to develop the F-86D all-weather version of the Sabre. These two interim designs bought time for Curtiss and Northrop to develop their more advanced interceptors. It was a good thing.[7]

Although the flight-test results being generated by the XF-87 and XF-89 were generally satisfactory, the Air Force ordered a fly-off between the XF-87, XF-89, and the Navy Douglas XF3D-1 Skyknight before deciding which interceptor to order into production. In October 1948, pilots from the Air Defense Command evaluated the three airplanes, and each came away with a mixed review. Unfortunately, by this time the requirements for a purely defensive interceptor had replaced those for an all-weather offensive fighter. Since the XF-87 had been designed to carry out an offensive mission with a 1,000-mile radius of action, it was considered excessively large and heavy for an interceptor. Nevertheless, the XF-87, with its side-by-side seating, was judged to have the best cockpit arrangement, with the XF3D-1 coming in second. The tandem seating of the XF-89 was thought to make communication between pilot and radar operator difficult. Maintenance was found to be easiest on the XF3D-1, with the XP-87 coming in second. However, although it was not outstanding in any particular area, the evaluation team judged the XF-89 as being the overall superior fighter and having the best development potential.[8]

Based on these results, on 15 October 1948 the Air Force cancelled the Curtiss XF-87 and subsequently ordered the F-89 into production. The failure of the XF-87 to win any production orders was the end of the line for the Aeroplane Division of Curtiss-Wright, which subsequently declared bankruptcy and sold its assets to North American.[9]

Curtiss XP-87 Blackhawk

The Curtiss-Wright Corporation, like all other American aircraft manufacturers, was hit hard by the massive cancellations that took place at the end of World War II. Unfortunately, Curtiss had no projects that were readily applicable to the civilian market, and none of its military aircraft fit postwar planning. Consequently, in 1946 Curtiss-Wright was forced to close all of its aircraft manufacturing plants except the government-owned facility in Columbus, Ohio, which had been built by the Navy for SB2C Helldiver production. All units of the Aeroplane Division were transferred to Columbus, and Curtiss-Wright valiantly tried to get back into the game.[10]

A year before the all-weather fighter competition, on 14 November 1944, the Army had awarded Curtiss-Wright a $105,895 contract (W33-038-ac-6266) for preliminary engineering data on a ground-attack aircraft. This was followed on 24 March 1945 by a supplemental contract for additional engineering data, a full-scale mockup, and various wind-tunnel models and tests. The Army was sufficiently impressed that on 27 June 1945 it ordered two XA-43 prototypes powered by General Electric TG-180 (XJ35) axial-flow turbojets.[11]

By the end of 1945, it had become obvious the TG-180 would not conform to its original specifications, resulting in the XA-43 not meeting its range guarantee. The 1,000-mile radius at 35,000 feet was met, but the desired radius at 10,000 feet would have required greatly increasing the amount of internal fuel to the point the airplane was no longer practical. In the meantime, Curtiss had proposed an all-weather offensive fighter meeting the November 1945 specification based loose-

The Curtiss XA-43 mockup shows only a passing resemblance to the XP-87. The tandem cockpit, slender fuselage, gun-equipped nose, vertical stabilizer, and oval engine nacelles are considerably different than those on the fighter. The XA-43 was also larger and 65-percent heavier than the XP-87. (Ray Wagner Collection via Bill Norton)

ly on the XA-43 design. Since the Army had lost interest in the XA-43, in January 1946 the remaining XA-43 funds were reallocated to the development of a single XP-87 (45-59600) as part of project MX-745.[12]

According to the official project history, "The fact that the XF-87s were built under the original XA-43 contract (W33-038-ac-6266) gave rise to the erroneous opinion of many that the XF-87 was in fact the XA-43 with a new model designation. Actually, the two airplanes were entirely dissimilar in size, equipment, and mission." All totaled, $863,959 had been spent on the XA-43.[13]

Consistent with the policy of providing at least two prototypes of a new design in case one was lost during testing, the Army added $3,082,280 to the original contract to cover a second XP-87 (46-0522) and additional testing. This change was approved on 16 January 1946, but the contract modification was not finalized until 17 May 1946.[14]

During the course of preliminary design, clarification of the definition of "all-weather fighter" was requested from the Army. Originally, both the Air Materiel Command and Curtiss-Wright had interpreted this as meaning both good and bad weather. Headquarters, however, clarified that it was meant to infer night and/or inclement weather only. This allowed the removal of the two-gun tail turret remotely controlled by a periscopic sight operated by the radar-observer that had been provided to provide a defense against interceptors during good weather.[15]

The configuration of the XP-87 was generally similar to the XA-43, but used four 3,000-lbf Westinghouse 24C (XJ34) axial-flow turbojets paired in large pods mounted under the wings. The size difference between the two airplanes was telling. For instance, the XA-43 had a wingspan of 77 feet, 7 inches compared to only 60 feet for the XP-87. The XA-43 was 74 feet, 10 inches long while the XP-87 was only 62 feet, 10 inches. The XA-43 had a design gross weight of 62,000 pounds, versus 37,350 pounds for the fighter. The pilot and radar-observer were seated side by side in a large cockpit, one of the most obvious changes from the XA-43 that had used tandem seating. The new nose turret under development at Martin was specified as the armament. However, it was evident that the fire-control system would not be delivered in time for the first XP-87, so plans were made to install it on the second prototype.[16]

On 29 May 1946, a meeting between the Army and Curtiss reviewed engine options for the XP-87 in case "prior commitments" prevented Westinghouse from delivering production quantities of the J34. The most attractive alternative was using two 4,000-lbf General Electric I-40 (XJ33) engines in lieu of the four J34s. The J33 allowed a lighter and less complex installation but only provided two-thirds the thrust. Curtiss was directed to proceed with the airplane mockup based on four J34s.[17]

It was anticipated that the greatest number of mockup comments would be centered on the cockpit due to the large number of instruments, radio, and radar equipment necessary to meet the military characteristics. At the Army's suggestion, in early July 1948, Curtiss held a preliminary cockpit mockup evaluation prior to the general airplane inspection. This greatly reduced the number of comments concerning the cockpit layout that were received during the mockup

This wind tunnel model of the XA-43 differs somewhat from the mockup, particularly the rounder cross-section fuselage. The engine nacelles are mid-mounted on the wing instead of being slung under the wing like the XP-87. (Jim Hawkins Collection)

inspection held 16-19 July 1948 at the Curtiss plant in Columbus. The most important changes were the deletion of the bomb bay and the complete redesign of the ejection seats based on requirements that had been formulated since the beginning of the XP-87 project.[18]

In August 1946, Curtiss requested the name Bat for the XP-87, but the Air Force rejected the name since it was already being used by the Navy ASM-N-2 (SWOD Mk 9) glide bomb. A month later Curtiss requested the XP-87 be named Blackhawk, which was subsequently approved.[19]

Since the development of the standard, all-weather fire-control system at the Glenn L. Martin Company was running even further behind than expected, the Army decided to equip the second XP-87 with a fixed-gun nose to allow a limited tactical evaluation. However, on 2 December 1946, Curtiss proposed installing a simulated turret to determine the aerodynamic effects of moving the guns on a high-speed airplane. This was subsequently approved, but the turret was not completed prior to the contract being terminated.[20]

During January 1947, the Army studied all airplanes then under development to determine which were the most suited for modification into tactical reconnaissance aircraft. The study determined that the XP-87 was the most readily adaptable of all fighter types, primarily due to the size of the nose section. Headquarters directed that one of the airplanes under construction be converted into a photo-reconnaissance prototype. A meeting in April 1947 concluded that both XP-87 airplanes would be completed as basic all-weather fighters, but that the second airplane would later be modified into an XRP-87 reconnaissance platform. The gun turret scheduled for the second airplane would instead be installed in the first prototype after it completed its Phase I flying tests and Phase II performance tests. The engineering work for the XRP-87 was completed prior to the Curtiss contract being cancelled, but little fabrication had been accomplished since the modifications were scheduled for eight months after the delivery of the second airplane, which never occurred.[21]

The issue of engines came up again in June 1947 when Curtiss proposed substituting two afterburning 7,500-lbf Allison J33-A-29 engines in lieu of the four J34s in the basic airplane. The afterburning J33 provided essentially the same thrust-to-weight ratio as the four J34s and resulted in a simpler installation with fewer maintenance requirements. The change was approved, but the modification of the nearly completed first prototype was postponed until the nose turret

was installed. The modified airplane would be redesignated XP-87A, and a separate contract (W33-038-ac-19837) was issued to cover the engine change as well as the turret modification and conversion of the second prototype into a reconnaissance airplane. All engineering work for the installation of the J33 engines was completed, and the nacelles had been fabricated prior to cancellation. The revised nacelles were not significantly different from the outside since they still had to house the main landing gear and other equipment.[22]

The safety-of-flight inspection of the first XP-87 took place on 7 October 1947, with only minor changes being suggested. Meanwhile, arrangements had been made to conduct the maiden flight at Muroc instead of Columbus as part of a new policy that all

The first XP-87 (45-49600) shortly after its roll-out at the Curtiss plant in Columbus, Ohio. The large canopy with side-by-side seating for the pilot and radar operator elicited favorable comments from Army evaluators, but the aircraft was large for an all-weather fighter since it had been designed as an "offensive fighter" capable of ground-attack missions. Note the Curtiss script on the nose and vertical stabilizer. (National Archives)

A walkaround of the first XP-87 (45-49600) showing the aircraft as it appeared for most of its flight-test program. On production airplanes, the four J34 engines would have been replaced by a pair of afterburning J33 engines in modified nacelles. Production models would also have used a swept-empennage to eliminate buffeting discovered during the flight-test program. Oddly, the Air Force briefly considered equipping the XP-87 with a track landing gear (similar to those tested on a P-40, C-82, B-36, and B-50) to allow it to operate from unprepared Arctic bases. (National Archives)

The engine nacelles seemed large to house the four Westinghouse J34s, but they also contained the main landing gear and hydraulic systems. (Terry Panopalis Collection)

first flights would take place at the desert test facility. After the inspection, Curtiss conducted low-speed taxi tests at Columbus along with various ground-systems tests.[23]

The first prototype was partially disassembled and, on 9 November 1947, loaded aboard a commercial truck for transport to Muroc. It did not get far. Unknown to the driver, the vertical stabilizer was too tall to clear the first overpass near the plant and sustained considerable damage when it contacted the structure. The airplane was returned to the plant where the vertical was removed and the fuselage inspected for other damage. Finding nothing of concern, on 10 November the convoy again headed for Muroc and progressed about 150 miles per day until it reached the vicinity of

Tulsa, Oklahoma. Approximately 16 miles east of Tulsa, the convoy was involved in a traffic accident that resulted in extensive damage to the left engine nacelle.[24]

The convoy was diverted to the Air National Guard hangar at the Tulsa Municipal Airport where the airplane was inspected by Curtiss engineers that had flown in from Columbus. It was determined the damage could be repaired at Muroc and the convoy left Tulsa, ultimately arriving at Muroc on 1 December where the repaired vertical stabilizer was waiting. Curtiss spent the next four months reassembling and repairing the airplane, as well as conducting additional ground tests and high-speed taxi tests.[25]

On 1 March 1948, Curtiss test pilots Lee Miller and W. P. Harrigan took the XP-87 on its 58-minute maiden flight. The flight was uneventful except for minor tail buffeting at approximately 190 mph that was later attributed to the main landing gear doors, which had been left unlocked and sagged open about eight inches. The flight reached 360 mph at 15,000 feet, and all systems performed normally. The next few flights also experienced tail buffeting, and engineers eventually determined this was caused by flow separation at the junction of the vertical and horizontal stabilizers, not from the landing gear doors. A 36-inch long, 13-inch diameter stinger was added at the junction, effectively curing the buffeting, although the critical Mach number of the empennage remained lower than that of the airplane as a whole. Curtiss proposed fixing this by installing swept vertical and horizontal stabilizers on production airplanes.[26]

The Army approved the change, and Curtiss began fabricating the new empennage as part of a production contract (W33-038-ac-20450) dated 29 March 1948. The modified airplane would have been redesignated XP-87B, and it would have been representative of an unspecified number of production airplanes.[27]

Curtiss conducted 55 flights totaling just over 47 hours during the Phase I contractor tests. One of these flights resulted in a wheels-up landing when the uplock on the left main gear failed. The damage was minor, and the airplane was quickly repaired. During these flights, the J34 engines had proven particularly unreliable and

The first XP-87 in storage at Wright Field during early 1949. No records can be found indicating the airplane flew after its arrival at Wright Field, and it was scrapped in late 1949. (NMUSAF Archives)

The XP-87 carried large tip tanks on at least a couple of occasions during the flight-test program. Each tank held 807 gallons, in addition to the 1,518 gallons carried internally. (National Records Center, St. Louis)

required numerous replacements and repairs, confirming the need to switch to J33 engines on production airplanes. Overall, the contractor flights had demonstrated the airplane was stable about all three axes, and that most airplane systems functioned satisfactorily. The tail buffeting was the major problem encountered, and kept the airplane from reaching its guaranteed top speed and altitude, but the swept-empennage was expected to solve this.[28]

The first flights by an Air Force pilot, on 3 June 1948, revealed that the stall speed was exceptionally high and could not be tolerated during operational service. It was also determined that the maneuverability at high altitude, although within contract specifications, needed improvement. Despite these problems, the Air Force placed a tentative order for 57 P-87B offensive fighters and 30 RP-87B photo-reconnaissance aircraft on 10 June 1948. The next day, all Air Force fighters traded their P-for-Pursuit designations for F-for-Fighter.[29]

The solution to both issues appeared to be a larger wing, and in July 1948, Curtiss proposed installing a 740 square foot wing (an increase of 140 square feet) on the second prototype at the same time the J33 engines were installed. This would reduce the stall speed from 130 mph to 110 mph and provide better maneuverability at high altitude, although it would result in a slight reduction in range. The Army approved the concept, and the second airplane was again redesignated, this time as the XRF-87C. This airplane would have used the same swept-empennage being developed for the XF-87B.[30]

Phase II performance testing took place between 24 September and 2 October 1948, racking up 19 flights in only seven days. The Air Force pilots considered the handling qualities satisfactory except for unusually high takeoff and landing speeds, and the known buffeting issue. The tests also showed that the climb performance was better than expected.[31]

However, based on the fly-off results that favored the Northrop XP-89, on 15 October 1948, the Air Force terminated the XF-87 effective later that month. The first prototype was ferried to Wright-Patterson AFB where it was formally accepted on 14 December 1948, although it appears to have never flown again. The airplane was salvaged between May 1949 and January 1950, having never received its swept-empennage, new engines, or larger wing. The second airplane was never completed and was used as spare parts for other projects. All totaled, $10,231,925 had been spent on the XF-87, in addition to the $863,959 spent on the XA-43.[32]

The loss of the F-87 contract was devastating for Curtiss-Wright. By this time, the company had completely run out of fresh ideas, and had finally reached the end of the line. With no orders forthcoming from the military, and with nothing even remotely promising for the civil market, Curtiss-Wright was forced to shut down its Airplane Division. All assets were sold to North American Aviation and the government-owned plant at Columbus was later used for the production of F-86 Sabres.

The first XP-87 was finished in overall black, like its Northrop XP-89 competitor. However, in contrast with the red used by Northrop, Curtiss used white for the markings. The man standing beside the airplane gives a sense of how large the XP-87 was, mostly because it had been designed to an early offensive-fighter requirement. (Stan Piet Collection)

Northrop XF-89 Scorpion

Although the Curtiss XP-87 was nominally the winner of the all-weather fighter competition, the Army was also intrigued by the Northrop proposal and issued a $4 million letter contract (W33-038-ac-14541) for two XP-89 prototypes (46-678/679) on 3 May 1946 as part of project MX-808. Unlike most of Jack Northrop's contemporary designs – the XP-79 and XB-35 flying wings – the XP-89 was fairly conventional. The aircraft was powered by a pair of General Electric TG-180 (XJ35) axial-flow turbojets, mounted one on either corner of the fuselage just underneath a 30-degree swept-wing. The Martin-designed nose turret being developed as MX-769 would be used when it became available, and various cannon installations were proposed for the interim.[33]

The XF-89 mockup was inspected on 25 September 1946, but the Air Force came away unimpressed. The inspection team wanted the radar operator moved closer to the pilot, the canopy redesigned, aluminum substituted for magnesium in the wings, and the oil and fuel systems simplified. At the same time, research in the Wright Field wind tunnel indicated that the 30-degree swept-wing had some undesirable handling characteristics and did not provide significantly better performance than a traditional straight wing. Northrop modified the design to address these issues, including using a larger, straight wing. Another mockup inspection was held on 17 December, after which Northrop was authorized to begin construction of the two experimental airplanes.[34]

The unarmed XP-89 (46-678), painted a sinister gloss black, rolled out of the Hawthorne, California, factory in early June 1948, nine months later than expected. It was powered by a pair of J35 engines built by Allison that produced only 3,750-lbf instead of the expected 4,000-lbf. Even before the new fighter made its maiden flight, the P-for-Pursuit designation was replaced by F-for-Fighter, and the airplane became the XF-89.[35]

Following ground taxi and brake tests at Hawthorne, the XF-89 was disassembled and trucked to Muroc on 26 July. Taxi tests commenced on 12 August, and Northrop test pilot Fred C. Bretcher took the XF-89 on its maiden flight on 16 August 1948. For the first 32 flights, conventional ailerons were fitted, but on 1 February 1949, Northrop-invented "decelerons" were installed. These two-part ailerons could split horizontally to act as speed brakes. The decelerons were used on all production F-89s and became a trademark of several Northrop designs including the B-2A Spirit.[36]

As a result of a 1948 evaluation of the XF-87, XF-89, and XF3D-1, on 4 January 1949, the Air Force issued a $51 million letter contract for

The XP-89 (46-678) was a completely conventional airplane, despite Jack Northrop's penchant for flying-wing designs. Two engines sat low in the fuselage, and contrary to most contemporary designs (P-80, P-84, and P-86), the fuselage was truncated at the engine exhaust instead of using a long tailpipe. This resulted in the scorpion-like appearance of a raised tail section. (Northrop via Tony Chong)

Northrop had originally proposed a 30-degree swept-wing, but wind-tunnel testing revealed the design had some undesirable handling characteristics and did not provide significantly better performance than a traditional straight wing. The airplane was quickly revised with a large straight wing optimized for high-altitude performance. (Northrop via Tony Chong)

48 F-89As (49-2431/2478) and directed Northrop to complete the second XF-89 as a service test aircraft under the designation YF-89A. In March 1949, the name Scorpion was approved, the suggestion originating with the ground crews at Edwards who thought the upward-curving rear fuselage and high tail looked a lot like the dangerous creature with the deadly stinger in its tail.[37]

Phase II performance testing began on 14 June 1949 on the 48th flight of the program. The testing was uneventful until 27 June, when the XF-89 crash-landed at Muroc on its 64th flight while being piloted by Lt. Col. L. C. Moon and Air Force civilian R. V. Coleman. Oddly, the left main landing gear had fallen off! The landing resulted in only minor damage to the airplane, which made its next flight on 15 October. In February 1950, the XF-89 was ferried to March Field to play the role of a secret enemy aircraft in the movie *Jet Pilot* starring John Wayne.[38]

Unfortunately, the January 1949 production commitment proved to be premature. On 22 February 1950, the XF-89 crashed on its 102nd flight when the right horizontal stabilizer separated during a 500-mph low-altitude pass over the Hawthorne plant and the aircraft tore apart in midair. Northrop test pilot Charles Tucker was thrown clear during the breakup and was able to parachute to safety, but Northrop flight engineer Arthur Turton was killed. Debris from the

XF-89 crashed onto Rosecrans Boulevard in Manhattan Beach, and one engine penetrated an oil storage tank, igniting a large fire.[39]

The subsequent investigation revealed that excessive tail flutter caused the horizontal stabilizer to fail. The ultimate fix was installing a series of external mass balance horns to the elevator hinge. The lines of the rear fuselage behind the jet pipes were also altered to eliminate the severe turbulence that had been encountered at high speeds.[40]

The YF-89A made its maiden flight, significantly delayed by the accident investigation, on 27 June 1950, finished in natural metal instead of overall black. A new nose added three feet to the fuselage to house the Hughes E-1 fire-control system. The air intakes were redesigned to include external boundary layer bleed ramps, and auxiliary pop-in doors were added to the nacelle sides to supply additional engine air during ground operations. Upgraded J35 engines were installed that actually produced 4,000-lbf. The development of the Martin nose turret was cancelled by the Air Force after several development delays were encountered. In its place, Northrop intended to use six T-31 20mm cannon, although the YF-89A was initially unarmed. The jettisonable 300-gallon wingtip tanks of the XF-89 were replaced by more streamlined, permanently attached 300-gallon tanks. The YF-89A made its maiden flight on 27 June 1950.[41]

The gloss black paint might have made the airplane look sinister, but it was undoubtedly uncomfortable for the crews in the high desert at the Muroc test base. What few markings the XP-89 carried were painted in red, except for the full-color national insignia. The large bullet in front of the horizontal stabilizer – used only on the XP-89 – stands out in this photo. Note the Boeing B-29s and North American B-45 in the background. (Northrop via Tony Chong)

The YF-89A (46-679) was used for armament trials at Edwards. Note the forward pointing cameras mounted in small fairings under the wings mid-way between the landing gear (shown partially retracted) and tip tanks. (Northrop Corporation)

At the time of the XF-89 accident, three F-89As (49-2431/2433) were nearing completion, and the Air Force decided to use these three airplanes, along with the YF-89A, for further testing. The first production F-89A was accepted by the Air Force on 28 September 1950, followed by the second and third examples a few weeks later. The three F-89As carried six 20mm T-31 (M24) cannon in the nose. Production of the remaining F-89As resumed in January 1951, although only eight A-models were ultimately built.[42]

Despite the concept of turret armament for the F-89 having been abandoned in 1950, a similar Martin D-1 four-gun swiveling turret was tested briefly on an F-89A (49-2434) during 1952. The entire nose section rotated as a unit, while the guns traversed through 105 degrees from the forward-facing position. The system proved difficult to use and maintenance intensive, and was not adopted for production F-89s.

Production soon shifted to 40 F-89Bs that differed only in various items of internal equipment, followed by 164 F-89Cs. However, during 1952, several F-89Cs crashed due to wing structural failure, including one spectacular crash in front of thousands of spectators at the International Aviation Exposition in Detroit, Michigan. On 22 September 1952, the entire F-89 fleet was grounded for seven months to work out the problems.[43]

The ground crew gives a good indication of the size of the XP-89 as they service it for a test flight from Edwards. Note the absence of mass balancers on the horizontal stabilizer – these would be added to production aircraft after the XP-89 crashed on 22 February 1950. The investigation revealed excessive tail flutter caused the horizontal stabilizer to fail. (Northrop via Tony Chong)

The YF-89A shows the original engine tailpipe configuration. The diverging area between the blast plates generated undesired vibrations, and was modified on production airplanes. (Northrop Corporation)

Following the loss of the XP-89, the Air Force decided to use the first three F-89As (49-2431 shown here), along with the YF-89A, for an extensive flight-test program. (AFFTC History Office Collection)

After an exhaustive series of flight tests, the problem was finally traced to a previously unknown effect, known as aero-elasticity. During high-g maneuvers, the wing tended to twist at the tip, exerting excessive strain on the wing attachment points and causing them eventually to fail. The large wingtip fuel tanks were found to be a significant factor in this twisting moment. A total of 194 F-89A, B, and C aircraft were shipped back to Northrop, where they were fitted with stronger wings with forged steel attachment points. At the same time, a small fin was added to the outboard rear of each wingtip tank to reduce the aerodynamic forces on the tank.[44]

YF-89D

A single F-89B (49-2463) became the prototype YF-89D with a longer nose housing a Hughes E-6 fire-control system. The F-89D replaced the six 20mm cannon with an all-rocket armament consisting of fifty-two 2.75-inch FFARs in the forward part of modified wingtip tanks, which also carried 308 gallons of fuel.

The maiden flight of the YF-89D was on 23 October 1951, and the first two production F-89Ds were delivered to the Air Force on 30 June 1952. Unfortunately, the YF-89D was lost on 20 October 1953, and the

The YF-89A undergoing maintenance. The sliding canopy was unusual for a two-seat airplane. Note the simple main landing gear strut and the large wheel and tire combination. (AFFTC History Office Collection)

The YF-89A showing the six 20mm cannon in the nose and the wide stance afforded by its landing gear. At this point, the cannon were the Scorpion's only armament. (AFFTC History Office Collection)

The YF-89D was converted from an F-89B (49-2463) and included a longer nose housing a Hughes E-6 fire-control system, and revised pods on the wingtips that carried fifty-two 2.75-inch rockets. The six 20mm cannon of the previous models were deleted to make room for the sophisticated Hughes electronics and radar. (AFFTC History Office Collection)

subsequent investigation did not uncover any specific cause, although the pilot had indicated the rocket armament was malfunctioning just prior to the accident. Eventually, 682 F-89Ds were accepted by the Air Force, of which 350 were subsequently modified into F-89Js.[45]

YF-89E

The F-89E was to have been an F-89D equipped with non-after-burning Allison J71 turbojets to provide a greater combat radius. A single F-89C (50-762) was modified into the YF-89E with a pair of 9,500-lbf YJ71-A-3 engines and larger air intakes with an additional lip on the upper surface for better high angle-of-attack performance. The YF-89E made its maiden flight on 10 June 1954, but did not offer much improved performance, and the project was abandoned before reaching production. The airplane continued to be tested until the program was terminated in 1955 when the total cost reached $5.7 million.[46]

YF-89H

The F-89H was an upgrade of the F-89D that used the Hughes E-9 fire-control system, which was a simplified version of the MA-1 being developed for the Convair F-102. The program was carried as part of WS-205B. A single F-89D (52-1938) became the prototype YF-89H, although two additional F-89Ds (52-1830 and 53-2449) were also modified to test the weapons system changes. The Air Force accepted the first production F-89H on 26 October 1955, but because of the rapid advances being made in the supersonic interceptor program, particularly with the F-102A and the follow-on F-102B (F-106) "Ultimate Interceptor," the service life of the F-89H with the Air Force was destined to be relatively brief.[47]

Eventually, the Air Force accepted 1,052 Scorpions, including 1 XP-89, 1 XF-89A, 8 F-89As, 40 F-89Bs, 164 F-89Cs, 682 F-89Ds, and 156 F-89Hs (the 350 F-89Js were modified F-89Ds).[48]

Lockheed YF-94

To solve its immediate need for a jet-powered, all-weather fighter while it waited for the P-87 and/or P-89, in March 1948 the Air Force approached Lockheed about fitting the TP-80C two-seat trainer with armament and a Hughes E-1 fire-control system. On 8 October 1948, the Air Force issued a General Operational Requirement (GOR) calling for the development of an interim all-weather interceptor. The Air Force was in a hurry, and wanted the first production aircraft to be available before the end of 1949. The concept was endorsed by the Secretary of Defense on 14 October 1948, and an amendment to the F-80 production contract (AF33(038)-1847) was issued in January 1949 for the development of the F-94.

Lockheed was, characteristically, enthusiastic in its response. Kelly Johnson entrusted the development of the new fighter to a team headed by Russ Daniell. Fortunately, the TF-80C airframe had sufficient volume to house the fire-control system in a modified nose and enough room in the aft cockpit for a radar operator and his equipment. Consequently, it appeared converting the trainer into an all-weather interceptor would be relatively straightforward.[49]

Two TF-80Cs were used as prototype interceptors. The first airplane (48-356) had been completed as a P-80C, and then converted into the first two-seater. Initially, the airplane was designated ETF-80C before it was redesignated YF-94 on 22 May 1950. (Lockheed Martin)

The first YF-94 used the wing and forward fuselage from its TF-80C roots, modified with a new nose and aft fuselage. The new nose was aerodynamically-representative of the radar-equipped version used on production airplanes but, at least initially, the prototype did not carry the radar. The modified aft fuselage housed an afterburning Allison J33 engine, still a relatively new concept at the time. (Lockheed Martin)

The second YF-94 (48-373) was also converted from a TF-80C, and was eventually redesignated EYF-94A. Like the first prototype, it originally flew without radar or armament, but both items were subsequently installed. (Lockheed Martin)

However, early design work soon indicated that the 3,825-lbf Allison J33 used in the TF-80C would not be powerful enough to accommodate the additional weight of the fire-control system and armament. In search of more power, Lockheed switched to the Allison J33-A-33, rated at 4,600-lbf dry and 6,000-lbf with afterburning. The afterburning concept had already been tested in the second XP-80A, but the engine required a longer and deeper rear fuselage, which pulled the center of gravity aft. Fortunately, this was offset by the weight of the fire-control system and radar installed in a longer forward fuselage with an upswept nose. An armament of six 0.50-caliber M3 machine guns had originally been planned, but space limited this to only four guns mounted in the lower nose section.[50]

Two TF-80Cs (48-356 and 48-373) were bailed to Lockheed as prototypes. The first airplane had been completed as a P-80C, and then converted to a two-seater. Initially, the airplanes were designated ETF-80C, which was later changed to ET-33A when the TF-80C became T-33A. Subsequent modifications to both airplanes resulted in them being redesignated YF-94 on 22 May 1950. The second airplane was redesignated EYF-94 in January 1953 and EYF-94A in September 1954. Both airplanes had the distinctive upturned nose that would

The first YF-94C (50-955) used a standard F-94A forward fuselage, a thinner wing, and a non-afterburning Rolls-Royce Tay engine. As shown here, the airplane has been fitted with the rocket-equipped nose used on production Starfires, although the metal radome indicates that the Hughes E-5 fire-control system is not installed. (Lockheed Martin)

The first YF-94C shows the non-standard tip tanks that differed in shape and also used a triangular fin instead of the later square-tip fin of production models. (National Archives)

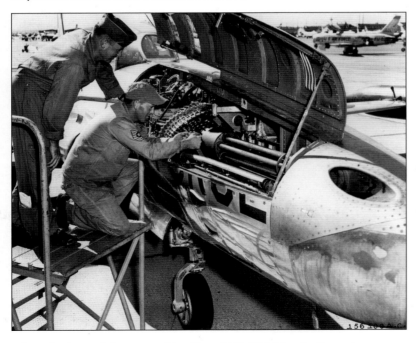

After the loss of the second Lockheed XF-104 (the dedicated weapons aircraft) on 14 April 1955, a modified F-94B (51-5500) was used as a testbed for the General Electric T-171 (M61A1) Vulcan 20mm cannon. The M61 first equipped the F-104, and has been used on almost every American fighter (and a few bombers) since. (National Archives)

characterize the future F-94A/B, and featured a frameless TF-80C-type canopy, F-80-style underwing fuel tanks, and the aft fuselage modifications for the new engine. Initially, at least, both airplanes lacked the radar, weapons, and most of the operational equipment that was to be fitted to production aircraft. Tony LeVier and Glenn Fulkerson made the maiden flight of the first ET-33A on 16 April 1949 from the Van Nuys airport.[51]

Initial flight tests proved that the handling characteristics with the different center-of-gravity were generally satisfactory. The afterburner, however, was a different story. At the time, afterburners were a relatively new concept, and the YF-94 engine suffered from frequent flameouts, often with very difficult relights. These problems were eventually solved by Allison and Lockheed engineers working together. The two YF-94s were used as testbeds for a few years before they were retired. The first YF-94 is on display at the Air Force Flight Test Center Museum at Edwards. The fate of the second airplane is unknown.[52]

The Air Force ordered 109 F-94As in January 1949, and despite the FY49 budget crisis, the order soon increased to 288. The F-94A was generally similar to the YF-94s, but carried full operational equipment. The F-94A was the first production fighter to be equipped with an afterburner as standard equipment, and it was the first jet-powered, all-weather interceptor to serve with the Air Force. The Soviet detonation of an atomic bomb in August 1949 resulted in yet another increase to 368 aircraft. Despite the large backorder, only 109 F-94As were built before production switched to the F-94B.[53]

There were no prototypes of the F-94B since it was a rather modest upgrade with more reliable electronics and engines, as well as a new instrument landing system to allow more efficient all-weather operations. Ultimately, 356 F-94Bs were manufactured, and the airplane entered service in January 1951.[54]

YF-94C Starfire

The F-94A/B all-weather interceptors were considered interim types to fill in the gap until the Northrop F-89 was available in quantity. Once its initial problems had been corrected, the F-94A/B proved to be reliable and relatively easy to maintain. However, the F-94A/B lacked sufficient range, climbing speed, and armament to make a truly satisfactory interceptor.[55]

In July 1948, several months before receiving the contract for the first production F-94As, Lockheed presented an unsolicited proposal for a more advanced airplane. A completely new wing with reduced thickness and greater dihedral would allow higher speeds using an afterburning Pratt & Whitney J48. This engine was a license-built version of the Rolls-Royce RB.44 Tay that also powered the Grumman F9F Panther. The increased thrust required larger air intakes and a completely new rear fuselage. The proposal also included a drag chute, a more advanced Hughes E-5 fire-control system, and an all-rocket armament mounted in the fuselage nose.[56]

The Air Force was not particularly interested in the Lockheed proposal, preferring to concentrate on the North American F-86D and the Northrop F-89. Undeterred by the lukewarm response, Lockheed management decided to build a company-funded demonstrator that would add the new wing to an F-94A fuselage. Since production of the J48 had not begun, the demonstrator was fitted with an imported non-afterburning version of the Tay.[57]

The unarmed demonstrator (civil registration N94C) made its maiden flight on 19 January 1950, with Tony LeVier at the controls. The Air Force was sufficiently impressed after a series of demonstrations that in February 1950 they purchased the airplane as the YF-97 and assigned it a military serial number (50-955). At the same time, the Air Force ordered a fully militarized YF-97A prototype (50-877) and 180 production F-97As.[58]

Initial trials with the YF-97 turned up several problems, all of which were fairly easily solved. The wing-root extension fillet was removed to improve stall characteristics during landing. The vertical stabilizer was made larger to increase directional stability at high speeds, and the original horizontal stabilizer was replaced by power-boosted swept surfaces to eliminate an annoying high-frequency vibration at high Mach numbers. Dampers were added to correct aileron buzzing, and spoilers improved roll control. When the American-built engine finally became available, the first YF-97 was re-engined with a J48-P-3 rated at 6,000-lbf dry and 8,000-lbf with afterburning.[59]

On 12 September 1950, the YF-97 was redesignated YF-94C for largely political reasons. Lockheed publicists applied the name

The new nose on the YF-94C housed a Hughes E-5 fire-control system and four groups of six 2.75-inch folding-fin aerial rockets. The upper left rocket tubes can be seen in their loading position on the far side of the air-data probe. By this time the aircraft had been equipped with production tip tanks. Contrary to popular belief, only the C-model F-94 was named Starfire. (Lockheed Martin)

The first YF-94C in natural metal without the orange markings shows the original F-94A-style forward fuselage. Note that the small wing root extension fillet found on all other P-80 variants was deleted from the new F-94C wing. The Starfire also used a swept-empennage to eliminate a high-frequency vibration at high Mach numbers. (National Archives)

Starfire to the F-94C, following the tradition of using the names of celestial objects. The C-model was the only Starfire, although as the years have passed, all F-94s seem to have inherited the name. The Starfire became the first all-weather fighter (as well as the first two-seater and first straight-wing aircraft) to break the sound barrier when test pilot Tony LeVier put his F-94C into a 60-degree dive from 45,000 feet. Later, Glenn Fulkerson became the first "passenger" to go supersonic.[60]

YF-94D

In January 1951, Lockheed received an Air Force contract for 113 F-94D single-seat fighter-bomber adaptations of the F-94C. The fuselage, empennage, and J48 engine of the F-94C were mated to a new wing with 50 percent more area, the rear seat was replaced by additional fuel tanks, and a retractable in-flight refueling probe was installed in the nose. The rocket armament in the nose was replaced by eight 0.50-caliber machine guns, along with 4,000 pounds of bombs or fuel tanks on underwing racks.[61]

Lockheed built two aerodynamic prototypes by mating the new F-94D nose to a pair of F-94Bs (51-5500/501), but without the new wing. These aircraft were generally called YF-94Ds, but it is unclear if this was an official designation. The single YF-94D (51-13604) in the production contract was almost complete when the Air Force cancelled the program on 15 October 1951. The uncompleted airframe was subsequently scrapped.

After the cancellation, one of the modified F-94Bs (51-5500) was used as a testbed for the General Electric T-171 (M61A1) Vulcan 20mm cannon that first equipped the Lockheed F-104. This became particularly important after the second XF-104 was lost on 14 April 1955, when Fish Salmon was forced to eject during gun-firing trials at 50,000 feet. That airplane had been allocated as the armament testbed for the F-104 program, and Lockheed engineers were forced to find an alternative. The modified F-94B fit the bill nicely.[62]

Ultimately, the Air Force accepted 109 F-94As, 356 F-94Bs,

2 YF-94Cs, and 385 F-94Cs. The original pair of YF-94s had been accepted as TF-80Cs. The last airplane was delivered in May 1954, and the type was phased out of Air Force service in February 1959 and from the Air National Guard in the mid-1960s.[63]

North American YF-95A (YF-86D) Sabre

The YF-95A was the initial designation of what was produced as the F-86D. For political reasons the designation of the F-95 was changed to F-86D on 24 July 1950. Details of the YF-86D may be found elsewhere in this book.

Lockheed YF-97A (YF-94C) Starfire

The YF-97A was the initial designation of what was produced as the F-94C. For political reasons, the designation of the F-97 was changed to F-94C on 12 September 1950. Details of the YF-94C may be found elsewhere in this book.

The first YF-94C was nothing if not colorful. As happened with so many early jet fighters, the development of the engine lagged the airframe, and the Pratt & Whitney J48 had a long and difficult gestation period, although it emerged as a decent powerplant. (AFFTC History Office Collection)

Chapter 4

Right: *The Convair XF-92A (46-682) in its final Air Force configuration and paint scheme. The aircraft was subsequently turned over to the NACA for further testing.* (AFFTC History Office Collection)

Below: *The second Republic XF-91 (46-681) shows one of its most distinctive features – its wings had a broader chord and thicker section at the tip than at the root. The landing gear also retracted backwards from most, with the wheels being housed in the wingtips. The goal was to reduce the wingtip stall characteristics.* (AFFTC History Office Collection)

POINT-DEFENSE INTERCEPTORS
EXTRAORDINARY PERFORMANCE

During mid-1945, the Army issued requests for proposals (RFP) for three new aircraft, including an all-weather offensive fighter, a point-defense interceptor, and a long-range penetration fighter. The point-defense interceptor RFP specified spectacular performance for the era, and the Army assumed it would be powered by liquid-propellant rocket engines. Oddly, despite the consensus from senior officers that 0.50-caliber machine guns were inadequate for the post-war era, the Army expected the point-defense interceptor to be armed with four of the weapons, presumably because weight and size constraints would preclude heavier armament.

In August 1945, the Army released tentative military characteristics for a supersonic (700-mph) interceptor capable of reaching 50,000 feet in four minutes and attacking both "enemy bombers and missiles," assumingly referring to cruise missiles. The perceived threat posed by Soviet bombers greatly worried the Army in the immediate post-war years, and project MX-809 was created to develop a high-speed, high-altitude daytime interceptor capable of "meeting and defeating any strategic bomber aircraft that any potential adversary might produce." These military characteristics were revised on 23 November 1945 and again on 5 February 1946. The Special Operational Requirement (SOR) released on 8 October 1946 called for an airplane capable of 25.5 minutes of combat operation, divided into a 2.5-minute to climb to 47,500 feet, 15 minutes of cruise at 535 mph, 3 minutes of combat at 760 mph, and 5 minutes of descent to landing. These were demanding requirements for the available technology.[1]

The Army ultimately received proposals from Bell, Consolidated-Vultee, Douglas, North American, and Northrop. On 12 April 1946, the Army announced that Convair had won the competition and awarded a contract for the XP-92. Oddly, although the Republic XP-91 had been submitted in response to the penetration fighter RFP, the Air Force believed it held greater potential as an interceptor. In a scenario that would later be replayed during the development of the F-102 and F-103, the Air Force was sufficiently impressed with the Republic design that it awarded a contract on 29 May 1946 for two prototype interceptors as a backup design in case the Convair airplane ran into development problems.[2]

Republic XP-91 "Thunderceptor"

During the development of the XP-84, Alexander Kartveli and his team at Republic began exploring the use of rocket power to provide extra speed during combat. Republic studied reports of the Messerschmitt Me 163 rocket interceptor and the Me 262C Heimatschutzer, the latter combining turbojet and rocket power, to gain information on the planned propulsion system. The Me 163 had demonstrated that spectacular performance could be attained with rocket propulsion at the expense of extremely short endurance. It seemed that one possible answer to the penetration fighter RFP was to use a relatively low-powered jet engine for cruise, coupled with rocket power during combat, conceptually similar to the Me 262C. Republic submitted its proposal on 30 October 1945. The design did not score well in the penetration fighter competition, but the Air Force thought a slightly modified version held potential as a point-defense interceptor. On 7 May 1946, the Air Force issued a $632,485

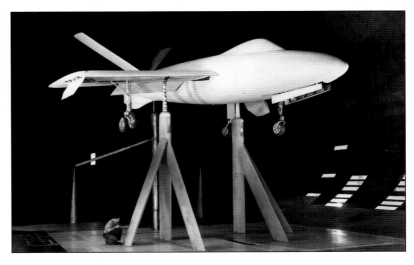

A 1:1-scale model of the XF-91 in the full-scale wind tunnel at the NACA Ames Aeronautical Laboratory shows the early V-tail configuration. Note the solid nose and absence of engine air intakes. (National Archives)

The first XF-91 (46-680) at Farmingdale. The tail of the mockup can be seen just ahead (left in the photo) of the prototype. At this point the aft fuselage was still configured for the XLR27 although there are no exhaust holes visible. (Cradle of Aviation Museum)

letter contract (W33-038-ac-14583) for a full-scale mockup and two XP-91 prototypes (46-680/681) as part of project MX-809. This was intended mostly as a fall-back in case the development of the radical Convair XP-92 ran into delays. Unusually, the definitive contract for $5,689,363 was not signed until 27 January 1949.[3]

Kartveli was assisted by R. G. Bowman, William J. O'Donnell, Costas E. Pappas, Werner Rankin, and Edwin Eddy. At first, Republic came up with an airplane powered by a single TG-190 (J47) axial-flow turbojet that generated 5,280-lbf and 6,000-lbf in afterburner. This was supplemented by four small rocket engines under development by Reaction Motors Incorporated (RMI). However, it soon became clear that the RMI rockets would not be ready when Republic needed them, so Kartveli selected a four-chamber Curtiss-Wright XLR27 instead.[4]

The fuselage had a general resemblance to the P-84, but only a few parts were interchangeable. An entirely new mid-mounted wing was swept back 35 degrees and had an angle of incidence that could be varied between –2 and +6 degrees to provide the most effective angle during takeoff, cruise, and landing. In contrast to the usual practice, the wing was thicker and wider (broader chord) at the tip than at the roots in the hope that it would provide greater lift outboard and reduce the tendency of the wingtips to stall at low speeds. An innovative V-tail was proposed to minimize drag where the stabilizers met the fuselage.[5]

The first XF-91 (46-680) in its final radar-nose configuration at the Air Force Museum. The airplane is not painted correctly (it was always in natural metal finish, not silver paint), but at least it is wearing the correct serial number. During the restoration, the museum applied an incorrect serial number (46-681) to the aircraft; after a couple of years the discrepancy was corrected. (Dennis R. Jenkins)

Unfortunately, the Curtiss-Wright XLR27 did not perform well during tests and was running significantly behind schedule. In response, Republic switched to the Reaction Motors XLR11 that had powered the X-1 series, although it is unclear if this was the same RMI engine Kartveli had originally wanted to use. The individual thrust chambers of the Curtiss-Wright engine were to have been positioned in vertical pairs above and below the jet exhaust, but all four XLR11 chambers were housed in an enlarged lower rocket housing that was lengthened two feet, extending slightly past the jet tailpipe. The installation of the XLR11 into the XF-91 was part of project MX-1658, and the engine was only installed in the second airplane, and then only for a few flights. The XLR11 generated 6,400-lbf at sea level and 7,180-lbf at 40,000 feet. Sufficient propellants were carried for a single chamber (1,600-lbf) to operate for 181 seconds, or for all four chambers to fire for 69.3 seconds.[6]

The mockup was inspected by the Air Force in May 1947 and resulted in the V-tail being replaced by a conventional empennage. A few months later, the Air Force decided against quantity production of the XP-91 or XP-92 because of a lack of funds. The two prototype XP-91s would be completed and used for "research purposes." This ended any real hopes of a production contract, although Republic would continue to offer versions of the F-91 to the Air Force.[7]

The first XF-91 (P changed to F in June 1948) was rolled out at Farmingdale on 24 February 1949. The usual ground and taxi tests were completed before the airplane was disassembled and shipped to Edwards on 2 April 1949 using two Fairchild C-82s and a Boeing C-97. Republic chief test pilot Carl Bellinger made the 40-minute maiden flight on 9 May 1949. The first flight that used the afterburner took place on 17 October. The inverse-taper wing, adopted to eliminate the wing-tip stall that had plagued first-generation swept-wing aircraft, worked as expected. The thin, narrow wing-root inevitably

The first XF-91 shows the original rear fuselage configuration for the Curtiss-Wright XLR27 rocket engine, with two exhausts above the jet tailpipe and two below. (Cradle of Aviation Museum)

stalled first, with a fully controllable nose-down pitching as a result. The first XF-91 completed its basic test program in March 1953 after 153 flights totaling 71 hours and 10 minutes.[8]

The second prototype was transported to Edwards in late July 1950 and made its maiden flight on 28 June 1951. During its third flight (on 30 June), an engine fire seriously damaged the aft fuselage. The aircraft was quickly repaired, and by the end of August had made six

The second prototype prior to its rollout. Note the XLR27 exhausts and the large external fuel tanks. Each main landing gear bogie used one wheel attached from the right and one attached from the left, and the entire assembly retracted outboard. Note the nose says "Number Two" under Republic. (National Records Center, St. Louis)

Models of the XF-91 were launched at the NACA Wallops Island facility to gather high-speed aerodynamic data. (Cradle of Aviation Museum)

Typical of many Republic airplanes, the anti-glare shield extended behind the cockpit canopy. (Cradle of Aviation Museum)

flights using the J47. The initial use of the rocket engine was not planned – on 11 September the J47 flamed-out during takeoff and the pilot ignited the rocket to gain altitude prior to a successful emergency landing. Exactly why the aircraft was carrying rocket propellant for a flight that did not intend to use the XLR11 was not explained. The first planned rocket flight was on 18 September. On 9 December 1952, the XF-91 became the first American combat aircraft to go supersonic in level flight when Republic test pilot Russell "Rusty" Roth hit Mach 1.07 using two of the four rocket-chambers. By March 1953, the second XF-91 had made ten successful rocket-powered flights, but a high-frequency vibration around Mach 1.18 prevented the aircraft from achieving its expected Mach 1.4 top speed.[9]

At low altitude, the XLR11 did not offer a significant increase in performance. For instance, with the J47 operating at military power at sea level, the airplane had a maximum speed of 536 mph, increasing to 606 mph with afterburner and 632 mph (Mach 0.957) with afterburner and the XLR11. It was a different story at high altitude. The J47 by itself could barely keep the XF-91 at 40,000 feet, so jet-only performance was only 517 mph; adding the XLR11 increased the maximum speed to 721 mph (Mach 1.253). As could be expected, the rate of climb improved significantly with the rocket engine. At military power, the XF-91 climbed at 3,580 feet per minute at sea level; adding the afterburner increased this to 8,850 feet per minute, and the XLR11 increased this to 28,250 feet per minute. Even at 40,000 feet, the XLR11 could keep the airplane climbing at 19,900 feet per minute.[10]

Late in the test program, the first prototype was used as the "Radar Armament Test Vehicle," (abbreviated R-A-T-V) and was redesignated XF-91A. The program was intended to test various weapons and electronic systems at high speed, including 2.75-inch and 5-inch FFARs, T-131 spin-stabilized rockets, the T-130 20mm cannon, and possibly GAR-1 Falcon missiles. To support these tests, the XF-91A received a chin-type air intake and a nose section suitable for installing a variety of radar systems. It is unclear exactly how much testing, and of what specific weapons and systems, was actually accomplished.[11]

Late in its life, the second prototype was modified with a V-shaped "butterfly" tail similar to the one originally shown on the mockup. The tests were intended to determine if the perceived aerodynamic benefits could be replicated in flight; apparently, they were not, since the design was not used again, although a similar configuration was proposed, and rejected, on the McDonnell XF-88 penetration fighter. The XLR11 was not installed during the V-tail tests, although the rocket fairing remained. The second prototype crashed at Edwards during the summer of 1951, when the engine suffered a catastrophic failure during takeoff with Carl Bellinger at the controls. As Bellinger retracted the landing gear after takeoff, Chuck Yeager, flying chase in an F-86, radioed flames were coming out of the engine. Bellinger landed immediately and exited the aircraft, but by the time fire equipment arrived, the airframe was destroyed.[12]

During 1950 Republic proposed a production variant of the XF-91 to the Air Force. Republic included several possible engine choices, including the Westinghouse X40-E8A, General Electric "advanced" J47 (J47-21), or Allison J35-A-23 used in conjunction

The second XF-91 shows the final aft fuselage configuration that housed a Reaction Motors XLR11 rocket engine with all four nozzles located below the jet tailpipe. The alcohol and liquid oxygen propellants are being loaded from the trailer at left. (AFFTC History Office Collection)

Although the XF-91 was completed with a conventional empennage, Alexander Kartveli had not given up on the concept of a V-tail. Late in its career, the second XF-91 was modified with a slightly revised V-tail that had a wider angle than the original design that had been tested in the NACA Ames wind-tunnel. Note that the serial number is written on both sides of the stabilizer. (AFFTC History Office Collection)

with two Aerojet AJ-24-2 or two Curtiss-Wright CW-482 rocket engines. Each of the jet engines provided approximately 9,000-lbf without afterburner and 13,000-lbf with reheat. The rocket engines added about 9,000-lbf more thrust. The nose intake used on the XF-91 was replaced by a pair of flush intakes on the fuselage sides, much like the North American XF-93. This configuration had already been tested on a modified F-84F.[13]

With the J47 engine and Aerojet rockets, Republic predicted a top speed of 1,180 mph at 50,000 feet and 803 mph at sea level. Cruising speed with two external tanks was 550 mph, increasing to 600 mph without the tanks. The interceptor would have a range of 432 miles when equipped with two external tanks. The combat ceiling was estimated as 53,500 feet. When using the jet engine without afterburner, the F-91 could climb at 6,700 feet per minute, increasing to 9,800 fpm with afterburner and 25,000 fpm with afterburner and the rockets.[14]

A solid nose housed a choice of Hughes, General Electric, or Westinghouse fire-control systems, although only the Hughes unit was expected to be compatible with the Falcon. The recommended

The two prototypes pose together near the end of the program. The first (left) had a radar nose and revised air intake, while the second had a V-tail. Each is carrying small external fuel tanks. The YRF-84F may be seen in the background. (AFFTC History Office Collection)

armament included four Hughes MX-904 Falcon missiles in the fuselage and two T-110 rocket launchers with thirty T-131 spin-stabilized rockets in the nose. An interim armament while the Falcon was being perfected could consist of four T-110 launchers with sixty T-131 rockets or four M24 20mm cannon with 800 rounds. The cannon would be installed in the same muzzle and trunnion mounts used by the rocket launchers, and the weapons were interchangeable in the field. At 1,000-yards range, the four T-110 launchers yielded an estimated kill probability of approximately "59 percent if the possibility of damage by fuel fires is included and approximately 48 percent if the possibility of fuel fires is excluded." At 2,000 yards, these probabilities fell to 38 and 27 percent, respectively.[15]

Reportedly, Republic reused much of the XF-91 design in the NP-48 proposal to the Navy, including the butterfly tail and wing with inverse taper but without the wing tanks or rocket engines. It also had a solid nose like those planned for the F-91A. In addition, a modified "F-91B" (not an official designation) was submitted by Republic as part of the "1954 Interceptor" competition that ultimately resulted in the Convair F-102 and Republic XF-103.[16]

The XF-91 contract was terminated on 23 September 1954 after a total expenditure of $11,644,974. On the sixth anniversary of its maiden flight, the first prototype was shipped to the Air Force Museum at Wright-Patterson AFB, where it can be seen today in its radar-nose configuration.[17]

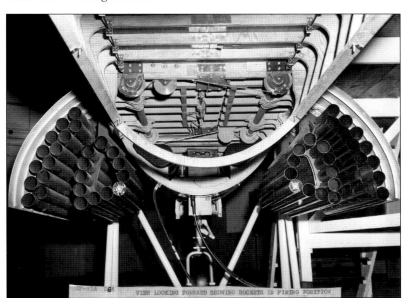

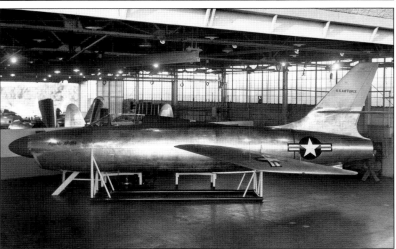

Republic completed a mockup of the proposed XF-91A that the company submitted in several Air Force (and Navy) competitions. The radar-equipped nose (upper left) featured a different air intake than that used on the second XF-91, while the entire aft fuselage was different (note the tapered jet tailpipe). The nitric acid tank (lower left) for the rocket engine was removable to ease loading operations. Although not generally listed as an option, the mockup had retractable bays with two dozen 2.75-inch FFARs per side. (Cradle of Aviation Museum)

Convair XF-92A

The Vultee Division of Consolidated-Vultee believed that a swept-wing airplane powered by a ducted rocket would be capable of meeting the point-defense interceptor requirements. The duct concept had its origins in research into liquid-cooled engine radiator designs Vultee had performed several years earlier. With the proper duct configuration, it was possible for the radiator heat mixing with the airflow to generate a positive thrust, a concept demonstrated – on a very small scale – on the North American P-51. In the Convair concept, a series of small rocket motors would provide the heat, and additional fuel would be added to the duct to create a pseudo-ramjet.[18]

On 13 October 1945, Convair submitted its proposal for a ducted rocket interceptor with a 35-degree swept-wing and a V-tail empennage to the Army. Convair described its concept as a "nonexpendable, inhabited missile with a pilot guiding it to its airborne target." In addition to the ducted rocket, four 1,200-lbf rockets were mounted around the circumference of the exhaust nozzle to provide initial acceleration, and a 1,560-lbf Westinghouse 19XB (XJ30) axial-flow turbojet provided power during the final approach and landing, and generated electrical and hydraulic power during the entire flight. The bicycle main landing gear had droppable outriggers, much like the later Lockheed U-2.[19]

On 12 April 1946, the Army announced that Convair had won the interceptor competition. An $850,000 letter contract for engineering data and wind-tunnel testing was issued on 2 May 1946 as part of project MX-813. This was followed on 25 June by a $5.3 million contract (W33-038-ac-14547) for a full-scale mockup, a structural test article, and two XP-92 prototypes. By 1 May 1947, the total funding for the XP-92 had increased to $7,142,586, although the scope of work remained the same.[20]

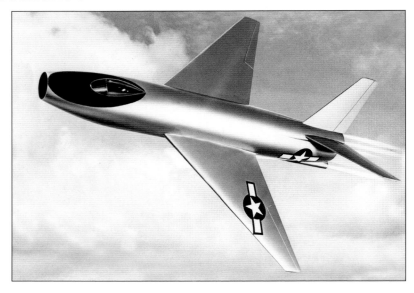

The first Convair design was for an airplane with a conventional canopy, 35-degree swept-wings, and a V-tail. Wind-tunnel testing revealed this configuration was less than ideal. (National Records Center, St. Louis)

The XP-92 team included chief engineer C. R. "Jack" Irvine, assistant chief engineer Frank W. Davis, chief of design Adolph Burstein, and chief of aerodynamics Ralph H. Shick. At the time, Chuck Yeager had not yet made his supersonic flight in the Bell X-1, but Convair had just committed to building an operational supersonic interceptor. The XP-92 was also the only rocket-powered combat aircraft under development by the Army at the time.[21]

The revised delta-wing XP-92 was tested using models boosted by small rockets from the NACA Wallops Island test facility. These models flew at velocities faster than wind tunnels could simulate. (National Archives)

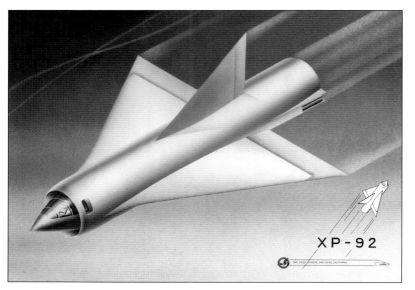

Artist concept of the revised XP-92 showing the cockpit within the center shock cone, and a pair of acceleration rockets on each side of the aft fuselage. The program logo is at lower right. (National Archives)

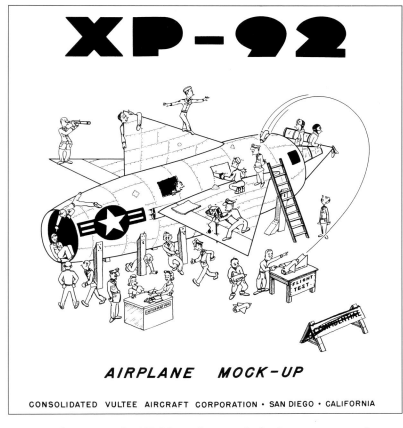

Apparently getting the XP-92 mockup ready for its government inspection was a fairly hectic activity, resulting in this cartoon by some unnamed Convair employee. (National Records Center, St. Louis)

Engineers realized the XP-92 presented two major challenges – the new aerodynamic configuration and the novel propulsion system. Convair suggested separating the two issues and building a dedicated aerodynamic test vehicle while developing the propulsion system using ground-based facilities. In September 1946, the Army approved the idea of a "flying mockup" to test the aerodynamic configuration using jet propulsion, and a single XP-92A aerodynamic demonstrator (46-682) replaced the previous structural test article. At the same time, serial numbers (46-683/684) were assigned to the pair of XP-92 interceptors. The demonstrator used a wing and vertical stabilizer identical to that planned for the XP-92 interceptor, but the ducted rocket and its large-diameter fuselage were replaced by a streamlined fuselage housing a single 4,000-lbf General Electric I-40 (XJ33) centrifugal-flow turbojet.[22]

By the time the full-scale mockup of the XP-92 was inspected on 17 April 1948, the swept-wing had been replaced by a delta planform. However, the inspection did not go well, with the Air Force commenting, "the airplane in its present configuration is highly impractical for any use other than a research aircraft." In June 1948, the Air Force decided to terminate the ducted-rocket portion of the project because of delays in the propulsion system and improvement in more conventional designs. In addition, the estimated cost of the project had increased to $16,243,000, and a great deal of development effort lay ahead. When the effort ended on 5 August 1948, $4,542,068 had been expended.[23]

However, the Air Force was still interested in the performance of delta-wing airplanes and allowed the XP-92A aerodynamic demonstrator to continue. The Army also agreed to loan Dr. Alexander Lippisch and several other German researchers to Convair for several weeks to further define the delta wing for the new airplane.

Oddly, no original photographs of the XP-92 mockup appear to have survived. All that remain are some "screened" pages in a variety of reports, such as this one. (National Records Center, St. Louis)

Desk model of the XP-92 showing one of the assigned serial numbers (46-683) that was also used on the full-scale mockup (see photo at left). (National Records Center, St. Louis)

The flying mockup is usually identified as the Convair Model 7002, but this clearly deviates from the standard Convair model-numbering scheme. Historian Robert E. Bradley deduced this number was actually taken from the engineering work order (EWO) that was used to record labor hours for the project. In reality the airplane was the Model 115, although it was later renumbered Model 1 when Convair changed its model-numbering scheme. Nevertheless, even in much of the official documentation it is referred to as the Model 7002.[24]

Contrary to many reports, the XF-92A was intended entirely for research purposes and was never intended to be a prototype of any production airplane. To save time and money, the main landing gear was taken from a North American FJ-1, the nosewheel was from a Bell P-63, the J33 engine, brakes, and hydraulics were from a Lockheed P-80, the ejection seat from the Convair XP-81, and the rudder pedals were from a BT-13 trainer.[25]

The XF-92A was manufactured, mostly, at the old Vultee Field plant in Downey, California. However, this facility was closed during the summer of 1947 and the 75-percent complete airframe was moved to the Consolidated plant in San Diego. The move caused considerable confusion, and the Air Force later attributed most of the 1-year delay in the XF-92A program to the change in location.[26]

Convair completed the airplane on 31 October 1947, and the XF-92A was shipped to San Francisco on the USS *Titania* (AKA-13) on 4 November 1947. From there it was trucked, sans engine, to the NACA Ames Aeronautical Laboratory, where it was installed in the full-scale wind tunnel on 29 November and tests run through 23 December. After these were complete, the airplane was shipped back to San Diego aboard the aircraft carrier USS *Boxer* (CV-21). The full-scale wind-tunnel tests generally confirmed the results of earlier sub-scale tests and analysis.[27]

Like many aircraft during the late 1940s and 1950s, the XP-92A was tested in the full-scale wind-tunnel at the NACA Ames Aeronautical Laboratory. Note the original frameless, clear canopy. (National Archives)

After arriving back in San Diego on 12 January 1948, the Allison J33-A-21 was installed, vibration tests conducted, and initial system runs performed. Provisions were also added for JATO rockets, although they were apparently never used during the test program. The airplane was loaded aboard a Navy LST on 26 March 1948 and taken to the port of Los Angeles, then trucked to Muroc for additional ground testing.[28]

The XP-92A (46-692) in final assembly. At this point, the vertical stabilizer had just been attached and several of the access panels are still open. The removable aft fuselage is evident. (National Records Center, St. Louis)

Still in its San Diego hangar, the XP-92A shows a pair of JATO bottles under the fuselage between the landing gear. There is no evidence these bottles were used at Muroc. (National Records Center, St. Louis)

The airplane arrived at Muroc on 9 April 1948, and the first taxi test by Convair test pilot Ellis D. "Sam" Shannon on 25 May revealed that the brakes were unsatisfactory, so the system was bled and retested. The second taxi test on 28 May showed the XF-92A tended to turn downwind in a 30-mph crosswind, something confirmed by the third taxi test on 4 June. The fourth taxi test on 8 June showed the airplane was very sensitive in longitudinal and lateral control at 165 mph. The following day, the fifth taxi test turned into a short hop, with the air-

plane flying about 2 miles at an altitude of 15 feet. The airplane exhibited rapid lateral and moderate longitudinal oscillations while in the air, so Shannon quickly landed.[29]

Convair decided to modify the control system to correct the instability observed during the taxi tests and short airborne hop. At the same time, the engine was replaced by a slightly more powerful J33-A-23 with water-alcohol injection (but no afterburner). A new high-speed canopy with bracing replaced the earlier clear canopy.

The XF-92A sees daylight for the first time, rolling out from the Convair facility in San Diego. The aircraft was in overall natural metal with unusually large national insignia and a black anti-glare panel. Like many of the early high-speed aircraft, the canopy was heavily reinforced since the art of blowing plexiglass enclosures was still in its infancy. (San Diego Air & Space Museum via Robert E. Bradley)

The XF-92A was painted in this unusual camouflage to play "MiG 23" in the movie Jet Pilot, *but in the end was not used in the film. The colors are black-green and sky blue with red lettering with a white outline. Note one wingtip is unpainted.* (AFFTC History Office Collection)

These modifications were completed on 15 September 1948, and the following day the sixth taxi test turned into another 2-mile hop that showed the longitudinal and lateral control were still very sensitive. Convair made a few minor adjustments before the last taxi test on 17 September, and although the controls were still sensitive during the 3-mile-long hop, Shannon was sufficiently satisfied to recommend a real flight. Overall, Shannon conducted 15 taxi tests.[30]

Sam Shannon took the XF-92A on the world's first powered delta-wing flight on 18 September 1948. Shannon reported an unexpected lag and a certain sensitivity in the control system, but otherwise the flight was uneventful. After the flight, the airplane was grounded for 10 days so that engineers could conduct a thorough inspection. Finding nothing of consequence, the second flight was on 29 September, and flights took place every few days for the next several months. After the 20th flight on 18 February 1949, the full-span elevons were replaced by a set of cut-off elevons in an attempt to improve the stability and control of the airplane. The first flight with these elevons was on 17 March, but Convair test pilot William "Bill"

Martin noted severe vibration above 399 mph. A second flight the same day confirmed the anomaly. After two more flights, on 21 April 1949, Convair decided to reinstall the full-span elevons. The airplane was formally accepted by the Air Force on 20 May, but Phase I contractor tests continued through 6 August, with 47 flights totaling 20.5 hours flown by Shannon and Martin.[31]

The Air Force conducted a safety-of-flight inspection on 7 September 1949, and Phase II performance tests began on 13 October 1949 with Maj. Charles E. Yeager at the controls. He was joined by Maj. Frank K. "Pete" Everest to evaluate the overall performance of the XF-92A, concentrating on stability and control of the delta wing. Phase II concluded on 28 December 1949 after 25 flights and 17 hours.[32]

In August 1949, Convair had proposed installing an afterburning J33-A-29 to increase overall performance, and the Air Force agreed to the change after the Phase II tests were completed. Most importantly, the new engine would shorten the takeoff runs and increase the margin of safety immediately after takeoff. Convair was obviously sure the Army would approve the modification; by the time they proposed it the company had already completed all engineering and manufactured more than 60 percent of the necessary parts. The modification also added 340 gallons of additional fuel; 250 gallons in new tankage and 90 gallons in the tank previously used for water-alcohol for the J33-A-23.[33]

Convair estimated the new engine would increase maximum speed at sea level from 552 mph to 718 mph. At 30,000 feet, maximum speed would increase from 589 mph to 669 mph. The rate of climb at sea level would increase from 5,580 feet per minute (with water) to 10,650 feet per minute. The takeoff distance would decrease from 5,400 feet to 3,900 feet, and the time to climb to 30,000 feet would decrease from 12.4 minutes to only 3.4 minutes. In

January 1950, the XF-92A returned to San Diego for 14 months of modifications that included lengthening the aft fuselage to accommodate the afterburner. The airplane was also painted overall white to facilitate optical tracking.[34]

The XF-92A returned to Muroc, and Chuck Yeager made its first flight with the new engine on 21 July 1951. Everest and Yeager made 21 flights for another 11 hours and 21 minutes before turning the XF-92A over to the NACA for research into delta wing stability. The test results with the afterburner were generally disappointing, with little overall performance gain over the earlier J33-A-23 engine. The XF-92A could only exceed Mach 1.0 in a dive, this being done at least once with Everest as the pilot.[35]

Above and Two Below: *The most publicized paint job was the all-white scheme the XF-92A wore at the end of its career. Note the deployed tail hook in the side view at top, and the tufts glued to the right wing and fuselage to study airflow.* (AFFTC History Office Collection)

The accident on 14 October 1953 ended the flying career of the XF-92A. While Scott Crossfield was landing on the lakebed, the nose wheel collapsed. Since the larger delta-wing Convair F-102 was scheduled to fly later that month, the XF-92A was permanently grounded. (NASA Dryden)

In late 1951, when Convair and the Air Force were negotiating the F-102 contract, some consideration was given to rebuilding the XF-92A as a proof-of-concept demonstrator for the new interceptor. It was decided that the modifications would be too expensive and no action was taken.[36]

The NACA replaced the engine with an improved J33-A-16 that made 8,600-lbf in afterburner. NACA test pilot A. Scott Crossfield flew the modified XF-92A for the first time on 9 April 1953, eventually making 25 flights totaling 13 hours and 13 minutes. These tests indicated a violent pitch-up tendency during high-speed turns, resulting in wing fences being added that only partially cured the problem.

On 14 October 1953, the nose wheel collapsed as Crossfield was landing at Edwards. Although comparatively minor damage resulted, the Air Force and the NACA agreed to permanently ground the XF-92A since the YF-102 was scheduled to fly only 10 days later. In all, the airplane made 118 flights of just over 62 hours.[37]

Following the accident, the XF-92A was carried in the Air Force inventory until March 1954. The airplane was used as a touring exhibit until 1962, when it was moved to the Air Force Museum where it is currently on display. The total cost of the XF-92A project was $4,436,170, not including the NACA flight-test program or the $4.5 million spent on the original XP-92 effort.[38]

After the accident, the XF-92A was used as a touring exhibit by the Air Force. Here the airplane is at the National Air Show at Cox Municipal Airport, Vandalia, Ohio, in September 1954. (National Archives)

The XF-92A on display in 1957 at a shopping center in Stoneham, Massachusetts. Note the nose markings. The airplane was transferred to the Air Force Museum in 1962. (AFFTC History Office Collection)

Bell S-1 Tactical Airplane Concept

Sometime during the mid 1940s, Bell Aircraft Company proposed building a tactical version of the XS-1 research airplane. It is unclear if this concept had any relationship to the proposal submitted for a point-defense interceptor on 12 April 1946 since all that was found was what could best be called an advertising brochure at the National Records Center in St. Louis.

This brochure described a "tactical airplane" based on the XS-1 airframe that was armed with four 0.50-caliber machine guns in the nose. The Reaction Motors XLR11 rocket engine from the XS-1 was retained, and Bell highlighted that the powerplant allowed takeoffs from the ground, eliminat-

ing the need for the Boeing B-29 carrier aircraft used at Muroc. There is some truth to this since Chuck Yeager made a single ground takeoff in the first X-1 (46-062) on 5 January 1947. The resulting flight was very short since almost all of the propellants had been used getting off the ground.

Using a ground takeoff, Bell estimated propellant exhaustion 20 miles from the base at 50,000 feet altitude. The S-1 would then glide another 20 miles, engage in one minute of combat at Mach 1.2, then glide home at 600 mph. Using an air-launch allowed the combat to take place 100 miles from base. Bell also proposed using the S-1 as a parasite fighter, in much the same role as the McDonnell XF-85 was designed to perform.

Several pages from the Bell brochure are reproduced below.

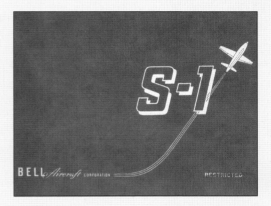

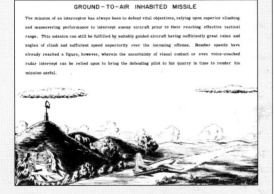
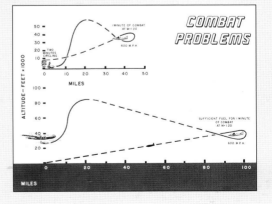
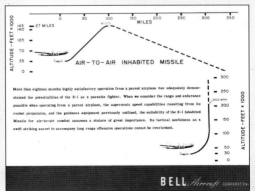

Chapter 5

Above: *The two McDonnell XF-88 prototypes were not identical, even after the first airplane gained its afterburning J34 engines. The most noticeable difference was the cannon muzzle fairings on the sides of the fuselage on the XF-88A.* (National Records Center, St. Louis)

Right: *The first Lockheed XF-90 (note the fuselage says "F-90") with a Lockheed F-80C (47-171). Although the two aircraft differed significantly in size and shape, their overall performance was similar.* (Lockheed Martin)

PENETRATION FIGHTERS
STILLBORN CONCEPT

During World War II, the Army had found escort fighters greatly enhanced the survival of bombers over enemy territory. Unfortunately, the first jet fighters lacked the range to escort the existing Boeing B-29s, not to mention the very long-range Northrop B-35 and Convair B-36 then on the drawing boards. The Army considered a variety of methods to increase the range of jet fighters, some bordering on the bizarre. One proposal was for the bombers to tow their escort fighters into the combat zone and release them when needed. Usually these proposals had the fighters "hard mated" to the bomber with nose or wingtip couplings, but a few concepts used towropes, much like gliders. To test one of the concepts, a Culver PQ-14 trainer was coupled with a Douglas C-47 and Republic F-84s were mated with Boeing B-29 and Convair B-36 carrier aircraft in projects TIP TOW and TOM TOM, respectively. None of these experiments proved successful, and several actually turned out to be extremely dangerous, resulting in the loss of a B-29 and two F-84s. Other proposals revived the parasite fighter concept of the 1930s, resulting in the McDonnell XF-85. Oddly, the concept of aerial refueling seems to have been largely ignored, initially, for fighters.

During mid-1945, the Army issued requests for proposals for three new aircraft including an all-weather fighter, a point-defense interceptor, and a long-range penetration fighter. The Army cautioned all potential bidders against the use of "paper" engines (i.e., ones that existed only as designs and had not yet proven themselves in flight or on the test stand) and recommended the use of at least two engines. Oddly, when the request for proposal for the penetration fighter was released on 28 August 1945, there were no firm requirements for such an aircraft.[1]

This oversight was cured on 23 November 1945 when the Army published a set of military characteristics for a "high performance, all purpose day fighter ... for destruction of enemy air forces and tactical targets." This "penetration fighter" was expected to replace all of the "day fighters," such as the P-80, P-84, and P-86, in the operational inventory. The requirements called for a top speed of 550 mph at 35,000 feet and 600 mph at sea level. The climb to 35,000 feet was to take less than 10 minutes and the aircraft was to have a combat radius of 900 miles. Armament was to include six fixed, forward-firing 0.60-caliber heavy machine guns or 20mm cannon and the airplane needed performance "capable of meeting or exceeding all opposing fighters." The Army expected the penetration fighter to be powered by a pair of 3,000-lbf gas turbine engines mounted as closely as possible to the aircraft centerline to provide optimum single-engine performance.[2]

Consolidated-Vultee, Curtiss-Wright, Goodyear, Lockheed, McDonnell, Northrop, and Republic all submitted proposals on 15 October 1945. Four of the eight proposals (Lockheed had submitted two) were eliminated immediately for not meeting the requirements of the competition. For instance, Lockheed's primary entry used L-1000 (XJ37) powerplants that the Army considered a "paper" engine since it had not yet run. The alternate Lockheed proposal was also eliminated since its TG-180 (XJ35) engines gave it performance similar to the F-86 it was designed to replace. Unusually, Lockheed was given an opportunity to submit a revised proposal, doing so in March 1946 using a pair of Westinghouse 24C (XJ34) engines.[3]

The source selection board selected Convair and McDonnell on 15 February 1946, but the Deputy Assistant Chief of the Air Staff, General Thomas S. Power, subsequently decided that each airframe manufacturer should only be allowed a single development contract from the three competitions. Given that Convair had also won the point-defense interceptor competition, in addition to the high-priority (and expensive) B-36 program, only the McDonnell XP-88 contract went forward. Somewhat belatedly, the Army decided it wanted two competitors and awarded Lockheed a contract for the XP-90 on 20 June 1946. This award seems to have been as much to preserve the Air Force industrial base as it was because the airplane met the requirements. A letter from the Air Materiel Command to Headquarters cautioned that if Lockheed was left out, "they will be out of the Army Air Forces development picture completely for the time being ... and ... the Navy will undoubtedly exploit the Lockheed facilities ..."[4]

In late 1947, North American entered the penetration fighter fray with a proposal for an extensively revised version of the P-86A. The Air Force ordered a pair of prototype P-86Cs (not YP-86Cs) using an amendment to the P-86A production contract. Interestingly, the Republic entry in the penetration fighter competition was ordered into development as the XP-91 point-defense interceptor.[5]

The military characteristics were revised at intervals during the ensuing two years. By 22 August 1947, the penetration fighter was required to operate at 50,000 feet with a top speed of 690 mph, climb to 50,000 feet in 10 minutes, and have a combat radius of 1,500 miles. The revised requirements called for a fire-control system with radar ranging and radar sighting during zero-visibility conditions. Air-to-air and air-to-ground guided missiles were also to be incorporated if possible.[6]

As it turned out, the first flights of the three penetration fighters were staggered every seven months, but this was more a reflection of when the contracts were approved than any particular plan on the part of the Air Force. The McDonnell XF-88 made its maiden flight on 20 October 1948, the Lockheed XF-90 flew on 3 June 1949, and the F-86C (it was not called YF-86C, but quickly became the YF-93A) took to the air on 25 January 1950.

The Air Force appeared to favor the North American design because of its commonality with other Sabre variants, and in June 1948, ordered 118 production aircraft. At that time, it was decided that there were so many differences between the F-86C and the production Sabre that it should be redesignated YF-93A. It seemed that the F-93 was headed for full-scale production when the contract was suddenly cancelled in February 1949, mostly because of a severe reduction in the military budget for FY50.[7]

On 12 May 1948, President Harry S. Truman had imposed a ceiling on FY50 military funds, although this was not announced publicly until the following January. In December 1948, General Joseph T. McNarney, the commander of the Air Materiel Command and chairman of the Defense Budget Advisory Committee, asked the Air Force to revise its FY49 and FY50 development and production programs to meet the reduced budget ceilings. The primary consideration was to optimize the nuclear-strike capability of the Strategic Air Command, both by providing escort fighters for the Convair B-36 fleet and developing nuclear-capable fighter-bombers. These decisions were in line with Truman's announced policy of using stored reserves of World War II airplanes before asking for funds for new aircraft.[8]

In addition, a Board of Senior Officers felt that production orders for penetration fighters should not be awarded until a competitive fly-off between the three contenders. The Air Materiel Command was unprepared to conduct this evaluation, but despite a general confusion, the $1 million fly-off took place between 29 June and 10 July 1950 at Muroc. This probably ranks as one of the most disorganized events in Air Force history, since none of the competitors was ready to be compared against each other due to continuing development problems. Nevertheless, there were nine major evaluation categories: tactical suitability, performance, design, producibility, maintenance, cost, delivery schedule, contractor capability, and growth potential.[9]

Surprisingly, given the initial favor extended to the North American entry, the Air Force notified McDonnell on 11 September 1950 that the F-88 had ranked first in the competition. However, it was a hollow victory since there were no funds to actually purchase penetration fighters. In addition, the pending development of long-range, high-speed jet bombers such as the B-47 and the B-52 eliminated any real need for penetration fighters.[10]

On 15 August 1950, the Air Materiel Command recommended that the McDonnell F-88 be given priority in any future decision to buy a penetration fighter, but Air Force Headquarters reiterated that none would be purchased in FY51. During the buildup for the Korean conflict, the Air Force briefly considered purchasing F-88s to escort B-29s and funded McDonnell to develop a production plan. Ultimately, however, the Air Force procured additional F-84s instead. The money spent on the F-88 planning would eventually be put to good use when the design was developed into the F-101 strategic fighter.[11]

McDonnell XF-88

The McDonnell design team, led by Kendall Perkins and Edward M. "Bud" Flesh, began with a design that used a fuselage almost identical to the XF2H-1 Banshee, which was then under development for the Navy. Other aspects of the design were also similar, including the use of two engines mounted in enlarged wing roots. The leading edge of the wing was swept 20 degrees, but the trailing edge was unswept, resulting in "a conservative delta." This configuration was abandoned when the designers could not determine if they could maintain good airflow over the wing roots at high speeds. The next idea moved the engines to the wingtips. Several advantages were immediately apparent, including excellent engine access, efficient inlet ducts, and engine exhaust that did not impinge on any part of the airframe. The primary disadvantage was a severe yawing moment if an engine failed at low speed, especially during takeoff or landing. There were also structural challenges to this engine location.[12]

In the design ultimately submitted to the Air Force, a pair of Westinghouse XJ34 axial-flow engines was located side by side in the lower central fuselage where they could be easily reached for maintenance. Air came from straight-through wing root intakes similar to

The original XP-88 mockup (shown here on 21 July 1947) featured a V-tail that McDonnell hoped would reduce compressibility effects. Note the XP-85 mockup in the foreground. (National Archives)

The second prototype (46-526) was designated XF-88A since it used afterburning Westinghouse J34 engines. Note the three cannon muzzle fairings on the side of the nose. (National Records Center, St. Louis)

effects by cutting the number of fuselage intersections from three to two, a theory also pursued by Alexander Kartveli at Republic on the XP-91. The cockpit was situated well forward of the wing, just behind the six 20mm cannon. The Air Force issued McDonnell a letter contract (W33-038-ac-14582) on 13 June 1946 for two XP-88 prototypes (46-525/526) and a full-scale mockup as part of project MX-881. The final contract was approved on 14 February 1947. [13]

The mockup inspection was held 21-23 August 1946, resulting in some major changes. The wing root intakes were swept back 40 degrees, and a boundary layer ramp was added to improve pressure recovery. Early wind-tunnel tests indicated that the V-tail would result in adverse rolling moments due to rudder action and would provide insufficient longitudinal stability near stall. Consequently, the V-tail was replaced by a conventional horizontal stabilizer mounted partway up the tail to keep it in undisturbed airflow. During the mockup inspection, the Air Force also requested McDonnell investigate adding afterburners to the second prototype, although this was not formally approved until 15 December 1947.[14]

On 11 June 1948, the XP-88 was redesignated XF-88 as part of the Air Force-wide reorientation of the designation system. Five days later, the safety-of-flight inspection of the first prototype was held in St. Louis, and the airplane was formally rolled-out on 11 August 1948. After various ground and taxi tests, the airplane was disassembled and transported to Muroc, where it made its maiden flight on 20 October 1948 with McDonnell chief test pilot Robert M. Edholm at the controls.[15]

those on the RF-84F, and the exhausts were under the rear fuselage. This configuration, it was hoped, would leave enough space in the fuselage for the fuel needed for the long-range penetration mission. The design used a relatively large 35-degree swept-wing for efficient cruise. McDonnell hoped that a V-tail would reduce compressibility

The first XF-88 (46-525) after it was rolled-out from the St. Louis factory on 11 August 1948. Note the stylized "XF-88" on the nose. Despite toying with a V-tail during the mockup stage, the two prototypes were completed with conventional three-surface empennages. A large pitot tube hangs beneath the fuselage just ahead of the nose landing gear doors. (Terry Panopalis Collection)

The first production F2H-1 (BuNo 122530) was bailed back to McDonnell as a testbed for the "short" afterburner being developed for the Westinghouse J34 engine. (National Records Center, St. Louis)

In January 1949, McDonnell compared a proposed production F-88 configuration against a hypothetical McDonnell Model 58A as an interceptor for the Air Defense Command. The Model 58A was a modified version of the Navy F3H Demon then under development. All equipment required for carrier operation, such as power wing folding, arresting hook, tail-skid, and nose-gear kneeling were removed. The airplane was powered by a single 7,310-lbf Westinghouse XJ40 with afterburner, and the armament consisted of two-dozen 2.75-inch folding-fin rockets.[16]

Two versions of the F-88 were considered, including one powered by 3,370-lbf Westinghouse J34 engines and another using 4,080-lbf Westinghouse J46s. Both powerplants were fitted with afterburners, resulting in 4,900-lbf and 6,100-lbf, respectively. Armament for both versions consisted of six 20mm cannon with sufficient ammunition for 20 seconds of firing.[17]

The analysis showed there was not much difference between the J46-equipped F-88 and the Model 58A. The maximum speed of the F-88 was 737 mph at sea level versus 739 mph for the Demon. At 45,000 feet, the figures were 646 mph and 651 mph. The J34-powered F-88 kept up reasonably well, with the estimates showing 727 mph at sea level and 610 mph at 45,000 feet. The rate of climb showed a much larger difference, with the J46-powered F-88 at 27,400 feet per minute at sea level, the Model 58A at 25,800 feet per minute, and the J34-powered F-88 at only at 17,010 feet per minute. The range of the J46 F-88 was 1,276 miles, the Model 58A was only 862 miles, and the J34 airplane was 1,064 miles. This analysis apparently did not support any specific Air Force decision, but provided an interesting comparison of the latest Air Force and Navy fighters.[18]

In the meantime, the performance of the first XF-88 was proving disappointing, mostly due to the weight increases that had taken place during development. McDonnell pilots made 41 flights totaling 35 hours and 43 minutes before turning the airplane over the Air Force for the Phase II performance tests at Edwards beginning on 15 March 1949. Air Force pilots made 17 flights totaling 17 hours and 57 minutes, including one night flight.[19]

The decision had already been made to fit afterburners to the second prototype to increase performance, but this proved more difficult than expected. Because of limited ground clearance, the afterburner needed to be less than 52 inches long. Westinghouse found that it could not develop a unit that could fit into the available space, forcing McDonnell to develop a "short afterburner" that was 30 inches long and weighed only 218 pounds. A Westinghouse J34 with a short afterburner was tested on the first production F2H-1 (BuNo 122530), which had been bailed back to McDonnell for use as a testbed.[20]

XF-88A

The designation of the second prototype (46-526) was changed to XF-88A to reflect the installation of the afterburner engines. To com-

The first prototype shows details of its landing gear, including the twin landing lights on the nose gear doors. Note the air-data probe on the nose. (National Archives)

The perforated speed brakes on the XF-88 were hinged at the rear. This was changed on the later F-101 to a forward hinged brake without perforations. (National Archives)

Because of the limited ground clearance of the XF-88 during rotation, McDonnell developed a "short" afterburner that was only 30-inches long. (National Records Center, St. Louis)

pensate for the appetite of the afterburning engines, McDonnell installed bladder fuel cells in the wings that increased internal fuel capacity to 834 gallons. The XF-88A made its maiden flight on 26 April 1949 from Lambert Field in St. Louis. The left-hand afterburner was ignited in-flight for the first time on 9 June, and both afterburners were used a few days later.[21]

On 26 August 1949, the first prototype was removed from flight status because the program was running out of money. Initially, the XF-88 was placed in standby storage at Muroc on 23 October, but the airplane was trucked to St. Louis later that year. Unfortunately, on 9 November the second prototype was damaged during an emergency

landing at Muroc and was subsequently trucked to St. Louis for repairs. The XF-88 had flown 93 times for a total of 82 hours and 33 minutes, and the XF-88A had made 41 flights for 28 hours and 8 minutes.[22]

Coupled with the usual wet lakebeds encountered during the winter months, the XF-88 test program did not pick up again until 27 March 1950, using the repaired second prototype. Additional funds were found to modify the first prototype with afterburning J34 engines, although the aircraft retained its XF-88 designation without a suffix (instead of becoming an XF-88A). The first flight of the modified airplane was in St. Louis on 1 May 1950, and the airplane flew to Muroc on 22 May.

Both XF-88 prototypes along with a number of F2H-2s (BuNo 125068 closest to camera). McDonnell had grand plans to produce 8,786 Navy Banshees and a staggering 15,046 Air Force F-88s. Fiscal realities kept this from happening and, ultimately, only 895 F2Hs were produced, along with the pair of XF-88 prototypes and 805 improved F-101s. (National Records Center, St. Louis)

Much of the forward fuselage of the fist prototype was reworked when it was modified with an Allison XT38 turboprop and converted into the XF-88B propeller research airplane. (National Records Center, St. Louis)

The XF-88B during its NACA testing. Note the large rake protruding from the fuselage to measure turbulence from the three-blade propeller and its abnormally large spinner. (Terry Panopalis Collection)

Phase II performance tests were conducted on the XF-88A between 5 May and 14 June 1950, using 18 flights totaling 12.5 hours. The performance improvement afforded by the afterburners allowed the maximum speed to increase from 630 mph at 15,000 feet to 693 mph. The maximum Mach number increased from 0.91 to 0.945 at 35,000 feet. Tests showed the XF-88A could easily exceed the speed of sound in a shallow dive (a maximum of Mach 1.18 was demonstrated) without encountering any significant buffeting.[23]

On 16 June 1950, the second airplane made a wheels-up landing at Muroc following an engine compressor failure. The XF-88A was trucked to St. Louis on 11 July, but it was never restored to flight status. It had made 105 flights totaling 82 hours and 45 minutes. The timing could not have been worse.[24]

The fly-off between the McDonnell XF-88, Lockheed XF-90 and North American YF-93A took place between 29 June and 10 July 1950 at Muroc. Given that the XF-88A – which had been scheduled to be used for the fly-off – had been damaged, it was a good thing that the first XF-88 had recently been modified with afterburners. During the evaluation, eight Air Force pilots made 26 flights totaling 16 hours in the XF-88. On 3 August 1950, the first prototype was flown to St. Louis, and all F-88 operations at Muroc ceased the following day. At this point, the first prototype had made 57 flights totaling 43 hours and 56 minutes.[25]

Surprisingly, given the initial favor extended to the North American entry, the Air Force notified McDonnell on 11 September 1950 that the F-88 had been ranked first in a competition that had no money to actually purchase any airplanes. Nevertheless, McDonnell submitted cost and schedule information for the proposed production F-88. The production airplane was substantially similar to the XF-88A, but used a 4.3-foot-long forward fuselage plug that contained an additional 944 gallons of internal fuel.[26]

McDonnell had been studying possible production schemes for some time. For instance, on 7 June 1949 the company had submitted an unsolicited proposal to produce 50 F-88s at a rate of five airplanes per month. Although the Air Force had informally asked for the data, no further action was taken. On 1 August, the Air Force again asked for production data, this time at a maximum rate of 15 airplanes per month. Another request on 22 August sought data for 108 airplanes, including 16 RF-88As, at a rate of 23 per month.[27]

However, the most grandiose plan came in October 1949, when McDonnell proposed ambitious production of the F2H-2 Banshee for the Navy and F-88A for the Air Force. Under this plan, McDonnell would control the engineering and produce both models, and it would license Goodyear Aircraft Corporation to manufacture the F2H-2 and General Motors to build the F-88A.[28]

McDonnell would attain a peak delivery rate of 150 F2H-2s per month by subcontracting half the work to a nearby Lincoln-Mercury plant and 150 F-88As per month by subcontracting half the work to the Fisher Body plant in St. Louis. In addition, Goodyear would produce 330 F2H-2s per month at its Akron plant and General Motors would produce 850 F-88As per month at three plants – 213 at Kansas City, 273 at Tulsa, and 364 at Cleveland. Westinghouse would produce J34 engines in Kansas City to supply McDonnell and the General Motors plants in Kansas City and Tulsa. Chrysler would produce J34s in Detroit to supply Goodyear and the General Motors plant in Cleveland. All totaled, McDonnell expected to produce the F2H-2 and F-88A for three years, resulting in 8,786 Navy and 15,046 Air Force airplanes.[29]

The XF-88B makes its maiden flight on 14 April 1953 from Lambert Field in St. Louis. The turboprop was not used on this flight. Compare this four-blade propeller and streamlined spinner with the one on the previous page. The afterburner installation on this airplane was cleaner than the original units used on the XF-88A, with the exhaust nozzles better faired into the fuselage. (National Archives)

Needless to say, this plan met a cold reception in Washington, where there was not sufficient funding to support this type of military buildup. For comparison, McDonnell eventually manufactured 895 Banshees between 1948 and September 1953, and 805 Voodoos between 1954 and March 1961 – a far cry from the numbers projected in the 1949 proposal.

XF-88B

After the first XF-88 returned to St. Louis on 3 August 1950, it was modified into the XF-88B propeller research vehicle. The airplane

The XF-88A poses with the first F-101A in St. Louis during 1954. The XF-88A had not flown since 16 June 1950 when it was involved in an accident while landing at Edwards. (National Archives)

had flown 126.49 hours during 160 flights before the conversion. The XF-88B had the distinction of being the last propeller-driven fighter in the Air Force designation series. Provisions were made for testing 27 different propellers using a 2,750-shp Allison XT38-A-5 turboprop mounted in the nose (essentially, half of the XT40 used in the Republic XF-84H). The engine was offset slightly to the left, and the nose wheel was moved to the right to accommodate the nose-mounted engine. The fuselage fuel capacity was reduced to 543 gallons to provide space for flight-test equipment, and 240 pounds of ballast was added to the rear fuselage to counter the turboprop in the nose.[30]

The turboprop installation was not completed until early 1952 after a long series of ground tests, and the modified airplane made its 42-minute maiden flight on 14 April 1953. A 10-foot-diameter, four-blade Curtiss propeller was used for the initial tests. The stability of the airplane was considered satisfactory over the entire speed range tested, except that between Mach 0.92 and Mach 0.95 a mild tuck-under tendency was noted. Stability returned above Mach 0.95 up to the maximum speed tested, Mach 0.97. Control was satisfactory under all conditions except that at low airspeeds with the turboprop at high-power settings, when very large rudder deflections were necessary to counteract torque. This led to a restriction against making takeoffs with the XT38 at high power because of insufficient rudder authority.[31]

The XF-88B spent most of its time at the NACA Langley Aeronautical Laboratory, and it was joined by the damaged second prototype on 24 February 1955 as a source of spare parts. Following the completion of its testing in 1956, the XF-88A sat in a junkyard at Langley AFB for several years, and both airplanes were eventually scrapped. The F-88 development program cost $5.3 million, including support for the NACA test program.[32]

Lockheed XP-90

The Lockheed XP-90 can trace its origins to mid-1945, when Kelly Johnson responded to an Army request for an advanced fighter design. The response to using the Lockheed-developed L-1000 engines was less than enthusiastic, and an alternate proposal using General Electric TG-180s offered no increase in performance over the F-86. In response, Johnson investigated using the Westinghouse 24C (XJ34) as an alternative. Regardless of which powerplant was used, Lockheed recognized that "tailpipe burning" – what is now called afterburning in the United States or reheat in Great Britain – would be required to provide any significant improvement in performance. Johnson arranged to have an experimental afterburning engine installed in the second XP-80A, and Tony LeVier conducted a short demonstration program. Things did not always go as planned, and LeVier had several harrowing moments, but fortunately, both pilot and aircraft survived intact.

The XF-90 project was assigned to Don Palmer, with Bill Ralston as his assistant, along with 36 engineers and shop mechanics. Lockheed submitted a proposal in October 1945 in response to the penetration fighter RFP, but it lost the competition to Convair and McDonnell. Political considerations subsequently resulted in the Air Force not awarding the Convair contract. Instead, the Air Force awarded contract W33-038-ac-14563 to Lockheed for two XP-90 prototypes (46-687/688) on 20 June 1946 as part of project MX-812. The definitive contract was signed on 25 January 1949.[33]

The original design called for fixed-angle swept-wings, but in November 1946 Lockheed changed to wings with outer sections incorporating variable sweep. Then, in December, this design was abandoned in favor of a delta wing. Wind-tunnel tests at the

The XP-90 full-scale mockup with a Westinghouse 24C (XJ34) engine in the back corner of the room. The two prototypes were generally similar to this mockup. (National Records Center, St. Louis)

California Institute of Technology indicated that the proposed delta-wing configuration did not provide the expected performance, exactly the opposite of what was being experienced at Convair on the XP-92 project. Consequently, in July 1947 work on the delta-winged prototype was halted, and those parts that had already been completed were scrapped. The fighter was completely redesigned, and the aircraft that finally emerged featured 35-degree swept-wings, a sharply

The vertical stabilizer being installed onto the first XF-90 at the Burbank plant. The XF-90 was overbuilt, using thick skins and a robust structure, that unfortunately also added considerable weight. (Lockheed Martin)

The first XF-90 (46-687) leaves the Lockheed Burbank plant bound for the trip over the foothills to Muroc in late April 1949. The rear fuselage followed on a second truck. (Lockheed Martin)

The six 20mm cannon were mounted below the air intakes, and the covered-over muzzle exits were just behind the intake leading edge. The shell casing ejection locations can be seen further back, just behind the wing leading edge line. (National Archives)

pointed nose, and two 3,000-lbf Westinghouse 24C (XJ34) axial-flow turbojets mounted side by side in the rear fuselage. Since Westinghouse had not perfected an afterburner for the XJ34, the first XP-90 would be powered by non-afterburning engines. The mockup was finally inspected by the Air Force on 2 December 1947, and the aircraft were redesignated XF-90 on 11 June 1948.[34]

By mid-1948 Kelly Johnson began to notice that the Skunk Works-type development effort that had worked so well for the XP-80 was running into considerable difficulty on the XF-90. Instead of Skunk Works building the prototypes, the aircraft were being built by the mainstream manufacturing organization, resulting in significantly increased requirements for drawings and meetings. Eventually, some compromises were reached, but the hands-on environment that had surrounded the XP-80, and would characterize future Skunk Works efforts, was missing, and the XF-90 represents one of the few missteps in the history of the design bureau.

Construction of the two aircraft continued, and the first airplane passed its engineering acceptance inspection in early April 1949. Lockheed test pilot Tony LeVier took the XF-90 on its maiden flight from Muroc on 3 June 1949. Although flight tests initially proceeded without serious problems, the performance of the XF-90 was rather sluggish because of its excess weight and the low power of its non-

The first prototype prior to being moved to Muroc. The XF-90 was an exceptionally clean looking airplane, and the twin Westinghouse engine exhausts were smoothly faired into the rear fuselage. Unfortunately, the engines were underpowered for such a large airplane and performance was disappointing. Note the large drop tanks on the wingtips that almost doubled the range of the XF-90. (Lockheed Martin)

Each drop tank had a triangular fin on it just ahead of where it met the leading edge of the wing. This fin was located slightly above the wing, but from this angle looks like a fillet extension. The airplane used relatively simple intakes, with a single boundary-air splitter and three bleed vents above the air intakes. (National Archives)

Kelly Johnson (behind wheel) discusses the XF-90 with members of the development team. By this time Johnson was a corporate executive and was not directly involved in the design effort. (Lockheed Martin)

Test pilot Tony LeVier in the cockpit of the XF-90. The airplane looked every inch the modern, high-performance fighter, but its heavy weight and low power produced disappointing results. (Lockheed Martin)

afterburning J34 engines. Seventeen flights were conducted over the next two months, but the aircraft was so underpowered that rocket-assisted take-off (RATO) bottles were required for almost every take-off. The flights revealed a variety of handling and performance problems that took the rest of the year to resolve.

Fortunately, Westinghouse finally delivered a set of afterburning XJ34 turbojets in September 1949. Each of these engines provided 2,920-lbf dry and 4,100-lbf with afterburning, but powerplant difficulties continued to plague the program. The afterburning engines allowed a maximum speed of 668 mph in level flight and Mach 1.12 in

It is uncertain if the XF-90 ever fired its six 20mm cannon in the air, but it did on the ground. Note the shell casings being ejected under the fuselage and the damage to the wing leading edge. (Lockheed Martin)

The wingtips of the XF-90s were rounded, and the drop tanks slipped over the tip, much like T-33 tanks. The pilot was located ahead of the large air intakes and had good visibility downward. (Lockheed Martin)

After the XF-90 lost the penetration fighter competition, the Air Force briefly ordered it into production as a fighter-bomber. Bomb-carrying trials had been accomplished during the earlier testing. (Lockheed Martin)

The first XF-90 at altitude with the landing gear down during a flight on 25 July 1949. All of the landing gear doors remained down while the landing gear was deployed. (Lockheed Martin)

A 500-pound bomb on a stub-pylon under the wing of an XF-90. (Lockheed Martin)

The XF-90 needed rocket assistance for almost every takeoff due to the combination of heavy weight and low power. Note the bombs in the left photo. (National Archives)

The only significant incident during the flight-test program was a wheels-up landing by the second XF-90 (46-688) on 11 May 1950. The pilot was not injured and the airframe suffered only minor damage. (National Records Center, St. Louis)

After the flight-test program, the second XF-90 was used as a nuclear weapon ground-test specimen during Operation TUMBLER/SNAPPER at the Nevada Test Site. The aircraft suffered comparatively minor damage, considering it was only a few miles from ground zero. (Fluid Tech, Inc.)

a dive. The second XF-90 made its maiden flight on 12 April 1950, equipped from the start with afterburning engines.[35]

The first XF-90 completed its 89th flight on 21 April, completing 52 of the required 56 test-hours for Phase I. Despite the slight short-fall in contractor test hours, the Air Force Phase II performance tests began on 22 May 1950. The only significant incident during the flight-test program was a wheels-up landing by the second airplane on 11 May 1950. The pilot was not injured and the airframe suffered only minor damage. On 23 June, the XF-90 entered the Penetration Fighter Evaluation program against the XF-88 and YF-93A. The last government flight was conducted on 8 July 1950 and by the end of September both aircraft were in storage at Edwards.[36]

On 11 September 1950, the Air Force announced that the F-88 had been ranked first in the penetration fighter competition. Separately, a Board of Senior Officers chaired by Lt. Gen. Ennis C. Whitehead met during July 1950 to consider a fighter-bomber to replace the F-84F. The board believed that the McDonnell F-88 "could not be strengthened to carry out the fighter-bomber role except by making it into a

new model" and recommended that the F-90 be placed into production. The Tactical Air Command established a requirement in line with this recommendation and the Air Force authorized the procurement of ten F-90s and a structural test article on 28 July 1950. This procurement was cancelled prior to a definitive contract being completed, and the exact intent of trying to make the F-90 (or F-88) into a fighter-bomber has never been explained.[37]

Since it had lost the competition, the XF-90 development contract was cancelled in September 1950 after an expenditure of $5,107,211. On 14 November 1950, the wooden mockup was disassembled and burned by the Air Force. The first XF-90 was sent to the Lewis Flight Propulsion Laboratory in Cleveland in September 1953 for use as a structural test article, and its fate is unknown. The second aircraft was used as a ground-test specimen during Operation TUMBLER/SNAPPER in Nevada during April 1952. The hulk has recently been decontaminated by Fluid Tech, Inc. (FTI) and sent to the National Museum of the United States Air Force, where it will eventually be featured in a diorama depicting the atomic testing.[38]

The XF-90 decontamination effort by Fluid Tech, Inc. was extensive, including completely disassembling both Westinghouse J34 engines. (Fluid Tech, Inc.)

After it was decontaminated, the second XF-90 was sent to the National Museum of the U.S. Air Force where it is in storage. Eventually the museum plans to use it in a diorama depicting nuclear testing and the effects of atomic weapons. There are no plans to restore the airplane to its flight-test condition. (Dennis R. Jenkins)

North American YF-93A (F-86C)

In late 1947, North American entered the penetration fighter fray with an extensively revised version of the P-86A. To keep costs down, the new airplane retained the swept-wing and the tail assembly of the P-86A, but almost everything else was different. This included a new Pratt & Whitney J48-P-1 centrifugal-flow turbojet that produced 6,250-lbf dry and 8,000-lbf in afterburner. The J48 was an American-built Rolls-Royce RB.44 Tay and was significantly larger than the J47, so the Sabre fuselage had to be increased in both width and length. The new fuselage featured a "necked down" center section that fore-shadowed the "coke bottle" fuselage championed by Richard Whitcomb at NACA Langley. The P-86C would carry six 20mm cannon with a search radar mounted in the nose, requiring the air intakes to be relocated to the sides of the fuselage. Initially, these used NACA-designed flush-mounted air scoops since wind-tunnel data showed they would significantly reduce aerodynamic drag. Two P-86C prototypes (48-317/318) were ordered as a supplement to an existing P-86A production contract (W33-038-ac-16013).[39]

In the penetration fighter competition, the Air Force initially favored the North American design because of its commonality with other Sabre variants. On 9 April 1948, North American submitted a

The first YF-93A (48-317) and the first YF-95A (YF-86D, 50-577) at Edwards. Both aircraft used the non-standard "YF" buzz numbers favored by North American Aviation for their prototypes. Note the B-45 in the background. (National Archives)

The first YF-93A poses on the lakebed at Edwards equipped with its original flush NACA-style intakes. The Sabre lineage is obvious in the empennage and canopy, but the rest of the fuselage was new to the YF-93A. All of the penetration fighters were large aircraft – note the dual main wheel landing gear used to support the North American entry. (AFFTC History Office Collection)

The original NACA-style intakes were expected to result in a significant reduction in drag, which they apparently did. However, they also did not provide sufficient air to the engine. (National Archives)

The final ducts used on both YF-93As at the NACA Ames Aeronautical Laboratory were much more conventional, giving up entirely on the idea of a flush intake for the main engine airflow. (National Archives)

$6,811,449 proposal for the two recently authorized P-86C prototypes and 118 production aircraft. The Air Force approved this on 29 May and authorized North American to procure production tooling for an ultimate fabrication rate of 180 aircraft per month under contract W33-038-ac-21672 worth $53,452,060. In September 1948, the Air Force decided there was so many differences from the production Sabre that the F-86C should be redesignated YF-93A, and the production airplanes became F-93As. However, F-93A production was suddenly cancelled on 25 February 1949, mostly because of a severe reduction in the military budget for FY50. Nevertheless, the F-93 was also considered for a variety of other roles. In 1948, it had received consideration as a tactical reconnaissance aircraft, in 1949 as an interceptor, and in 1950 as an escort fighter. None of these ideas resulted in a production contract.[40]

While at NACA Ames, several intake modifications were made in an attempt to find the best compromise between reducing drag and providing adequate airflow for the engine. This version kept some of the basic contours of the flush installation, but had a smoother opening and protruded further from the fuselage centerline. It still did not provide enough air for the engine to operate efficiently. (National Archives)

The contours of the rear fuselage around the engine exhaust also changed during the test program. At left is the original straight-cut rear fuselage on the first airplane, while the later, tapered-cut on the second airplane is at right. (National Archives)

The YF-93A was the last of the three penetration fighter competitors to take to the air. The first YF-93A did not roll out of the factory until late 1949, and it was trucked out to Muroc where North American test pilot "Wheaties" Welch made its maiden flight on 25 January 1950. During the following months, no major problems were experienced by the airplanes. However, on the last scheduled flight of the first YF-93, on 5 June 1950, the pilot landed after a 73-minute flight and attempted a second takeoff. This was interrupted by an explosion and fire that severely damaged the aft fuselage. The cause was later traced to a broken afterburner fuel manifold drain line.[41]

The second aircraft arrived at Edwards in May 1950 and entered the penetration fighter evaluation on 23 June where it ranked third. The Air Force concluded that the YF-93A had insufficient range and endurance, and could not be successfully operated above 25,000 feet without use of the afterburner. The maximum altitude, even with afterburner, was only 32,000 feet. Furthermore, the evaluation flights revealed that airspeed deteriorated rapidly during maneuvers, even with the engine at full power. The airplane had a maximum speed of only Mach 0.94, and at speeds above Mach 0.80 tended to snake, much like the P-59. Finally, pilots found that the airplane could not sustain level flight with the landing gear and flaps extended.[42]

The first YF-93A as it was marked while at NACA Ames. Note the Air Force serial number has been removed and "NACA 139" applied to the rear fuselage, along with a "1" on the nose and tail. (National Archives)

The second YF-93A at NACA Ames. Interestingly, the rear fuselage is from the first airplane – note the "1" on the tail and the "NACA 139" on the rear fuselage, despite the "2" on the nose. (National Archives)

The first YF-93A with its final intakes, although it is still wearing Air Force markings, not NACA ones. The slight Area Rule applied to the fuselage (pinched at the wing) is evident from this angle. Note the large air-data probes on the wingtips, and a smaller one protruding under the nose. By this time the airplane had received the "USAF" markings on top of the wing. (AFFTC History Office Collection)

On 11 September 1950, the Air Force announced the F-88 had ranked first in the penetration fighter competition and the North American contract was terminated. Oddly, given their derivative roots, the two YF-93As were by far the most expensive of the penetration fighters. By the time the various contracts had been sorted out, $7,329,816 had been spent building the two prototypes, and an additional $4,167,568 was spent on spare parts, special ground equipment, and contract termination costs.[43]

After the competition, the first airplane was repaired and returned to flight status. The second YF-93A was returned to North American where the radar and gunsight were removed and an all moving horizontal stabilizer installed. The flight program officially ended in December 1950. The first aircraft was accepted by the Air Force on 6 February 1951 at Edwards, and the second airplane was accepted on 26 February at the North American plant.[44]

In June 1951, both YF-93As were turned over to the NACA Ames Aeronautical Laboratory for tests of the flush air intakes.

After a series of experiments, the NACA eventually fitted both prototypes with conventional air intakes that proved more efficient at high speeds. Although the air intakes created more drag, they allowed the engines to produce more power, overcoming the additional drag. At some point, both aircraft had their rear fuselages modified to accept a production F-86D tailpipe and stabilizer housing. They were used by NACA as flight-test and chase aircraft well into the mid-1950s, and played an important role in testing components for most of the Century Series fighters. Both were retired and scrapped in the late 1950s.[45]

Republic XF-96A (XF-84F) Thunderstreak

The YF-96A was the initial designation of what was produced as the swept-wing F-84F. For political reasons, the designation of the F-96 was changed to F-84F on 9 August 1950. Details of the YF-84F may be found elsewhere in this book.

Chapter 6

Right: *A Boeing YIM-99A Bomarc launches from Pad 4 at the Cape Canaveral Missile Test Annex, Florida, on 28 October 1959. By this time, production representative missiles were also rolling off the Boeing production line.* (45th Space Wing History Office)

Below: *An early Hughes GAR-1 on its ground launcher at the White Sands Missile Range in New Mexico. The forward fins are taking on the shape used by production Falcons, but the aft aero surfaces are still considerably different than later missiles.* (National Archives)

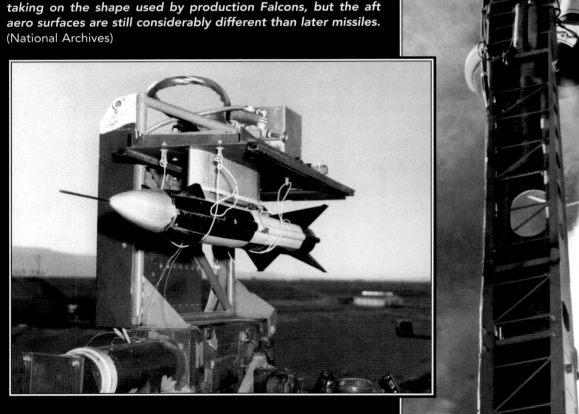

MISSILES ?
UNMANNED FIGHTERS AND INTERCEPTORS

Surprisingly, not all "F" designations were assigned to manned aircraft. In 1951, an "unmanned fighter" and an "unmanned interceptor" were assigned designations within the traditional fighter series since it was expected that their functions would eventually supplement, if not supplant, manned aircraft. This decision was rather quickly reversed in 1955, and no missiles entered operational service with an F designation.

Hughes XF-98 Falcon

In 1947, the Army released requests for proposals for two aircraft armament systems. The first was to study a radar-based airborne fire-control system for manned interceptors, and the second was to develop an air-to-air guided missile, initially to be used as a bomber defense missile as part of project MX-798. Both contracts were awarded to Hughes Aircraft Corporation of Culver City, California, although the effort spawned similar contracts to Ryan

Aeronautical (MX-799), M.W. Kellogg (MX-800), Bendix (MX-801), and General Electric (MX-802).[1]

In 1947, the AAM-A-2 (Air-to-Air Missile – Army) designation was assigned to the Hughes missile, which was later named Falcon. The first experimental XAAM-A-2 missiles were ground launched in 1948 in a long-lived investigation of various aerodynamic configurations. In 1950, the Army largely dropped the idea of a bomber defense missile, although it was shortly revived during the B-70 competition. Therefore, the Falcon was redirected as an anti-bomber missile to be launched by a new generation of interceptors, and the development was moved to project MX-904. A year later, the missile was redesignated XF-98 and XF-98A to reflect its new-found importance. (Some sources indicate the XF-98A was briefly designated XF-104 but these could not be confirmed.)

The XF-98 used a rocket motor that provided 5,560-lbf for 1.2 seconds and boosted the missile to about Mach 2, after which the missile glided to its target. This variant was intended for subsonic fighters

The Falcon was originally conceived as a bomber defense missile, and several bomber proposals during the late 1940s (here a B-52 from 22 August 1949) included launching tubes for the missile. (National Archives)

When the Falcon was reoriented toward arming interceptors, such as this early F-89, the first concepts still used the tube-launching techniques developed for the bomber defense missile. (National Archives)

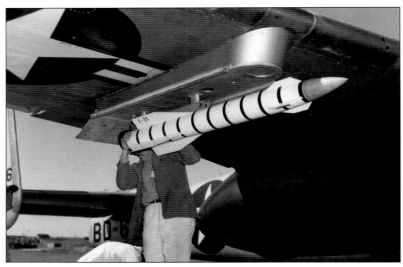

These photos show the evolution of the MX-904 airframe shape between 9 November 1950 (left) and 26 April 1951. In both cases the missile is mounted under the wing of a North American B-25 that was used during ground launch trials and later air launches. Note that early missiles had a fairly conventional aero surface arrangement, but the missile slowly evolved into the canard-and-delta that became the Falcon. (National Archives)

such as the Northrop F-89 against subsonic bombers. Many different XF-98 configurations were tested in wind tunnels and ground launched in an attempt to find an aerodynamic configuration that provided suitable stability and control. Eventually, as increased emphasis was placed on supersonic launch platforms, the XF-98 variant was dropped, and all efforts concentrated on the XF-98A.[2]

Besides the subsonic F-89, the intended launch platforms for the F-98A were the Convair F-102 and Republic F-103, airplanes with decidedly different performance characteristics. The F-103 was expected to be faster than the F-102 at all altitudes, but particularly above 50,000 feet. The F-98A would need to be launched at speeds ranging from subsonic to over Mach 3.0 at altitudes from 5,000 to 60,000 feet. This meant the missile would need to operate at speeds between Mach 1.6 and 3.8 at altitudes from essentially sea level to 100,000 feet.[3]

The XF-98A was intended for use by subsonic and supersonic fighters, still against subsonic bombers. The missile speed at the end of the boost phase was highly dependent on the speed of the interceptor at launch since missile speed was launch speed plus the acceleration from the booster motor. Development of the XF-98 had been dropped since, when launched from a supersonic interceptor, the mis-

These two photographs do not depict the same event, but the outcome was largely the same. The undated photo at left shows an early MX-904 streaking toward a QB-17 drone; the 21 October 1953 photo at right shows the results of a later test. (National Archives)

sile attained excessive speeds because of the burn characteristics of the rocket motor. The XF-98A used a booster-sustainer rocket motor that produced 4,500-lbf for 0.7-second, reduced to 900-lbf for 1.0 second, and then gradually tapered to zero over the next four seconds. This reduction was achieved by contouring the solid propellant grain.

The XF-98A was an aerodynamic and propulsion test vehicle only, and did not carry a guidance system or warhead. Many XF-98A configurations were ground launched at various locations, primarily White Sands Missile Range, while Hughes engineers struggled to find a workable aerodynamic configuration. The YF-98A added a guidance system and was generally air launched. Both variants were 83 inches long, 6.4 inches in diameter, and weighed 132 pounds.[4]

By June 1952, nineteen YF-98As had been launched, including ten from a North American B-25 flying at 17,000 feet. Four of these were air-launched in June alone, scoring one "statistically equivalent hit" and three physical hits on the QB-17 target aircraft. The ground-launched missiles were fired against simulated aircraft structures several miles from the launch site. Some of the missiles used magnetic fuzes in the nose, but most used the tail-fin proximity fuzes that were ultimately featured on production models. None of these missiles carried a warhead, and the fuze generally detonated a smoke bomb instead. June also saw the first attempts to record radar cross-section data (called radar target signal scintillation data at the time) on an F-86 and QB-17.[5]

Not all of the tests were successful, but all yielded valuable data. For instance, four motor storage surveillance missiles were launched to determine the effects of having the solid rocket motors stored under different conditions. The motor of missile M-421 failed to ignite when it was fired, but the igniter blast sheared the attachment bolt and the missile fell off the launcher. The motor on missile M-422 did not come up to full thrust until three seconds after ignition, although the rest of the flight appeared normal. The other two test missiles performed as expected.[6]

The Falcon was not a particularly maneuverable missile, and needed to be pointed in generally the right direction at launch. This meant that the fire-control system in the interceptor needed to guide the aircraft into the proper position to launch the missile. This was a demanding navigation problem in an era before high-speed digital computers and partially explains the delays encountered by the Northrop F-89 and Convair F-102 fire-control systems. Initially, the missile could attack targets flying up to 5,000 feet above the launch platform but, in 1952, Hughes began studying methods to attack targets up to 15,000 feet higher using a "snap-up" mode. This markedly reduced the time required for the interceptor to reach an attack position, especially at high altitude. However, this proved considerably more difficult than originally thought, since the fire-control system had to determine precisely the proper moment for

Another series of photos illustrating the configuration evolution of the MX-904 missile. At left, an early design from 13 July 1950; in center, the beginning of the Falcon on 10 January 1951; at right, a slightly later Falcon on 15 February 1951. (National Archives)

the snap-up maneuver and when to launch the missile. By May 1955, after nearly three years of study and extensive tests, a primitive snap-up computer was installed in the F-89.[7]

Initially, snap-up trials with the F-89 were not particularly successful, but they did provide valuable data for further development. This is not to say that there weren't successes along the way. In one test, three of five Falcons launched in the snap-up mode scored direct hits, and another was a near miss. In September 1955, Hughes was directed to incorporate the snap-up mode into the improved E-9 fire-control system for the Northrop F-89H. [8]

Testing of YF-98A prototypes continued, and the first production-representative F-98A was delivered in 1954. However, in 1955, the Air Force stopped using aircraft designations for missiles, and the Falcon was again redesignated. The XF-98A, YF-98A, and F-98A became the XGAR-1, YGAR-1, and GAR-1, respectively (GAR standing for Guided Aircraft Rocket).[9]

The final members of the extended Falcon family included the AIM-26 Super Falcon (on ground), the AIM-47 for the F-108 and YF-12A (at right), and the XAIM-54 Phoenix for the F-14 (at left). (National Archives)

An armed GAR-1 was fired from a modified Northrop F-89D on 27 January 1955, downing a QB-17 drone, marking the first GAR-1 armed with a live warhead to strike an airborne aircraft. Hughes went on to build several variants of the Falcon with different types of guidance systems and subtle aerodynamic changes.[10]

The development by Hughes of a workable passive infrared sensor in 1954 apparently took everybody by surprise, including the Strategic Air Command. The appearance of the infrared-guided GAR-2 was one of the factors that prompted Brig. Gen. George E. Price, the director of requirements, to declare that defense against infrared missiles was an "urgent task requiring immediate action." The defenses proposed were very far-sighted and mirror the countermeasures still used (or being developed) 50 years later. These included confusing the missile with heat-radiating decoys, flares, or towed targets, and blinding the infrared sensor with intense outputs of heat (effectively what the current laser units do). A more far-fetched idea was to restrict the heat output from the bomber (target) by using "plastic smoke" consisting of low-density particles that settled rapidly to screen the engine exhaust.[11]

By August 1955, Hughes had accomplished the preliminary engineering to integrate the GAR-2 with the E-9 fire-control system in the Northrop F-89H. The E-9, however, was running into problems that called in question the readiness of the F-89H in general. For instance, during 1956, two F-89Hs at Eglin AFB, Florida, launched 30 Falcons (both radar and infrared), scoring zero hits. Worse, only nine of the radar-guided GAR-1s had displayed any control whatsoever. This was partially the fault of the Air Force, since the two test F-89Hs did not incorporate many of the fixes to the E-9 that had already been identified by Hughes. Once these changes were incorporated, 12 additional missiles were launched and all guided properly, although only three scored direct hits.[12]

A year later, in May 1957, tests at Eglin during Project Quick Draw showed that the radar-guided GAR-1D worked well. However, the July 1957 Quick Draw tests of the infrared-guided GAR-2 launched from an F-102 were not nearly as satisfactory, since not a single missile tracked its target. This should not have been a surprise, since tests during December 1956 had resulted in only one hit from 20 launches. The initial diagnosis placed the blame on excessive background noise that confused the infrared sensor. Eventually, Hughes and the Air Force recognized that much of the background noise came from atmospheric or terrain phenomena that were outside of their control, so Hughes went back to the drawing board to work on filters and other techniques to minimize the distractions. Although Hughes developed an improved infrared detector for the GAR-2A, it did not work significantly better during operational testing. The problem was not satisfactorily resolved until the improved GAR-4A entered service.[13]

The GAR series of missiles was subsequently redesignated AIM (Air Intercept Missile) in 1962, with the GAR-1, GAR-2, and GAR-3 Falcons becoming part of the AIM-4 family. Eventually, more than 60,200 Falcon missiles of various versions were built, with 48,000 of them being delivered to the U.S. Air Force.[14]

The GAR-9 (AIM-47A) was the ultimate version of the Falcon, designed for use with the advanced ASG-18 radar on the North

American F-108 interceptor. Development began in 1958, and the first ground launch took place in August 1961. The missile had an effective range of 115 miles and featured both semi-active radar and infrared homing. When the F-108 program was cancelled in 1959, the GAR-9 project was transferred to the Lockheed YF-12A program and later formed the engineering basis for the AIM-54 Phoenix for the Navy/Grumman F-14 Tomcat.[15]

Boeing/MARC XF-99 Bomarc

In June 1945, Boeing began studying surface-to-air (SAM) guided missiles as part of project MX-606 under the name Condor. On 30 January, the Air Force awarded Boeing a one-year contract (W33-038-ac-13875) for the development of a military weapon based on the results of the Condor study. The resulting weapon was supposed to intercept enemy aircraft flying 700 mph at 60,000 feet. The missile would be vertically launched, boosted by solid-propellant rockets, and sustained by ramjets. By July 1946, the missile had been renamed GAPA (Ground-to-Air Pilotless Aircraft) and was 21.5-feet long, 2 feet in diameter, and weighed 6,900 pounds at launch. By 1950, Boeing had launched more than 100 test missiles in various configurations, all under the XSAM-A-1 designation. Some of the missiles reached 1,500 mph during the generally successful tests conducted at Holloman AFB, New Mexico.[16]

In 1949, the Air Force awarded Boeing a development contract for a "pilotless interceptor" as part of project MX-1599. The MX-1599 missile was to be a nuclear-armed, ramjet-powered, long-range surface-to-air missile to defend North America from Soviet bombers.[17]

The Michigan Aerospace Research Center (MARC) was added to the project during 1950 to develop the warning and control system that linked the launch bases, and this gave the new missile its Bomarc (for BOeing and MARC) name. In 1951, the Air Force decided to emphasize that missiles were nothing more than pilotless aircraft by assigning aircraft designators. Anti-aircraft missiles received F-for-Fighter designations, and Bomarc became F-99 (several offensive missiles were designated in the bomber series). The Bomarc was the only surface-to-air missile deployed by the U.S. Air Force; all other U.S. land-based SAMs were developed by the U.S. Army.

Two different types of test missiles were manufactured. Experimental XF-99 propulsion test vehicles were used to evaluate the liquid-fueled booster that would accelerate the interceptor to ramjet ignition speed. XF-99 tests began at the Air Force Missile Test Center (AFMTC) at Cape Canaveral on 10 September 1952 and continued through early 1955. Launches were intermittent due to Boeing's insistence that engineers in Seattle analyze the flight data before the next missile was fired. The second Bomarc was launched from Cape Canaveral on 23 January 1953, and the third followed nearly five months later, on 10 June. Two more XF-99s were launched during the summer of 1953, and three were launched in 1954. In February 1955, the XF-99 propulsion test vehicles began using live ramjets, but still no guidance system or warhead. [18]

The YF-99 designation was reserved for missiles that included prototype guidance systems, but in August 1955, before any YF-99s could be built, the Air Force discontinued the use of aircraft-type designators for missiles. The tremendous differences in operations and maintenance between fighter aircraft and missiles led Bomarc to be redesignated IM-99 (for Intercept Missile). The XF-99 and YF-99 became XIM-99 and YIM-99, respectively. Originally, the Air Force had allocated the designation IM-69, but this was changed (possibly at Boeing's request to keep number 99) to IM-99.[19]

Predating the SAGE network, Bomarc was developed with its own command and control segment, although by the time it was built it had been integrated into the SAGE environment. (National Archives)

The Bomarc guidance radar and electronics were tested on a Lockheed F-94B (51-5502, above) and a Martin B-57B (52-1497). Both aircraft included extended Bomarc noses. (National Archives)

The fifth YIM-99A (56-4031) in Hangar I at Cape Canaveral on 25 August 1958. This missile was known as "XY-3," although no documentation was located that explained why. A warning is stenciled on the wingtip, "Danger: Stand Clear of Surface at all times." (45th Space Wing History Office)

The first XF-99 propulsion test vehicle at Cape Canaveral about three weeks prior to the first launch. The missile was successfully launched on 10 September 1952. (45th Space Wing History Office)

The second propulsion test vehicle being prepared for launch on 23 January 1953. The Bomarc airframe changed in only minor details during the test program. (45th Space Wing History Office)

Ultimately, 41 XIM-99 propulsion test vehicles were manufactured, followed by 38 YIM-99 guidance test missiles and 7 YIM-99A (56-4027/4033) operational test missiles that used production-representative engines and guidance systems. Later, 20 YIM-99B service-test examples of the improved B-model Bomarc were manufactured.[20]

On 2 October 1957, the first production-representative YIM-99A was launched from Cape Canaveral and passed within kill distance of a North American X-10 target traveling at Mach 2 and 48,000 feet; notably, the SAGE (Semi-Automatic Ground Environment) site at Kingston, New York, controlled the intercept. Twenty-five more Bomarcs were launched from Cape Canaveral before the Air Force announced plans, in September 1958, to transfer the program to the Air Proving Ground Center test site at Santa Rosa Island near Eglin AFB, Florida. The first launch from Santa Rosa – from a production-representative Type I shelter – took place on 15 January 1959. Boeing conducted its last Bomarc launch from Cape Canaveral on 15 April 1960.[21]

The first production IM-99A Bomarc rolled out at Seattle on 30 December 1957. Boeing delivered 366 production IM-99As that equipped five sites in the northeastern United States and 349 IM-99Bs stationed at six sites in the United States and two in Canada. In June 1963, the IM-99A and IM-99B missiles were redesignated CIM-10A and CIM-10B, respectively, with the "C" indicating its basing mode, in this case "coffin." The Bomarc A was retired soon afterwards, with the last CIM-10A being phased out in December 1964. Withdrawal of the CIM-10B also began in the mid-1960s, and by 1969, most missile sites had been deactivated. Finally, in April 1972, the last Bomarc B was retired. Designed to intercept relatively slow manned bombers, the Bomarc had little chance of countering intercontinental ballistic missiles.[22]

Unsurprisingly, not all Bomarc launches were successful. This would have been the 70th launch from Cape Canaveral, but the missile exploded on Pad 4 on 5 March 1960. (45th Space Wing History Office)

An early Bomarc intercepts a QB-17 drone off the coast of Cape Canaveral. The "spotting charge" at upper right shows where the missile would have detonated. (45th Space Wing History Office)

The interceptors that defended North America during the late 1950s and early 1960s included the Avro CF-100 Mk 5 Canuck (18680), IM-99A Bomarc (59-1976), and Convair F-102A (56-1235). (National Archives)

Chapter 7

Left: *The first North American F-107A (55-5118). Despite popular writings, there was never any real "competition" between the F-105 and F-107, with the latter being a long-shot contingency in case the F-105 failed.* (AFFTC History Office Collection)

Below: *The second Lockheed XF-104 (53-7787) shows the early, and unimaginative, nose markings. The air intakes on the two experimental airplanes lacked the center-body shock cones of later aircraft since their Wright J67 engines did not allow Mach 2 performance.* (Lockheed Martin)

CENTURY SERIES FIGHTERS
SUPERSONIC OPERATIONS

At the beginning of the turbojet revolution, Pratt & Whitney had been producing Rolls-Royce designs under license, instead of developing its own designs, and the company decided that it was at least five years behind the other major turbojet companies in development expertise. In 1946, Pratt & Whitney made a strategic decision to invest substantial amounts of its own funds in new research and test facilities to catch up with its competitors.

The focus of the research was aimed at solving the two most significant shortcomings of existing turbojets: low thrust and high fuel consumption. At the end of World War II, the best production engines developed about 4,000-lbf, so Pratt & Whitney decided to leap-frog the competition by developing a 10,000-lbf engine that was significantly more fuel efficient. The company focused on the military market but recognized the possibility of later commercial applications.

Of the five main U.S. jet-engine companies, only Pratt & Whitney believed that dramatically increasing the compressor pressure ratio was the solution to the thrust- and fuel-consumption issues. In response, Pratt & Whitney engineers developed a "twin spool" engine that incorporated two different sets of compressor and turbine combinations in the same engine. A low-pressure compressor at the front of the engine was driven by a low-pressure turbine connected by a rotating shaft inside a second rotating shaft. The outer shaft connected a high-pressure compressor behind the low-pressure compressor to a high-pressure turbine located in front of the low-pressure turbine. This promised a substantial increase in the overall efficiency of the engine, although it also significantly increased the complexity of the axial-flow turbojet.

The Pratt & Whitney J57 (JT3) first ran in 1950 and proved to be the revolutionary advance that made supersonic flight possible. The J57 developed up to 18,000-lbf and powered the North American F-100, McDonnell F-101, Convair F-102, Boeing B-52, Boeing KC-135, and Lockheed U-2, in addition to several Navy and commercial aircraft, including versions of the Boeing 707 and Douglas DC-8. The larger J75 (JT4) used the same principles as the J57 and produced up to 25,000-lbf. This engine powered the Republic F-105, Convair F-106, North American F-107, and Martin P6M Seamaster.

However, these high-pressure-ratio engines presented designers with a new set of challenges. As pressure ratios increased for optimal efficiency at cruise conditions, problems arose with the compressor operating efficiently at low speeds, especially during acceleration when airflow patterns over the compressor airfoils were very different from what they were under their design conditions.

General Electric solved this problem by developing variable-geometry stators that change their angle of attack for different airflow conditions. The General Electric X24A concept emerged in response to an Air Force requirement for a high-thrust, fuel-efficient, Mach 2 engine. In 1952, General Electric began development of an advanced variant of the J47/J71 that incorporated the variable stator concept. Flight-testing of the J79 began in mid-1955, and the engine was used on the Convair B-58, the first Mach 2 bomber, and Lockheed F-104, the first Mach 2 fighter. The J79 also powered several Navy aircraft, most importantly the McDonnell F-4.

The Pratt & Whitney J75 was the most powerful turbojet of its era, but it proved troublesome in initial service. The engine would mature into a responsive powerplant for both the Republic F-105 and Convair F-106. (Air Force Historical Research Agency)

Development Lament

It is difficult for anybody watching the snail's pace of fighter development in the early 21st century to appreciate fully how things were 50 years ago. During the 1950s, the future was always just a day away. Anything that could be dreamed could be developed, or at least that is how it appeared. When World War II ended, fighter aircraft had a maximum speed of less than 500 mph. Two years later, Chuck Yeager broke the sound barrier in the rocket-powered X-1 research airplane, but everybody understood that fighters would soon be flying that fast as a matter of routine.

The North American F-100, powered by the revolutionary Pratt & Whitney J57, was the first of a new breed that was capable of supersonic speeds in level flight. The F-100 would lend its designation to the "Century Series" of fighters that defined American airpower during the early part of the Cold War. Between May 1953 and December 1956, seven different operational fighter designs – the F-100, McDonnell F-101, Convair F-102, Lockheed F-104, Republic F-105, and Convair F-106 – made their first flights, expanding the speed envelope well past Mach 2. Two other highly-advanced designs, the Republic XF-103 and North American XF-108, would have pushed the envelope out past Mach 3 had those programs not been cancelled, one for technical delays and the other for largely political reasons.

The pace of development was truly remarkable. The Air Force awarded the development contract for the F-100 on 1 November 1951, and the first aircraft made its maiden flight on 25 May 1953. Production F-100s were delivered in November 1953, with the 479th Fighter (Day) Group becoming operational on 29 September 1954. From contract to operational service was an unbelievably short three years.

The last large, multi-role fighter to become operational with the Air Force was the McDonnell Douglas F-15. That development contract was signed on 23 December 1969, and the F-15 made its maiden flight on 27 July 1972. Deliveries began in November 1974, and the 1st Tactical Fighter Wing became operational in June 1976. Six-and-one-half years from contract to operations, double the time taken by the F-100.

Contrast that with how things are done today. The first request for information for the Advanced Tactical Fighter (ATF) was issued in June 1981 and the contract awards for a two-company fly-off were made on 31 October 1986. The maiden flight of the first YF-22 was on 29 September 1990 and the aircraft was subsequently declared the winner of the fly-off. A full-scale development contract was awarded to Lockheed on 3 August 1991, and the maiden flight of the F-22A took place on 7 September 1997. Deliveries of production-representative examples began in 2003, and the Raptor became operational with the 1st Fighter Wing on 15 December 2005. Taken from the contract award for the fly-off, this is a 19-year gestation period; from the development contract award to Lockheed, it is 14 years. The more-recent F-35 is perhaps even more worrisome since the Air Force announced in 2007 that the systems development phase is scheduled to last more than 12 years, this after more than a dozen years of studies and a fly-off. The unfortunate consequence is that the engineers and designers never have

a chance to get good at their jobs. Alexander Kartveli and Kelly Johnson designed dozens of aircraft during their careers; most current designers will be lucky to develop a single design.

Of course, aircraft have gotten immensely more complex during that time, but so have the tools available to designers and engineers. Control cables and aluminum have been replaced with fly-by-wire and composite structures. Slide rules and drafting tables have given way to computational fluid dynamics and CATIA@designware. Computer numerical control (CNC) milling machines have replaced labor-intensive hand shaping of prototype parts.

On the brighter side, aircraft have also become much safer. Over the course of its career, the F-100 flew 5,471,047 hours in U.S. service, and 889 aircraft were lost to non-combat causes, killing 391 crewmembers. This works out to 16.25 aircraft destroyed per 100,000 flight hours. No current U.S. fighter has flown quite as many flight hours, so let's look at a point in time (5 million flight hours) where we can make some reasonable comparisons.

It took 20 years for the F-100 to accumulate 4,999,107 flight hours. During that time, 853 aircraft and 310 crewmembers were lost. This equates to a rate of 17.06 aircraft destroyed to non-combat causes per 100,000 flight hours. Recently, it has taken 33 years for the F-15 to accumulate 4,998,072 hours. During that time, 107 aircraft and 45 crewmembers were lost to non-combat causes. This equates to a loss rate of 2.14 aircraft per 100,000 flight hours, a tremendous improvement over the F-100. The other modern fighter for which statistics are available is the Lockheed F-16, which took 22 years to get to 4,891,291 hours, with a loss of 214 aircraft and 70 crewmembers. This equates to a rate of 4.37 losses per 100,000 hours. Obviously, twin-engine aircraft (F-15) are safer than single-engine ones (F-16), but both modern aircraft are remarkably safer than the F-100 was just 40 years earlier. Notably, the ratio of crewmembers killed to aircraft lost has not changed significantly, despite dramatic improvements in ejection seat technology. [1]

Although not directly comparable, it is interesting to note that in the 10 years since it entered service, the Boeing 777 airliner has accumulated 7.7 million flight hours with no losses, a tribute to the age of the digital airplane and the safety of commercial aviation.

The Cook-Craigie Plan

The Century Series were the first combat aircraft to be procured under the concept of "concurrency" developed during the late 1940s by Lt. Gen. Orval R. Cook, Deputy Chief of Staff for Materiel, and Lt. Gen. Laurence C. Craigie, Deputy Chief of Staff for Development. The idea was to reduce the time between the start of a program and the initial operational capability (IOC) of the resulting weapon.[2]

Past practice had been to purchase one or two experimental ("X") models that were essentially hand-built. The contractor would perform the initial Phase I airworthiness tests on these airplanes, and then turn them over to the Air Force for Phase II performance tests. If these proved satisfactory, the government would purchase a limited number of service test prototypes ("Y" models)

The first five operational Century Series designs, on 22 June 1956 at Edwards. Clockwise from bottom, Lockheed XF-104 (53-7786), North American F-100A (53-0663), Convair F-102A (53-1805), McDonnell F-101A (53-2430), and Republic YF-105 (54-0099). (AFFTC History Office Collection)

that incorporated all of the lessons learned from the experimental models. In most cases, the prototypes would be manufactured on production-representative tooling to get ready for mass production. The tooling required to mass-produce an airplane was a significant development effort in itself, and generally consumed 26 months before the first prototype could be delivered.[3]

Under the Cook-Craigie plan there would not be any experimental models. The contractor would develop the production tooling simultaneously with the design of the airplane and use this tooling to build the initial aircraft. For the first year, the production rate would be limited to a couple of airplanes per month, and the first 25-50 examples (for fighters; fewer for bombers and transports) would be dedicated to an accelerated flight-test program. Any deficiencies found during testing would be incorporated into production aircraft intended for operational use. Early aircraft would be modified to the same standard and be issued to operational squadrons.[4]

The Air Materiel Command and Air Research and Development Command initially concurred in principle with the new plan, but by May 1952 were beginning to voice concerns. Maj. Gen. Mark E. Bradley, the AMC Director of Procurement and Production, warned that extreme caution was necessary before using the Cook-Craigie concept. The cost risk could be great should the airplane prove unsatisfactory and be cancelled, since the significant investment in production tooling would already have been made. Even more likely were major configuration changes resulting from flight tests that could – and ultimately did – make early tooling obsolete.[5]

The same idea would surface again in the late 1960s and early 1970s, when programs became so expensive that prototype efforts could not be afforded. A similar concept was revived for the Lockheed Martin F-22 and Bell-Boeing V-22. Unfortunately, the idea has a major flaw – it assumes that any problems found will be minor in nature, clearly understood, and easily corrected. As would be discovered, this was seldom the case.

North American YF-100 Super Sabre

The quest for a supersonic fighter began in February 1949, when Raymond Rice and Edgar Schmued of North American Aviation began an in-house design study for a supersonic version of the F-86. The first conceptual design increased the wing sweep to 45 degrees, but wind-tunnel studies indicated that this brought only a relatively small increase in speed due to the steep rise in aerodynamic drag at transonic velocities. Clearly, aerodynamic changes alone would not be sufficient and more power would be needed – a lot more power. After a series of studies centered around various versions of the General Electric J47, North American began looking at an airplane powered by the new twin-spool Pratt & Whitney J57.[6]

After considerable study, North American came up with the J57-powered Sabre 45 that had an estimated speed of 860 mph (Mach 1.3) at 35,000 feet. In October 1951, the Air Force authorized the development of the new fighter as part of project MX-1894, despite the misgivings of key personnel that much of the technology and aerodynamics was not well understood. In a move that would ultimately prove costly, the Air Force decided to procure the F-100 using the Cook-Craigie concept of concurrency, and on 1 November 1951, issued a letter contract for two YF-100 prototypes (52-5754/5755) and 110 production aircraft. Given the use of the Cook-Craigie plan, there was no XF-100 despite the significant technological advances embodied in the aircraft.[7]

The mockup was inspected on 7 November 1951, resulting in more than 100 configuration changes. One of the most important was to move the horizontal stabilizer below the plane of the wing to keep it out of the wing wake at high angles of attack. This would prevent the dangerous tendency of a swept-wing aircraft to pitch up suddenly and violently following a stall. This sometimes-deadly phenomenon had become known as the "Sabre dance," and was the cause of numerous accidents in the F-86. North American modified the first YF-86D (50-577) to evaluate this new low-set horizontal tail arrangement.[8]

The first YF-100A (52-5754) shows the extremely long air-data probe used by several early supersonic aircraft. Researchers wanted to ensure the instruments were in clean air. (National Records Center, St. Louis)

The first YF-100A on a truck heading between the North American plant in Inglewood, at the Los Angeles Airport, and Edwards. By this time the aircraft had a traditional buzz number. (National Records Center, St. Louis)

Test pilot George S. Welch broke the sound barrier on the maiden flight of the first YF-100A on 25 May 1953. Two weeks later, the first production F-100A rolled off the line. (National Records Center, St. Louis)

The first YF-100A shows its clean lines. Given its size and the power available from the Pratt & Whitney J57, it was a tribute to the engineers that the aircraft was as fast as it was. (AFFTC History Office Collection)

North American also changed the air-intake lip so that it had a sharp edge to improve the airflow, extended the nose nine inches to improve the fineness ratio, and replaced the original F-86-style canopy with an elongated clamshell design to minimize drag. But most importantly, North American increased the chord of the vertical stabilizer while simultaneously making it shorter. This last change was made too late to appear on the two YF-100 prototypes, but it was incorporated, untested, on production aircraft. The changes were present, however, on the F-100A mockup during the second inspection on 21 March 1952. This time there were few comments of consequence. On 26 August 1952, the Air Force authorized the procurement of 250 additional F-100s, long before the YF-100 flew.[9]

The YF-100 that finally emerged from these changes was sufficiently different from the original design that it was redesignated YF-100A. As the first airplane was nearing completion, the Air Force recognized that two prototypes would not be sufficient for the test program, and it authorized the use of the first 10 F-100As as well. The first YF-100A was completed on 24 April 1953, and after the customary ground tests it was disassembled and transported to Edwards for taxi tests.

Everybody was impressed on 25 May 1953 when North American chief test pilot George S. "Wheaties" Welch took the YF-100A past Mach 1 on its 57-minute maiden flight. On that same afternoon, Welch took the airplane on its second consecutive supersonic sortie. These flights were seven months earlier than specified

The first YF-100A on 4 November 1953. Note the configuration of the vertical stabilizer and rudder compared to the later "short" and "tall" versions seen at right. (National Records Center, St. Louis)

The original production "short" vertical stabilizer (right) and the taller tail recommended by the NACA that largely cured the inertial roll-coupling problems encountered by the Super Sabre. (NASA Dryden)

in the contract. By late 1953, the airplane had demonstrated its guaranteed speed by reaching Mach 1.34 during level flight at 35,000 feet. Clearly, the airplane was fast.[10]

However, all was not going as well as it appeared. Pilots found the YF-100A outperformed all other production fighters in the Air Force, but there were serious shortcomings that might cause problems in operational service. In particular, the longitudinal stability at high speeds was inadequate, the low-speed handling was poor, and there was a tendency to yaw and pitch near stall with the left wing dropping uncontrollably. Rudder flutter was encountered on many early test flights,

although it was easily corrected by the installation of hydraulic dampers. Despite the problems, production continued unabated.[11]

Scientists and engineers were rapidly expanding the performance envelope without the benefit of the tools modern designers take for granted. Although the first supersonic flight had taken place six years before, and wind tunnels had been simulating the environment years before that, there was remarkably little data on the pitfalls of high-speed flight. Part of this was the fact that it took a long time – years in some cases – for test data to be reduced into useable information since there were no high-speed digital computers. Data reduction was

During the final design stage, North American engineers made several changes to the YF-100A to reduce drag and increase engine thrust. These included modifying the air intake lip with a sharp edge to improve airflow to the engine at supersonic speeds and making the nose 9 inches longer. Note the full-span leading edge slats and all-moving horizontal stabilizer. (AFFTC History Office Collection)

done manually, or using – by modern standards – agonizingly slow analog computers. Another issue was that only a limited amount of data was acquired from each test. Today, it is not uncommon for thousands of parameters to be monitored at once; during the 1950s, monitoring more than a few dozen was considered exceptional. Most were recorded on optical (film) recorders in analog (line-trace) form.

Despite the deficiencies, the Phase II performance tests were completed on 15 September 1953, at which time the first YF-100A had made 39 flights lasting 19 hours and 42 minutes. The second YF-100A flew on 14 October 1953, and the Air Force decided to use it to break the 3-kilometer speed record of 753.4 mph held by the Douglas XF4D-1. To set a new record, the YF-100A had to top the previous mark by at least one percent, which meant the aircraft had to average at least 760.9 mph over the 3-km course. On his first attempt, Lt. Col. Frank K. "Pete" Everest averaged 757.75 mph on the required four runs, which was faster than the XF4D-1, but not by one percent. The Air Force switched to a 15-km course where the one-percent Fédération Aéronautique Internationale (FAI) rule did not apply and the fastest speed over either course counted as a world speed record. On 29 October 1953, Everest averaged 755.149 mph while keeping the YF-100A within 100 feet of the ground. Not much of a victory (less than 2 mph), but a new record nonetheless.[12]

The production F-100A was similar in most respects to the YF-100A, but had the shorter vertical stabilizer developed after the mockup inspection. The first three F-100As were delivered to the 436th Fighter Squadron (Day) at George AFB, California, in November 1953, and the squadron became operational less than a year later, on 27 September 1954. Serious trouble soon began.[13]

During 1954, a new aerodynamic phenomenon – inertial roll coupling – made itself known in a series of F-100A accidents. The first occurred on 2 October 1954 during a high-speed dive followed by a high-g pullout when the ninth production F-100A disintegrated in midair. Although George Welch was able to eject over Rosamond Dry Lake, his injuries proved fatal. Three weeks later, on 8 November, RAF Air Commodore Geoffrey D. Stephenson, Commandant of the Central Fighter Establishment, was killed at Elgin AFB when his F-100A went out of control and crashed before Stephenson could eject. The following day an F-100A piloted by Maj. Frank Emory was lost over Nevada, but fortunately, Emory was able to eject safely. In response to these accidents, the Air Force grounded the 68 remaining F-100As on 10 November, and deferred acceptance of 112 additional airplanes under production.

Although it caught everyone by surprise, Leonard Sternfield and William Phillips at the NACA Langley Memorial Aeronautical Laboratory had predicted the inertial roll coupling phenomenon six years earlier. In a series of 1947 and 1948 reports, Sternfield and Phillips had predicted that aircraft with heavily loaded fuselages and reduced stability would become victims of inertial roll coupling. It took a few years for aircraft performance to catch up, but the theories put forth by the NACA researchers proved remarkably accurate.[14]

The F-100A had a high-fineness-ratio fuselage and sufficient thrust to attain supersonic speed in level flight and Mach 1.48 in shal-

The second YF-100A (52-5755) shows that the initial versions of the F-100 did not have landing flaps on the trailing edge of the wing. The later D- and F-models did. (AFFTC History Office Collection)

low dives. The NACA research into inertial roll coupling, previously thought to have been of only academic interest, was now a key to solving the problem being experienced by the F-100A and Douglas X-3 research airplane. The short answer was that high-speed aircraft needed more vertical stabilizer surface area than previously thought.

During early 1954, the NACA High-Speed Flight Station at Edwards received an F-100A, and NACA test pilot A. Scott Crossfield tested the inertial coupling boundaries of the original tail as well as two larger vertical stabilizers (one of increased chord, the other of increased height). What is ironic is that the two YF-100As had used a vertical stabilizer 16 feet, 3 inches tall. After the mockup inspection, North American reduced aerodynamic drag by making the vertical wider (broader chord) and shorter (15 feet, 8 inches), directly leading to the problems being encountered by the early-production aircraft. Based on the results of the NACA tests, North American decided that the easiest solution would be to retain the broad chord that had been installed on the 180 aircraft already manufactured, but to extend the height back to the original 16 feet 3 inches. This resulted in a 27-percent increase in total area. Under pressure from the Air Force, North American cut its delivery schedule for the first modification kit from 90 days to just 9 days. The larger vertical stabilizer was not incorporated on the production line until the 184th aircraft, but all earlier aircraft were ultimately modified with the new tail.[15]

The F-100B was originally proposed as an improved F-100A day fighter, but on 8 July 1954, the Air Force changed the designation to F-107A, and it is covered in more detail elsewhere in this book.

F-100 production eventually totaled 2,249 aircraft. The Air Force accepted 2 YF-100A prototypes, 203 F-100As, 476 F-100Cs, 1,274 F-100Ds, and 294 two-seat F-100Fs.

McDonnell F-101 Voodoo

Despite winning the penetration fighter competition, the McDonnell F-88 had been unsuccessful in attracting any production orders, mostly because of the austere military budget for FY50 and FY51. However, during the Korean conflict, the Air Force had found the straight-wing Republic F-84s were incapable of protecting Boeing B-29s against the faster, swept-wing MiG-15. Unfortunately, the more capable North American F-86 lacked the range to provide effective escort. The Air Force procured additional swept-wing Republic F-84Fs as long-range escort fighters, but Strategic Air Command (SAC) wanted a much longer-range "strategic fighter," one with sufficient range to accompany the Convair B-36 over the Soviet Union if the need ever arose.[16]

On 6 February 1951, the Air Force issued a General Operational Requirement for a long-range strategic fighter, followed by a request for proposals a few weeks later. Lockheed submitted versions of the F-90 and F-94, North American resubmitted the F-93, and Northrop proposed an escort version of the F-89. Republic came up with three separate submissions, a modified F-84F, the F-91, plus another version of the F-84F powered by a turboprop engine (essentially the XF-84H). As its entry, McDonnell proposed a larger and more powerful version of the F-88.[17]

In May 1951, the Air Force announced that McDonnell had won the competition without a fly-off. In October 1951, the Air Force released FY52 funds previously allocated to the F-84F and F-86F programs to cover the development of the new fighter, which would be

The first production F-101A (53-2418) in final assembly during August 1954, a month before its maiden flight. The markings on the vertical stabilizer were later moved to the nose. (Terry Panopalis Collection)

procured using the Cook-Craigie concept of concurrency. The revised F-88 was designated F-101 on 30 November 1951, and a development contract was issued on 3 January 1952.[18]

The McDonnell team, led by Edward M. "Bud" Flesh, had proposed an airplane using a pair of afterburning Allison J71 turbojets, but the Air Force preferred the new Pratt & Whitney J57, despite a very modest improvement in thrust or fuel consumption. This made sense, given that SAC's latest aircraft, the Boeing B-52 and KC-135, both used versions of the J57, as did the F-100.

The mockup was inspected on 21 July 1952, with few major changes being requested. The end of the Korean conflict made the Air Force reconsider its intended use for the F-101, and ordered McDonnell to add a nuclear-strike capability to the strategic fighter. An atomic weapons mockup inspection was held 17-18 March 1953, again with few major changes being requested. The Air Force issued an initial production contract for 39 F-101As on 28 May 1953, without ordering any experimental prototypes (XF-101) or service test aircraft (YF-101). A year later, however, the Air Force directed McDonnell to only complete a single aircraft until Category II flight tests were completed.[19]

The first F-101A (53-2418) was rolled out in August 1954, and after completing ground trials in St. Louis, it was shipped to Edwards. McDonnell test pilot Robert C. Little took the F-101A on its maiden flight on 29 September 1954, reaching Mach 0.9 at 35,000 feet. Less than a month later, the maximum speed had been extended to Mach 1.4.[20]

In the meantime, the Air Force had changed its mind yet again about its requirements. It now concluded that the range of the F-101A, impressive as it was, was not nearly enough to escort bombers all the way to the target. Consequently, SAC lost interest in the aircraft as a strategic fighter. Ordinarily, this would have been the end of the F-101A, which would have been consigned to history along with its F-88 predecessor. Fortunately, the Tactical Air

The XF-88A (46-526) and the first F-101A (53-2418). Note the Voodoo markings on the tail of the F-101 and compare with the nose and tail markings during flight-test (facing page). (Gerald H. Balzer Collection)

While under construction, the 16th and 17th F-101A airframes (54-149 and 54-150) were converted into YRF-101A photo-reconnaissance aircraft. The major changes were to the nose, deleting the armament and adding oblique and vertical cameras. The first YRF-101A made its maiden flight on 30 June 1955 and was the first supersonic reconnaissance aircraft to enter Air Force service. (National Records Center, St. Louis)

Command (TAC) saw the potential of the aircraft as a nuclear-armed fighter-bomber and acquired the F-101A as Weapon System WS-105A. Consequently, the "tactical fighter" that finally emerged became a hybrid aircraft, fitted with the MA-7 fire-control system for the air-to-air role, and a Low-Altitude Bombing System (LABS) to deliver nuclear weapons.[21]

YRF-101A

In January 1953, as part of contract AF33(600)-8743, the Air Force authorized McDonnell to develop an unarmed photographic reconnaissance version of the F-101A as WS-105L to replace the Republic RF-84F. The 16th and 17th F-101A airframes (54-149/150) were converted into YRF-101A photo-reconnaissance aircraft with a redesigned and longer nose housing four low-altitude cameras. In addition, two high-altitude cameras were mounted behind the cockpit in place of the ammunition boxes of the fighter variant. Robert Little took the YRF-101A on its maiden flight on 30 June 1955. McDonnell built 35 production aircraft, which were the first operational supersonic reconnaissance aircraft.[22]

Ultimately, the Air Force purchased 883 Voodoos, including 75 F-101As (29 later became RF-101Gs), 2 YRF-101As, 35 RF-101As, 479 F-101Bs, 47 F-101Cs (32 later became RF-101Hs), 166 RF-101Cs, and 79 F-101F trainers (originally called TF-101Bs or TF-101Fs).[23]

The first F-101A shows its faired-over cannon muzzles and the nose art it carried for most of its early flight-test career. Note the open speed-brakes on the aft fuselage. (Gerald H. Balzer Collection)

After completing its flight-test program, the first F-101A was bailed to General Electric where it was fitted with J79 engines. Note "J-79 Voodoo" on the nose and band on the tail. (Terry Panopalis Collection)

Lockheed XF-104 Starfighter

On 2 July 1951, the Air Force announced that Convair, Lockheed, and Republic had been selected to conduct a preliminary design for the "1954 Interceptor" that eventually became the F-102. Within a couple of months, however, events over Korea had convinced the Air Force that it needed a new lightweight, day superiority fighter. Lockheed was directed to shift its efforts from the 1954 Interceptor to a new lightweight fighter.

In December 1951, Kelly Johnson from Lockheed, John L. "Lee" Atwood from North American Aviation, and Lt. Gen. Benjamin W. Chidlaw, chief of the Air Materiel Command, visited Korea to talk with combat fighter pilots. The general consensus was that the trend toward ever-increasing weight and complexity had gotten out of hand, and the pilots wanted a lightweight fighter with improved speed, ceiling, rate of climb, and maneuverability.[24]

Johnson and a small group of engineers began evaluating possible designs, many taking their inspiration from the lightweight MiGs being encountered over Korea. More than 100 concepts were considered and rejected before the team began working on a series of studies that weighed only 9,000 pounds empty. By November 1952, this concept had the basic shape and layout of what eventually emerged as the F-104.[25]

In early December 1952, Johnson and members of the design team traveled to Wright-Patterson AFB to brief the Air Force; afterwards Johnson went to the Pentagon to share the idea with Lt. Gen. Donald L. Putt, the vice commander of the Air Research and Development Command. The Air Force was impressed and issued a General Operational Requirement on 12 December 1952 for a lightweight air-superiority fighter to replace the North American F-100 in the Tactical Air Command beginning in 1956. Interestingly, Lockheed turned down a sole-source procurement offer from the Air Force since a clause in the contract assigned all rights to the government and permitted the Air Force to let other companies produce the airplane. Similar clauses had been included in the initial North American F-100, McDonnell F-101, and Convair F-102 contracts, and the manufacturers all declined to sign the definitive contracts until the clauses were removed.[26]

Given the failure of the sole-source contract, government regulations dictated a competitive procurement, and the Air Force issued a request for proposals in January 1953. In response, North American submitted an advanced version of the F-100, which eventually emerged as the F-107A. Northrop submitted the J79-powered N-102 Fang, and Republic submitted a modified XF-91 with a solid, rounded nose and NACA-style flush air intakes.

The Air Force selected the Lockheed proposal, although it appears to have been as much because the government wanted to preserve the industrial base as any other reason. Unlike the F-100, F-101, and F-102 programs, in which production was initiated before flight tests were completed (or even begun), the Air Force proceeded cautiously with the Lockheed airplane. On 12 March 1953, the Air Force issued a letter contract for two XF-104 prototypes (53-7786/787) as WS-303A (also listed as part of project MX-1853). Since the proposed General Electric J79 engine was not yet ready, the two XF-104s would use less-powerful Wright J65 engines. The fixed-geometry air intakes of the two XF-104s did not incorporate the half-cones used on later aircraft since the J65-powered aircraft were incapable of Mach-2 performance.[27]

Under the guidance of Kelly Johnson and project engineer William P. Ralston, the F-104 rapidly moved ahead. The mockup was inspected on 30 April 1953, and the Air Force directed a single 20mm General Electric T-171 Vulcan cannon be substituted for the two 30mm cannon originally proposed. The T-171 (later redesignated M61) was capable of firing 6,000 rounds per minute, and the F-104 was the first aircraft to use the cannon that became standard on most every American fighter for the next 50 years.[28]

The full-scale wooden mockup of the XF-104 at Burbank. The two experimental aircraft were faithful to this mockup, including the use of air intakes without the center shock cones used later. (Lockheed Martin)

Assembly of the second XF-104. Note the sign on the back wall indicating the "March 1st, 1954 9:00 AM" maiden flight target date for the first prototype. They came very close. (Lockheed Martin)

The second XF-104 (53-7787) on 7 April 1955. This aircraft was lost during gun-firing trials on 14 April 1955, but fortunately Fish Salmon ejected successfully. The tests of the T-171 (M61) rotary cannon continued using a modified F-94B (51-5500). (Lockheed Martin)

On 16 April 1956, the second YF-104A (55-2956) was used for the roll-out ceremony in Burbank, marking the first time the F-104 had been shown to the public. The engine air intakes were covered with temporary fairings since the half-cones were classified. (National Archives)

The first XF-104 (53-7786) at Edwards prior to a flight. The first prototype was unarmed and the cannon muzzle was faired-over. The equipment compartment behind the cockpit was accessed by a flip-up cover on the XF-104s; this changed to a side-hinged cover on the YF-104s. Note the protective screens over the air intakes and the taped-on covers on the sharp wing leading edge. (Lockheed Martin)

Construction of the first prototype began in the summer of 1953 at the Lockheed facility in Burbank. The second prototype proceeded at a slower pace in case revisions were needed based on early flight-test results. The first XF-104 was trucked to Edwards North Base during the night of 24-25 January 1954. Taxi tests began on 27 February 1954, and the following day the XF-104 made a scheduled short hop 5 feet off the ground during a high-speed taxi test. The official maiden flight took place on 4 March 1954, with Lockheed test pilot Anthony W. "Tony" LeVier at the controls. Unfortunately, the landing gear would not retract, and after a 20-minute low-speed flight, LeVier landed. Some adjustments were made, and LeVier took off again, but the landing gear still would not retract. The problem turned out to be low pressure in the hydraulic system, which was fairly easy to correct. However, inclement weather kept the XF-104 on the ground until 26 March, when the third and fourth flights showed the landing gear was capable of retracting.[29]

The XF-104 could not exceed Mach 1 in level flight when powered by the non-afterburning J65-W-6 turbojet. However, the airplane was supersonic in a shallow dive, and the transonic transition was smooth. In July 1954, the J65-W-6 was replaced by an afterburning J65-W-7, and the performance of the XF-104 was markedly improved.[30]

The second prototype made its maiden flight on 5 October 1954 with an afterburning J65-W-7 from the start. Ultimately, the second XF-104 achieved Mach 1.79 at 60,000 feet on 25 March 1955, with Lockheed test pilot J. Ray Goudey at the controls. This was the highest speed achieved by either of the XF-104 prototypes. The second XF-104 was lost on 14 April 1955 when Lockheed test pilot Herman R. "Fish" Salmon was forced to eject during gun-firing trials at 50,000 feet. With the loss of the armament testbed, Lockheed engineers were forced to find an alternative, and they settled on one of the modified F-94Bs (51-5500) prepared for the YF-94D development effort.[31]

The Air Force accepted the first XF-104 in November 1955, but the airplane was lost on 11 July 1957 when it developed an uncontrollable tail flutter while flying chase for an F-104A. Lockheed test pilot William M. "Bill" Park ejected successfully. The two XF-104s had accumulated approximately 250 flight hours.[32]

YF-104A

Still cautious despite the successful early flights of the XF-104, in July 1954 the Air Force ordered 17 YF-104A service test aircraft (55-2955/2971) for further flight tests. The YF-104As were 5.5 feet longer to accommodate XJ79 engines instead of the J65s used in the two XF-104s. A forward-retracting nosewheel replaced the earlier rearward-retracting unit to provide improved ejection-seat clearance out of the bottom of the aircraft. The air intakes were modified in shape and were fitted with the half-cone center bodies that had been omitted from the two XF-104s. The fixed-geometry central intake shock cone had an internal bleed slot that routed some intake air through the fuselage for afterburner cooling and helped to reduce base drag.[33]

The first YF-104A made its maiden flight at Edwards on 17 February 1956, with Tony LeVier at the controls. The J79, with its revolutionary variable stators, provided a spectacular improvement in performance, and the first YF-104A exceeded Mach 2 on 28 February 1956, becoming the first American fighter capable of doing so in level flight.[34]

The first XF-104 is checked-out by Lockheed engineers and technicians on 27 February 1954 prior to its first taxi test by Lockheed test pilot Tony LeVier. Note the national insignia on the rear fuselage instead of on the air intake. (Lockheed Martin)

On 16 April 1956, the second YF-104A was used for the official rollout ceremony in Burbank, marking the first time the Starfighter had been shown to the public. The engine air intakes were covered with temporary fairings since the half-cones were classified. The first photographs were released in the spring 1956, limited to air-to-air shots of the first XF-104 and ground photos of the first YF-104A with the intake fairings still fitted. It was another six months before the air intakes were finally revealed to the public.[35]

All seventeen YF-104As, together with the first 35 F-104As, were used during the flight test program and to evaluate improved versions of the J79, T-171 Vulcan cannon, GAR-8 (later AIM-9) Sidewinder air-to-air missile, and wingtip-mounted fuel tanks. By the beginning of 1957, continuing difficulties with the T-171 cannon were offset by "the phenomenal successes" with the Sidewinder missile. As a result, the Air Force decided that the GAR-8 would be the F-104's primary air-to-air weapon, with the T-171 relegated to a "secondary" capacity.[36]

A later photo of the first XF-104 showing the production-style national insignia and buzz number. Note the "Lockheed Starfighter XF-104" logos on the nose and tail, and the pair of dice on the forward fuselage just over the "e" in Air Force. (AFFTC History Office Collection)

On 7 May 1958, Maj. Howard C. Johnson took a YF-104A to 91,249 feet in a zoom climb over Edwards, setting a new altitude record. A week later, on 16 May 1958, Capt. Walter W. Irwin set a new speed record of 1,404.19 mph flying over a 15/25-kilometer course at Edwards in another YF-104A. For the first time, the same aircraft type held both the world speed and altitude records simultaneously. The Air Force and Lockheed were justifiably proud.[37]

Several YF-104As were lost in crashes during the test program. For instance, the second airplane crashed at NAS China Lake, the fourth YF-104A made a crash landing at Palmdale on 15 February 1957, and the eighth airplane crashed west of Barstow on 1 May 1957. In August 1958, the fifteenth YF-104A was bailed to General Electric for flight testing the J79, and was eventually returned in August 1961. The surviving YF-104As were brought up to F-104A standard and were turned over to Air Force squadrons. Following the withdrawal of the F-104A from active service in 1960, at least four of the ex-YF-104As (55-2956, 2957, 2969, and 2971) were converted into QF-104A target drones.[38]

The first YF-104A was involved in a landing accident on 25 April 1957, resulting in the fuselage breaking just behind the cockpit. Note the nose art just below the windscreen. (Lockheed Martin)

Part of the Starfighter test fleet on 28 March 1957. From the front, the tenth YF-104A (55-2964), eighth YF-104A (55-2962), sixth production F-104A (56-0735), first YF-104A (55-2955), fifteenth YF-104A (55-2969), and the first XF-104 (53-7786). Note that the prototypes have light grey upper surfaces on the wings, whereas all production aircraft had white wings. (Lockheed Martin)

After the completion of its test program, the second YF-104A (55-2956) was refurbished and issued to an operational squadron. It ended its career as a QF-104A target drone. (AFFTC History Office Collection)

Only two YF-104As are known to survive. The seventh YF-104A was transferred to the NACA High-Speed Flight Station in August 1956 (initially as tail-number 018, then as civil registration N818NA) and was retired to the National Air and Space Museum in November 1975. The thirteenth YF-104A is on display at the Air Force Academy in Colorado Springs, Colorado.

The Starfighter was destined to serve only briefly and in relatively small numbers with the U.S. Air Force, which accepted only 296 aircraft. These included the 2 XF-104s, 170 F-104As, 26 similar two-seat F-104Bs, 77 tactical F-104C versions, and 21 two-seat F-104Ds. However, the F-104 won a NATO contract for a multi-role fighter capable of delivering nuclear weapons, and was built in large numbers by a European consortium, Canada, and Japan. Ultimately, 2,580 F-104s were manufactured and served with the air forces of Belgium, Canada, Denmark, Greece, Italy, Japan, Jordan, Netherlands, Norway, Pakistan, Spain, Taiwan, Turkey, and West Germany. The last Starfighter was finally retired from Italian service in 2004, marking the end of a long career for the "missile with a man in it."[39]

The fifteenth YF-104A (55-2969) was also brought up to production standards and issued to an operational squadron. It, too, ended its career as a QF-104A target drone, shown here at Eglin AFB in December 1969. The leading "0-" in the serial number on the vertical stabilizer indicated the aircraft was more than ten years old. (Jack D. Morris via the Terry Panopalis Collection)

Republic YF-105 Thunderchief

During the late 1940s, Alexander Kartveli, the legendary chief engineer at Republic, began studying how to incorporate a weapons bay into the swept-wing F-84F. This proved to be a dead end, since the increased airframe weight quickly negated the additional thrust from any of the available engines.[40]

At the same time, work began on a new design using the General Electric J73. Although it was an entirely new aircraft, it bore a distinct resemblance to the RF-84F. An internal weapons bay could carry two 1,000-pound bombs, or a single 3,400-pound "special" weapon. Four 0.60-caliber heavy machine guns were mounted in the wing roots. The aircraft had an estimated maximum speed of 920 mph at 35,000 feet.[41]

The design was presented to the Air Force during February 1952, but at some point just prior to submittal, the J73 was replaced with an Allison J71. On 25 September 1952, Republic received a $13 million letter contract, AF33(600)-22512, for the development and production of 199 F-105As as part of WS-306A, with a scheduled initial operational capability in early 1955. The contract did not include any XF or YF aircraft since it was being procured using a modified version of the Cook-Craigie concept of concurrency. The F-105 was also one of the first Air Force aircraft to be developed using the "weapons system" concept, in which Republic was the prime contractor responsible for the entire development and integration effort, including airframe, armament, engine, and all subsystems.[42]

However, on 20 March 1953 the Air Force unexpectedly cut the program back to 37 F-105As to be delivered at a rate of three per month beginning in April 1955. The definitive contract for 37 F-105s and 9 RF-105s (as WS-306L) was signed on 25 September 1953, however it was already obvious that the J71 would not meet either the thrust or schedule requirements, so plans were made to temporarily install the new Pratt & Whitney J57 until the J71 matured. The F-105 mockup was inspected on 27 October 1953,

resulting in 152 changes, most of them minor. Republic still expected to meet the 1955 IOC date, but in December 1953 the Air Force suspended WS-306A entirely due to development delays, unexpected increases in gross weight, and the lack of a suitable engine.[43]

The increase in gross weight and development delays were largely byproducts of the Air Force continuing to ask for more elaborate equipment and subsystems to enhance the strike capabilities. What began as a relatively simple fighter was rapidly becoming the most sophisticated aircraft of its era, incorporating several electronic systems that would not have been possible a few years earlier. In an effort to find a suitable engine, the Air Force approached Pratt & Whitney to see if the experimental J75 could be fitted to the F-105. The 16,000-lbf engine was already destined to power the Convair F-102B (F-106A), and the engine company was sure it could be adapted to the Republic aircraft.[44]

In February 1954, the program was reinstated with $49.9 million of FY54 funding for 14 YF-105As and a single YRF-105A fitted with J57 engines. The switch to a less powerful engine for the YF-105As was an attempt to get the initial aircraft into flight test as early as possible. Unexpectedly, on 2 September 1954, Air Force Headquarters cut the program back to three aircraft, all powered by the J57. This was prompted by a review that concluded "… a general lack of confidence in this contractor fulfilling his commitments and meeting the performance guarantees on the F-105 weapon system." The order allowed local Air Force management to authorize the construction of "two or three additional aircraft if this is considered desirable." The actual stop-work order was issued on 9 September, limiting production to two J57-powered YF-105As and a single YJ75-powered YF-105B. Three weeks later, this was amended to include three additional F-105Bs, and on 26 October a structural test article was also authorized.[45]

On 19 January 1955, the Air Force changed this to two J57-powered YF-105A prototypes, ten YJ75-powered YF-105B service-test aircraft, and three YRF-105B reconnaissance variants. All 15 aircraft would be procured under the Cook-Craigie concept of concurrency.[46]

The end of a short test career. The first YF-105A (54-0098) made its maiden flight on 22 October 1955, and a crash landing at Edwards on 16 December 1955. (Mike Machat Collection)

Many published reports indicate the YF-105As (54-0099 shown here) did not have the ventral fin of production aircraft, but every available photo of both prototypes shows it installed. (Mike Machat Collection)

YF-105A

Not truly prototypes of the production configuration, the two YF-105As (54-0098/099) were powered by Pratt & Whitney J57-P-25 engines. Although readily identifiable as F-105s, they still had subsonic, elliptical engine inlets similar to those found on the RF-84F and the fuselage was 2 feet shorter, 1 foot narrower, and 3 inches shallower than the later F-105B.

Immediately after it was completed, the first YF-105A was disassembled and shipped to Edwards, Republic not even conducting an engine run-up test at the factory. The fuselage and miscellaneous parts were placed in one Douglas C-124 that departed Long Island on 28 September 1955, while the wings, empennage, engines, and more parts were placed in a second C-124 that departed the following day.

On 22 October 1955, the first YF-105A made its maiden flight with Republic chief test pilot Russell M. "Rusty" Roth at the controls. A brief Republic press release stated that the aircraft had exceeded Mach 1, but given the aerodynamics and power available, it could not have been by much. By the end of November, the aircraft had made 12 flights and been formally accepted by the Air Force. On 16 December 1955, the first YF-105A was performing a series of high-speed tests to evaluate maneuvering stability, including straight and level dashes followed by high-g turns and a complete roll. After completing several successful runs, the aircraft was traveling approximately 530 knots in a 5.5-g turn when the right main landing gear extended suddenly and was promptly torn off. Roth managed to recover and made a hard landing at Edwards, breaking the back of the aircraft in the process. The airplane had logged approximately 22 hours during 29 flights, and was returned to the factory for repairs. It never returned to flight status, and its fate remains unknown.[47]

The second YF-105A was also transported from Long Island to Edwards inside two C-124s, departing from the Republic plant on 8 and 9 December 1955. The aircraft made its maiden flight on 28 January

The third YF-105B (54-0102) shows the orange markings on the vertical stabilizers and the long air-data probe initially used by the prototypes. (AFFTC History Office Collection)

1956 with Rusty Roth again at the controls. The differences between the two aircraft were limited to the second having a smooth exhaust, while the first had the four-petal speedbrake system that became standard on production F-105s. The aircraft participated for a short time in the flight-test program, but no record as to its fate has surfaced.

YF-105B

Republic built the 15 aircraft from the original contract under the Cook-Craigie plan with the expectation that all of them would be used in the flight-test program. By the time the aircraft flew, the WS-306L reconnaissance program had been cancelled, so the three

The four YF-105Bs (54-0102 shown here) had a glazed panel behind the canopy to improve rearward vision. For reasons unknown, this panel was deleted from production aircraft. (Mike Machat Collection)

The third YF-105B shows the logo on the nose that originally adorned all of the B-model prototypes, and the non-standard "F-105" buzz number on the forward fuselage. (Cradle of Aviation Museum)

YRF-105Bs had been redesignated as JF-105B test aircraft and only the first four B-models were designated YF-105B, the others becoming F-105Bs. As accepted by the Air Force, the 15 aircraft were two YF-105As (54-0098/099), four YF-105B-1-REs (54-0100/103), two JF-105B-1-REs (54-0105 and 54-0108), a single JF-105B-2-RE (54-0112), five F-105B-5-REs (54-0104, 0106/107, and 0109/110), and a single F-105B-6-RE (54-0111).

The F-105B was powered by the 23,500-lbf Pratt & Whitney J75, and the airframe was revised to take full advantage of the new engine. In addition, the fuselage was reconfigured according to the Area Rule devised by Richard Whitcomb at the NACA Langley Aeronautical Laboratory. On 14 March 1956, the first J75 was delivered to Republic and was installed in the first YF-105B, which was subsequently airlifted to Edwards on 29 April 1956. The aircraft made a 64-minute maiden flight on 26 May, with Republic test pilot Henry G. "Hank" Beaird, Jr. at the controls. Upon returning for landing, Beaird discovered that

the nose gear would not extend and was forced to make a "fast and flat" emergency landing on the dry lakebed. The YF-105B was not seriously damaged during the landing, but a crane operator managed to drop the aircraft while retrieving it and cracked the fuselage. This necessitated major repairs, and the aircraft was out of service for several weeks.

On 19 June 1956, Republic officially asked the Air Force to approve the name Thunderchief, and on 25 July, the Air Force agreed. This continued a long-standing Republic tradition – Thunderbolt, Thunderjet, Thunderstreak, Thunderflash, and now Thunderchief.

The second YF-105B was airlifted to Edwards on 8 December 1956 and made its maiden flight on 28 December. The first Thunderchief to make its maiden flight from Farmingdale was the third YF-105B, which did so on 29 April 1957.[48]

The Air Force conducted the Category II flight tests between 8 January and 7 March 1957 using 18 flights totaling 13 hours and 45 minutes. According to the flight-test report, the YF-105B "… has the

The third YF-105B (54-0102) refuels from a buddy store on the second YF-105A (54-0099), but the technique was not adopted by the F-105 fleet. The orange markings varied somewhat between each airplane – note that the YF-105A has orange on its air intakes. The second YF-105A features a smooth exhaust area instead of the four-petal speedbrake used on the first prototype and all subsequent aircraft. (Mike Machat Collection)

The two YF-105As used an elliptical intake that was reminiscent of the RF-84F. This was not optimized for supersonic flight and was replaced by a forward-swept intake on production aircraft. (Mike Machat Collection)

The last YF-105B (54-0103) shows the Air Force Flight Test Center (AFFTC) markings on the vertical stabilizer that were carried by most test aircraft during the 1950s. (AFFTC History Office Collection)

potential of becoming an excellent fighter-bomber. But it needs a large number of improvements before it could be considered acceptable for operational use." The report disclosed that the YF-105B "is capable of 1.95 Mach number in level flight at 35,000 feet and 1.49 Mach number at 20,000 feet under standard day conditions." However, the report went on to say that Mach numbers in excess of 1.8 were "not considered useable because of poor acceleration characteristics." This was borne out by the fact that the YF-105B required nearly 9 minutes to accelerate from Mach 1 to Mach 1.95 at 35,000 feet. Noteworthy was the fact that fuel reserves were nearly depleted by the time the aircraft reached its maximum speed. The tests concluded that the aircraft had a useable combat ceiling of 46,500 feet, but could be zoom-climbed to 63,000 feet with a significant loss in speed.[49]

By 15 April 1958, 643 flight tests had been completed, including 163 flights by 20 different Air Force pilots, with seven different Republic pilots accumulating the remaining 480 flights. Republic had 1,300 engineers working on the project and had produced more than 10,000 engineering drawings. A press release noted that there were more than 65,000 individual components on the aircraft and that in excess of 5 million man-hours of engineering had been used to develop it.

Ultimately, the Air Force accepted 833 F-105s, including the pair of YF-105As, 4 YF-105Bs, 3 JF-105Bs, 71 F-105Bs, 610 F-105Ds, and 143 F-105Fs. The F-105G Wild Weasels were modified F-models. The proposed two-seat F-105C and F-105E versions were cancelled before any aircraft were completed.

Looking less colorful than its sister at the top of the page, the third YF-105B made its maiden flight at Edwards on 28 December 1956. Later aircraft would make their first flights at Farmingdale. (National Archives)

Technically not prototypes, the three JF-105Bs (54-0105, 0108, and 0112) were used extensively in various test programs. The first aircraft is in the foreground with the second behind it. (Mike Machat Collection)

North American F-107A (F-100B) "Ultra Sabre"

On 4 March 1952, North American began an in-house study of a possible follow-on to the F-100A. The "F-100B" (a made-up designation not yet approved by the Air Force) retained the swept-wing of the F-100A but had a thinner cross-section with a 5-percent thickness/chord ratio rather than the 7-percent of the F-100A. The design used a 16,000-lbf Pratt & Whitney J57-P-25 engine with a variable-area inlet duct and convergent-divergent exhaust nozzle. The area-rule fuselage had an increased fineness ratio over the F-100A, and all the internal fuel was carried in integral wing tanks, with no provisions made for carrying external fuel tanks. A maximum speed of Mach 1.80 at high altitude was anticipated.[50]

At the same time, North American began to study the feasibility of adapting the F-100 as an all-weather interceptor. The project became known as the F-100I (I for interceptor) or F-100BI, although these were not official Air Force designations.[51] This aircraft was similar in overall configuration to the F-100B except for a modified cockpit and nose radome. To accommodate the radome, the variable-area air intake was mounted under the nose, similar to the later F-16. Provisions were made for underwing drop tanks and an all-rocket armament. The F-100BI was intended to bear much the same relation to the F-100B as the F-86D did to the F-86A.[52]

Unfortunately, neither the F-100B nor F-100BI attracted much interest from the Air Force. Consequently, on 15 January 1954, North American president Lee Atwood abandoned plans to undertake full development and the program was scaled back to an engineering study. On 16 May 1954, work on the interceptor project was terminated and efforts turned to a fighter-bomber derivative that had been briefly studied as early as November 1953.

The original mockup of the "F-100BI" shows the air intake mounted under the cockpit and the short vertical stabilizer used by early production F-100s. (Boeing Historical Archives)

The Air Force finally expressed some interest in the North American concept, mostly as a contingency in case the Republic F-105 ran into insurmountable problems. On 11 June 1954, the Air Force issued contract AF33(600)-27787 for 33 F-100B fighter-bombers, but on 8 July notified North American that the designation had been changed to F-107A. On 29 February 1956, the order was cut back to three prototypes (55-5118/5120) and nine service test aircraft (that apparently did not have serial numbers assigned). Given they were described as "experimental prototypes," the aircraft should have been

The first prototype (55-1118) being prepared for painting on 14 June 1956. A few weeks later, it would be trucked to Edwards AFB and make its first flight on 10 September 1956. (National Records Center, St. Louis)

The second F-107A (55-5119) at the end of the production line before it was painted. The cannon ports differentiated the second prototype from the first. (National Records Center, St. Louis)

The first F-107A suffered a nose gear collapse during landing at Edwards. This pointed out one advantage to the intake location – there was no foreign object damage to the engine. (Terr Panopalis Collection)

designated XF-107A, but since the aircraft were purchased with production funds, the aircraft carried a straight F-107A designation.[53]

The first F-107A made its maiden flight on 10 September 1956 at Edwards with North American test pilot J. Robert Baker at the controls. It went supersonic on this flight, although there was minor damage upon landing when the drag chute malfunctioned and the aircraft overran the end of the concrete runway and ended up in a ditch. The aircraft was quickly repaired and flew again three days later.

By mid-1956, the Air Force was debating cancelling the F-105 and ordering the F-107 into production, largely because of financial and managerial concerns at Republic. But even under ideal circumstances the F-107 could not be ready as quickly as the F-105, and there was the possibility that the F-107 would run into its own development problems, as later became evident with the variable-geometry inlet. On 15 March 1957, the Air Force decided to stay with the F-105. The three F-107As were relegated to aerodynamic testing, and the nine service test aircraft were cancelled. Contrary to popular belief, there was no fly-off or real "competition" between the F-105 and F-107, the latter being developed strictly as a contingency. Interestingly, the entire

The first F-107A (55-5118) at Edwards AFB on 9 July 1956, prior to its maiden flight. Note how the canopy opens in front of the air intake. Similar to the initial F-105s, there are small glazed panels behind the canopy to increase rearward vision. (National Archives)

The third F-107A (55-5120) takes off from Los Angeles Airport. This airplane had an automatic variable-geometry intake that was supposed to increase performance, but seldom worked. (National Archives)

The first F-107A shows the markings on the bottom of the wing. In general the wing was similar to that used by the F-100D/F, including landing flaps on the inboard trailing edge. (Terry Panopalis Collection)

$105.8 million cost for the F-107 project had been paid for out of procurement support funds instead of the more normal RDT&E funds.[54]

At the completion of the Air Force test program, the first and third F-107As were turned over to NACA, with the first arriving on 6 November 1957. However, it was so mechanically unreliable that it was grounded by NACA after only four flights and was scavenged for spare parts to keep the third airplane flying.

The third F-107A arrived at NACA in February 1958. Originally, NACA was interested in evaluating the variable-geometry intake, but this was abandoned because of mechanical problems. Eventually, NACA gave up on the variable-geometry inlet altogether and bolted it in a fixed position, limiting the top speed to Mach 1.2. The F-107As completed 40 test flights for NACA/NASA during 1958-59, with many being used to evaluate a prototype of the side-stick planned for the X-15 research airplane. The third F-107A was damaged on 1 September 1959, when test pilot Scott Crossfield was forced to abort a takeoff because of control problems. Both tires blew and the left brake burst into flames. Crossfield was uninjured, but the resulting damage to the F-107A was deemed too severe for economical repair, and NASA decided to scrap the aircraft.

After being retired by NASA, the first F-107A was eventually acquired by the Pima Air and Space Museum in Tucson, Arizona, where it is now on display. The second F-107A is on display at the National Museum of the U.S. Air Force.

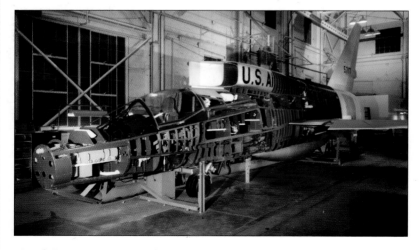

The full-scale mockup of the F-107A. Note the retractable refueling probe just behind the canopy, as well as the location of the 20mm cannon under the probe. (Boeing Historical Archives)

North American proposed a two-seat F-107 that used an extended fuselage to accommodate a second crewmember under a single canopy. None were built. (Boeing Historical Archives)

The first F-107A shows its unique markings – note the size and location of the "F-107A" on the fuselage compared to the second (below) and third (facing page) prototypes. (AFFTC History Office Collection)

One of the features of the F-107A was its all-moving vertical stabilizer. There was no separate rudder. Likewise, the all-moving horizontal stabilizers did not have separate elevators. (National Archives)

The F-107A was intended to be a nuclear fighter-bomber. Unlike the Republic F-105, which had an internal weapons bay, the F-107A carried its nuclear store semi-submerged under the fuselage. Additional hardpoints on the wings could carry fuel or weapons. Note the muzzle ports for the 20mm cannon (two per side), unlike the F-105's single 20mm M61 gatling gun. (Boeing Historical Archives)

XF-109

Throughout the 1950s, there were published reports that the F-109 designation had been assigned to a vertical-takeoff aircraft based on the Ryan X-13. However, the X-13 was never intended as an operational aircraft, and there is no official documentation showing an operational designation was ever requested, let alone assigned. It is hard to see how the diminutive X-13 could have been used as an effective fighter or reconnaissance aircraft in any case.

In 1955, McDonnell proposed a two-seat, all-weather interceptor variant of the F-101 called the F-109, and a "Standard Aircraft Characteristics" chart was even issued showing this designation on 12 May 1955. This is somewhat of a mystery, since the next available designation at the time was F-108, which was subsequently used by the North American Mach 3 interceptor. Nevertheless, there was a note indicating, "Headquarters Air Force has been requested to assign the designation F-109 to this modification of the F-101A into an interceptor type." This request was apparently cancelled at an early stage, because no written documentation about it exists in the Air Force nomenclature records. Eventually, however, Headquarters decided to call the new interceptor the F-101B instead.[55]

The F-109 designation is usually attributed to the Bell D188A supersonic vertical takeoff and landing (VTOL) fighter project. However, although Bell and the Air Research and Development Command requested the YF-109 designation for this project in January and again in October 1958, Air Force Headquarters turned down both requests. It therefore appears that the F-109 designation was never officially assigned.[56]

The Bell D188A was a private venture for a Mach 2+ VTOL fighter. This proposal called for a high-winged aircraft powered by eight General Electric J85-GE-5 turbojets. Two engines were mounted horizontally in the rear fuselage and fed by cheek-type air intakes mounted on the sides of the rear fuselage. Two other J85s were mounted vertically in the fuselage behind the cockpit to provide lift during vertical takeoff and landing, but they were shut down for ordinary horizontal flight. The other four engines were mounted in two pairs in moveable pods at the wingtips. The pods rotated into a vertical position for takeoff and landing, and rotated horizontally for level flight. Projected performance included a top speed of Mach 2.3 and a maximum altitude of "over 60,000 feet" while carrying over 8,000 pounds of armament.[57]

Bell reported, "The XF-109 represents the high-water mark in high performance V/STOL aircraft development in the United States." The Air Force and Navy had provided approximately $17 million in Phase I funds for the program, resulting in a full-scale mockup, 600,000 engineering manhours, and 3,500 wind-tunnel hours. Nevertheless, the Air Force did not fund further development of the D188A, although the general concept was later taken up by West Germany in the E.W.R-Sud VJ-101C.[58]

Several published reports show two serial numbers (59-2109 and 60-2715) being assigned to the D188A prototypes. This is unlikely, given that the first number is in the middle of a production run of

A Standard Aircraft Characteristics was issued for the proposed two-seat version of the McDonnell Voodoo using the F-109 designation. Eventually the Air Force used F-101B instead. (NMUSAF Collection)

Boeing IM-99A Bomarc surface-to-air missiles and the second is in the middle of a batch of Martin AGM-12 Bullpup air-to-ground missiles. There is no evidence that the Air Force was sufficiently interested in the D188A to assign it a designation or serial numbers.[59]

BELL AEROSYSTEMS COMPANY

D188A/XF-109 In-Flight — This supersonic aircraft has a propulsion system using J85 afterburning lightweight turbojet engines. This highly efficient propulsion system results in an aircraft with an excellent useful load to gross weight ratio. The XF-109 represents the highwater mark in high performance V/STOL aircraft development in the United States. The program was funded jointly through Phase I by the Air Force and Navy. Total government and Bell funding approaches $17 million to date. Aircraft features include full weapon system capability, utilizing an integrated Avionics system with forward looking radar, doppler and inertial navigation, CNI system and all purpose digital computer and integrated cockpit display system. A wide variety of air-to-air and air-to-ground stores are carried internally. Provisions for reconnaissance packages have been made. A mockup exists and the program is backed by 600,000 engineering manhours and 3500 wind tunnel test hours.

Most press releases from Bell Aerosystems talking about the D188A also used the XF-109 designation. As near as can be determined, the Air Force never approved this usage. (Scott Lowther Collection)

Bell completed a full-scale mockup of the D188A, as well as several display models (above). The cutaway drawing (below) shows the location of the eight J85 engines. Interestingly, the data block on the mockup says "XF-109, A.F. Serial No. 59-2109." (Jay Miller Collection)

Chapter 8

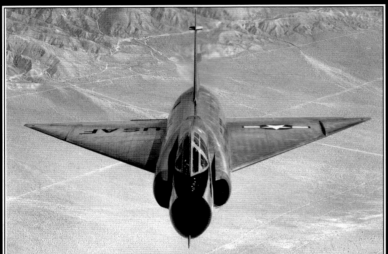

Left: *The sixth YF-102 (53-1782) shows the relatively straight fuselage that largely ignored the NACA Area Rule principle. Given the large expanse of delta wing, this was a critical flaw and severely restricted performance.* (National Archives)

Below: *One of two full-scale metal mockups of the XF-103 constructed by Republic in Farmingdale, New York. This mockup had a cockpit with a conventional canopy (note the fairing on top of the forward fuselage), while the other had a controversial flush canopy.* (Cradle of Aviation Museum)

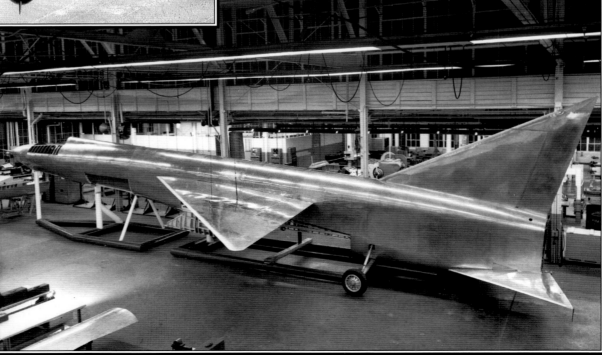

CENTURY SERIES INTERCEPTORS
DELTA-WINGS TO DEFEND AMERICA

The concept of dedicated interceptors had come to fruition during World War II – the Messerschmitt Me 163 being an early example of an aircraft intended solely to shoot down enemy bombers over its home territory. After the war it seemed that all things became more specialized, furthering the concept of dedicated interceptors. This was helped in the U.S. Air Force by the fact that there were two operating commands – the Air Defense Command (ADC) and the Tactical Air Command (TAC). Each wanted its "own" aircraft, and so defensive interceptors and tactical fighters began to diverge in design and capabilities. Even the weapons carried by each began to diverge: the ADC pressed the development of the Falcon family of air-to-air guided missiles, while TAC fielded the Sparrow and Sidewinder, both, ironically, developed by the Navy.

Following the end of the war in Europe, relations between the United States and the Soviet Union rapidly deteriorated. However, at that time, there seemed to be little direct threat from the Soviet Union to the continental United States itself. This changed in October 1947, when several Tupolev Tu-4 heavy bombers (reverse-engineered B-29s) appeared at the Tushino air display, and the newly organized U.S. Air Force was now faced with a potential strategic bombing threat from the Soviet Union.

In early 1949, the Air Force issued a request for proposals for a supersonic interceptor to replace the Northrop F-89 that was just entering development. This program came to be known as the "1954 Interceptor," after the year that the new aircraft was scheduled to enter operational service.[1]

At the time, the Air Force recognized that the increasing complexity of modern weapons meant it was no longer practical to develop the airframe, electronics, and engines in isolation and then expect them to work properly when they were put together. In response, the Air Force introduced the "weapons system" concept where a single prime contractor would manage the entire development effort, making sure that the various systems would be compatible with each other when they were incorporated into the final aircraft. (The highly touted "system-of-systems" concept from the first part of the 21st century is a reincarnation of this concept.) The 1954 Interceptor was assigned the first "air-defense system" (interceptor) moniker in the

new scheme – WS-201A. As originally conceived, WS-201A consisted of a new air-to-air guided missile, an all-weather fire-control system, a new engine, and an airframe optimized for supersonic flight.[2]

The weapons system concept notwithstanding, the Air Force had begun studying an advanced electronics package in February 1949, with a goal of having it ready to equip the 1954 Interceptor. In January 1950, the Air Force solicited bids from 18 electronics contractors for the system: only Bendix, General Electric, Hughes Aircraft Company, North American Aviation, Sperry Gyroscope, and Westinghouse responded. On 7 July 1950, the Air Force announced that Hughes had won the contract to develop what would become the MA-1 fire-control system as project MX-1179. The system was intended to "direct some type of air-to-air guided missile," although the exact nature of this weapon was unknown during the bidding. Separately, Hughes had already won the competition to develop the Falcon as project MX-904, and this missile was subsequently selected for use with the MX-1179, mainly because it could meet the 1954 operational date.[3]

The airframe for WS-201A was project MX-1554, and the Air Force issued a request for proposals on 18 June 1950; the winner would also become the "weapons system integrator." (This is another concept that has found renewed interest in the new millennium, although nobody will admit it is a 50-year-old idea.) By the January 1951 deadline, nine different proposals were submitted by six airframe manufacturers – Chance-Vought, Convair, Douglas, and Lockheed each submitted a single design, North American two, and Republic had three separate proposals. On 2 July 1951, the Air Force announced that Convair, Lockheed, and Republic had been selected to continue development through the mockup stage, with the design deemed most promising at that time being awarded a production contract.

A short while later, the Air Force decided that it also needed a lightweight fighter to combat the new MiG day-fighters that were being encountered over Korea. The Lockheed effort was redirected toward a day superiority fighter that ultimately became the F-104, with Convair and Republic continuing on MX-1554.[4]

On 31 August 1951, the Air Force issued letter contract AF33(600)-5942 to Convair for the preliminary development work on the F-102 delta-wing interceptor. The definitive contract was

SAGE employed the first production digital computer as well as innovative devices such as light pens and data links. The system could control aircraft and missiles thousands of miles away. (National Archives)

signed on 17 December 1952. Work on one of the competing Republic designs was also authorized as the XF-103, since it potentially offered vastly superior performance to any other fighter then under development. However, Alexander Kartveli's concept was so far ahead of the state of the art that it was not thought to be a serious contender for the 1954 Interceptor project, which made the F-102 for all practical purposes the winner of the competition.[5]

Almost as soon as the development of the F-102 began, it was obvious that the design would not meet the original performance requirements, and a revised aircraft – the F-102B "Ultimate Interceptor" – began to be studied. The MX-1179 also ran into problems, forcing a "universal computer fire-control system" (originally the MG-3; later the MG-10) to be substituted in the F-102A. Not surprisingly, there were any number of problems encountered during the development and early operational service with the F-102 and its electronics and weapons. Nevertheless, the Delta Dagger would go on to a fairly long, if undistinguished, career in the air forces of several countries. The Ultimate Interceptor eventually emerged as the Convair F-106 Delta Dart.[6]

SAGE

In October 1952, the Air Force initiated a project to develop the Semi-Automatic Ground Environment (SAGE) to protect the airspace over North America. SAGE was an integrated set of radar, surface-to-air missiles, and interceptor aircraft tied together by digital computers and long-distance communication networks. This was by far the most technologically demanding project yet attempted, surpassing even the development of the atomic bomb in size and complexity. When the program began, there was only a single digital computer in the world – the Whirlwind at the Massachusetts Institute of Technology (MIT). As the major development effort associated with SAGE, the International Business Machines Corporation (IBM) won a contract in April 1953 to design and build the Whirlwind II, designated AN/FSQ-7 by the military.[7]

The FSQ-7 was, for all practical purposes, the first "production" digital computer and weighed 275 tons, used 919 miles of cables, had approximately 50,000 vacuum tubes, 7,300 pluggable units, and 170,000 diodes. It consumed 3 megawatts of power, enough for a city with 15,000 inhabitants. The FSQ-7 processed radar and other data, and then presented the information to 100 operators on cathode ray tubes: one of the first uses of this device to display computer-generated data. Light pens were used to interact with the data on the CRTs.[8]

At the heart of the system that eventually emerged were 24 hardened-concrete "Direction Centers" across the United States and Canada. An extensive series of radar sites scattered around the periphery of the continent would detect Soviet bombers and guide friendly fighters or Bomarc and Nike missiles to intercept them. The fighters were connected to SAGE by a radio data link, allowing them to fly intercepts with only minimal action from the pilot.[9]

Each Direction Center was linked to more than 100 air defense elements by long-distance telephone lines, requiring system integration on a scale previously unimagined. It is estimated that SAGE cost almost $12 billion in 1964 dollars (about $79 billion in 2008 dollars) – the single most expensive defense project of the era, except, perhaps, the development of the intercontinental ballistic missile (ICBM). The first Direction Center came online at McGuire AFB, New Jersey, in November 1956; the last was completed in 1962. They would operate continuously until SAGE was formally decommissioned in 1983. Today, only a few remnants of the Direction Centers remain, most having been torn down to make room for newer facilities.[10]

Almost unbelievably, given its 275 tons of electronics, the FSQ-7 did not have the raw processing power that is currently available in a Palm Pilot that weighs less than a pound. Nevertheless, the system showed the way to the future. The basic computer and communications architecture was reused by the FAA air-traffic control system and the SABRE airline reservation system. What had been learned in developing the FSQ-7 itself was instrumental in the design of the IBM System/360 considered by most to be the most successful mainframe of its era. The communications system laid the groundwork for the Internet; the cathode ray tubes and their light pens showed the way to modern displays and input devices such as mice.[11]

Because of the processing power provided by SAGE, it was possible to extend the defensive perimeter further toward potential enemies, allowing more time to counter whatever hostile advances they might make. This led directly to placing radars and surface-to-air missiles in remote locations, and for a desire to have a manned interceptor that could destroy enemy bombers farther from the populated areas of North America.

Convair YF-102 Delta Dagger

The winning Convair entry was closely related to the XF-92A demonstrator that Convair had built in 1948 since Convair had become convinced that the delta configuration was well suited to supersonic flight. Unlike the XF-92A, the 1954 Interceptor had a solid nose to accommodate a large search radar, and used side-mounted intakes to feed a single 10,000-lbf Wright J67 turbojet (a license-built version of the Bristol Olympus). A single pilot sat under a highly streamlined canopy with a two-pane, V-shaped windscreen.

By December 1951, it was apparent that the Wright J67 engine and Hughes MA-1 fire-control system would not be ready in time. This forced the Air Force to proceed with an interim version of its 1954 Interceptor, one that could be introduced into service at an early date, pending availability of the fully developed version. The interim version was designated F-102A, with the fully developed advanced version being the F-102B. The F-102B ultimately turned out to be so different from the F-102A that it was redesignated F-106 in 1956.[12]

In January 1952, the Air Force amended the Convair contract to authorize the manufacture of two YF-102 airplanes (52-7994/995) and added eight more (53-1779/1786) in February. Although having different Convair model numbers, there were few differences between these two batches of YF-102s. The contract, in accordance with the Cook-Craigie plan, was a combined development, production, and flight test program. The basic $99,554,105 contract included $85,554,145 for ten prototype YF-102s and 32 production F-102s, but only $12 million was allocated to research and development.[13]

Initially, the Air Force and Convair agreed to use the 7,500-lbf Westinghouse J40 as an interim powerplant, but in early 1952 this was changed to the new 10,000-lbf Pratt & Whitney J57. In retrospect, this change was extremely fortuitous, since the J40 proved so

troublesome that it was eventually cancelled. As it turned out, the J67 also never materialized, and the J57 became the only engine used by the F-102. Nevertheless, the changes required to use the J57 resulted in a five-month schedule slip.[14]

The F-102A full-scale mockup was inspected by the Air Force on 18 November 1952 and a number of alterations were recommended. The major changes included adding the ability to carry external stores (primarily fuel tanks, but also future armament that would not fit in the weapons bay) and rearranging the cockpit components of the fire-control system.[15]

However, the delays in the engine and fire-control system were soon overshadowed by a major problem that became evident in

The first YF-102 (52-7994) at the end of the assembly line. One sign in front of the aircraft lists the scheduled dates and shows the "First Airplane Completed" on "2 Oct 53" while the other sign indicates it is, indeed, Oct. 2. (Terry Panopalis Collection)

Some of the models launched from the NACA Wallops Island facility were quite large. This is a self-powered one-fifth-scale model of the original YF-102 configuration. It would be boosted to high speed by the attached 6,000-lbf solid-propellant rocket. (National Archives)

The sixth YF-102 (53-1782) shows the reinforced windscreen and canopy that were a direct evolution of the XF-92A. Note the short, stubby nose compared to the later YF-102A aircraft. (Terry Panopalis Collection)

early 1953. Wind tunnel testing showed the initial drag characteristics of the YF-102 had been significantly underestimated. Even with 10,000-lbf (using either the J57 or J67), the F-102 would be unable to exceed Mach 1 instead of the Mach 1.3 that had been predicted originally. In addition, the maximum altitude would be only 52,400 feet, versus the predicted 57,600 feet. Despite these wind tunnel results, it was not until August 1953 that Convair reluctantly accepted the implications of the "NACA ideal body theory" and embraced the concept of the Area Rule. By that time, it was too late to incorporate the required changes in the first ten YF-102 aircraft.[16]

The fifth YF-102 being towed across the desert at Edwards. Oddly the access ladder is still attached to the far side of the aircraft. The desolate dry lakebeds were perfect runways. (Terry Panopalis Collection)

The nose of the first YF-102A contained flight test equipment and recorders instead of the Hughes E-9 (MG-3) fire-control system that would be eventually installed in lieu of MX-1179. (National Archives)

A good comparison of several YF-102 prototypes. From the front, the fifth (53-1781), fourth (53-1780), second (52-7995), and seventh (53-1783) aircraft. Note that the second YF-102 (52-7995) has a long, pointed nose and a early set of bulges around the engine exhaust, the beginning of the Area Rule subsequently introduced on the four YF-102A prototypes. Also note the lack of "ears" on the vertical stabilizer of 995. (National Archives)

The first YF-102 was completed during the summer of 1953 and the initial ground tests were conducted at the Convair facility at Lindbergh Field in San Diego. After being trucked to Edwards, Convair test pilot Richard L. Johnson took the airplane on its maiden flight on 24 October 1953. The initial tests showed the YF-102 handled decently, but the airplane was written off on 2 November following an engine failure during takeoff on its seventh flight. Richard Johnson was seriously injured, and the cause of the accident was eventually traced to a failure in the Bendix fuel-control system.[17]

The second YF-102 made its maiden flight on 11 January 1954, again at Edwards. In initial tests, severe buffeting was encountered at Mach 0.9 and the aircraft was drag-limited to Mach 0.98 with a 48,000-foot ceiling. Nevertheless, on 27 January 1954, the airplane managed Mach 1.06 in a shallow dive. The second YF-102 was modified with cambered wing leading edges and a new elevon-to-fuselage fillet to improve altitude performance and reduce buffeting in the transonic regime. The modifications were completed on 14 April 1954, and on 2 May the airplane reached Mach 1.29 in a 30-degree dive, but still could not go supersonic in level flight.[18]

Fortunately, the weapons-system tests were going better, and on 9 September 1954, a YF-102 successfully fired a GAR-1 Falcon at 25,000 feet. Two months later, four 2.75-inch FFAR rockets were fired at a similar altitude.[19]

Despite the performance issues, testing continued. The first of the second batch of YF-102s made its maiden flight on 28 April 1954. Given that the airplane was essentially identical to the first two YF-102s, there was no increase in performance. Between 4 May and 1 June 1954, ten Air Force pilots and one NACA pilot conducted the Phase II performance tests using the second YF-102. These found that the performance of the YF-102 was not all that much better than the F-86D Sabre, which was already in production. The F-102 program was in serious trouble.[20]

The sixth YF-102 streaks over the desert around Edwards. The heavily reinforced windscreen and canopy on the initial prototypes severely restricted vision and would be replaced by improved units on the YF-102As and production aircraft. (National Archives)

The first YF-102 flies with an F-86A (48-0209) and an F-80B (45-8478). The main landing gear on the YF-102 is retracting and the speedbrakes on the F-86 are deployed. (AFFTC History Office Collection)

When new Air Force markings were introduced, they did not fit well on the YF-102s – note how "U.S. Air Force" is bent on the air intake and the national insignia is on the aft fuselage. (AFFTC History Office Collection)

YF-102A

The wind-tunnel results had finally convinced Convair to embark on a major redesign of the F-102. The urgency of this effort was reinforced by the early flight tests of the YF-102s. The most obvious change to the airframe was incorporating the Area Rule devised by NACA researcher Richard Whitcomb. According to the Area Rule, the total cross-sectional area along the direction of flight should be a

constant in order to achieve minimum transonic drag. To achieve this, the fuselage needed to be narrower in the area of the wing, resulting in a characteristic "wasp-waist" or "Coke-bottle" shape. This as especially important for a delta-wing aircraft since the wing intersected a large portion of the fuselage. Since it was too late to completely redesign the fuselage, Convair was forced to use a pair of fairings around the extreme aft fuselage to provide sufficient area. These fairings extended beyond the end of the afterburner to minimize turbu-

The NACA High-Speed Flight Station operated the ninth YF-102, shown here on 11 May 1955. Note the NACA winged stripe on the vertical stabilizer. All other markings were typical Air Force. (NASA Dryden)

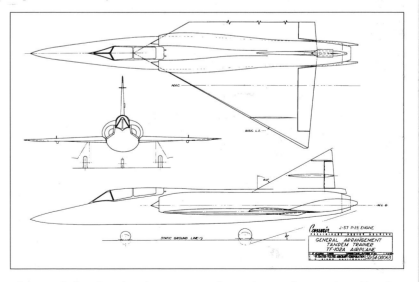

The initial sketches for the TF-102A showed a tandem cockpit like that later used on the F-106B. Instead, the production TF-102A used side-by-side seating that resulted in a truly ungainly airplane. (National Archives)

The first YF-102A (53-1787) featured a completely revised fuselage that was in accordance with the NACA Area Rule. This aircraft has been retrofitted with a clear canopy and windscreen. (National Archives)

Looking much like an early production aircraft in its overall light grey paint scheme, the third YF-102A (53-1789) still has the reinforced canopy and windscreen used on the earlier YF-102s. (National Archives)

lence off the fuselage. Other modifications included lengthening the fuselage 11 feet and changing the profile of the nose. Initially the four YF-102As used the same reinforced windscreen and canopy as the earlier YF-102s, but most of the prototypes eventually received clear canopies that afforded better vision. New, more sharply pointed windscreens reduced drag, at the cost of some forward vision.[21]

The first of four YF-102As (53-1787/790) was trucked to Edwards and made its maiden flight on 15 December 1954, with a recovered Richard Johnson at the controls. On its second flight, the YF-102A easily exceeded Mach 1 in level flight and a week later reached Mach 1.22 at 35,000 feet. On 29 December 1954, the first YF-102A exceeded 52,000 feet, and by the end of January pushed this to 55,130 feet.[22]

According to the NACA Area Rule, the total cross-sectional area along the direction of flight should be a constant to achieve minimum transonic drag. To achieve this, the fuselage needed to be narrowed where the wing roots attached, then broadened at the wing trailing edge resulting in a Coke-bottle shape. On the YF-102As, the length of the fuselage was increased 11 feet and a pair of aerodynamic tail fairings were added aft of the trailing edge, extending beyond the end of the afterburner exhaust. These fairings served no other purpose. (National Archives)

The YF-102As also introduced cambered leading edges to improve the behavior of the thin delta-wing at high angles of attack as well as revised wingtips. Production aircraft would receive taller vertical stabilizers and have noses that were another five feet longer. (National Archives)

Weapons system testing continued and, on 8 July 1955, a YF-102A fired six Falcon missiles and two-dozen 2.75-inch FFAR rockets in less than 10 seconds. None of these were aimed at a target, but the test demonstrated the airplane could salvo all of its weapons at the required intervals. Eventually the system was tested against live targets, and, on 11 May 1956, a GAR-1 launched from a YF-102A scored a direct hit on a drone over Edwards.[23]

For a while, the Air Force considered equipping the F-102A with the Genie rockets. Nevertheless, on 22 December 1955, a dummy MB-1 was jettisoned from a fixed-wing pylon on the second YF-102, and, on 1 May 1956, a live Genie was fired from the wing pylon. On 14 May 1956, an aerodynamic dummy of an MB-1 was jettisoned from a modified launcher in the weapons bay. By early 1957, however, the Air Force decided not to use the Genie on the F-102, although it was integrated into some versions of the Northrop F-89, McDonnell F-101, and later Convair F-106.[24]

The problems experienced by the F-102 program showed just how much could go wrong with the Cook-Craigie concept of concurrency. A cost review in April 1955 revealed that 32,000 tools had been completed based on the original YF-102 design, but more than 24,000 of them had to be discarded because of the major changes to the YF-102A. The total cost for design and manufacture of these tools had been $40,442,000, and $19,362,000 had been wasted by throwing the tools away. This was in addition to the $34 million that had been spent on research and development.[25]

Following the costly re-tooling, full production of the F-102A began at the Convair plant in San Diego. The first production F-102A (53-1791) made its maiden flight on 24 June 1955 and was delivered to the Air Force five days later. The first delivery to an operational Air Defense Command unit took place on 1 May 1956, almost three years later than originally expected. Ultimately the Air Force accepted 875 F-102As (889 including the prototypes) and 111 two-seat TF-102A trainers, with the last being delivered in September 1958. An early plan to manufacture three YTF-102As was cancelled in March 1954, and all two-seaters were considered production models. The popular name Delta Dagger was not chosen until 1957. The development costs totaled $101,920,000, and each production airplane cost $1.2 million.[26]

Republic XF-103

The requests for proposals for the 1954 Interceptor competition had included relatively few hard requirements, instead relying on the aviation industry to propose solutions to the problem. The Air Force did, however, describe the expected threat as Soviet bombers capable of Mach 1.3 at 55,000 feet. Alexander Kartveli at Republic did not believe this was realistic, given that the United States already had Mach 2 fighter-bombers and medium-range bombers on the drawing boards, with even more advanced aircraft under conceptual study. Therefore, one of the three proposals submitted by Republic was for an airplane capable of defending against a Mach 2 threat flying at 55,000 feet.[27]

By September 1951, it was obvious that the Kartveli design was far too advanced to become operational in the near term, but at the same time, it promised such a leap in performance that the Air Force felt the project had to continue. Concurrent with the Convair design being selected for further development as WS-201A, Republic received letter contract AF33(600)-6034 for WS-204A, with the airframe designated XF-103. It would use the same Hughes MX-1179 fire-control system and MX-904 Falcon missiles as the F-102 and, in fact, the projected performance of the XF-103 drove significant aspects of the XF-98A design. The Republic airplane also used a variation of the Wright J67 engine that was initially selected for the Convair airplane.[28]

Although the entire XF-103 was extremely futuristic, perhaps its most notable feature was the dual-cycle propulsion system developed as project MX-1787.[29] There was nothing particularly noteworthy about the 10,000-lbf Wright XJ67 turbojet engine itself, being a license-built version of the Bristol Olympus. What was notable was its installation. The engine is usually described as having an afterburner, but this is not truly the case for the XF-103, at least not in the conventional sense. The afterburner was a separate unit (eventually designated XRJ55-W-1) located several feet behind the engine. The XRJ55 could be used as a traditional afterburner – hot exhaust gas from the J67 was ducted into it, mixed with fresh fuel, and ignited. It could also be used as a ramjet where the turbojet was shut down and all incoming air was ducted directly into the XRJ55, fuel was injected, and the mixture ignited. In the ramjet mode, internal ducting completely sealed off the J67 from the inlet airflow and the turbojet was shut down.[30]

This was a novel approach to a propulsion system. The turbine inlet (compressor output) temperature of the J67 was limited to about 1,500 degrees Fahrenheit because of the materials used to manufacture the engine. This temperature limitation made it difficult to maintain Mach 2.5 for any length of time, or to achieve higher speeds, without destroying the engine. The dual-cycle approach eliminated this problem by removing the J67 from the propulsion system at high speeds.[31]

It should be noted that the ramjet provided somewhat less thrust than the J67, and used more fuel while doing so. This was not, however, considered a major liability. The F-103 would take off and climb using the J67, with the XRJ55 functioning as a normal afterburner. As the aircraft approached Mach 2.25, the combination was generating approximately 19,500-lbf. At this point, the pilot opened the exhaust nozzle, disengaged the turbojet, and bypassed all incoming air to the XRJ55. In less than one second the thrust fell to about 14,000-lbf – the XRJ55 was now using bypass air, but it was doing so less efficiently

The mockup of the massive Wright MX-1787 powerplant for the XF-103. The 10,000-lbf XJ67 turbojet is at the right (behind the man), while the XRJ55 ramjet/afterburner is on the extreme left. Above the MX-1787 sign is the air valve that could select exhaust from the jet engine or fresh air (from the unoccupied scoop on top) that was bypassed around the J67. (National Records Center, St. Louis)

The primary XF-103 mockup during the Air Force inspection on 3 June 1953. This mockup featured a flush canopy while a second full mockup in the same room had a more conventional canopy. There were also two separate forward fuselage mockups that allowed detailed evaluation of the cockpit arrangement, ejection capsule, and MX-1179 weapons system components. (National Records Center, St. Louis)

than it had been using engine exhaust. About six seconds later the air-flow and temperature stabilized, the fuel flow into the XRJ55 was increased, and thrust came up to about 16,000-lbf. The entire transition took 10 seconds, and the aircraft continued to accelerate to its Mach 3 design speed. Thrust reportedly increased to 18,800-lbf at 55,000 feet. The concept was successfully demonstrated several times in test cells at the Air Force Arnold Engineering Development Center.[32]

A Ferri-type two-dimensional air intake with a sharply forward-swept lip was located under the fuselage. The intake divided into two separate ducts; the lower one fed the J67 during turbojet operations, and the upper bypass duct fed air directly into the remotely located XRJ55. The two-dimensional exhaust nozzle had variable throat and exit surfaces moving within fixed side plates. In most versions of the design, the exhaust nozzle incorporated dive brakes at the sides and was designed to be the outer structure of the aft fuselage, much like the later Republic F-105.[33]

Despite some initial Mach 4 estimates, as the concept progressed Kartveli came to realize that the structural design of the aircraft – or more precisely, the materials being used in its construction – would limit the XF-103 to just over Mach 3 due to aerothermal concerns. An independent performance evaluation conducted by the Air Materiel Command showed a sustained speed of just over Mach 2.5 (1,438 knots), still a fast airplane for the time. The rate of climb at 45,000 feet was projected to be almost 70,000 feet per minute, equal to Mach 1.2 straight up, using the ramjet. Even at lower altitude while using the normal afterburner, the initial rate of climb would be more than 40,000 feet per minute. Total time to climb to 60,000 feet was a little more than 7 minutes from brake release. A service ceiling in excess of 75,000 feet

The two XF-103 forward fuselage mockups. Each mockup used the same size radar antenna, but the contours were significantly different because of the cockpit arrangements. (Cradle of Aviation Collection)

was expected using the ramjet. These performance estimates were one reason the Hughes XF-98A Falcon missile was redesigned during its development to allow for higher launch speeds and altitudes.[34]

The armament of the XF-103 changed several times during development, although it always included MX-904 (XF-98/GAR-1) Falcons. All armament was carried internally to reduce drag. At the time of the mockup inspection on 3 June 1953, the armament consisted of four Falcons, plus two 18-rocket pods of 2.75-inch FFARs. One rocket pod was located just behind the lower Falcon on each side. (National Records Center, St. Louis)

The Wright XJ67 engine was low to the ground, providing awkward access for ground crews. Additionally, the aircraft would have to be jacked up to remove the engine. (National Records Center, St. Louis)

A full-scale metal mockup of the XF-103 was inspected on 3 June 1953 with encouraging results. Actually, two mockups were presented at the inspection, one with the flush canopy favored by Kartveli and another with a more traditional canopy. Both designs were functionally identical, and both appear to have been carried for the entire development effort. An 18-month extension of the Phase I contract was used for further studies of titanium fabrication, high-temperature hydraulics, escape capsules, and periscopic sights.

Although development money was hard to come by, the Air Force decided that the interceptor held so much promise that the program continued to be funded despite a variety of technical problems. By July 1954, the design had advanced to the point that the Air Force awarded Republic a contract to manufacture three XF-103 prototypes, although no serial numbers appear to have been allocated.[35]

Another innovative feature of the XF-103 was its escape capsule. Kartveli believed that in order to survive a Mach 3 escape, some sort of capsule was necessary – a view not universally shared in the aircraft industry, although the use of a capsule in all new aircraft was briefly codified by the Air Force during the late 1950s. The use of a capsule also addressed another problem – how to get into the XF-103, the cockpit of which sat fairly high off the ground. The solution was to have the capsule lower on a rail to ground level where the pilot got in. Escape was from the bottom, making it useless at low level or during takeoff and landing (much like early F-104s).[36]

The XF-103 was one of the first programs to investigate the widespread use of titanium, paving the way for the Lockheed Blackbirds and North American XB-70 later in the decade. Actually, Republic investigated four different construction techniques: all Ti-150B titanium, all 4130 steel, a combination that used Ti-150B titanium alloy outer skins and a 4130 stainless-steel inner structure, and an all-aluminum (24S-T86) structure. The aluminum aircraft was limited to

The exhaust nozzle was as unconventional as the rest of the aircraft. Ramps provided a variable-area exit while the outer side petals were used as speedbrakes. (National Records Center, St. Louis)

Getting air into the powerplant at Mach 3+ presented a challenge for the engineers, especially considering the different requirements of the turbojet and ramjet. (National Records Center, St. Louis)

In 1955, the XF-103 forward vision concept was tested on a modified F-84G (51-843) that accumulated nearly 50 hours of flight testing including at least one cross-country flight. (National Archives)

were capable of sustained Mach 3 operation. A great deal was learned about the manufacture of high-strength titanium alloy and the fabrication of aircraft parts out of it during the course of the XF-103 program, although neither Lockheed nor North American acknowledged the contribution to their later programs.[38]

Despite a low priority and little funding, the program continued to advance, albeit slowly. Full-scale test articles of the wings and horizontal stabilizers were built and tested in heat chambers. A few major subcontracts for the three prototypes were issued, primarily for the landing gear and various pieces of titanium tooling. However, it was becoming obvious that the XF-103 was never going to fly. The effort was experiencing serious difficulties by 1955, but the Air Force still felt a need for an interceptor with higher performance than the upcoming Ultimate Interceptor. It was the beginning of the search for the elusive Mach 3 interceptor.[39]

On 6 October 1955, the Air Defense Command released GOR-114 for the Mach 3 Long-Range Interceptor, Experimental (LRI-X) program. In anticipation of the LRI-X program entering development, during early 1957, the XF-103 was cut back to a single prototype and two flight engines. In this role, the Republic aircraft was to be an advanced research vehicle for the LRI-X program, but was no longer considered a possible operational aircraft. The design evolved considerably during this period, with more than a little assistance from Hughes, which intended to use it as a demonstrator for a new long-range radar and Falcon missile. External changes included a more slab-sided shape for the rear fuselage, a refined variable-geometry inlet, and a rearrangement of the armament. Hughes proposed a weapons load of four GAR-1 Falcons in individual bays (two on each side, one above the other) and two GAR-9 long-range missiles, located in bays behind the upper GAR-1s. Little progress had been made by 21 August 1957, when the XF-103 and Wright engine were cancelled entirely. The program had cost $104 million over nine years.[40]

Mach 2.8 (375 degrees Fahrenheit), and also turned out to be the heaviest at 10,250 pounds (empty airframe weight); it was quickly dropped from consideration. Not surprisingly, the all-titanium structure was the lightest (8,750 pounds), with the combination structure being second (9,400 pounds). The all-steel structure was 100 pounds lighter than the all-aluminum design.[37] Both the steel and titanium aircraft

This was the field-of-view from the XF-103 cockpit as seen from a mockup placed atop a truck and driven around the airfield at Farmingdale. Overall, forward vision was not significantly worse than several contemporary fighters, and side vision was excellent. Rearward vision, on the other hand, was nonexistent. In addition to eliminating drag, the flush canopy offered superior heat and radiation protection for the pilot (the effects of radiation at high altitude was not yet understood). (National Records Center, St. Louis)

Since the Convair F-106 was a derivative of the earlier F-102, there were no prototypes or service test aircraft built. This is the first production F-106A (56-451). (AFFTC History Office Collection)

The "Ultimate Interceptor" was originally the F-102B but this was soon changed to F-106A. This is the second aircraft (56-452) with the new designation on the nose. (National Archives)

Convair F-106A Delta Dart

By December 1951, it was apparent that the Wright J67 engine and the MA-1 fire-control system for the Convair F-102 would not be ready as early as originally thought. This forced the Air Force to proceed with an interim version of its 1954 Interceptor, one that could be introduced into service more-or-less on schedule, pending the availability of the fully developed version at a later time. The interim version was designated F-102A, and the fully developed advanced version became the F-102B.[41]

The F-102B mockup was inspected in December 1955 and resulted in several major changes, particularly to the cockpit. On 18 April 1956, the Air Force ordered 17 service-test aircraft, and on 17 June 1956, the designation was changed to F-106A. Interestingly, the service test aircraft were not called YF-106A.[42]

On 28 September 1956, the Air Force issued a new system-development directive that required the F-106A to be available by August 1958 (some four years later than initially planned) and be compatible with the Semi-Automatic Ground Environment (SAGE). The interceptor would be capable of destroying hostile aircraft within a radius of 430 miles and at altitudes as high as 70,000 feet. Interceptions would be accomplished at speeds of up to Mach 2 at 35,000 feet. It was to be capable of launching Falcon guided missiles and nuclear-armed Genie rockets under the control of the Hughes MA-1 fire-control system.[43]

The first F-106A (56-451) made its maiden flight at Edwards on 26 December 1956, with Convair test pilot Richard L. Johnson at the controls, only 38 months after the first flight of the F-102. The second airplane made its maiden flight on 26 February 1957. The test program proved problematic, although the F-106 turned out to be a capable interceptor that enjoyed a long service career. Ultimately, only 275 F-106As and 63 two-seat F-106Bs were built, not the 1,000 airplanes originally envisioned.[44]

YF-106C

At one point, Convair and the Air Force discussed a follow-on F-106C (and its accompanying F-106D two-seater) with a "look-down, shoot-down" fire-control system with a 40-inch radar antenna. The Air Force considered acquiring 350 of these advanced interceptors, but the project was cancelled on 25 September 1958. Nevertheless, two production F-106As (57-0239/240) were modified as YF-106Cs to test the five-foot nose extension that would house the new radar antenna (the test aircraft carried ballast instead of a radar). Only the first airplane actually flew, and 10 flights were made with the new nose before the flight-test program was cancelled on 10 February 1959. The aircraft was later tested to destruction during a series of fatigue tests at Wright-Patterson AFB. The second airplane reverted to standard F-106A configuration.[45]

Two YF-106Cs were converted from standard F-106As to test a 40-inch radar antenna in an enlongated nose. This aircraft (57-0240) never flew in this configuration. (Terry Panopalis Collection)

Chapter 9

Above: *The first Lockheed YF-12A (60-6934) on the ramp at Edwards on 28 September 1964. At this point the aircraft still had the infrared sensors on the chines. Note the open missile bay doors and the streamlined camera pods under the engine nacelles.* (AFFTC History Office Collection)

Right: *The North American XF-108A mockup as it was inspected by the Air Force on 5 January 1959. Note the infrared sensor at the wing root. There is little physical resemblance to the XB-70A bomber, but many subsystems would have been shared between the two designs.* (National Archives)

LONG-RANGE INTERCEPTORS
MACH 3+

Despite the relative success of the Ultimate Interceptor (F-106A), the search for the elusive Mach 3 interceptor continued. Air Force Headquarters formally approved the development of a new long-range interceptor on 20 July 1955 to replace the 1954 Interceptor (F-102/F-106). In response, the Air Force released GOR-114 on 6 October 1955 for the Long-Range Interceptor, Experimental (LRI-X). The aircraft was to have a service ceiling of 60,000 feet (65,000 desired), a speed of Mach 1.7 at 40,000 feet, a 1,000-nautical-mile radius, a two-man crew, and at least two engines ("at least" so as not to exclude variants of the Convair B-58). It was also to have an integrated fire-control system capable of detecting a B-47-size target at 60 nautical miles (100 desired), and the ability to kill three bombers per mission.[1]

At least eight companies expressed an interest in the LRI-X competition, including Boeing, Douglas, Grumman, Lockheed, McDonnell, North American, Northrop, and Republic. On 11 October 1955, study contracts were issued to Lockheed, North American, and Northrop that included fabricating full-scale mockups of their proposed designs. One of the contractors would be eliminated from competition after the mockup review, with the other two manufacturing prototype aircraft for a fly-off. Simultaneously, contracts were awarded to Hughes and Sperry for advanced fire-control system studies.[2]

By early 1956, each company had completed its preliminary study, and the Air Force was evaluating the results. It was expected that each company would begin building their mockups after incorporating the comments from the review, but it would never get that far. The original plan notwithstanding, funding constraints forced the Air Force to down-select to a single contractor even before the mockups were completed, and the North American design offered the most promise.[3]

In the meantime, however, the Air Defense Command requested that the Pentagon cancel the long-range interceptor program and replace it with a new, medium-range aircraft with a 350-nautical mile radius. The North American selection was put on hold while this new wrinkle was sorted out. The situation was further complicated when factions within the Air Defense Command began supporting the concept of a lightweight interceptor modeled after the Lockheed F-104. It now appeared that both the medium- and long-range interceptors might fall by the wayside. On 9 May 1956, the Pentagon formally cancelled the long-range interceptor due to "questions which had arisen regarding the utility and desirability" of such a weapons system.[4]

Despite the confusion over what type of aircraft the Air Defense Command really wanted, the termination order allowed the two fire-control system development efforts to continue. Sperry had signed its development contract in December 1955, and Hughes followed two months later. Each company was to produce preliminary designs for an advanced fire-control system for the now-cancelled, long-range interceptor. A lack of progress at Sperry led to that contract being cancelled in May 1956. The Hughes design seemed to be progressing well, and the company was working with Ramo-Wooldridge (which later became TRW) to further define the required capabilities, with special consideration being given to using the system on an unlikely production version of the Republic F-103. Despite the seemingly good progress at Hughes, the Air Force awarded a similar development contract to RCA during September 1956 to replace the cancelled Sperry effort.[5]

With the entire matter of what type of interceptor was needed still undecided, the Air Defense Command proposed yet a different set of requirements during the summer 1956. This time the command wanted a Mach 2.5 aircraft capable of 70,000 feet altitude with a 300-nautical mile radius flown by a single pilot operating a modified MX-1179 fire-control system. Interestingly, this aircraft was called a "long range" interceptor, although its radius was less than the previous "medium range" requirements.

Amid this confusion, the Pentagon intervened, deciding that the original long-range interceptor really was what the Air Force needed, but that it should now be equipped with an advanced GAR-X air-to-air missile in addition to the new fire-control system. A special "generals board" chaired by Maj. Gen. Albert Boyd, the commander of the Wright Air Development Center[6] reported directly to the Air Force Chief of Staff that a, "two-place manned interceptor, capable of attaining a speed of Mach 3, altitudes of 70,000 feet plus, and a radius of action of 1,000 miles … is essential to the defense of the United States." The envisioned fire-control system had an 80- to 100-nautical-mile range, and the GAR-X missile would have a range of 15 to 25 nautical miles with interchangeable nuclear and high explosive warheads.[7]

North American XF-108A Rapier

The Air Force had already selected North American during the original LRI-X competition, and this was reaffirmed for the revived airplane during a series of meetings at Wright Field. On 6 June 1957, North American was issued contract AF33(600)-35605 for two XF-108A experimental interceptors as part of WS-202A. An additional 31 YF-108A service-test aircraft were also ordered, but apparently, no serial numbers were allocated for any of them. The stated Air Force requirement was for 480 production aircraft. Reports that the F-108 was intended to be a long-range "escort fighter" for the soon-to-enter-development B-70 appear to be unfounded, although the aircraft would certainly have been capable of such missions.[8]

The mockup inspection of the radar and missile was held at the Hughes plant in Culver City, California, on 15-17 April 1958, and the Air Force concluded that the design approach was both "feasible and acceptable." After successfully passing this milestone, the Hughes XY-1 fire-control system was designated AN/ASG-18 and the GAR-X missile became the GAR-9. At the same time, it was decided that Hughes would provide an infrared search and track (IRST) system as a secondary sensor for the F-108. Exactly why an IRST was specified is uncertain, since the only weapons carried by the aircraft were radar-guided (not IR) missiles that could not take cues from the optical system. Similar, but less sophisticated, systems were being installed on the F-101 and F-102 interceptors.[9]

On 19 November 1958, the operational date for the F-108 was pushed back to mid-1963 due to budgetary issues. A little more than a month later, on 30 December, the number of service-test aircraft was cut from 31 to 20, and the first flight date was delayed three months to April 1961.[10]

A detailed presentation was made to the Air Force development engineering inspection team the week of 5 January 1959, and the F-108

An early artist rendering of the F-108 shows a delta canard and three vertical stabilizers. This concept was continually refined into the design that was shown at the mockup inspection. (Boeing Historical Archives)

mockup was inspected the week of 26 January. The chairman of the team was Col. Linus F. Upson, Jr. and a notable member was double-ace (at the time, later a triple ace) Lt. Col. Robin Olds. In addition to a full-scale mockup of the entire aircraft, a metal mockup of the forward fuselage was provided to demonstrate the fitment of the ASG-18, and a wooden "vision" mockup was constructed to show the view from the cockpit.[11]

North American stated "this high performance air vehicle cruises and combats at Mach 3 with a 1,000-nautical-mile radius on internal fuel. It has a [combat] ceiling in excess of 77,000 feet and a zoom-climb ceiling in excess of 100,000 feet. Under normal loading and weather, the air vehicle requires runway lengths of only 3,200 feet for takeoff and landing. It can be operated from 6,000-foot runways in all weather conditions. From a nominal 70,000-foot combat altitude, missile launch can be accomplished against any air-breathing target flying at altitudes from sea level to 100,000 feet." The accompanying charts showed a maximum speed of 1,980 mph at altitudes up to 81,800 feet.[12]

The major change between the December 1958 configuration and that presented at the mockup inspection was the powerplant. The J93-GE-1 engines that had been carried as a baseline since the beginning of the program were replaced with J93-GE-3R variants that produced 17,500-lbf normal and 27,200-lbf with afterburners. These finally included the thrust reversers that had long been desired, adding 345 pounds to each engine. Testing of the thrust reverser had begun at Edwards in January 1959, using a scaled-down reverser attached to a J79 engine; these tests indicated that the design would meet the performance requirements.[13]

As could be expected, the F-108 was being looked at to fill roles other than the long-range interceptor it had been designed as. Perhaps the most important was as a gap-filler for the Distant Early Warning (DEW) radars. If a few aircraft were based at remote arctic

The General Electric XJ93 turbojet from the XB-70A would have powered the XF-108A, although the fighter engine was equipped with thrust reversers. This is a mockup engine. (National Archives)

The two photos at top show the mockup shortly after the inspection on 5 January 1959, having traded its original silver paint for a new coat of gloss white. The lower photo is later still, and shows the rear window has been changed from rectangular to a circle. The mockup was quite detailed and included the radar and electronic boxes required for the advanced Hughes ASG-18 fire-control system. (National Archives)

airstrips, a sufficient number of them could be constantly airborne to eliminate the gaps that existed in radar coverage. Each F-108 could scan about 278,000 square miles – an area a little larger than Texas – per hour. In addition to basic radar coverage, the F-108 would also provide positive identification of targets and act as a radar and communications relay for other F-108s scrambled to intercept the bombers. It was noted that the ambient temperatures encountered by the F-108 at the arctic (Zone of Interior – ZI – or continental United States) bases would "not last longer than 36 hours below –25°F or 2 hours below –40°F." Separately, it had already been decided that the performance of the F-108 was sufficient to allow it to intercept any known target well outside the air defense identification zone (ADIZ), with the exception of a small area of the southern United States where there was very limited radar coverage, hence preventing early detection of possible targets.[14]

The long-range interceptor was gathering support during early 1959 based on its apparent successful development, but this was outweighed by an increasing funding problem. The Joint Chiefs of Staff evaluated the F-108 against yet-another Convair B-58 interceptor concept and an "I-70" interceptor version of the North American B-70 bomber, and substantiated the value of the F-108. It was pointed out that the F-108 program was paying for the development of systems for the B-70, and that these costs would not go away even if the F-108 were eliminated. The aircraft was named Rapier on 15 May 1959, continuing a short-lived tradition of naming North American fighters after swords. [15]

The cost of the program, however, would eventually overshadow all of the technical progress. The Air Force could not come up with the funds to continue, and the F-108 was cancelled on 23 September 1959.[16]

The Pentagon did, however, continue development of the ASG-18 fire-control system and GAR-9 missile. Since the requirement for a

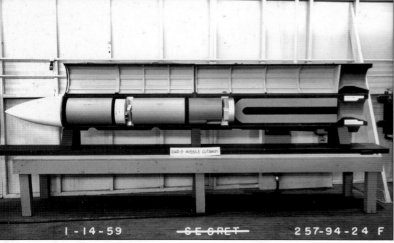

Hughes presented several mockups of the GAR-9 (AIM-47) missile at the XF-108A mockup inspection. The bottom photo shows a cutaway of the missile: from left is the warhead, stable platform, electronics, umbilical interfaces, and the rocket motor. (National Archives)

Unlike the later Lockheed YF-12A, which had a separate weapons bay for each of the three GAR-9 missiles, the XF-108A would have used a rotary launcher that carried three missiles in a single bay. Here one missile is in the launch position, with another above it. (National Archives)

The large radar antenna for the Hughes ASG-18 fire-control system was located just ahead of the windscreen, with the rest of the radome serving aerodynamic purposes only. (National Archives)

North American built a series of models depicting the arrangement of ground support equipment around the F-108A. This is the nominal turnaround model. Note the missiles at right. (National Archives)

long-range interceptor had not gone away, the Air Force investigated using the ASG-18 and GAR-9 on another aircraft. In the end, they found that only the F-108 could do the job, and recommended that the North American effort be reinstated, or that the fire-control system be cancelled also. The Pentagon disagreed, and funds were provided to continue the Hughes effort through 30 June 1960. With these decisions, the most likely candidate for a Mach 3 interceptor faded from the scene.[17]

The cockpit mockup was quite detailed and showed the tape-style instruments planned for the F-108. The same type of instruments were used on the Lockheed YF-12A, the only Blackbird to use them. This is the front cockpit, showing that the pilot was concerned only with flying the airplane – all weapons systems controls were in the back cockpit. (National Archives)

Lockheed YF-12A

There was, however, one other possible Mach 3 interceptor.

Always looking for new opportunities, Kelly Johnson had periodically proposed a high-speed interceptor, based on the CIA's A-12 design, to the Air Force. Inside Lockheed, the interceptor was referred to as the AF-12, and in late October 1960 the Air Force awarded Lockheed a $1 million contract under Project Kedlock. Lockheed's vision, not necessarily shared by the Air Force, was that a fleet of 93 high-speed interceptors could adequately protect the North American continent against most expected Soviet threats from directions other than those expected (and well-defended) over the North Pole.[18]

As originally conceived by Lockheed, the AF-12 was an A-12 modified with the Hughes AN/ASG-18 fire-control system from the cancelled North American F-108 and three Hughes GAR-9 missiles. The pilot's seat was raised for better visibility, and a second seat (for the radar officer) was added in a deeper forward fuselage. This bulged canopy gave the AF-12 a distinctive appearance among the Blackbirds. To minimize radar signal distortion, the aerodynamic chines on the extreme nose were deleted and the radome lengthened, although the aircraft was slightly shorter overall. The modified chines accommodated a pair of infrared search and track (IRST) sensors, also from the F-108. The aft fuselage, wings, nacelles, and engines were identical to the A-12.

On 31 May 1961, a mockup of the AF-12 forward fuselage was inspected by the Air Force with no serious comments. Unfortunately, by June 1961, wind-tunnel tests had revealed that the revised nose chines and cockpit configuration caused directional stability problems at high Mach numbers. A large folding ventral stabilizer was added under the aft fuselage, and a small, fixed ventral fin was added under each engine nacelle, giving the AF-12 a distinctive in-flight appearance among Blackbirds. Although these ventral stabilizers significantly increased the radar cross section of the AF-12, stealth was not of particular concern since the aircraft would always operate over North American territory.[19]

The Air Force finally ordered three AF-12s and negotiated with the CIA to use the seventh, eighth, and ninth A-12 airframes to speed the project along. By August 1962, the major elements of the first AF-12 were in the assembly jigs. The first AF-12 was trucked to Groom Lake in July 1963, and on 7 August Lockheed test pilot Jim Eastham made the maiden flight. On 29 February 1964, part of the Blackbird's security blanket was removed when President Johnson announced, "The United States has successfully developed an advanced experimental jet aircraft, the A-11, which has been tested in sustained flight at more than 2,000 miles an hour and at altitudes in excess of 70,000 feet.[20]

"The performance of the A-11 far exceeds that of any other aircraft in the world today. The development of this aircraft has been made possible by major advances in aircraft technology of great significance to both military and commercial application. Several A-11 aircraft are now being flight tested at Edwards Air Force Base in California … The A-11 aircraft now at Edwards Air Force Base are undergoing extensive tests to determine their capabilities as long-range interceptors. … In view of the continuing importance of these developments to our national security, the detailed performance of the A-11 will remain strictly classified and all individuals associated with the program have been directed to refrain from making any further disclosure concerning this program." At the same time, the Air Force assigned the YF-12A designation to the airplanes, along with proper serial numbers (60-6934/936).[21]

Of course, this statement contained two non-truths. First, the reference to the A-11 (instead of A-12) was at Kelly Johnson's suggestion to

The first YF-12A (60-6934) as it appeared prior to its maiden flight on 7 August 1963, taken at the Test Site in Nevada. Note the silver fuselage chines (instead of black) and the lack of any markings except a serial number on the vertical stabilizer. (Central Intelligence Agency)

A Hughes AIM-47 being loaded into the second YF-12A (60-6935) on 26 February 1965. The fighter had three weapons bays, each capable of carrying a single missile. (Lockheed Martin)

On 1 May 1965, the first and third YF-12As were used to set a series of world records for speed and altitude. Skunk Works were justifiably proud. Note Kelly's signature at right. (AFFTC History Office Collection)

mislead intelligence sources. Second, there were no Blackbirds of any description at Edwards. The test team had been caught off guard by the Presidential announcement, and two of the YF-12s were hastily flown from Groom Lake to Edwards by Lockheed test pilots Louis W. "Lou" Schalk and William C. "Bill" Park. In the rush to get the two aircraft out of public view, they made a direct approach to Edwards and taxied directly to the hangar. Park taxied straight in, but Schalk had some difficulty making a turn, so he advanced the throttles a bit to assist. The hot blast from the engines set off the fire deluge system and alarms, covering the aircraft and ground crew with water. As they are trained to do, the flight-line crash crews responded quickly to what was, in reality, a non-event. So much for a quiet arrival.[22]

The first YF-12A in front of the old Edwards control tower at its first public display. Note there is not an Air Defense Command (ADC) badge on the vertical stabilizer. (AFFTC History Office Collection)

The first YF-12A on 26 February 1965, complete with the ADC logos on the tail. Note the buzz number on the upper engine nacelle, completely defeating its purpose. (AFFTC History Office Collection)

Flight tests at Edwards proceeded with increased frequency, and relatively few problems were uncovered. Since most of the aerodynamics had already been verified on the A-12, the YF-12 test team concentrated on evaluating the fire-control and missile systems. On 16 April 1964, the first XAIM-47 (as the GAR-9 had been redesignated) inert verification shape was ejected from a YF-12A in flight. The launch was generally successful in that the missile separated cleanly from the aircraft, but its ejection angle left a great deal to be desired. If the missile had been powered, it would have immediately flown through the YF-12 cockpit. Jim Eastham had warned the engineers this would happen, based on his previous experience at Hughes developing other air-to-air missiles, but his warnings went unheeded. Obviously more work was needed.

After the necessary modifications were made to the missile ejection system, all future launches were relatively uneventful. Ultimately, on 18 March 1965, a YF-12A launched a single YAIM-47 and hit a drone flying 36 miles away with a closure rate of more than 2,000 mph.

Earlier that year, on 9 January, Jim Eastham had taken the first YF-12A to Mach 3.23, and sustained Mach 3.2 for more than 5 minutes. The various Blackbirds were routinely breaking just about every Fédération Aéronautique Internationale (FAI) speed record in existence, but nobody knew due to the security restrictions surrounding the programs. On 12 August 1964, the Air Force asked Lockheed to come up with a program to use one of the YF-12As to publicly break the FAI records. The YF-12A was chosen primarily because it was the Blackbird with the greatest public exposure and was also the one with the least design and technology sensitivity. Not to mention, it was also easier to understand why the Air Force needed such a high-speed aircraft while it was more difficult to explain the CIA's need, or indeed, why the CIA even had an air force.[23]

On 1 May 1965 the first and third YF-12As were used to set several FAI Class C-1 Group 3 (turbojet-powered landplanes) absolute records, including: sustained altitude – 80,257.65 feet (Col. Robert Stephens and Lt. Col. Daniel Andre); speed over a 15/25-km closed course – 2,070.101 mph (Col. Robert Stephens and Lt. Col. Daniel Andre); speed over a 500-km closed-course – 1,643.042 mph (Maj. Walter Daniel and Maj. Noel Warner); and three 1,000-km closed-course (without payload, with 1,000ikilogram payload, and with 2,000-kilogram payload) speed records – 1,688.893 mph (Maj. Walter Daniel and Capt. James Cooney). The records were nowhere near the maximum capability of the aircraft. Unfortunately, four of the speed records did not stand for long – the Soviet Union used a modified MiG-25 (E-266) to break them on 27 October 1967 (averaging 1,852.618 mph for the 500-km run, and 1,814.820 mph for the 1,000-km categories). The other records would be broken by an SR-71A in 1976.

The YF-12 program took a step closer to production on 14 May 1965, when the Air Force provided $500,000 for engineering development of the follow-on F-12B. This would have been the operational configuration of the YF-12A, and was designed to be deployed without the need for the extensive ground systems required of the A-12 and YF-12A prototypes. An additional $500,000 was released to Lockheed on 10 November 1965 for continued engineering work on the F-12B. Externally the F-12B would more closely resemble the A-12, since careful shaping of the radome allowed the addition of small chines, improving the aerodynamics and eliminating the large ventral fins.[24]

The first YF-12A was damaged beyond repair by fire at Edwards during a landing mishap on 14 August 1966. The rear fuselage and wings were salvaged and combined with the front half of a Lockheed static test airframe to create the only SR-71C. That aircraft is currently on display at the Hill Aerospace Museum near Ogden, Utah.

The first YF-12A at the test site in Nevada. Note the black fuselage chines, something that was changed sometime after the first flight. The location of the buzz number is different than it was when the aircraft was painted all-black. (Lockheed Martin)

If it looks like an SR-71, that is because it is. After the third YF-12A was lost on 24 June 1971, the Air Force made the second SR-71A (61-7951) available to NASA under the YF-12C designation with a fictitious serial number of 60-6937. (NASA Dryden)

The second YF-12A (60-6935) in NASA markings. This aircraft was used to test a center ventral fin manufactured from Lockalloy, a high-temperature-resistant alloy developed by Lockheed for very high-speed aircraft and lifting-reentry spacecraft. (NASA Dryden)

Like the CIA A-12s, the YF-12As had a short rear fuselage that did not protrude past the trailing edge of the wing (which the SR-71's did). The cut-off chines are clearly evident from this angle, although production F-12Bs would have used chines extending to the nose. (NASA Dryden)

But it was all not to be – the Air Force had run out of money and ordered the two surviving YF-12s placed into flyable storage at Edwards. By August 1967, Lockheed had lain off or reassigned more than half of the F-12 test team, retaining just enough personnel to put the aircraft into storage and clean up the documentation. By Christmas, the Air Force had decided not to pursue the F-12B follow-on program.

On 5 January 1968, a formal order was issued by the Air Force Systems Command that shut down the F-12B program in its entirety. A similar notice for the YF-12A program followed on 1 February 1968, including orders to destroy all tooling for both the fighter and reconnaissance (SR-71) variants. To comply with this order, the large assembly jigs were cut up and sold to local scrap dealers for seven cents per pound. However, a majority of the smaller tools and fixtures were placed in storage at nearby Norton AFB, California, and supported the manufacture of spare parts for the SR-71s for several decades.

The Air Force had finally found its elusive Mach 3 interceptor, and built exactly three of them.

Blackbirds with NASA

After the interceptor program was cancelled, the Air Force offered NASA the use of the second and third YF-12A (60-6935 and 6936), then in storage at Edwards. A memorandum of understanding was signed 5 June 1969 followed by a public announcement on 18 July. NASA and Air Force technicians spent three months getting the second YF-12A ready for flight, and the joint flight research program got under way with a successful maiden flight on 11 December 1969. The first flight with a NASA crew was on 5 March

1970, using the third YF-12A, with Fitzhugh L. "Fitz" Fulton and Victor W. Horton at the controls.[25]

The third YF-12A was lost on 24 June 1971 when a fuel line failed from fatigue, resulting in a fire in the right engine nacelle. Lt. Col. Ronald J. Layton and Maj. Billy A. Curtis debated whether they could land the burning Blackbird, but wisely elected to eject. The YF-12A crashed in the desert just east of the runway and the remains were later moved to a commercial scrap yard in nearby Rosamond.

NASA had wanted to add a third aircraft to the test program solely for propulsion tests. A month after the loss of the third YF-12A, the Air Force made the second SR-71 (61-7951) available to NASA. Because the SR-71 program was still shrouded in secrecy, this aircraft was fictitiously designated YF-12C and carried the equally fictitious serial number 60-6937 (confusingly, this serial number was also used by an A-12). On 24 May 1972 the YF-12C made its first flight with a NASA crew. The NASA Blackbirds flew an average of once a week, and program expenses averaged $3.1 million per year.

By the early part of 1977, the NASA Blackbirds had completed more than 175 flights, with a good percentage of them at or above Mach 3. However, the cost of flying the two high-performance aircraft became too great a burden for the Flight Research Center and in the spring of 1977 NASA decided to retire the YF-12A and return the YF-12C to the Air Force. The YF-12C was flown to Palmdale on 27 October 1978 and made one last flight on 22 December 1978 before being placed in storage at Plant 42 along with the nine remaining A-12s, and is currently on display at the Pima Air and Space Museum in Tucson. The sole remaining YF-12A made its final flight to the Air Force Museum on 7 November 1979 and is currently on display there.

Chapter 10

Left: *The second F-111A (63-9767) was heavily involved in the test program after its maiden flight on 25 February 1965. This aircraft was initially unpainted, highlighting one of the last mostly-aluminum airframes on an Air Force fighter.* (National Archives)

Below: *The first YF-5F (73-0889) two-seater was used for weapons trials, and is seen carrying an impressive load of Maverick missiles and fuel tanks. Small orange cameras are mounted on the nose and rear fuselage.* (National Archives)

THE END OF AN ERA ...
AFTER THE CENTURY SERIES

The Century Series took 1950 technology about as far as possible. The Pratt & Whitney J57, Pratt & Whitney J75, General Electric J79, and General Electric J93 represented the pinnacle of military turbojet engine development, while the Republic F-105 and Convair F-106 showed the limits of discrete-component electronic systems.

By the end of the 1950s, U.S. engine developers began focusing on new military engines that combined unprecedented thrust-to-weight ratios and specific fuel consumption provided by turbofan technology. These engines pushed the edge of the feasible technical and performance envelopes. As a result, the early augmented turbofan engines, especially the Pratt & Whitney TF30, experienced serious development problems, mostly involving inlet airflow and compressor stall. Pratt & Whitney had experimented with a duct-burning turbofan in 1956, but the TF30 burned both fan and turbine exhaust air in the same afterburner. The TF30 began development in 1959 in support of what later became the TFX program that resulted in the General Dynamics F-111.

The single-function electronics of earlier aircraft began to be replaced with integrated fire-control systems. This began as far back as the MX-1179 fire-control system designed for the Convair F-102, but required greater computer power than had been available at the time. Advances in airborne computers, such as the highly successful IBM 4Pi/AP-101 series, allowed unprecedented navigation accuracies and set the stage for the introduction of smart weapons, such as laser-guided bombs. Only much later would the ultimate advances – such as the laser-ring gyros and the Global Positioning System (GPS) – become available. As automated and accurate as the original Republic F-105 weapons system had seemed at the time, it paled in comparison to the one developed for the F-111, although many of the newer systems were later retrofitted into the earlier fighters.

As a result of these advances, the last of the Century Series – the McDonnell F-110 and General Dynamics F-111 – were either a dignified end, or a crude beginning, depending on where one sat. The next generation, the McDonnell Douglas F-15 and General Dynamics F-16, would be in a class of their own.

The first F-110A was really a Navy F4H-1 (BuNo 149405), and the last five digits of the BuNo were painted on the vertical stabilizer. (These would have translated to 64-9405, which was in the middle of a run of Martin AGM-12 Bullpup missiles.) (National Archives)

Likewise, the second aircraft was also a Navy F4H-1 (BuNo 149406). Eventually these two F-110As received real Air Force serial numbers (62-12168/169). Note the Sparrow and Sidewinder missiles carried on the inboard wing stations of the two aircraft. (National Archives)

McDonnell F-110 Spectre

During the early 1960s, the Air Force began to investigate new aircraft to replace the Republic F-105 as a tactical fighter and Convair F-106 as an interceptor. Although traditionally reluctant to look at Navy aircraft, the impressive performance of the McDonnell F4H-1 was difficult to ignore. Under pressure from Secretary of Defense Robert S. McNamara, who wanted to reduce defense expenditures by achieving greater commonality between the services, the Air Force agreed to evaluate the F4H-1 against the F-106 as part of Operation HIGHSPEED. On 24 January 1962, a pair of Navy F4H-1s (BuNos 149405/406) arrived at Langley AFB painted in standard Navy grey and white. The aircraft carried Air Force markings with their new F-110A designation prominently displayed on the nose and subsequently received Air Force serial numbers (62-12168/12169). They were named, in accordance with McDonnell's fascination with the supernatural, Spectre.[1]

Since the Navy had developed the F4H-1 as an interceptor, that is how the Air Force evaluated it. It was found that the F-110A had better overall speed, altitude, and range than the F-106A as well as a 25 percent greater radar range. Later, the Air Force also looked into using the airplane as a tactical fighter and found the F-110A more versatile than the Republic F-105 since it could carry similar external loads and was potentially a better air superiority fighter due to its more favorable wing and power loadings.[2]

The Department of Defense subsequently announced that the F-110A would become the standard Air Force tactical fighter, and on 30 March 1962 issued McDonnell a letter contract for a single F-110A (62-12199) and two RF-110A reconnaissance variants (62-12200/201). Since the F-110A was a derivative of a Navy production aircraft, there were no XF-110A or YF-110A variants. However, a full-scale mockup was inspected in April 1962 to verify the Air Force-specific electronics and cockpit configurations. To formalize the F-110A project, the Air Force issued Specific Operational Requirement 200 on 29 August 1962 calling for an aircraft based on the F4H-1 but with added ground-attack capability.[3]

On 18 September 1962, the Department of Defense directed the use of a common designation system for all Air Force, Army, and Navy aircraft. The F4H-1 was redesignated F-4B and the F-110A became the F-4C. At the same time, all F-4s were named Phantom II. Therefore, no aircraft were actually built as F-110As, and only the original pair of borrowed F4H-1s carried that designation.[4]

The first F-4C made its maiden flight on 27 May 1963. The F-4C was externally identical to the F-4B but carried substantially different electronics and was fitted with flight controls in both cockpits (the Navy back seater was strictly a weapons-system operator). Bulges above and below the inner wing panels accommodated wider wheels and low-pressure tires, marking one of the major exterior differences between F-4Bs and F-4Cs. The Navy probe-and-drogue aerial refueling equipment was replaced by a boom-type system with a refueling receptacle mounted on top of the fuselage behind the rear cockpit.[5]

In November 1963, the Navy temporarily loaned 27 F-4Bs to the 4453rd Combat Crew Training Wing at MacDill AFB (including BuNos 150480, 150486, 150493, 150630, 150634, 150643, 150649, 150650, 150652, 150653, 150994, 150995, 150997, 150999, 151000, 151002, 151003, 151004, 151006, 151007, 151009, 151011, 151014, 151016, 151017, 151020, and 151021). It is difficult to determine if the Air Force called these aircraft F-4C or just used the Navy F-4B designation, but they were never called F-110A since that designation had been abolished a year before they were delivered. The aircraft were assigned Air Force serial numbers (62-1270/196). As production F-4Cs became available, the borrowed F-4Bs were returned to the Navy.[6]

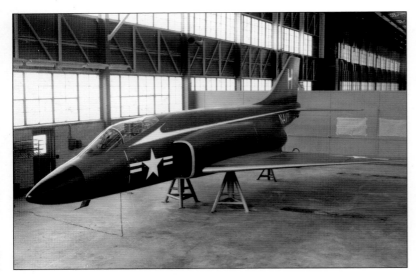

This is the F3H-G/H mockup that led to the F4H (F-4) series. The basic shape is readily identifiable despite the single-seat cockpit and the unbent wingtips and horizontal stabilizer. (National Archives)

One of the ex-Navy aircraft (BuNo 149405) with its new Air Force serial number (62-12168). Other than the markings, this was a standard Navy F-4H-1 (F-4B). (AFFTC History Office Collection)

A total of 583 F-4Cs were built, the last rolling off the production line on 4 May 1966. The Air Force also accepted 793 F-4Ds and 993 F-4Es (and its 116 F-4G conversions) before the last Phantom (an F-4G) left Air Force service on 20 April 1996. Many more F-4s were manufactured for the Navy and foreign users, and the F-4 served in the air forces of Australia, Egypt, Germany, Greece, Iran, Israel, Japan, South Korea, Spain, Turkey, and the United Kingdom (the only other operator of Navy variants). Ultimately, 5,195 Phantom IIs were manufactured.[7]

YRF-4C / YF-4E

While McDonnell was developing the Air Force-specific changes for the F-110A, the company also proposed a reconnaissance variant based on preliminary work accomplished for the Marine F4H-1P. The RF-110A offered better performance than the RF-101A/C along with the ability to support nighttime photographic missions, which the Voodoo lacked. The Air Force was impressed and ordered a pair of reconnaissance prototypes (62-12200/12201) at the same time they ordered the first F-110A. Since there was no equivalent Navy version, these aircraft were designated YRF-110A.[8]

On 31 December 1962, nine months after the recce prototypes had been ordered, the Air Force released Specific Operational Requirement (SOR) 196 for a tactical reconnaissance aircraft. The major modification to the recce version was a longer, pointed nose that housed cameras, mapping radar, and infrared imaging equipment. A mockup of the revised forward fuselage was inspected on 29 October 1962 to verify the new reconnaissance nose and the removal of the forward pair of AIM-7 missile wells. The aft missile wells remained, but the aircraft lacked the equipment needed to carry or launch Sparrows. Testing of optical and electronic reconnaissance

systems was conducted at Holloman AFB, New Mexico, during 1963 using an early F-4A (BuNo 145310) bailed from the Navy.[9]

On 18 September 1962, the Department of Defense directed the use of a common designation system, and the Marine F4H-1P reconnaissance variant was redesignated RF-4B and the Air Force RF-110A became the RF-4C.[10]

By the time the first Air Force reconnaissance variant was completed during the summer of 1963, the designation had changed, so no RF-110As were built. The first YRF-4C made its maiden flight on 8 August 1963 with McDonnell test pilot William S. Ross at the controls. The aircraft still had the "thin wing" (no main landing gear bulges) used on the Navy F-4B and did not carry any cameras or other reconnaissance equipment and was delivered to Edwards on 22 August by McDonnell test pilot George Eaton. It is interesting to note that this was 18 months before the first Marine Corps RF-4B (BuNo 151975) made its maiden flight (on 12 March 1965).[11]

The second YRF-4C made its maiden flight on 30 September 1963. This aircraft was fitted with high and low panoramic and frame cameras but still lacked most of the other production systems. The second YRF-4C was bailed to General Electric in January 1966 for continued testing of advanced versions of the J79 engine. The airplane was returned to the Air Force in June 1972 and was used at the Chanute Technical Training Center in the Fuel Specialist course. It is currently on loan to Octave Chanute Aerospace Museum from the National Museum of the United States Air Force. Eventually, 503 production RF-4Cs followed.[12]

After the completion of the reconnaissance test program, the first YRF-4C was modified as the prototype of the cannon-armed Tactical Strike Fighter that became the F-4E. The installation of the M61 20mm cannon was not as clean as the final F-4E design because the Air Force and McDonnell wanted to use as much of the existing nose

The second YF-4E (63-7445) with a terrain following radar system mounted in a modified TMU-2B pod on the left wing station. The right wing station carries a fuel tank. (National Archives)

The first YRF-4C (62-12200) in its control-configured vehicle (CCV) configuration on 5 July 1974. Note the large canards mounted on top of the air intakes. (AFFTC History Office Collection)

structure as possible to minimize cost and get the aircraft into the air as soon as possible. The redesignated YF-4E made its maiden flight on 7 August 1965 from St. Louis, piloted by McDonnell test pilots Joe Dobronski and Ed Rosenmeyer.[13]

The first YF-4E was later used in Project Agile Eagle to test the leading-edge maneuvering slats and slotted horizontal stabilizer that were fitted to late production F-4Es. Still later, the airplane was used to flight-test various composite material components such as a light-weight beryllium rudder.[14]

In April 1972, the YF-4E was modified with a fly-by-wire (FBW) control system as part of the Precision Aircraft Control Technology (PACT) project. For the initial flight tests, the fly-by-wire system was backed up by conventional mechanical controls, but as confidence grew during flight-testing, this backup was eliminated. The PACT

The first F-110A (BuNo 149405/62-12168) as it was originally delivered to the Air Force, including the "thin" wing that did not have the bump added later for the wider wheels and tires of the Air Force F-4C. Note that "Phantom II" has been added to the nose markings (compare to page 209). This brings into question the exact timing of the name change from Spectre versus the designation change to F-4C. (National Archives)

The first YRF-4C (62-12200) in its reconnaissance configuration on 15 January 1964. Although this was only five months after the first flight, the aircraft has been modified with the wing bulges needed to clear the Air Force wheels and tires. (AFFTC History Office Collection)

The third YF-4E prototype was converted from an F-4D (65-0713), and was much closer to the production configuration than the YRF-4C had been. This photo was taken above Edwards on 29 January 1968. (AFFTC History Office Collection)

demonstrator made its first fully FBW flight on 22 January 1973, and 30 flights were made.

The first YF-4E was later rebuilt as a Control Configured Vehicle (CCV) with large canards mounted on the upper edges of the air intakes. The aircraft made its first flight in the new configuration on 29 April 1974. During the flight-test program, lead ballast was added to the rear fuselage to move the center of gravity aft to destabilize the aircraft in pitch. On 5 December 1978, the first YRF-4C/YF-4E was retired to the Air Force Museum, where it is now on display. The airplane had made 737 flights totaling 952.1 flight hours.[15]

The results with the first YF-4E were sufficiently encouraging that the Secretary of Defense authorized the production of the F-4E on

22 July 1966. McDonnell subsequently produced two other YF-4Es by modifying an F-4C (63-7445) and an F-4D (65-0713). Ironically, this particular F-4C had been used to test a pod-mounted cannon system for the Phantom prior to the Tactical Strike Fighter program being approved. These two aircraft had the M61 20mm cannon installed in a nose that closely resembled the final configuration, rather than the modified recce nose of the first prototype. The second YF-4E, rolled out on 1 March 1967, had the cannon but no radar, and the third had both cannon and radar. Both prototypes were ultimately assigned to Edwards as general-purpose test and chase aircraft. It is uncertain what happened to the second YF-4E, but the third airplane is currently on display at the Air Force Flight Test Center Museum at Edwards.[16]

The first YRF-4C (62-12200) at its roll out in its fly-by-wire configuration. The nose shows its recce heritage with the hastily-converted YF-4E gun fairing under it. (National Archives)

By the time it became the CCV testbed, the YRF-4C/YF-4E had received the leading edge slats and the slotted horizontal stabilizer from the late E-models. (AFFTC History Office Collection)

General Dynamics F-111 Aardvark

The General Dynamics F-111 is probably the most controversial combat aircraft in American history. Perhaps no other aircraft before or since has been so bitterly criticized in the media and by Congress. It suffered a protracted development program with numerous serious problems and cost overruns that soon became front-page news. Of the several thousand aircraft originally planned, only 562 examples of seven different variants were ultimately completed.

After a particularly protracted and difficult proposal period, and amid great controversy, on 21 December 1962, the Department of Defense awarded General Dynamics a production contract for 18 Air Force F-111As (63-9766/782) and 5 Navy F-111Bs (BuNos 151970/151974). Under the procurement system championed by Secretary of Defense Robert S. McNamara – but closely resembling the Cook-Craigie concept of concurrency – these were not considered experimental or prototype models and were not designated XF-111 or YF-111. They were, however, expected to be dedicated to research, development, test, and evaluation (RDT&E) flights.[17]

The F-111A mockup was inspected in September 1963 with only relatively minor changes requested. The first RDT&E F-111A (63-9766) rolled out of the General Dynamics plant in Fort Worth on 15 October 1964, 37 months after the go-ahead decision and two weeks ahead of schedule. The aircraft made its maiden flight from the adjacent Carswell AFB on 21 December, with General Dynamics test pilots Richard L. Johnson and Val Prahl at the controls. Although the flight was shortened to 22 minutes because of a flap malfunction, the results were generally satisfactory. On its second flight, on 6 January 1965, the wings were swept from the 16-degree full-forward position to the 72.5-degree full-aft position.[18]

Oddly, there appear to have been two aircraft designated YF-111A, but they were never delivered. When the Royal Air Force cancelled its

An Air Force F-111A (63-9769) carrying Navy AIM-54 Phoenix missiles? This was the dedicated spin-test aircraft, and it carried a variety of external stores, including Navy ones, during the tests. (National Archives)

F-111K order on 17 January 1968, the first two aircraft (67-0149/150) were in final assembly. These were reportedly redesignated YF-111A for possible use by the Air Force, but were scrapped prior to being completed. Their RAF serials were XV884 and XV885.[19]

After a prolonged gestation period, amid a very public controversy, the F-111 turned out to be one of the most effective all-weather interdiction aircraft ever built. Although vilified by some as unsafe and dangerous, the F-111 established the best safety record of any of the Century Series fighters, with only 115 aircraft being lost in 1,876,503 flight hours. Although the aircraft has left U.S. service, it still serves with the Royal Australian Air Force and may very well continue until 2020.[20]

The first F-111A (63-9766) seen at the General Dynamics facility in Ft. Worth after its maiden flight on 21 December 1964. A malfunctioning flap shortened the otherwise successful flight. (National Archives)

The fourth F-111A (63-9769) was the dedicated spin-test aircraft. Note the recovery parachute container protruding behind the vertical stabilizer. The aircraft was unpainted for much of its career. (National Archives)

Northrop F-5 Freedom Fighter

Development of what became the F-5 began when a Northrop team toured Europe and Asia during 1954 to examine the defense needs of NATO and SEATO countries. This resulted in a 1955 in-house design study for a lightweight supersonic fighter that would be relatively inexpensive, easy to maintain, and capable of operating from short runways. The aircraft would use the General Electric J85 turbojet being developed for the McDonnell GAM-72 Quail decoy. The design went through several configurations before the final N-156F fighter and N-156T two-seat trainer were selected. It was much the same philosophy being used by Lockheed for the F-104, except Northrop was not aiming to develop a maximum-performance aircraft; the N-156F would be supersonic, but nowhere near as fast as the Mach 2+ Starfighter.[21]

The Air Force had little interest in the N-156F since it perceived no need for a lightweight fighter. However, it did need a new trainer to replace the Lockheed T-33, and in June 1956, awarded a contract for three prototype N-156Ts under the T-38 designation. The first T-38A, named Talon, made its maiden flight on 10 April 1959, and ultimately 1,187 were built.[22]

Undaunted, on 25 February 1958, Northrop decided to proceed with the development of the N-156F as a private venture, drawing heavily on the design of the T-38. Unlike the trainer, the N-156F wing had a forward-angled fillet at each root and continuous-hinge flaps on the leading edges. The N-156F also had larger air intakes equipped with square-shaped perforated splitter plates to bleed the boundary layer airflow.[23]

Although it still lacked a requirement for a lightweight fighter, the Air Force inspected the N-156F mockup and on 25 February 1958 ordered three prototypes (59-4987/4989). Oddly, no military designation was assigned, most likely because the Air Force never expected to operate the type. The first N-156F was rolled out on 31 May 1959 and

shipped to Edwards for ground tests. Afterburning versions of the J85 were not yet available, so the first (and second) N-156F used unaugmented versions of the engine. The airplane made its maiden flight on 30 July 1959 with Northrop test pilot Lewis A. "Lew" Nelson at the controls. Despite the lack of afterburning engines, the aircraft went supersonic on its first flight. The second N-156F made its maiden flight on 31 July 1963, piloted by Northrop test pilot Henry E. "Hank" Chouteau. Completion of the third N-156F was held in abeyance pending a decision by the Air Force on a production contract.[24]

Early test flights were generally encouraging, and the N-156F outperformed the North American F-100 in nearly every category. Nevertheless, in August 1960, the Air Force concluded that it still had no requirement for the aircraft. This soon changed under the administration of John F. Kennedy that wanted to fund sales of advanced aircraft to allied nations. The Air Force supported versions of the Lockheed F-104, but the Department of Defense and the International Security Affairs Agency preferred the Northrop aircraft. On 25 April 1962, the Department of Defense announced that it had chosen the N-156F as the standard Foreign Military Sales (FMS) fighter.[25]

On 9 August 1962, the N-156F was designated F-5A and named Freedom Fighter. At the same time, a two-seat combat trainer version was ordered under the designation F-5B. It looked a lot like the T-38A, but retained the full combat capability of the F-5A. There were no XF-5A or YF-5A aircraft, although it is common practice to call the three original N-156F airplanes YF-5As (some sources indicate the third aircraft was actually designated YF-5A, but this could not be confirmed).[26]

Trials with the first two N-156F prototypes indicated the need for a beefier landing gear and a stronger wing structure that could accommodate an additional stores station on each side. These changes were built into the third N-156F (59-4989) along with afterburning J85-GE-13 engines. The third airplane made its maiden

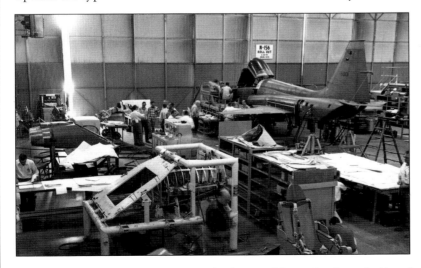

The first N-156F (59-4987) during final assembly at Northrop in Hawthorne. Each prototype was essentially hand-built, with little in the way of hard tooling used since it was uncertain if there would be any production contracts forthcoming. As it turned out, the F-5 series was extremely successful gathering international customers and went on to a long career. (Northrop Corporation)

The second N-156F (59-4988) at the 1960 Edwards air show. The large can on the air-data probe protected the instruments from damage while the aircraft was on the ground. (Terry Panopalis Collection)

By the time of this 29 July 1963 photo, the third N-156F had been designated YF-5A (59-4989) and looked much more like a combat aircraft in its official paint scheme. (AFFTC History Office Collection)

flight on 31 July 1963 with Hank Chouteau at the controls. The first overseas order for F-5As was from Norway, which ordered 64 aircraft plus four attrition replacements on 28 February 1964. Eventually, 1,197 F-5A/B/C/D aircraft were manufactured.[27]

F-5E Tiger II

In the meantime, the Air Force had bailed the sixth F-5B (63-8445) to General Electric as a testbed for the more powerful YJ85-GE-21

The first N-156F (59-4987) at the 1962 Edwards air show with a French Nord AS20 air-to-surface missile on each wing and a larger AS30 on the centerline. These missiles were used by the British, French, German, South African, and Swiss air forces during the 1960s. Northrop demonstrated the early F-5s with a variety of weapons to increase its sales potential for various countries. (Terry Panopalis Collection)

engines, unofficially becoming the F-5B-21 demonstrator. The aircraft made its maiden flight with the new engines from the General Electric facility at Edwards on 28 March 1969, with General Electric test pilot John M. Fritz at the controls.[28]

On 26 February 1970, the Air Force released a request for proposals for an Advanced International Fighter (later changed to International Fighter Aircraft) to be the successor to the F-5A. Eight companies initially expressed interest, but only four actually submitted proposals: Ling-Temco-Vought with a lightweight development of the Navy F-8, Lockheed with a development of the F-104, McDonnell Douglas with a simplified version of the F-4, and Northrop with a J85-GE-21-powered F-5-21.[29]

The F-5-21 had larger air intakes, the fuselage was wider to accommodate the new J85-GE-21 engines, and rear-fuselage auxiliary louvered doors were added to prevent compressor starvation at low speeds. To enhance airflow over the wing at high angles of attack, the wing root leading-edge extensions (LEX) were enlarged. Compared to the F-5A, the new aircraft had a 23 percent improvement in sea-level rate of climb, a 7 percent improvement in instantaneous turn rate, a 17 percent improvement in sustained turn rate, and a 39 percent improvement in turn radius. Maximum speed increased from Mach 1.4 to Mach 1.6.[30]

On 20 November 1970, the Air Force awarded Northrop a fixed-price contract for 5 development and 325 production aircraft. These were designated F-5E on 28 December. Again, there would be no XF-5E or YF-5E, although the first two aircraft are generally called YF-5Es. The aircraft was named Tiger II after the nickname the F-5A acquired in Vietnam during Operation SKOSHI TIGER.[31]

The first F-5E (71-1417) was rolled out at Hawthorne on 23 June 1972 and made its maiden flight on 11 August 1972 with Hank Chouteau at the controls. The J85-GE-21 engines proved less reliable than had been hoped and led to flight-testing being suspended between

Northrop test pilot Dick Thomas took the first YF-5F (73-0889) on its maiden flight on 25 September 1974. Note the tiger head logo on the vertical stabilizer. (AFFTC History Office Collection)

19 September and 16 December. Although flight-testing resumed, the engines were not really ready until the end of April 1973. In the meantime, the second F-5E made its maiden flight on 29 December 1972.[32]

YF-5F

Northrop had not originally planned to offer a two-seat version of the Tiger II, but after initial flight-tests it became clear that the increased performance of the F-5E required a transition trainer. On 15 May 1973, the Air Force gained Congressional approval to evaluate a Northrop proposal for a combat-capable two-seater. The Air

There were no experimental or prototype F-5Es, and the first production aircraft (71-1417) was used for the test program. Hank Chouteau made the maiden flight on 11 August 1972. (Northrop Corporation)

The third YF-5F (73-0891) was used for spin testing at Edwards. Each side of the vertical stabilizer was a different color, as was each wing. This helped when reviewing films of the spins. (Dennis R. Jenkins)

The second F-20A (82-0063/N3986B) in its air defense fighter configuration carrying a pair of AIM-7 Sparrows under the wings and an AIM-9 Sidewinder on each wingtip. (Northrop Corporation)

The first F-20A (82-0062/N4416T) in its red and white paint scheme. This later gave way to a light grey. Although looking like earlier F-5s, the F-20A was a much more advanced fighter. (National Archives)

Force subsequently ordered three two-seat YF-5Fs (73-0889/891) as an amendment to the F-5E production contract.

Instead of squeezing in the second crewmember by pushing the front cockpit further forward in the nose (as had been done in the T-38 and F-5B), the entire fuselage was lengthened by 3.5 feet. The fire-control system was retained, and aside from the deletion of the starboard 20mm cannon, the F-5F retained the full combat capability of the single-seat F-5E. The first YF-5F made its maiden flight at Edwards on 25 September 1974, with Northrop test pilot Dick Thomas at the controls.[33]

Ultimately, more than 2,600 F-5s were built, including those manufactured under license in Canada, South Korea, Spain, Switzerland, and Taiwan. Over the years, F-5s have been operated by Austria, Bahrain, Botswana, Brazil, Canada, Chile, Ethiopia, Greece, Honduras, Indonesia, Iran, Jordan, Kenya, Libya, Malaysia, Mexico, Morocco, The Netherlands, Norway, The Philippines, Saudi Arabia, Singapore, South Korea, South Vietnam, Spain, Sudan, Switzerland, Taiwan, Thailand, Tunisia, Turkey, the United States (Air Force, Marines, and Navy), Venezuela, and Yeman.[34]

F-5G/F-20A

After the success of the F-5A and F-5E, in January 1980 Northrop embarked on the in-house development of a significantly improved aircraft. Northrop received approval for the development of the F-5G from the State Department, which issued a specification for an Intermediate Export Fighter and made it clear that there would be no financial help from the government. The new aircraft was intended to bring the F-5 series up-market from its original austere roots and offer performance comparable to the General Dynamics (now Lockheed Martin) F-16.

The F-5G drew heavily on a version of the F-5 that Northrop had designed, but never built, for Taiwan. The twin J85s of the F-5E were replaced by a single 16,000-lbf General Electric F404 turbofan. Although the new engine was heavier than the pair of J85s it replaced, the empty weight of the F-5G was only 17 percent greater than the F-5E but generated 60 percent more thrust. Therefore, the F-5G offered a significant increase in performance. The rear fuselage was narrower than the F-5E because of the powerplant change, but the longitudinal stability characteristics of the earlier F-5s were retained by adding a flat shelf on either side of the lower rear fuselage that provided the same shape as that of the twin-engine F-5. Internal fuel capacity was unchanged, but the lower specific fuel consumption of the F404 gave the F-5G a 10 percent increase in combat radius.[35]

The first F-20A was painted in German Luftwaffe markings (sort of) during an October 1983 sales campaign. This aircraft crashed in Korea on 10 October 1984, killing Darrell Cornell. (Dennis R. Jenkins Collection)

The Air Force was sufficiently interested that it ordered four F-5Gs (82-0062/065) for evaluation; again, there were no XF-5G or YF-5G aircraft. The first F-5G, carrying civil registration N4416T, made its maiden flight from Edwards on 30 August 1982, with Northrop test pilot Russell J. Scott at the controls. It achieved Mach 1.04 on its first flight.[36]

The Air Force had assigned it the F-5G designation mostly for political reasons since it implied the aircraft was simply an extension of proven design, one which had already been cleared for export. This avoided confusion with new fighters such as the McDonnell Douglas F-15 or General Dynamics F-16, which were kept off the foreign market to avoid arms proliferation. However, under the new administration of President Ronald Reagan, there was less reluctance to export advanced weapons, and it soon became clear that the F-16 would be made available for export. The F-5G designation was now thought to be a disadvantage, and Northrop requested a new designation.

In November 1982, the F-5G was redesignated F-20A and named Tigershark. Various references indicate that F-19 had been deliberately skipped at Northrop's request because the number 20 made for better advertising copy: "Northrop F-20: first of a new series of fighters …" The first order for F-20As was placed by Bahrain in early 1983, but the order for only four aircraft was too small to justify production. The F-20A was shown at the Paris Air Show in 1983 and at Farnborough in 1984 but failed to attract any further orders. Although the performance of the F-20A was attractive, it soon became obvious that nobody wanted to buy an aircraft that the United States military was not operating.[37]

By April 1983, work was well under way on the second F-20A (82-0063/N3986B), powered by the improved F404-GE-100 and fitted with the General Electric APG-67 radar. The aircraft made its maiden flight on 11 August 1983. The third F-20A (82-0064/N44671) made its maiden flight on 12 May 1984 and conducted numerous

All three F-20 prototypes in formation. Only the third aircraft survived the test (and sales) program and is currently on display at the California Science Center in Los Angeles. (Northrop Corporation)

The F-5G (F-20) mockup displayed a few differences from the three aircraft that were built. For instance, the leading edge extensions extended farther forward and the canopy was larger. (Northrop Corporation)

weapons trials including Sparrow missile launches and Harpoon anti-shipping missile compatibility tests.[38]

On 10 October 1984, Northrop test pilot Darrell Cornell was killed in the first F-20A while flying a demonstration at Suwon Air Base, Korea. Cornell had put the F-20A into a climbing roll with flaps and landing gear extended, when it stalled and crashed. Five months later, on 14 May 1985, the second F-20A crashed while performing a similar maneuver at Goose Bay, Labrador, killing Northrop test pilot David Barnes. The Canadian F-20A accident report ascribed g-induced pilot loss of consciousness as the cause. Neither report indicated any mechanical failure or design deficiency.[39]

By this time, the Air Force had settled on a high-low mix of fighters, with the F-15 filling the high end and the F-16 the low end. Therefore, an Air Force order for the F-20A was considered unlikely. However, it was becoming obvious that the F-15 and F-16 were becoming increasingly expensive. When the Air Force announced in April 1985 that it was seeking 270 Air Defense Fighters, Northrop proposed building F-20s at a cost of $15 million each. Unfortunately, the Air Force ultimately decided to modify 270 older F-16As as air defense fighters instead of ordering either F-20As or new F-16Cs.[40]

After having spent more than $1 billion, Northrop officially terminated the program on 17 November 1986. All work on the uncompleted fourth prototype was abandoned. The sole surviving F-20A now hangs in the California Science Center in Los Angeles.[41]

Chapter 11

Right: *The first Northrop YF-17 (72-1569) was an outstanding performer in the vertical, and was the first aircraft announced to have gone supersonic straight up (although the F-15 and F-16 had also accomplished the feat). The YF-17 was also the first American fighter to go supersonic in level flight without using an afterburner.* (NMUSAF Collection)

Below: *The McDonnell Douglas F-15A (72-0119), named Streak Eagle, was used to set eight world time-to-climb records between 16 January and February 1975. These flights showed the performance of the new generation of fighters, reaching 98,430 feet in 207.80 seconds.* (National Archives)

ANOTHER REVOLUTION
THE EAGLE AND VIPER

The Pratt & Whitney TF30 demonstrated that turbofan engines were the wave of the future and in the mid-1960s the Air Force began funding efforts to develop a second-generation high-performance afterburning turbofan. However, the unhappy TF30 experience led the Air Force to be more receptive to recreating the multiple, concurrent engine development programs that had routinely happened during the 1950s and 1960s.

The story begins with the formulation of requirements for new Navy (the VFX, ultimately the Grumman F-14), and Air Force (the F-X, which became the McDonnell Douglas F-15) fighters. The Department of Defense mandated that both aircraft use the same basic engine, the last remnants of the McNamara commonality philosophy. The new engine would be the first to use a new designation, F-for-Fan (turbofan), although oddly enough, the series began at 100 for the Air Force and 400 for the Navy.

The Air Force took the lead because the Aero Propulsion Laboratory had already initiated the Advanced Turbine Engine Gas Generator (ATEGG) demonstrator that brought together prototype components from Allison, General Electric, and Pratt & Whitney.

In 1967, the Air Force released a request for proposals for the Advanced Technology Engine in early 1968, and Allison, General Electric, and Pratt & Whitney submitted proposals. The Air Force selected General Electric and Pratt & Whitney to demonstrate prototype engines and in early 1970 selected the Pratt & Whitney JTF-22 as the F100 turbofan. Ironically, Pratt & Whitney won the competition at least in part because of its greater understanding of engine/inlet compatibility phenomena, which was acquired through years of problems with the TF30 on the F-111 (with yet more to come on the F-14A).

The F100 was an extremely innovative engine that pushed the limit of available technology, especially in exotic high-temperature materials. A tight Air Force schedule and budget left little room for dealing with the inevitable technical problems and cost growth. In June 1971, the Navy pulled out of the program because of continuing technical problems, further increasing cost because of a smaller production base. Unfortunately, the difficulties continued throughout flight-testing and the engine went into production before development was completed.

Continued problems with the F100 led the Air Force to fund an alternative engine development and production program for both the

The second-generation Pratt & Whitney F100 turbofan (shown), and its General Electric F110 competitor were the key to the phenomenal performance of the McDonnell F-15 and Lockheed Martin F-16. These engines provided the new generation of fighters with a thrust-to-weight ratio of greater than 1:1, allowing them to accelerate through the speed of sound while climbing vertical. (Pratt & Whitney)

F-15 and F-16. The obvious source was the losing General Electric entry in the Advanced Technology Engine competition, which had become the basis of the F101 selected to power the Rockwell International B-1 bomber. Learning from the F100 development problems, General Electric decided to assume less performance risk on its F101 and focus on reliability and maintainability. In 1979, the Air Force ordered further development of the F101, designated F110, as an alternative to the F100.

The Air Force had originally viewed its support of the F101 as a ploy to force Pratt & Whitney to be more responsive about fixing the F100. However, Congress soon entered the fray and mandated that the Air Force and Navy fund competitive engine programs to supplement both the TF30 and F100. By 1980, this had become the Alternate Fighter Engine program with the General Electric F110 and improved Pratt & Whitney F100-PW-220. Between 1984 and 1989, the Air Force competed the two engines against each other for new F-16 orders (but oddly, not the F-15). Each year, the engine buy was split between the two companies, but the percentage shares varied widely. Yet, at the end of the six years of the "Great Engine War," each contractor ended up receiving almost half of the total overall orders.

As early as 1965, the Air Force had begun concept formulation studies of new high-performance fighters to use the second-generation turbofans. These included the heavy F-X air-superiority fighter and the lightweight Advanced Day Fighter (ADF). The F-X was to be a 40,000-pound class fighter equipped with an advanced long-range radar and air-to-air missiles. The ADF was to be in the 25,000-pound range and was to better the performance of the MiG-21 by at least 25 percent. The general concept behind the ADF was much the same as had led to the Lockheed F-104.[1]

The appearance of the MiG-25 in 1967 (thought to be the MiG-23 at the time) prompted a redirection in Air Force fighter plans, with high performance becoming the primary concern. This accelerated work on the F-X and resulted in the ADF being temporarily shelved. The F-X emerged as the McDonnell Douglas F-15, procured without a competitive fly-off and with no experimental or prototype models being ordered. The ADF concept, however, was kept alive by former fighter instructor Maj. John Boyd and Pierre M. Sprey, a civilian working in the office of the Assistant Secretary of Defense for Systems Analysis.[2]

Deputy Defense Secretary David A. Packard (who came in with the Nixon Administration in 1969) was a strong advocate of returning to competitive prototyping as a way to control the costs of new weapons systems. During the 1960s, Secretary of Defense Robert S. McNamara had implemented the Total Procurement Package philosophy, in which an aircraft was committed to production even before the first example had flown and without any competitive fly-off against rival designs. The general idea was extremely similar to the unsuccessful Cook-Craigie concurrency concept in the 1950s, and had led to the controversial Lockheed C-5A and General Dynamics F-111 programs, which had both encountered expensive and time-consuming developmental problems and extensive cost overruns. The F-15 was already in development under the old scheme, so the ADF would be the first fighter to benefit from the Packard competitive prototyping process.

In the meantime, the ADF program was renamed Light Weight Fighter (LWF) to better reflect its position in the Air Force high-low fighter mix. The LWF request for proposals was released on 16 January 1971, and Boeing, General Dynamics, and Northrop ultimately responded. On 13 April 1972, the Air Force issued contracts for two General Dynamics YF-16s and two Northrop YF-17s.

The fly-off between the General Dynamics YF-16 and the Northrop YF-17 began as soon as flight-testing started and there was an attempt to get as many pilots as possible to fly both aircraft types. The prototypes never flew against each other, but they did fly against all current Air Force fighters as well as against MiG-17s and MiG-21s that had been acquired by the United States.

Within the Air Force, there was a strong institutional bias against the LWF, since it was perceived as a threat to the F-15, which was proving to be the most capable fighter in the world. To deflect this suspicion, the program was renamed yet again, this time as the Air Combat Fighter (ACF). In the meantime, the governments of Belgium, Denmark, Netherlands, and Norway had begun to consider possible replacements for their Lockheed F-104s, and the winner of the ACF contest in the United States would be the favored candidate.[3]

In the meantime, the Navy initiated the VFAX to explore a low-cost aircraft to supplement the Grumman F-14, which was suffering from cost overruns. In August 1974, Congress directed these efforts toward the Navy Air Combat Fighter (NACF) to be based on the Air Force ACF. In September 1974, the Navy announced that it would select a single contractor to begin engineering development of the NACF and requested bids from the industry. In response, on 27 September 1974, General Dynamics announced it was teaming with Ling-Temco-Vought to propose a variant of the YF-16, and Northrop teamed with McDonnell Douglas to promote a version of its YF-17. On 2 May 1975, the Navy announced that it had selected the Northrop proposal, which was eventually to emerge as the McDonnell Douglas F/A-18, although the one-time teammates spent a considerable amount of time in court arguing about work-share and intellectual property rights.

The first F-15A (71-0280) in final assembly showing the different materials used in construction. Note the 4,261st F-4 being manufactured in the background. (National Archives)

McDonnell F-15 Eagle

The Air Force released the F-X request for proposals on 30 September 1968, with Boeing, Fairchild-Republic, General Dynamics, Grumman, Lockheed, McDonnell Douglas, North American, and Northrop responding. On 23 December 1969, the Air Force announced that the McDonnell Douglas proposal had been selected. The F-15 was ordered "off the drawing board" without any XF-15 or YF-15 aircraft. The initial contract called for 20 full-scale development (FSD) aircraft – a preliminary batch of ten single-seat F-15As (71-0280/0289) and two TF-15A two-seaters (71-0290/0291) Category I versions, plus eight single-seat F-15A (72-0113/0120) Category II aircraft. McDonnell Douglas would conduct Category I flight tests, while Category II testing would be accomplished by an Air Force joint test force consisting of pilots from Air Systems Command and Tactical Air Command. These aircraft are frequently called YF-15s, but this was never an official designation. Several of the single seaters went to the Israeli Defense Force and the rest ended their careers as GF-15 ground instructional trainers. The two-seaters had much more interesting careers.[4]

The first F-15A (71-0280) was rolled out in St Louis on 26 June 1972, disassembled, loaded aboard a Lockheed C-5A, and transported to Edwards. The airplane made its maiden flight on 27 July 1972 with McDonnell test pilot Irving W. Burrows at the controls.[5]

By 29 October 1973, eleven F-15s had flown, reaching a maximum speed of Mach 2.3 and an altitude of 60,000 feet. Remarkably, especially given the performance offered by the aircraft, few significant problems were encountered during flight-testing and all 20 development aircraft survived. However, minor problems existed with buffeting and wing loading at certain altitudes, resulting in four square feet of the wingtip being removed. A flutter problem discovered during wind tunnel testing required a dogtooth be cut into the leading edge of the horizontal stabilizer. The dorsal airbrake was found to cause buffeting in the fully open position, resulting in its area being increased so that the required drag could be achieved with lower extension angles.[6]

The first production TF-15A (73-0108) was accepted by the 555th Tactical Fighter Training Squadron at Luke AFB on 4 November 1974 in a ceremony presided over by President Gerald R. Ford.[7]

During the winter of 1974-75, a surplus Cat II F-15A (72-0119) was used to set eight world time-to-climb records as Operation STREAK EAGLE. To save weight, all non-mission critical systems were deleted, including the flaps and the speedbrake, armament, radar, and the fire-control system. The paint was even stripped off, leaving an aircraft that weighed 1,800 pounds less than a stock F-15A. The flights were carried out at Grand Forks AFB, North Dakota, to take advantage of the cold temperatures. During the record attempts, only enough fuel was carried to make the specific flight and return to base. The aircraft broke eight existing time-to-climb records previously held by the F-4B and MiG-25. As an example, *Streak Eagle* climbed to 65,620 feet (20,000 meters) in 122.94 seconds (just over 2 minutes). The airplane eventually went to 98,430 feet (30,000 meters) in 207.80 seconds (3.46 minutes). Most of these records were later broken by the Soviet "P-42," which was a prototype for the Sukhoi Su-27 multi-role fighter.[8]

The first TF-15A (71-0290) has enjoyed a long career, including use as a control-configured demonstrator equipped with two different types of vectorable engine exhaust nozzles. (AFFTC History Office Collection)

McDonnell Douglas made a significant effort early in the program to sell the F-15 to international customers, but initially only Israel signed up. Here is the second TF-15A (71-0291) in French markings during a sales demonstration. More recently, the Strike Eagle variant has had significant international sales. (Dennis R. Jenkins)

The seventh F-15A (71-0286) with the seldom-seen outboard pylon carrying an ALQ-119 ECM pod. This station has some flutter issues and is not used operationally. (AFFTC History Office Collection)

General Dynamics YF-16 Fighting Falcon

The first YF-16 (72-1567) was rolled out at Fort Worth on 13 December 1973 and, after preliminary ground tests, was disassembled and transported to Edwards by a Lockheed C-5A on 8 January 1974. Its first flight was an unintended short hop around the pattern on 21 January 1974 at the hands of General Dynamics test pilot Phil Oestricher. During high-speed taxi tests, the empennage inadvertently scraped on the runway and caused a violent lateral oscillation. Oestricher decided to take off and regain control in the air, making a six-minute flight and uneventful landing. The scheduled maiden flight was delayed until a new right stabilator could be fitted and finally took place on 2 February 1974, with Oestricher at the controls. The second YF-16 (72-1568) made its maiden flight on 9 March 1974, with General Dynamics test pilot Neil R. Anderson at the controls.[9]

On 13 January 1975, Secretary of the Air Force John McLucas announced that the YF-16 had won the ACF contest, and the Air Force tentatively ordered 15 full-scale development (FSD) aircraft. McLucas indicated that lower operating costs, longer range, and better transient maneuverability had won the competition. Another advantage, as far as the Air Force was concerned, was that the F-16 used the same F100 engine as the McDonnell Douglas F-15.[10]

The second YF-16 had been scheduled to go to the Paris Air Show in 1975. However, before it could go, it was damaged when Neil Anderson made a belly landing in the grass beside the Carswell AFB runway next to the General Dynamic plant. Although only slightly damaged, the aircraft eventually ended up in non-flying test duties at Rome Air Development Center in New York.[11]

In its place, the first YF-16 made a transatlantic sales tour to potential NATO customers, and briefly visited the Paris Air Show. On 7 June 1975, armed with the assurance of an Air Force commitment to the type, Belgium, Netherlands, Denmark, and Norway announced that they would acquire the F-16 as a replacement for the F-104.[12]

In December 1975, the first YF-16 was rebuilt into a Control Configured Vehicle (CCV) with twin canted-canards underneath the air intake. This was a follow-on to the YF-4E/CCV program. The flight controls were modified to use the wing trailing edge flaperons acting in combination with the all-moving stabilator to allow the aircraft to maneuver in one plane without movement in another.

The YF-16/CCV flew for the first time on 16 March 1976, piloted by General Dynamics test pilot David J. Thigpen. On 24 June 1976, the airplane was damaged in a crash landing after its engine failed during a landing approach. The aircraft was repaired, and the flight test program resumed. On 31 June 1977 the YF-16/CCV made the last of its 87 flights for a total of 125 hours. The first YF-16 was restored to its original prototype configuration and is now on display at the Hampton Roads History Center in Virginia.[13]

YF-16A

The original order for 15 full-scale development aircraft was reduced to six single-seat YF-16As (75-0745/0750) and a pair of two-seat YF-16Bs (75-0751/0752). The full-scale development aircraft were 13 inches longer than the YF-16 to accommodate the Westinghouse APG-66 radar and additional fuel. The wing area was increased by 20 square feet, and an additional underwing hardpoint was fitted.

The first YF-16A made its maiden flight on 8 December 1976 with Neil Anderson at the controls. The first two-seat YF-16B (the fourth FSD aircraft) made its maiden flight on 8 August 1977, with Neil Anderson and Phil Oestricher in the cockpit. The flight test program, like that of the F-15, was remarkably uneventful.

After the completion of the flight-test program, the first airplane was modified as the F-16/101 with a General Electric F101 engine; it is currently on display at Wright-Patterson AFB marked as a production F-16A (79-0317). The second YF-16A is in storage at the Lockheed facility in Fort Worth. The third and fifth aircraft were modified with

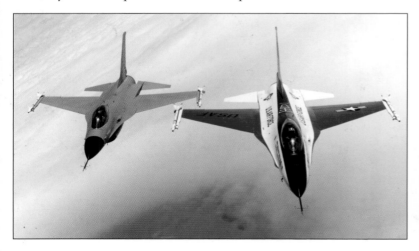

The first two YF-16As seen during 1977. The "broken sky" camouflage on the second YF-16 had not worked well, so most of the FSD aircraft used the overall light grey shown here. (National Archives)

The second YF-16 (72-1568) carrying a quartet of AIM-7 Sparrow missiles on 11 January 1975. For some reason the YF-16s and YF-17s carried non-standard serial numbers with a leading zero. (National Archives)

As is becoming a tradition, Ronald Stephano came up with a caricature for this book. The painting depicts the second YF-16 (72-1568) in front of the old Edwards AFB control tower. (Original Artwork by Ronald Stephano, ©2007)

The second YF-16 shortly after its roll-out in Ft. Worth. As delivered, the aircraft wore an innovative "broken sky" camouflage that combined a light blue (similar to the Air Superiority Blue worn by the early F-15s) with patches of white that were supposed to resemble clouds. The paint scheme was not deemed effective and was soon replaced by an overall light grey and later by red, white, and blue. (National Archives)

cranked-arrow wings as F-16XLs, and both were subsequently transferred to NASA. The fourth YF-16A is on display at the Air Force Academy. The last YF-16A was modified as an Advanced Fighter Technology Integration (AFTI) demonstrator, and the aircraft is currently stored at the National Museum of the U.S. Air Force.[14]

The first YF-16B is on display at Edwards AFB, and the second aircraft was modified as a Wild Weasel demonstrator and later as the export-intended F-16/79 with a General Electric J79 engine.

F-16XL

In 1977, Harry Hillaker at General Dynamics began the F-16 SCAMP (Supersonic Cruise and Maneuver Prototype) program to demonstrate the applicability of supersonic transport technologies to military aircraft. Working closely with the NASA Langley Research Center, the company used in-house funds for wind-tunnel testing and a preliminary design effort. In February 1980, General Dynamics proposed fitting a radically modified wing to one of the YF-16As to validate what had been learned in the wind tunnel. The "cranked-arrow" wing doubled the standard F-16 wing area and would hopefully allow supersonic cruise performance.[15]

In late 1980, the Air Force agreed to a cooperative test program and provided the third and fifth YF-16As for modification into F-16XL prototypes. The first F-16XL was converted from the fifth YF-16A (75-0749) using a Pratt & Whitney F100 turbofan. It flew for the first time on 3 July 1982, with General Dynamics test pilot James A. McKinney at the controls. The second F-16XL was originally the third FSD F-16A (75-0747) that had been damaged in a landing accident. It was modified with a two-seat F-16B cockpit and used a General Electric F110 turbofan. It first flew on 29 October 1982, piloted by General Dynamics test pilots Alex Wolf and Jim McKinney.[16]

The first YF-16 (72-1567) and first YF-17 (72-1569) during the competition. One selling point for the F-16 was that it used the same engine as the F-15, simplifying logistics and lowering cost. (National Archives)

In March 1981, the Air Force announced that it would be developing a new tactical fighter to replace the F-111 in the low-level interdiction role. The competition was limited to aircraft already flying and included the crank-arrow General Dynamics F-16XL and a modified McDonnell Douglas F-15 called Strike Eagle. In February 1984, the Air Force announced that it had selected the McDonnell Douglas entry as the F-15E.

The first full-scale development YF-16A (75-0745) wore the same paint scheme used by the first YF-16 during the competition. The flags of the initial customers were painted under the canopy. (National Archives)

Late in its career, as part of a series of tests for the Joint Strike Fighter, the last YF-16A (75-0750) was the first aircraft to fly with all-electric flight-control actuation and no mechanical backup. (National Archives)

The second F-16XL (75-0747) wore a Ferris deceptive paint scheme for a period. This is the bottom – note the false canopy (with helmets!) and refueling receptacle outline. (AFFTC History Office Collection)

After the loss to McDonnell Douglas, both F-16XLs were placed in storage at Fort Worth, having made 437 and 361 flights, respectively. Although supersonic cruise without afterburner had been an original goal of the F-16XL program, the aircraft never achieved this feat.[17]

In late 1988, the F-16XLs were turned over to the NASA Dryden Flight Research Center to evaluate aerodynamics concepts to improve wing airflow during sustained supersonic flight. The first F-16XL was delivered to NASA on 9 March 1989. It was subsequently fitted with an active suction titanium glove encasing the left wing that had thousands of 0.0025-inch-diameter laser-cut holes intended to suck away turbulent airflow over the wing, restoring laminar flow and reducing drag. NASA later used this aircraft in a sonic boom research project with an SR-71 and in a Cranked-Arrow Wing Aerodynamics Project (CAWAP) to test boundary layer pressures and distribution. In 1997, NASA replaced the analog fly-by-wire flight-control system with a digital system and planned to use the aircraft as a testbed for autonomous systems to be employed in spacecraft. Funding for this project never materialized, and the aircraft was placed in storage at Dryden.[18]

The second F-16XL was modified with a passive fiberglass and foam glove on the right wing and an active glove on the left wing to test supersonic laminar flow. The second F-16XL flew 45 times between 13 October 1995 and 26 November 1996. NASA research pilot Dana D. Purifoy flew 38 of the missions, with NASA research pilot Mark P. Stucky flying the others.[19]

After sitting in storage for a decade, in 2007 NASA proposed using the first F-16XL to conduct a variety of propulsion related tests. On 29 June 2007, for the first time in seven years, the first F-16XL moved under its own power. Using a spare F-15 engine, it was taxied from the Dryden ramp to the Edwards tower and back as a final systems check. It remains to be seen if funding can be found to fly the aircraft.[20]

The first F-16XL (75-0749) on 18 August 1982. Note the semi-conformal stub pylons used to carry the bombs. Four AIM-7s and two AIM-9s could be carried with any weapon load. (AFFTC History Office Collection)

The first F-16XL in its striking black, white, and gold paint scheme used at the NASA Dryden Flight Research Center. Note that the aircraft does not have an engine installed. (NASA Dryden)

Northrop YF-17 Cobra

The first YF-17A (72-1569) was rolled out at Hawthorne on 4 April 1974, and was trucked over the foothills to Edwards. The aircraft made its 61-minute maiden flight on 9 June 1974 with Northrop test pilot Henry E. "Hank" Chouteau at the controls. On 11 June, the YF-17 became the first American fighter to exceed the speed of sound in level flight without using an afterburner. The second YF-17A made its maiden flight on 21 August 1974, again piloted by Chouteau. During the course of the flight tests, the YF-17 was found to perform well and generally in accordance with the Northrop performance guarantees. The last flights of the competition were in mid-December 1974.[21]

Although the Northrop contender demonstrated remarkable handling qualities and was actually superior in certain areas, on 13 January 1975, Secretary of the Air Force John McLucas announced that the YF-16 had been selected as the winner of the ACF contest. The YF-16 was a little faster than the YF-17 and its F100 engine was used in the F-15, simplifying logistics and, in theory, lowering procurement costs through larger quantities. The J101 engine was a new, relatively untried powerplant that would require enormous investment in tooling, spare parts, and documentation. In addition, the YF-16 had better specific fuel consumption and cost $250,000 less per aircraft. The YF-16 was also, according to reports, the near unanimous choice of the pilots.[22]

That might have been the end of the line for the Northrop design, but on 2 May 1975 the Navy announced that it had selected the Northrop-McDonnell Douglas version of the YF-17 to become the F/A-18. The Navy liked the two-engine design, its apparent mission adaptability, and the airframe's inherent room for growth. The second YF-17 was earmarked for development work as the "F-18 prototype," although a real F/A-18 did not fly until 18 November 1978. Despite

Part of the NASA Dryden test fleet in 1976. From the left, one of the Lockheed F-104Ns (N812NA), the eighth F-15A (72-0287) that had been used for spin tests, and the first YF-17A (72-1569). (NASA Dryden)

the superficial resemblance to the YF-17, the F/A-18 does not share a single dimension and is a completely different aircraft.[23]

During the LWF/ACF program, the two YF-17s logged 288 flights that totaled 345.5 hours, including 13 hours at supersonic speeds. The first prototype is currently on display at the Western Museum of Flight in Hawthorne, California, and the second is on display at the U.S. Naval Aviation Museum in Pensacola, Florida.[24]

The first YF-17 on 11 June 1976 as it is readied for its 200th flight. Note the "YF-1776" on the fuselage spine. By this time the aircraft had been turned over to the Navy for the F-18 program. (NASA Dryden)

The first YF-17 drops a 2,000-pound bomb over the Edwards range. The YF-17 proved to be a stable and accurate weapons platform in both air-to-air and air-to-ground modes. (National Archives)

A Boeing KC-97L (52-0903) refuels the second YF-16 while the first YF-16 and first YF-17 await their turn on 30 October 1974. The piston-powered KC-97 would be largely retired before the F-16 entered operational service. (AFFTC History Office Collection)

The second YF-17 (72-1570) in the two-tone camouflage worn during the competition. Note the large spin recovery parachute container on the fuselage between the vertical stabilizers. (National Archives)

The "F-18 Prototype" was the second YF-17 used for limited testing and several promotional (i.e., sales) campaigns after the end of the LWF/ACF competition before a real F/A-18 became available. (National Archives)

Chapter 12

Left: *The Boeing X-32B STOVL variant made its maiden flight on 29 March 2001, with Boeing test pilot Dennis O'Donoghue at the controls of a 50-minute conventional flight from Palmdale to Edwards AFB.* (U.S. Air Force)

Below: *The two Northrop YF-23s together over Edwards on 29 November 1990. The dark grey first aircraft (called PAV-1, 87-800) is at the top while the lighter grey PAV-2 (87-801) is at the bottom.* (Northrop Grumman)

THE STEALTH GENERATION
HIDING IN PLAIN SIGHT

In 1974, the Defense Advanced Research Projects Agency (DARPA) requested several aerospace companies to study what reduction in radar cross-section (RCS) was necessary to ensure the survival of an aircraft in a high-threat environment, particularly around the Warsaw Pact and Soviet Union. Fairchild-Republic, General Dynamics, Grumman, McDonnell Douglas, and Northrop were asked to participate, although Fairchild and Grumman declined due to a shortage of available engineering resources. General Dynamics reported that it did not believe RCS reduction alone could achieve the results the agency was looking for and asked DARPA to consider active jamming along with RCS reduction. DARPA was unwilling to compromise, and General Dynamics bowed out.

This left Northrop and McDonnell Douglas, both of which were awarded $100,000 study contracts. Hughes Aircraft, which contrary to its name does not build aircraft, but rather the radar systems that equip them, was also funded to evaluate various aspects of the study. It should be noted that the magnitude of the problem was large. In order to reduce the detection range by a factor of 10, the RCS of the target has to be reduced by a factor of 10,000. Previous efforts had managed RCS reductions of less than 50 percent – barely noticeable in real terms. These initial studies were classified confidential, the lowest of the three security levels (confidential, secret, and top secret).[1]

Lockheed had not been asked to participate simply because nobody thought the company was still in the tactical aircraft business. The F-104 was the last fighter that had been produced by Lockheed, and production had ended almost 10 years earlier. However, when Kelly Johnson found out about the studies, he approached the CIA for permission to brief DARPA on the RCS-reduction techniques tried on the U-2 and A-12. Since the aircraft were public knowledge by this time, the CIA voiced no particular objections, and DARPA soon included Lockheed in the studies.

The McDonnell Douglas concept relied too heavily on active jamming and was eliminated early in the process, resulting in Lockheed and Northrop being selected on 1 November 1975 for Phase I of the Experimental Survivable Testbed (XST) program.[2] This would involve building full-scale models of their designs for testing at a radar measuring facility, designing an actual flight vehi-cle, flight-control simulation, and wind-tunnel testing. Building an actual prototype was part of Phase II.

The final tests revealed that the Lockheed design enjoyed a slight edge over the Northrop concept from most directions, including the all-important frontal aspect. In itself, this was probably not enough to swing the decision, but combined with Skunk Works' known track record with "black" (secret) projects and experience with advanced composite materials, there was a consensus that Lockheed was most likely to succeed. In April 1976, Lockheed was awarded a $19.2 million Phase II contract to cover the manufacture of two Have Blue flight demonstrators. Lockheed would contribute up to $10 million of its own money to the program (Northrop had agreed to do the same). In the end, Have Blue cost a total of $43 million; $10.4 million from Lockheed and the rest from the U.S. government.

Program management for Phase II was transferred from DARPA to the Air Force, which promptly imposed a "special access" classification on the program, meaning that little would be known outside of those directly involved. Even budget requests would be hidden in such a manner that the majority of Congress and the Office of Management and Budget would not know the Have Blue demonstrators were being developed. Special access is above and beyond the normal three-tier classification levels, and essentially these programs do not exist.

The Pratt & Whitney F119 is a third-generation turbofan engine designed for the Lockheed F-22. One key to the performance of the new fighter is the two-dimensional thrust vectoring nozzle. (Pratt & Whitney)

Lockheed Stealth Fighter

If you accept the premise that it was logical to designate the Lockheed stealth fighter the F-117, then the Have Blue demonstrators that preceded it should logically have been called XF-117s, and the full-scale development (FSD) aircraft should have been YF-117As. Of course, bureaucratic logic was not high on the stealth program's priority list, so that is not the way it happened, and there were no XF-117 or YF-117 aircraft.

Have Blue Demonstrators

The word demonstrator is important. Have Blue was never intended to produce an operational aircraft, or even a true prototype of one. The project was meant simply to demonstrate the concept of radically altering the shape of an aircraft could achieve a significant reduction in radar cross section and that the resulting aircraft could actually fly. The aircraft were never assigned an official designation or Air Force serial numbers. Internally they were known as HB1001 (BLUE-01) and HB1002 (BLUE-02).[3]

By November 1977, the first aircraft had been completed and powered up inside the hangar at Burbank where it was built. On 16 November, the aircraft was partially disassembled, loaded into a Lockheed C-5A, and transported to the old U-2 base at Groom Lake, north of Las Vegas. Once at Groom Lake, the aircraft conducted four taxi tests before making its maiden flight on 1 December 1977, with Lockheed test pilot William C. "Bill" Park at the controls. It had only been 20 months since Lockheed had been awarded the Have Blue contract. The two J85s did not really provide sufficient power for the rather heavy demonstrator, and its aerodynamic performance was mediocre, at best. Nevertheless, Have Blue quickly proved that the shape could fly.[4]

Flight tests of the Have Blue initially went fairly smoothly, but on 4 May 1978, HB1001 landed excessively hard, jamming the right main landing gear in a semi-retracted position. Bill Park pulled the aircraft back into the air, and tried to shake the gear back down. After his third attempt failed, he took the aircraft up to 10,000 feet and ejected. As he exited the aircraft, Park hit his head and was knocked unconscious. Unable to control his parachute during landing, Park severely injured his back on impact. The aircraft was written off, and Bill Park was forced to retire from flying as a result.

The second Have Blue made its maiden flight on 20 July 1978, with Maj. Norman "Ken" Dyson at the controls. This aircraft did not have the flight-test instrument boom or spin-recovery parachute, and it was covered with radar absorbing material (RAM) to minimize its radar signature. HB1002 proved to be essentially undetectable by airborne radars except the Boeing E-3 AWACS, which could only acquire the aircraft at short ranges. Most ground-based missile-tracking radars could detect the Have Blue only after it was well inside the minimum range of their surface-to-air missiles. It was found that the best tactic to avoid radar detection was to approach the radar site head on, presenting the Have Blue's small nose-on signature.[5]

The first HAVE BLUE on the ramp at the Nevada test site with "Nice" Mike Kammerer in the cockpit. The camouflage paint scheme was just one of many that were tested on the two HAVE BLUE prototypes during the course of the program. (Lockheed Martin)

The only known photo of the Northrop XST pole model taken at the Air Force Radar Target Scatter (RATSCAT) facility in New Mexico in February 1976. The Northrop model had a significantly higher radar cross-section (RCS) than the Lockheed design. (Northrop)

Originally the program had scheduled 55 flights for the second aircraft, but on 11 July 1979, during its 52nd flight, the aircraft suffered a double hydraulic failure and fire. Ken Dyson successfully ejected and was not injured, but the aircraft was a total loss. Since the project was winding down in any case, the loss of the aircraft had minimal impact. Both Have Blues were buried somewhere on the Groom Lake reservation.

F-117A

On 10 October 1977, even before the first Have Blue had flown, DARPA awarded Lockheed a contract to explore possible production versions. The results of these studies were sufficiently promising that the Air Force issued a development contract on 16 November 1977 under the name Senior Trend. Although initially based on the Have Blue configuration, Senior Trend rapidly diverged in several important ways. First, the wing sweep was reduced to solve the center-of-gravity problems experienced during wind-tunnel testing (and subsequent flight testing) of the Have Blue design. The forward fuselage was made shorter to allow the pilot and planned sensors to have a better view over the nose. However, the most visible change was that the vertical stabilizers canted outboard from the centerline instead of canting inboard from the outer parts of the body.[6]

Unlike the Have Blue designs, which had carried minimal equipment, the Senior Trend was intended to be an operational attack aircraft. Provisions were made for a pair of weapons bays under the fuselage and sensors in the nose. Each of the weapons bays was sized to accommodate a single 2,000-pound laser-guided bomb, although other weapons could be carried, including a B61 tactical nuclear weapon. When Senior Trend emerged from the black world, it wore the unlikely F-117 designation.

The initial order was for five full-scale development (FSD) aircraft, although the Tactical Air Command quickly established a requirement for 20 production versions. Some reports have called the FSD aircraft YF-117As, but there is no official confirmation of this. Ultimately, 59 F-117As were manufactured.[7]

When the Senior Trend program had begun, it was expected that the first aircraft would fly in July 1980. However, Lockheed ran into some difficulties assembling the aircraft, and the program ran a year behind schedule. In May 1981, the first Senior Trend (Lockheed number 780) was finally shipped to Groom Lake inside a Lockheed C-5A, much like the Have Blues before it. Ground testing revealed serious fuel leaks, delaying the first flight by several weeks. Finally, on 18 June 1981, Lockheed test pilot Harold "Hal" Farley, Jr. took the first Senior Trend on its maiden flight.

During initial flight testing it was noted that directional stability was less than ideal, and after the tenth flight the aircraft was modified with larger vertical stabilizers. The second aircraft made its maiden flight on 24 September 1981, also with the small verticals, but received the larger units after its fourth flight. The last FSD aircraft (784) made its maiden flight on 10 April 1982.

The first F-117A (780) in the light grey paint it wore for most of its flight-test career. The five pitot tubes on the nose show up well from this angle, as do the engine exhausts. (Lockheed Martin photo by Les Keute)

There has been a great deal of controversy over the serial numbers of the Senior Trend aircraft. The first aircraft was simply called "780," seemingly a reference to its originally planned first flight date. Subsequent aircraft were sequentially numbered through 844. However, it appears that bureaucracy got the better of the program after it emerged from the black world, and the sequential numbers were converted to serial numbers (by simply assigning a fiscal year prefix to them) after the fact. Most Air force documentation now lists them as standard "FY-xxxx" serial numbers beginning with 79-1780, and this is what is currently seen painted on the tail of each aircraft. Interestingly, the new serial numbers span five fiscal years, but the last three digits remain in sequence, an unlikely occurrence.

Advanced Tactical Fighter

In 1969-70, even before the F-15, F-16, and A-10 had entered service, the Tactical Air Command began exploring what their successors might look like. This led to a 1971 study of an Advanced Tactical Fighter (ATF), sometimes also called the Advanced Offensive Strike Fighter (AOSF). In early 1975, the Air Force Systems Command developed a plan to conduct a fly-off between two sets of ATF prototypes, but there were no funds available for such an effort.[8]

In 1978, the Air Force defined two projects, the near-term Enhanced Tactical Fighter (ETF) and the longer-term Advanced Tactical Attack System (ATAS). Initially, the emphasis would be on the ground-attack mission, since it was assumed that the F-15 and F-16 would be able to maintain air superiority for the foreseeable future. These programs morphed into the competition that ultimately resulted in the McDonnell Douglas F-15E.

However, the appearance of a new generation of Soviet fighters resulted in the Air Force also initiating the Advanced Tactical Fighter

(ATF) program for a general-purpose fighter capable of air-to-ground and air-to-air missions. In June 1981, the first request for information (RFI) for the Advanced Tactical Fighter was issued and seven companies, Boeing, General Dynamics, Grumman, Lockheed, McDonnell Douglas, Northrop, and Rockwell, responded.[9]

A request for proposals was issued in May 1983 for the concept definition investigation (CDI) phase of the ATF program. In September 1983, nine-month, $1 million concept-definition contracts were issued to the seven companies that had responded to the RFI with 19 conceptual designs ranging from lightweight fighters smaller than the F-16 to heavyweight aircraft larger than the YF-12A.

Once again, the primary competitors for the engine contract were General Electric and Pratt & Whitney. Ironically, it can be argued that the companies switched strategies compared to those used in the "Great Engine War" competition for the F-16. In view of the painful developmental problems that had plagued both the TF30 and F100 programs, Pratt & Whitney emphasized lower-risk technology and high reliability at a slight cost in performance. Yet General Electric had lost the previous initial FX/VFX competition to in part because of the perceived technological virtuosity of the Pratt & Whitney design. General Electric was then forced to struggle for more than 10 years to reenter the high-end fighter engine market, which it finally did by stressing the reliability and simplicity of its F110 and F404 engines. This time, General Electric management was determined to win the initial competition and concluded that it could do so by demonstrating very high performance and unparalleled technological sophistication.

In September 1983, General Electric and Pratt & Whitney were awarded contracts to develop 30,000-lbf ground-test engines with two-dimensional nozzles and the ability to supercruise. These demonstrator prototypes did not have to meet the weight requirements necessary for flight-testing and had no particular fuel consumption goals. The Pratt & Whitney XF119 focused on technical issues such as reducing the number of compressor stages to lower costs, reduce weight, and increase reliability. The General Electric XF120 moved ahead using a more complex variable-cycle concept with a vaneless interface between the high-pressure and low-pressure turbines. Both designs employed counter-rotating spools.

Initially, the Air Force wanted to develop the ATF through a "Demonstration and Validation" (Dem/Val) process rather than by having a competitive fly-off like the YF-16/YF-17. The Dem/Val phase would include mockups, wind tunnel testing, radar cross-section testing – everything short of building a flyable prototype. On 8 October 1985, the Air Force released a request for proposals for the Dem/Val phase to the seven contractors that had taken part in the CDI phase. The winner of the Dem/Val phase would be awarded a full-scale development contract for a flyable prototype.[10]

In May 1986, the Air Force changed its mind and announced that instead of proceeding toward a single contractor at the end of the Dem/Val phase, two contractors would build a pair of demonstrators for a competitive fly-off for the FSD contract. The Packard Commission had advocated flight testing prototypes in military procurements, and the Air Force was under strong pressure to accept the

recommendation since the memories of cost overruns and delays in the Lockheed C-5A and General Dynamics F-111 were still fresh.[11]

The decision to fly competitive prototypes also affected the engine manufacturers. This meant redesigning the demonstrator engines to flight-weight standards. This became even more complex in 1987, when the two airframe contractors concluded they needed more powerful 35,000-lbf engines. Given the lateness of the emerging requirements, the engine contractors were allowed considerable latitude on what would be demonstrated on the ground versus in flight.[12]

The Pratt & Whitney YF119 flight demonstrator was only slightly different from the XF119 ground demonstrator and did not meet the higher thrust requirement. The General Electric YF120 engine, by comparison, was far closer to its proposed FSD design, including meeting the 35,000-lbf requirements. Because of these different approaches, both the Lockheed YF-22 and the Northrop YF-23 demonstrators ultimately showed higher performance with the General Electric engine than with the Pratt & Whitney engine.

On 28 July 1986, the five remaining airframe companies (Grumman and Rockwell had dropped out for various reasons) submitted their proposals to the Air Force. While the proposals were being written, the contractors began a multi-billion dollar kabuki dance in an attempt to team with other competitors to ensure each company would retain a piece of the action. Lockheed teamed with Boeing and General Dynamics, while Northrop chose its arch-friend, McDonnell Douglas, despite pending court cases over F/A-18 work share. In each case, whichever company's proposal was selected by the Air Force would become the leader of the consortium, with the other teammates receiving work-share based on complex formulas and agreements.[13]

Whether it was planned, or if it just worked out that way, the two winning designs were from different consortia. On 31 October 1986, the Air Force awarded Dem/Val contracts to Lockheed for the YF-22 and Northrop for the YF-23. Each company would build two demonstrators, one powered by Pratt & Whitney F119s and the other by General Electric F120s. However, the Air Force did not consider the competition to be a performance "fly-off" but rather a demonstration of the technical and management capability needed to meet the program objectives with the least technical risk and lowest cost. At the completion of the competition, one of the teams would be awarded a full-scale development contract (a term soon replaced by engineering, manufacturing, and development – EMD). Each team was allocated $691 million, which included $100 million for radar and electro-optical sensor development and $200 million for avionics development.[14]

On 23 April 1991, Secretary of the Air Force Donald Rice announced that Lockheed and Pratt & Whitney had been selected to proceed into the EMD phase. It appears that Lockheed and Pratt & Whitney won because their proposals represented lower technical risk and lower cost. General Electric's variable-cycle approach and vaneless interface concepts were perceived as new technical approaches that were less than fully proven and complex, and brought increased technical risk. Although detailed comparisons between the YF-22 and the YF-23 are still classified, the consensus is that the YF-23 was the faster and stealthier of the two designs, particularly from the side and the rear.

Lockheed Martin YF-22

Lockheed would seem to be an unlikely entrant into the ATF competition, and even less likely to have won since the company had not mass-produced a fighter since the F-104. However, the Advanced Development Projects Division, better known as the Skunk Works, had made a series of breakthroughs in low-observables technology during the mid-1970s that had culminated in the F-117A. Boeing also seemed an unlikely entrant in the ATF contest since it had never built a manned supersonic aircraft nor a jet fighter, although it had a wealth of production experience with commercial airliners. General Dynamics, on the other hand, had successfully developed the F-111 and F-16, bringing a wealth of recent fighter experience.

Since the Lockheed proposal won the competition, it became the leader of the consortium. Skunk Works assumed responsibility for the overall design of the YF-22, and would manufacture the forward fuselage and cockpit. It would also handle most of the specialized stealth development and final assembly in its facility at Palmdale, California. Boeing would build the wings and the aft fuselage, while General Dynamics would handle the center fuselage, weapons bays, empennage, and undercarriage.[15]

The first YF-22 was rolled out in Palmdale on 29 August 1990. Rather unusually, the aircraft bore civilian registry N22YF rather than its Air Force serial number (87-0700). Neither YF-22 carried radar, nor were they equipped with the M61 20mm cannon. However, they were capable of carrying and launching AIM-9 Sidewinder and AIM-120 AMRAAM missiles, unlike the competing Northrop YF-23. The first aircraft made its maiden flight, a short hop from Palmdale to Edwards, on 29 September 1990, with Lockheed test pilot David L. Ferguson at the controls. The aircraft went supersonic on 25 October during the ninth test flight, and the first aerial refueling was on the 11th flight on 26 October. In early November 1990, the first YF-22 attained Mach 1.58 without using afterburners.[16]

The second YF-22 (87-0701/N22YX) shows that almost the entire underside of the fuselage was taken up by weapons bay or landing gear doors, all with serrated edges to reduce the RCS. (Lockheed Martin)

The second YF-22 (87-0701/N22YX) followed on 30 October, with Lockheed test pilot Tom Morgenfeld at the controls. The weapons bay doors were opened in flight for the first time on 20 November, and on 28 November Jon Beesley fired an AIM-9M Sidewinder over China Lake during the 11th flight. This was followed by Morgenfeld firing an AIM-120 AMRAAM over the Pacific Missile Range on 20 December. These were the only missiles fired during the Dem/Val phase.[17]

The first thrust-vectoring was performed by Dave Ferguson in the first YF-22 on 15 November 1990. With two-dimensional thrust vectoring, the aircraft could achieve supersonic roll and pitch rates

The first YF-22 (87-0700/N22YF) was used for spin testing and was equipped with a large, orange recovery parachute container between the vertical stabilizers. (Lockheed Martin)

Jon Beesley launched an AIM-9 Sidewinder from the second YF-22 over the China Lake range on 28 November 1990. This aircraft also launched an AIM-120 three weeks later. (Lockheed Martin)

The two YF-22 prototypes were easy to tell apart – the first aircraft (87-0700/N22YF) had red, white, and blue stripes on the vertical stabilizer, while the second aircraft (87-0701/N22YX) had blue, white, and red stripes (the reverse order). In addition, the first aircraft used an italic font for the "YF-22" on the tail, while the second YF-22 used a roman font. (AFFTC History Office Collection)

better than those achievable by earlier fighters at subsonic speeds. At speeds above Mach 1.4, the two-dimensional nozzles improved turning rates about 35 percent.[18] Optimal supercruise speed was Mach 1.58 for the YF120-powered N22YF and Mach 1.43 for the YF119-powered N22YX. With afterburning, both aircraft could exceed Mach 2 at 50,000 feet. It should be noted that supercruise, in itself, is not a new development. The Convair B-58 was capable of maintaining Mach 1 without afterburner at some altitudes, but required afterburners to break through the transonic flight regime. Similarly, the F-15 and YF-17 had already demonstrated the ability to go supersonic without using afterburners, although neither aircraft could sustain a supersonic cruise without reheat.[19]

On 23 April 1991, the Air Force announced that Lockheed and Pratt & Whitney had won the Dem/Val phase, and on 3 August 1991, the Air Force formally awarded engineering, manufacturing, and development (EMD) contracts to the two companies.[20]

The second YF-22 with its YF119 engines resumed flying on 30 October 1991, with Tom Morgenfeld at the controls. Lockheed intended to add about 100 hours to expand the envelope and explore some flight regimes in greater detail. Unfortunately, after about 60 hours, the YF-22 was involved in an accident on 25 April 1992 when it belly-flopped onto the runway after 8 seconds of violent pilot-induced oscillations. It slid several thousand feet down the runway and caught fire, destroying some 25 percent of the airframe. Tom Morgenfeld was uninjured, but the aircraft was too badly damaged for economical repair. At the time of the accident, the aircraft had logged 100.4 flight hours. The aircraft was ultimately rebuilt, but not to flight standards, and became an antenna testbed at the Rome Air Development Center.[21]

The General Electric-powered first aircraft was stripped of its engines and moved to the Lockheed Martin plant in Marietta, Georgia, for use as an engineering mockup. It was subsequently transferred to the Air Force Museum where it is currently on display.

Northrop YF-23

Although Northrop and McDonnell Douglas had unchallenged technical credentials, their teaming seemed odd since they were still involved in various lawsuits concerning work share and intellectual property rights on the F/A-18 program. Nevertheless, the teaming agreement held that Northrop would perform most of the design and engineering work, systems integration, final assembly, construction of the aft fuselage and empennage, and the development of the defensive avionics and flight-control system. McDonnell Douglas would produce the forward and center fuselage, the landing gear, and the wings, along with the development of the fuel and armament systems and offensive avionics.[22]

The two YF-23s were more bare bones than their Lockheed counterparts. To save money, the main landing gear used modified F/A-18 components and the nose gear was from an F-15. The cockpit was from an F-15, and the big-screen monitors proposed for production aircraft were not fitted. Northrop did not redesign the aft fuselage when the Air Force dropped the thrust-reverser requirement, and the engine bays were broader and deeper than that planned for production aircraft. Northrop did not plan to do high-angle-of-attack maneuvers with the prototypes, but wind-tunnel tests at the NASA Langley Research Center showed that the aircraft could perform tail slides, had no angle-of-attack limits, and could self-recover from any spin except when the weapons doors were open.[23]

The YF-23 was seven feet longer and more slender than the Lockheed YF-22. The leading edge of the YF-23 wing was swept back 40 degrees, and the trailing edge was swept forward at the same angle, resulting in a clipped triangle planform. Every line of the planform was parallel to one or the other of the wing leading edges. Northrop elect-

ed not to use thrust vectoring for aerodynamic control to save weight and to achieve better all-aspect stealth, especially from the rear. The large chine on the forward fuselage helped maintain pitch and yaw stability at high angles of attack and also shed a vortex at high angles of attack that acted as a fence, stabilizing the overwing airflow.[24]

The forward section of the fuselage underbelly was flat, with a weapons bay immediately aft of the nose gear that could accommodate four AIM-120 AMRAAM air-to-air missiles. Production F-23As would have a stretched forebody to accommodate an extra missile bay for a pair of AIM-9 Sidewinders or AIM-132 ASRAAMs in front of the AMRAAM bay. Neither YF-23 was equipped with radar, although McDonnell Douglas did build a complete prototype avionics system that was test flown in Westinghouse's BAC-111. Unlike Lockheed, Northrop did not intend to fire missiles during the Dem/Val phase, and neither prototype was equipped with the 20mm cannon intended for production aircraft.[25]

The YF119-powered first YF-23 (87-0800/N231YF), named *Gray Ghost*, was shipped to Edwards in late 1989 for final preparations, and was rolled out in a public ceremony on 22 June 1990. The aircraft made its maiden flight on 27 August 1990, with Northrop test pilot Alfred P. "Paul" Metz at the controls. The first aerial refueling was completed on the fourth flight on 14 September, and Mach 1.43 supercruise was attained on 18 September. The first YF-23 ended its flight-test program on 30 November with a "combat surge" demonstration that included six missions in less than 10 hours. The shortest turn-around time was 18 minutes and included simulated missile and gun rearming.[26]

The second YF-23 (87-0801/N232YF), named *Spider*, was powered by YF120 engines and made its maiden flight on 26 October, piloted by Jim Sandberg. Progress was just as rapid, with Mach 1.6 supercruise being demonstrated on 29 November 1990.[27]

A temporary truce while the first YF-22 (87-0700/N22YF) and second YF-23 (87-0801/N232YF) fly in formation over Edwards on 18 December 1990. (U.S. Air Force photo by SSgt. D. J. Thompson)

The first YF-23 (87-0800/N231YF) during its rollout at Edwards on 22 June 1990. This YF-23 was seven feet longer than the Lockheed aircraft, but looked even bigger because of its large wing. (Tony R. Landis)

On 23 April 1991, the Air Force announced that Lockheed had won the competition. The two YF-23s were mothballed and remained in a fenced area near the B-2 facility at Edwards until they were given to the NASA Dryden Flight Research Center for stress-analysis testing that never materialized. They then sat deteriorating in the desert by Dryden for years.

The first YF-23 flew 34 times, accumulating 44.3 hours in the air. Its last flight was on 30 November 1990, with Paul Metz at the controls. The airplane remained at Edwards until March 2000, when it was transferred to the Air Force Museum where it is currently on display.[28]

The second YF-23 flew 16 times for a total of 21.6 hours. Its last flight was on 18 December 1990, with Ron Johnston at the controls. In 1996, the airplane was pulled into a hangar at Edwards, disassembled by three Northrop Grumman employees, and shipped to Hawthorne, where it was restored by a team of volunteers and put on display at the Western Museum of Flight under loan from NASA. Unfortunately, the condition of the airplane has steadily deteriorated since 1996, and Northrop Grumman is in the process of preparing it for a fresh restoration.[29]

The angle between the YF-23's vertical stabilizers show up well in the rear view of the first prototype air vehicle (PAV-1) landing at Edwards. Note the thrust vectoring nozzles on the engines. (Northrop Corporation)

Both competitors for the Advanced Tactical Fighter contract demonstrated aerial refueling during the competition, here using the first YF-22 and second YF-23 over Edwards on 18 December 1990 with a Boeing KC-135E. This YF-23 used a variation of the Compass Ghost scheme found on the F-15, while this YF-22 used a darker scheme similar to that used by the F-16. (U.S. Air Force photo by SSgt. D. J. Thompson)

A family portrait of Northrop jet fighters at the Western Museum of Flight in 2004. The YF-23 is at the upper left, followed by (clockwise), the YF-17, F-5A, and F-20. (Tony Chong)

Another Northrop family portrait. A B-2A Spirit stealth bomber lands at Edwards while the first YF-23 awaits its turn to use the main runway. (AFFTC History Office Collection)

The YF-23 pole model in storage at the RATSCAT range in New Mexico in 2003. Plans to transfer the pole model to the AFFTC Museum at Edwards were put on hold due to lack of funding. (U.S. Air Force)

The diamond-shape of the YF-23 wing and its long engine exhausts both show up well in the overhead photo. Markings and serial numbers were on the top and bottom of the vertical stabilizers. (Northrop Corporation)

Joint Strike Fighter

Logically, the X-32 and X-35 should have been the XF-24 and XF-25. However, at least this time there was a mostly logical explanation for why the prototypes were designated as they were. That said, there is no logic whatsoever behind the resulting F-35 designation for production aircraft (which should have been F-24).

During 1986, the Defense Advanced Research Projects Agency (DARPA) began collaborating with the British on an Advanced Short Takeoff and Vertical Landing (ASTOVL) aircraft as a possible replacement for the Harrier. Between 1989 and 1991, DARPA funded airframe studies by General Dynamics, Lockheed, and McDonnell Douglas, as well as propulsion studies by General Electric and Pratt & Whitney.[30]

DARPA planned to have multiple contractors conduct design studies for about a year, then down-select to two contractors for a three-year critical technologies validation (CTV) program beginning in March 1993. The CTV would build large-scale (approximately 80-percent of full-size) models and test them in a variety of facilities such as the hover laboratory at the NASA Ames Research Center. This would be followed in mid-1996 by the selection of a single contractor to build two full-scale prototypes, after which the program would be turned over to the Navy for the development of production models.

However, before this happened, DARPA determined that its preliminary design could be adapted to meet the short takeoff-vertical landing (STOVL) needs of the Marine Corps and the strike aircraft requirements of the Air Force and Navy. One of DARPA's missions was to reduce the cost of weapons systems, and a revival of the "commonality" concept that had played so poorly during the McNamara regime appeared to offer a chance of success this time around.

Given this, the name of the program was changed from ASTOVL to CALF – Common Affordable Lightweight Fighter. Four companies, Boeing, Lockheed, McDonnell Douglas, and Northrop, were invited to bid on two demonstrator aircraft – one STOVL and one conventional takeoff and landing (CTOL). The CALF contracts were awarded to Lockheed and McDonnell Douglas in March 1993. Since only one company would be down-selected to build actual prototypes, DARPA assigned a single designation to the program: X-32.

At the same time, the Department of Defense conducted a Bottom-Up Review (BUR) that recommended initiating a Joint Advanced Strike Technology (JAST) program to develop the next-generation strike aircraft for all three U.S. air arms. By late 1994, the same four companies studying the CALF concept were actively competing for JAST contracts. The government subsequently announced that it would select two contractors to build two flyable demonstrators each.

Subsequently, CALF and JAST were combined into the Joint Strike Fighter (JSF) program, reflecting a newfound production aspiration instead of being strictly a technology demonstration. A request for proposals was released in March 1996, and on 16 November 1996, Secretary of Defense William Perry announced that Boeing and Lockheed Martin had been selected to build the JSF prototypes.

The Boeing design reused the X-32 designation originally assigned to the CALF program; Lockheed Martin was assigned X-35 for its aircraft (X-33 and X-34 having been used by NASA in the meantime). Since CALF had been intended as a technology demonstrator, not a production prototype, it had not been assigned an "XF" designation. Apparently, none of the four aircraft received official Air Force serial numbers, Navy bureau numbers, or civil registrations (N-numbers).

The fly-off took place during the middle of 2001, and on 26 October, the Department of Defense announced that Lockheed Martin had won the JSF competition. One of the main reasons for this appears to have been the method of achieving STOVL flight, with the Department of Defense judging that the higher performance of the lift fan system was worth the extra risk.

Boeing X-32

Beauty is in the eye of the beholder, but many people rank the X-32 as one of the most ungainly aircraft ever built in the United States. The X-32A CTOL demonstrator made its maiden flight from Palmdale on 18 September 2000 with Boeing test pilot Fred Knox at the controls. During the flight, Knox put the X-32A through initial airworthiness tests, including flying qualities and sub-systems checkout. On 15 November 2000, the X-32A began field carrier landing practice tests to demonstrate low-speed aircraft carrier approaches. Commander Phillip "Rowdy" Yates and Fred Knox demonstrated simulated carrier landings using a Fresnel lens to provide pilot cues during their approaches to a simulated carrier deck outlined on a runway at Edwards. The tests included 97 approaches and 74 actual touchdowns. Ultimately, the X-32A completed approximately 50 flights totaling about 100 hours.[31]

The X-32B made its maiden flight on 29 March 2001, with Boeing test pilot Dennis O'Donoghue at the controls of a 50-minute conventional flight from Palmdale to Edwards. During the flight, the X-32B was subjected to a series of initial airworthiness tests, including flying qualities and subsystems checkout. Following the conclusion of sev-

A quiet Edwards sunrise shows the two Joint Strike Fighter (JSF) competitors, with the Boeing X-32 on the left and the Lockheed Martin X-35 on the right. (AFFTC History Office Collection)

A heavily-retouched photo shows the major components of the X-32B "direct lift system" that, much like Harrier, used a single engine and movable nozzles to enable vertical takeoffs and landings. (DARPA)

The X-32A shows a 1,000-pound bomb and AIM-120 AMRAAM air-to-air missile in one of its weapons bays. Note the JSF logo under the cockpit and the Pratt & Whitney logo on the nose. (DARPA)

eral in-air STOVL tests, the X-32B was prepared for a ferry flight to NAS Patuxent River, Maryland. The X-32B departed Edwards on 4 May and made six refueling stops en route to Pax River since the aircraft was not certified for air-to-air refuelings. The X-32B arrived at Pax River on 11 May and immediately began V/STOVL tests.[32]

On 24 June, during the 44th flight, Phil O'Donoghue transitioned the X-32B from fully wing-borne (conventional) to jet-borne (STOVL) flight and then decelerated the X-32B to a steady hover about 250 feet above the ground. O'Donoghue then accelerated out of the hover and transitioned back to conventional flight before making a "slow landing." During four other flights the same day, the X-32B

completed three additional hovers and numerous transitions to STOVL flight. In total, the X-32B hovered for 8 minutes that day, the single longest sustained hover lasting 2 minutes and 42 seconds. The final flight of the X-32B took place on 28 July 2001 with Royal Navy test pilot Lieutenant Commander Paul Stone at the controls. The flight included a series of supersonic dashes up to Mach 1.05.[33]

In 2005, after 66 flights, the X-32A was transferred to the National Museum of the United States Air Force, where it remains in storage. The X-32B is now in the permanent collection of the United States Association for Naval Aviation and is on loan to the Patuxent River Naval Air Museum in Lexington Park, Maryland.[34]

The X-32B at Edwards has the doors to its direct-lift nozzles open under the fuselage (the landing gear retracts into the wings). Note the Pratt & Whitney and Rolls-Royce logos on the nose. (Tony R. Landis)

One of the few angles that the X-32 did not look ungainly from. Unfortunately, production aircraft would have used a different wing planform along with conventional horizontal stabilizers. (DARPA)

Lockheed X-35

The X-35A CTOL demonstrator (aircraft 301) made its maiden flight from Palmdale on 24 October 2000. The aircraft climbed to an altitude of 10,000 feet, and maintained an airspeed of 250 knots while accomplishing a series of figure-eight maneuvers to demonstrate key handling qualities and to validate design predictions. The X-35A made its last CTOL flight on 22 November 2000, arriving in Palmdale, where it was converted into the X-35B STOVL variant.[35]

On 16 December 2000, Lockheed test pilot Joe Sweeney took the X-35C (300) carrier version on its maiden flight from Palmdale to Edwards. Sweeney cycled the landing gear and performed aircraft flying-qualities evaluations, including rolls, sideslips, and overall systems checks. The primary differences from the X-35A included a larger wing and control surfaces, the addition of ailerons, a special structure to absorb high-impact landings, and stronger landing gear.[36]

Lockheed Martin completed installing the shaft-driven lift fan and main engine in the X-35B on 12 May 2001. The aircraft was towed to the hover pit and British Aerospace test pilot Simon Hargreaves began preliminary systems checks on 24 May. The X-35B conducted its first "press-up" on 23 June 2001, marking the first time that a shaft-driven lift fan propulsion system had lifted an aircraft. Hargreaves took the aircraft up between 15 and 20 feet for several minutes and then conducted a vertical landing. The following day, Hargreaves again engaged the lift-fan propulsion system, and the aircraft rose straight up to a stabilized position at an altitude of about 25 feet, while he checked to ensure the flight controls responded properly before he landed.[37]

Following the completion of their flight tests, the X-35s were retired to museums. The X-35A/B is now in the collection of the Smithsonian Institution and is on display at the Stephen F. Udvar-

The STOVL X-35B (301) hovers at Edwards on 21 July 2001 with RAF Squadron Leader Justin Paines in the cockpit. The X-35 used a separate lift engine just behind the cockpit. (Lockheed Martin)

Hazy Center near the Dulles International Airport in Virginia. The X-35C was donated to the United States Association for Naval Aviation and is on loan to the Patuxent River Naval Air Museum in Lexington Park, Maryland.[38]

On 19 February 2006, the first full-scale development F-35A (Air Force version) was rolled out in Fort Worth. The aircraft subsequently underwent extensive ground testing at Fort Worth Joint Reserve Base before making its maiden flight on 15 December 2006. The flight test program is expected to last until the end of 2012.

A giant American flag served as the backdrop for the X-35 rollout ceremony. Like most prototypes, the X-35 had a long air-data boom on its nose to help calibrate the normal static-pitot system. (Lockheed Martin)

The X-35A (301) in afterburner during throttle transient testing in Palmdale, California, on 17 August 2000. Note the shock diamonds in the exhaust. (Lockheed Martin photo by Peter A. Torres)

The X-35C (300) with Navy LCdr. Brian Goszkowicz in the cockpit on 11 January 2001 over Edwards during flight 15. The Navy variant included a heavier structure, larger wing, and the addition of ailerons. Note the tail hook under the fuselage. (Lockheed Martin photo by Tom Reynolds)

The conventional takeoff and landing X-35A (301) shows its speed brakes and lack of a tail hook. The trailing edge of the wing was a single control surface, without individual ailerons. (Lockheed Martin)

The X-35A on its maiden flight from Palmdale to Edwards on 24 October 2000. Note the small Skunk Works logo on the vertical stabilizer just under the hyphen in X-35. (AFFTC History Office Collection)

Appendices

Left: *One of the Bell XP-59As being maintained in the desert at Muroc. Note the mostly empty forward fuselage – this space would be used by the cannon and ammunition on production aircraft.* (AFFTC History Office Collection)

Below: *The two Northrop YF-23s show just how far jet fighter aircraft have come in the 60 years since the XP-59A first flew. The YF-23s, and all modern fighters, have performance that was not even dreamed of by Larry Bell and the designers of the Airacomet.* (Northrop via Tony Chong)

APPENDIX A
COMPANY HISTORIES

What follows are extremely brief histories of the major companies that have built the fighter aircraft discussed in this book. These histories are courtesy of the National Air and Space Museum and www.pilotfriend.com, with a little embellishment and correction where it seemed appropriate. The reader will undoubtedly note that the story may be more confusing than enlightening.

In the early days, it seems that almost everybody either did, or would, work for just about everybody else at some time. Then the creation of a couple of large holding companies meant that everybody bought or sold just about everybody else. Legislation and the pressures of World War II eventually gave rise to the holding companies disbanding and the establishment of mostly independent aircraft manufacturers. Later, a downturn in government business led to a new series of mergers that has left only a handful of players, and many of the legendary names disappeared. Hopefully, this brief history gives a sense of how dynamic the aviation industry has been during its 100-year history.

AVCO Corporation: T. Higbeen Embry and John Paul Riddle created the Embry-Riddle Company in Cincinnati that sold and maintained aircraft, operated a flying school, and ran an air-taxi service. In 1927, the company was awarded an Air Mail contract, but by late 1928 needed additional funds to continue. The Curtiss Aeroplane and Motor Company approached Embry-Riddle with an offer of financial support if Embry-Riddle stopped selling Fairchild aircraft and instead became a Curtiss dealer. Not wanting to lose a successful partner, Fairchild countered the offer and created the Aviation Corporation holding company to finance Embry-Riddle and other aviation companies in the Great Lakes area. Thanks to the aviation craze created by Charles Lindbergh's 1927 trans-Atlantic flight, AVCO had no problem raising more than $35 million, a significant sum of money at the time.

By the end of 1929, AVCO had bought its parent company, Fairchild, along with Embry-Riddle, and acquired interests in more than 90 aviation-related companies, including at least 13 airlines. On 1 February 1930, AVCO formed American Airways, which took control of all the airlines in the company except Embry-Riddle. In April 1932,

Errett L. Cord sold two airlines to AVCO and became a member of the board of directors. This brought the Airplane Development Corporation into AVCO, which established the Aviation Manufacturing Corporation in early 1934 to manage the Airplane Development Corporation (really Vultee, and later Consolidated-Vultee), the Lycoming Manufacturing Company, and Stinson Aircraft.

The Air Mail Act of 1934 forced the reorganization of holding companies such as AVCO. Embry-Riddle was spun off and eventually emerged as the Embry-Riddle Aeronautical University. The airlines were spun off as American Airlines. The airframe and engine manufacturers were retained within the newly renamed Avco Manufacturing Corporation, which became the Avco Corporation in 1959. In December 1984, Avco was purchased by Textron and renamed Avco Systems Textron, becoming Textron Defense Systems in 1985. Over the years, Avco had gradually sold most of its aircraft interests until, by 1985, it was primarily a financial institution centered around the insurance business.

Avion, Inc.: After proving himself as an aircraft designer for Loughead, Davis-Douglas, and Lockheed, John K. "Jack" Northrop formed the Avion Corporation in 1927 in partnership with Kenneth Jay. The company lacked sufficient funds and contracts to continue independent operations, however, and United Aircraft & Transport Corporation (UATC) acquired Avion in October 1929. Avion became the Northrop Corporation, a division of UATC, with Jack Northrop as its president. On 1 September 1931, UATC consolidated Northrop with Stearman Aircraft and moved the operation to Wichita, Kansas. Northrop had no desire to relocate to the Midwest, so he exercised a clause in his contract and quit UATC. The Northrop division again became Avion, Inc., still a subsidiary of UATC. The company's fate is somewhat of a mystery, although it existed as late as World War II when it was a subcontractor to Northrop on the XP-79 project.

Bell Aircraft Corporation: In 1935, Lawrence D. Bell and several other former Consolidated employees, along with Robert J. Woods, formed the Bell Aircraft Corporation in Buffalo, New York. In 1941, Larry Bell saw a helicopter model crafted by Arthur

Middleton Young, and was impressed enough to set up a small shop for the inventor in Gardenville, New York, leading to a separate helicopter division being established in Fort Worth during 1951. The corporate structure saw few changes until 1957, when Bell Aircraft and Bell Helicopters became divisions of the newly established Bell Aerosystems. In 1960, Bell Aerosystems was again reorganized as Bell Aerospace, a wholly owned subsidiary of Textron, Inc., and in 1982, Bell Helicopter was renamed Bell Helicopter Textron. By this time, Bell Aircraft had ceased to exist.

The Boeing Company: William E. Boeing founded Pacific Aero Products in 1915, reforming as the Boeing Airplane Company in 1917. Ten years later, Boeing formed Boeing Air Transport (BAT) to carry air mail and passengers, and soon purchased Pacific Air Transport and merged it with BAT. On 1 February 1929, Boeing Airplane Company, Boeing Air Transport, and Pratt & Whitney merged into the United Aircraft and Transport Corporation (UATC). In 1934, Congress passed legislation that forced aircraft manufacturers to separate from airline companies. At the time, the transport group consisting of Boeing Air Transport, National Air Transport, Varney, Stout Airlines, and several others; these were split off to form United Air Lines.

As part of the divestiture, Boeing regained its independence as the Boeing Aircraft Company, although it took the remnants of Stearman with it. This changed back to the Boeing Airplane Company in 1947. In 1961, the parent company was renamed The Boeing Company (with a capital The), reflecting more diversified corporate interests. A reorganization at the end of 1972 resulted in the formation of three largely autonomous companies: Boeing Commercial Airplane, Boeing Aerospace, and Boeing Vertol. In December 1996, Boeing purchased the aerospace and defense units of Rockwell International, including the one-time North American Aviation. On 15 December 1996, Boeing surprised industry observers by announcing the acquisition of McDonnell Douglas Corporation, and on 1 August 1997, Boeing and McDonnell Douglas began operating as a single company under the Boeing name (but using the McDonnell Douglas logo).

Chance Vought: On 18 June 1917, Birdseye Lewis and Chauncey "Chance" Milton Vought established Lewis & Vought Corporation and in 1918, began producing military aircraft. In 1924 the company was renamed Chance Vought Corporation, and when Vought died in 1930, it became a division of the United Aircraft and Transport Corporation (UATC). In 1935 the division was renamed Chance Vought Aircraft and in 1939 merged with Sikorsky to form the Vought-Sikorsky Division of United Aircraft Corporation (as UATC has become). The operation split again in 1943, with the Sikorsky Division concentrating on helicopter development and the Chance Vought Aircraft Division producing combat aircraft. On 1 July 1954, Chance Vought Aircraft became a subsidiary (no longer a division) of United Aircraft. On 31 December 1960, the company became Chance Vought Corporation, merging in 1961 with Ling-Temco Electronics, Inc. to form Ling-Temco-Vought, Inc. (LTV).

Consolidated Aircraft Corporation: On 29 May 1923, Maj. Reuben H. Fleet founded the Consolidated Aircraft Corporation to build Dayton-Wright TW-3s in a building leased from the Gallaudet Aircraft Corporation in East Greenwich, Rhode Island. Fleet soon took over Gallaudet Aircraft and acquired the rights to Dayton-Wright Company designs from General Motors, which left the aviation business. In February 1929, Reuben Fleet formed Fleet Aircraft in Buffalo, New York. Consolidated purchased Fleet Aircraft in August 1929, but continued production under the Fleet name. At the same time, Consolidated acquired Thomas-Morse Aircraft Corporation as a subsidiary. In late 1941, under increasing pressure to retire, Fleet sold his 34 percent stock holding to Vultee Aircraft, a subsidiary of AVCO, for $10 million. Vultee subsequently purchased a controlling interest in Consolidated and formed the Consolidated-Vultee Aircraft Corporation, still within AVCO.

Consolidated-Vultee Aircraft Corporation: Vultee purchased a controlling interest in Consolidated Aircraft Corporation in November 1942, forming Consolidated-Vultee Aircraft Corporation on 17 March 1943. Both companies had been operating independently for more than a year under the AVCO umbrella. The new company was known internally as CVAC or Convair, although this name was not trademarked or otherwise official. On 12 April 1946, Reuben Fleet resigned from the Consolidated-Vultee board, finally ending his involvement with the company he built.

The company flourished during World War II and caught the interest of multimillionaire investor Floyd B. Odlum. In 1946, Odlum began buying AVCO stock through his Atlas Corporation and on 4 September 1947, Odlum swapped his AVCO stock for the Consolidated-Vultee aviation operations in San Diego, Fort Worth, and Detroit. Atlas Corporation took control of Consolidated-Vultee in November 1947. Odlum was primarily interested in making money, and subsequently negotiated a merger between Consolidated-Vultee and the Electric Boat Company, a submarine manufacturer. The two firms officially merged on 29 April 1954 to create General Dynamics Corporation, with an Electric Boat division and a Convair division, the name finally becoming official and a registered trademark. The Convair division would operate over the next quarter century primarily as an independent company under the General Dynamics corporate umbrella. In 1985, the Convair space efforts were split off to form General Dynamics Space Systems Division. In 1993, the General Dynamics Space Division (in effect, the San Diego operations) was sold to Martin Marietta, and the fixed-wing aircraft business (in effect, Fort Worth operations) was sold to Lockheed. In 1994, the Aerostructures unit was sold to McDonnell Douglas, and in 1996 the Convair division ceased to exist.

Curtiss-Wright Corporation: The merger of Curtiss Aeroplane and Motor Company, and Wright Aeronautical in August 1929 created the Curtiss-Wright Corporation. There were three main divisions: the Airplane Division for military aircraft, Curtiss-Wright Airplane for civil aircraft, and Wright Aeronautical for engines. Curtiss-Wright remained the largest aircraft firm throughout World War II in terms of total business. But despite its wartime importance, the company faced severe post-war difficulties. It failed to sell any of its post-war designs to the military, and the Curtiss Airplane Division closed in March 1951, as the company focused on engine and propeller manufacturing. Unfortunately, the end of the piston-engine era also largely spelled the end for Curtiss-Wright. The company's unsuccessful foray into jet engines – the J65 and J67 – ended in 1960 when the government removed Curtiss-Wright from the list of approved engine providers. The company continued to diversify, entering the electricity-generating business and nuclear-product industry, and servicing and providing components for jet engines. By the early 1980s, the company had become a diversified, multi-industry, multinational concern, but was no longer a significant player in the aerospace industry.

Douglas Aircraft Company: Donald Douglas began his career as a consultant to the Connecticut Aircraft Company. He then joined the Glenn L. Martin Company as chief engineer, but left in 1916 when Martin merged with the Wright Company. When Martin re-established his company in 1918, Douglas joined him. Two years later, Douglas left Martin and established the Davis-Douglas Company on 22 July 1920 with David R. Davis. By July 1921, Davis had lost interest in aircraft manufacturing and Douglas reorganized the company with new financial backing as the Douglas Company. In November 1928, he again restructured the company, forming the Douglas Aircraft Company. In January 1932, Douglas Aircraft financed 51 percent of Jack Northrop's second Northrop Corporation (the first having been renamed Avion under UATC). When Northrop experienced labor problems in 1937, Douglas Aircraft acquired the remaining Northrop stock and dissolved the company in September 1937, absorbing the operations as the El Segundo Division of Douglas Aircraft. In 1 October 1945, Douglas set up Project RAND (Research and Development) as a think-tank for the Air Force; this division separated from Douglas on 14 May 1948 as the independent RAND Corporation (all caps, although it is no longer an acronym). Employment and profits rose dramatically during the 1950s as a result of large military orders, and net sales reached an all-time high in 1958. However, the coming of the Jet Age saw a significant reduction in commercial orders as Boeing cornered the majority of the jet airliner market and military orders largely dried up. On 28 April 1967, the financially troubled Douglas Aircraft Corporation merged with the McDonnell Company to form McDonnell Douglas Corporation.

General Dynamics Corporation: Formed in 1952 through the combination of Electric Boat Company and Canadair, General Dynamics did not emerge as an operating company until it merged with Consolidated-Vultee Aircraft Corporation in 1954. At that time, the company was comprised of two major divisions, Electric Boat and Convair. In 1992, General Dynamics sold its Missile Systems business to Hughes Aircraft and Cessna Aircraft to Textron. In 1993, the former Convair space business (essentially, the San Diego operations) was sold to Martin Marietta and the fixed-wing aircraft business (largely, the Fort Worth operation) to Lockheed. The Aerostructures business was sold to McDonnell Douglas in 1995.

Beginning in 1995, the company expanded the Electric Boat and Land Systems divisions by purchasing other shipyards and combat vehicle-related businesses. In 1997, General Dynamics began acquiring companies with expertise in information technology products and services, particularly in the command, control, communications, computing, intelligence, surveillance and reconnaissance (C4ISR) arena. In 1999, the company purchased Gulfstream Aerospace Corporation, a business-jet aircraft and aviation support-services company.

Glenn L. Martin Company: Glenn Martin established the Glenn L. Martin Aircraft Company in Santa Ana, California, in 1912. However, in 1916, Martin accepted a merger offer from the Wright Company, creating the Wright-Martin Aircraft Company in September. This apparently did not go well, and Martin left to form a second Glenn L. Martin Company on 10 September 1917, this time based in Cleveland, Ohio. When Martin sold his Cleveland plant in 1929, he built a new facility in Middle River, Maryland. This was the first plant designed for metal aircraft construction and, during the 1930s, was regarded as the most modern factory in the United States. Martin merged with the American-Marietta Corporation in 1961 to form the Martin Marietta Corporation. In 1982, Martin Marietta was subject to a hostile takeover bid by the Bendix Corporation that purchased the majority of Martin Marietta shares and, in effect, owned the company. However, Martin Marietta management used the short time separating ownership and control to sell non-core businesses and launch its own hostile takeover of Bendix (an action known as the Pac-Man defense). The end of this extraordinarily bitter battle saw Martin Marietta survive and Bendix being bought by Allied Corporation. Martin Marietta merged with the Lockheed Corporation in 1995 to form Lockheed Martin Corporation.

Grumman Aircraft Engineering Corporation: In December 1929, Leroy Grumman, William Schwendler, and Leon "Jake" Swirbul organized Grumman Aircraft Engineering Corporation in Bethpage, New York. In 1969, after diversifying into a variety of non-aviation industries, the company was renamed Grumman Corporation, with aviation-related work being centered in the Grumman Aerospace subsidiary. In 1973, the civil aviation work (primarily, the Gulfstream program) was merged with American Aviation Corporation to form Grumman American Aviation Corporation, while government work continued at Grumman Aerospace. In 1978, the company sold Grumman American to American Jet Industries, forming Gulfstream American Corporation, which was later renamed Gulfstream Aerospace Corporation, and still later, purchased by General Dynamics. In 1994, Grumman Corporation was acquired by Northrop Corporation, with the new company being named Northrop Grumman Corporation.

Hughes Aircraft Company: In 1933, the Hughes Tool Company began working on its first aircraft, and during 1936 the aviation staff was reorganized as the Hughes Aircraft Company. During World War II, Hughes Aircraft created the Hughes Electronics division that soon hired two very promising engineers – Simon Ramo and Dean Wooldridge – who had a concept for an innovative electronic fire-control system (and later left to form TRW). In 1953, Howard Hughes donated Hughes Aircraft to the newly formed Howard Hughes Medical Institute, allegedly as a way of avoiding taxes on its huge income. Left behind at Hughes Tools, was Hughes Helicopters, which moved to Summa Corporation in 1972, to Hughes Corporation (as Hughes Helicopter, Inc.) in 1981, and to McDonnell Douglas Corporation in 1984 as the McDonnell Douglas Helicopter Company. On 1 August 1997, McDonnell Douglas merged with Boeing, but Boeing's plans to sell the civil helicopter products to Bell Helicopters in 1998 were thwarted by the U.S. Federal Trade Commission (FTC). In 1999, Boeing completed the sale of the civilian helicopters to MD Helicopter Holdings Inc., an indirect subsidiary of the Dutch company, RDM Holding Inc. Boeing maintained the AH-64 line of helicopters. After suffering dismal commercial performance, the company was purchased in 2005 by Patriarch Partners, LLC, an investment fund. The company was recapitalized as an independent company, MD Helicopters, Inc. in Mesa, Arizona.

Hughes Aircraft remained a separate company until 31 December 1985, when it was acquired by General Motors and merged with the Delco Electronics unit to form Hughes Electronics Corporation, an independent subsidiary. The group then consisted of: Delco Electronics Corporation, Hughes Aircraft Company, Hughes Space and Communications Company, Hughes Network Systems, and DirecTV. Hughes Aircraft now existed within Hughes Electronics, instead of the other way around. In 1997, Hughes Electronics was sold to the Raytheon Company.

Ling-Temco-Vought: In 1961, the Chance Vought Corporation merged with Ling-Temco Electronics to form Ling-Temco-Vought (LTV). In 1965, a further reorganization created three operating divisions: LTV Aerosystems, primarily the old Chance Vought; LTV Electrosystems; and LTV Ling-Altec. The firm became LTV Corporation on 5 May 1971. Under the LTV Corporation was LTV Aerospace, which housed Vought Aeronautics and Vought Helicopters (the marketing subsidiary for French Aerospatiale helicopters).

On 1 January 1976, LTV Aerospace was renamed Vought Corporation. In April 1983, it was renamed LTV Aerospace and Defense Company, divided into a Missiles and Advanced Programs Division and an Aero Products Division. The company filed for bankruptcy in July 1986. In 1992, Loral Corporation purchased the LTV Missiles Division (primarily the Grand Prairie, Texas operation) and named it Loral Vought Systems. Also in 1992 LTV, Lockheed Corporation, and Martin Marietta Corporation reached an agreement that resulted in the sale of the LTV Aerospace and Defense Company to the Carlyle Group and its minority (49 percent) partner, Northrop Grumman. In September 1994, Northrop Grumman exercised its option to acquire Carlyle's interest and absorbed all of Vought as an operating unit focusing on aerostructures. In 1996, Lockheed Martin purchased the majority of Loral's defense businesses, including the newly renamed Lockheed Martin Vought Systems. Three years later Vought Systems and the former Martin Marietta Electronics and Missiles division merged to form Lockheed Martin Missiles and Fire Control. In July 2000, Northrop Grumman sold its aerostructures business back to the Carlyle Group, and Vought Aircraft Industries once again became an independent company, as a subsidiary of the Carlyle Group.

Lockheed Corporation: In 1912, Allan and Malcolm Loughead, in partnership with Max Mamlock, established the Alco Hydro-Aeroplane Company to construct an aircraft of Allan's design. Following the crash of the first airplane, the company became dormant. In 1916 the brothers established the Loughead Aircraft Manufacturing Company in Santa Barbara, with John K. "Jack" Northrop as their chief engineer. The company reorganized in 1919, but continuing financial problems forced its liquidation in 1921. In 1926 the brothers established the Lockheed Aircraft Company, again with Northrop as the chief engineer. In July 1929, Fred E. Keeler, an investor who owned 51 percent of Lockheed, decided to sell 87 percent of his assets to Detroit Aircraft Company, a holding company. Lockheed became a division of that company until 1931, when it was forced into receivership by the Great Depression. The company locked its doors in 1932.

Five days after the Lockheed Division of Detroit Aircraft failed, a group of investors – Walter Varney, Mr. and Mrs. Cyril Chappellet, R. C. Walker, and Thomas Fortune Ryan III – led by Robert Gross bailed the company out and purchased Lockheed's assets for $40,000, forming the new Lockheed Aircraft Corporation with Lloyd C. Stearman as president. Gross also attracted a young engineer named Clarence L. "Kelly" Johnson, who would soon help make Lockheed's reputation.

In 1937, Lockheed established a new AiRover Aircraft subsidiary to give Lockheed a place in the personal aviation market. AiRover became Vega Airplane Company in June 1938, which converted to military activity when the war began. At the end of 1941, Vega Airplane became Vega Aircraft Corporation, and Lockheed absorbed it on 30 November 1943. In January 1951, Lockheed reopened a government-built plant at Marietta, Georgia, and the complex was used to build Boeing B-47 Stratojets, C-130 Hercules, and JetStar aircraft. In 1961, the Lockheed-Georgia Division was reorganized as the Lockheed-Georgia Company while the west coast operations became the Lockheed-California Company. Meanwhile, on 1 January 1954, Lockheed had established a Missile Systems Division, soon renamed the Lockheed Missiles and Space Company (LMSC). On 1 September 1977 the overarching company was renamed Lockheed Corporation to reflect the diversification of its interest. In 1993, Lockheed acquired the Fort Worth Division of General Dynamics as the Lockheed Fort Worth Division. In 1994, Lockheed merged with Martin Marietta, forming the Lockheed Martin Corporation.

Lockheed Martin Corporation: In 1994, the Lockheed Corporation merged with Martin Marietta to create Lockheed Martin Corporation. Two years later, Lockheed Martin acquired the majority of Loral Corporation's defense business, and Vought Systems became Lockheed Martin Vought Systems. In 1998, Lockheed Martin abandoned plans to merge with Northrop Grumman due to government concerns over the potential strength of the new group (the new company would have received over a quarter of the Department of Defense procurement budget). In 2000, Lockheed Martin sold its Control Systems and Aerospace Electronic Systems businesses to BAE Systems. This group encompassed Sanders Associates, Fairchild Systems, and Lockheed Martin Space Electronics & Communications. Lockheed Martin is currently comprised of four major business areas: Aeronautics, Electronic Systems, Information Systems, and Space Systems.

McDonnell Aircraft Corporation: In 1928, James S. McDonnell Jr, and two colleagues, Constantine Zakhartchenko and James Cowling, decided to leave Hamilton Aero Manufacturing Company, which was being absorbed by the United Aircraft and Transportation Corporation, and organize J. S. McDonnell Jr. & Associates. A lack of funding and the Great Depression doomed the company, leading McDonnell to join the Glenn L. Martin Company as chief engineer. In 1938, however, he again set out on his own and established McDonnell Aircraft Company in St. Louis on 6 July 1939. In 1942, the company gained an interest in the Platt-LePage Aircraft Company, and acquired LePage outright in 1944 before liquidating it in 1946. In 1966, the company was renamed McDonnell Company to reflect its growing diversification. At the same time, McDonnell acquired control of the Douglas Aircraft Company, and on 28 April 1967, the two companies merged to form McDonnell Douglas Corporation.

McDonnell Douglas Corporation: In 1966, the McDonnell Company bought the Douglas Aircraft Company and on 28 April 1967, the two companies merged to form the McDonnell Douglas Corporation, with McDonnell Aircraft Company (McAir) and Douglas Aircraft Company (DAC) as operating divisions. The merger did not stem the flow of red ink from the commercial airplane sector, and McDonnell Douglas began selling off its non-aviation related subsidiaries. In 1984, McDonnell Douglas purchased Hughes Helicopters and 10 years later acquired the aerostructures business from General Dynamics. The red ink, however continued to accumulate, despite several profitable fighter (F-15, F/A-18, AV-8) production contracts. On 15 December 1996, Boeing offered to purchase McDonnell Douglas, and the acquisition was completed on 1 August 1997.

Menasco Manufacturing Company: Menasco was established by Albert Menasco in Los Angeles in 1926. The company's first product was an air-cooled rebuild of a Salmson radial. In 1929, Menasco introduced the 4-A, the first of what was to become its main product line, the inverted, in-line engine. Menasco was deeply involved with air racing, and his products were popular with racers looking for small-displacement engines. Menasco attempted to enter the gas turbine engine business as the primary subcontractor to Lockheed for the L-1000 (XJ37) axial-flow turbojet, but this project ultimately failed to produce anything useful. The company ended engine development and manufacturing after World War II. Most recently, Menasco Aerospace was known for its landing gear and, as part of Coltec Industries, was acquired by Goodrich Aerospace in 1999.

North American Aviation: In December 1928, Clement Keys established North American Aviation as a holding company to invest in a range of aviation businesses with no intent to become an aircraft manufacturer. Its first years were spent buying and selling interests in a number of aviation and airline companies through a series of complicated transactions. The Air Mail Act of 1934, however, forced aviation holding companies to break up the manufacturing and airline operations (although North American was able to retain Eastern Air Lines until 1938). One of the new companies retained the North American Aviation name and recruited James H. "Dutch" Kindelberger from Douglas Aircraft as its president.

In 1955, North American created the Rocketdyne division, which would become the premier American producer of liquid-fuelled rocket engines. Its new Missile Development division became the Space and Information Systems Division in 1960. Another division, Autonetics, focused on guidance systems. The company name remained unchanged until a 1967 merger with Rockwell-Standard Corporation created North American Rockwell Corporation. In 1973, the company became Rockwell International Corporation with the North American name remaining in the North American Aerospace Operations Division. In 1996, The Boeing Company purchased North American operations. The North American name was briefly retained on some operating units, but eventually disappeared into the Boeing culture.

Northrop Corporation: In January 1932, after the unhappy merger of Avion and UATC, John K. "Jack" Northrop partnered with Donald Douglas and formed the Northrop Corporation, with Douglas holding 51 percent of the stock. Douglas experienced labor problems that affected the Northrop Corporation and eventually caused Douglas to buy Northrop's 49 percent of the business and to dissolve Northrop completely on 8 September 1937. Jack Northrop remained with Douglas until 1 January 1938, when he formed Northrop Aircraft, Inc., which was renamed Northrop Corporation in 1959.

The company purchased Grumman Corporation in 1994, resulting in the Northrop Grumman Corporation. A series of acquisitions followed the merger. In 1994, Northrop Grumman added the remaining 51 percent of Vought Aircraft Company, an aerostructure producer, to the 49 percent that Northrop had acquired in 1992. It held Vought until 2000 when it was sold back to its previous owners, the Carlyle Group. In 1996, Northrop Grumman acquired the defense electronics and systems business of Westinghouse Electric Corporation. In August 1997, Northrop Grumman and Logicon

Inc., an information technology company, merged. In 1999, the company acquired Ryan Aeronautical, focusing on unmanned aerial vehicles. In April 2001, Northrop Grumman acquired Litton Industries, a major information technology supplier to the federal government. The acquisition also added shipbuilding to Northrop Grumman's array of capabilities. In October 2001, it purchased Aerojet. In November 2001, it acquired Newport News Shipbuilding Inc., creating the world's largest naval shipbuilder.

Republic Aviation Corporation: Republic Aviation was established on 13 October 1939 when the board of directors of Seversky Aircraft ousted Alexander de Seversky as company president because of mounting losses and changed its name to Republic Aviation. The company attempted to diversify, establishing a helicopter division in December 1957 to build the French Alouette helicopter under license. Republic acquired a minority interest in the Dutch aircraft firm Fokker and attempted to market an attack plane in 1960. None of these efforts was successful. Republic was purchased by Fairchild Hiller Corporation in July 1965 and became the Republic Aviation Division. Reorganized again in 1971, the division became the Fairchild Republic Company, a subsidiary of Fairchild Industries.

Seversky Aircraft Corporation: A former Russian aviator, Alexander P. de Seversky formed the Seversky Aero Corporation in 1923 to produce aircraft parts and instruments but not complete airplanes. The small company did not survive the stock market crash of 1929. In the meantime, he attracted the backing of millionaire Paul Moore and other investors, and in February 1931, formed the new Seversky Aircraft Corporation on Long Island to produce military aircraft. He was elected president and quickly surrounded himself with expatriate Russian engineers including one of the most innovative designers of all time, Alexander Kartveli. De Seversky was ousted during a 1939 reorganization, and the company was renamed Republic Aviation Corporation.

United Aircraft and Transport Corporation: In the fall of 1928, William E. Boeing, the founder of Boeing Airplane Company, and Fred Rentschler, the president of Pratt & Whitney, agreed to merge the Boeing Airplane Company, Boeing Air Transport, and Pratt & Whitney into a consolidated holding company. On 1 February 1929, the United Aircraft and Transport Corporation (UATC) was incorporated. UATC also included Hamilton Metalplane Company, which had become a division of Boeing earlier in the year, and Chance Vought Corporation. On 30 July 1929, Sikorsky Aviation joined UATC and was soon followed by Stearman Aircraft and Avion, Inc. in October 1929. Standard Steel Propellers of Pittsburgh was acquired in September 1929, and was merged with Hamilton to become the Hamilton Standard Division of UATC. The airline interests were soon grouped under a new management company known as United Air Lines, Inc. However, the individual airlines (as well as the individual companies held by United) continued to operate under their own names.

In 1934, the U.S. government concluded that large holding companies such as United Aircraft and Transport and the Aviation Corporation (AVCO) were anti-competitive, and new antitrust laws were passed forbidding airframe or engine manufacturers from having interests in airlines. As a consequence, UATC was broken up. Its manufacturing interests east of the Mississippi River (Pratt & Whitney, Sikorsky, Vought, and Hamilton Standard Propeller Company) were organized into a new United Aircraft Corporation. Boeing acquired the western manufacturing interests and again became an independent company. United Airlines also became an independent company.

Vought was spun off as an independent business in 1954, but otherwise, United Aircraft maintained its original corporate structure and concentration in the aerospace and defense industries well into the 1970s. United Aircraft changed its name to United Technologies Corporation (UTC) in 1975, and the next year acquired Otis Elevator. In 1979, Carrier Refrigeration and Mostek were acquired; Mostek was sold in 1985 to the French electronics company Thomson. United Technologies acquired Sundstrand in 1999, and merged it into the Hamilton Standard unit to form Hamilton Sundstrand. Two years later, UTC entered the fire and security business by purchasing Chubb Security, which was followed in 2005 by Kidde. Also in 2005, United Technologies acquired Boeing's Rocketdyne division, a remnant of North American Aviation, which was merged into the Pratt & Whitney business unit, creating Pratt & Whitney Rocketdyne (PWR).

Vultee Aircraft Corporation: Gerard "Jerry" Vultee and Vance Breese had started the Airplane Development Corporation in early 1932 after American Airlines showed great interest in their six-passenger V-1 design. Soon after, Errett Cord bought all 500 shares of stock in the company and Airplane Development Corporation became a Cord subsidiary in 1934. AVCO then established the Aviation Manufacturing Corporation (AMC) in 1934 through the acquisition of Cord's holdings including the Airplane Development Corporation. The timing was fortuitous, since the Air Mail Act of 1934 forced the large holding companies to split up their assets into airline companies and aircraft companies. AMC was liquidated on 1 January 1936 and Vultee Aircraft Division was formed as an autonomous subsidiary of AVCO in November 1937. Vultee acquired control of AVCO's Stinson Aircraft Corporation subsidiary in October 1939, creating the Stinson Division of Vultee.

Vultee Aircraft, Inc. was established in November 1939, acquiring the assets of Aviation Manufacturing Corporation – including Lycoming and Stinson – but remaining an AVCO subsidiary. Vultee purchased a controlling interest in Consolidated Aircraft Corporation in November 1942, forming Consolidated-Vultee Aircraft Corporation on 17 March 1943.

As we said, more confusing than enlightening.

APPENDIX B
Notes & Citations

Introduction – Enter, The Jet Fighter

1. There seems to be great confusion and debate over World War II production numbers. The ones used here came from: http://www.nationalmuseum.af.mil/factsheets/factsheet.asp?id=22 13 (P-47) and http://www.nationalmuseum.af.mil/factsheets/factsheet.asp?id=22 14 (P-51). They disagree with other published sources, but nevertheless illustrate the point.
2. "Case History of the L-1000 (XJ37-1) Jet Propulsion Engine," prepared by the Historical Division, Intelligence, T-2, Air Materiel Command, June 1946, p. 1.
3. Ibid, p. 4.
4. Ibid, p.1.
5. Ibid, pp. 1-2.
6. Ibid, p. 2.
7. *United States Air Force Dictionary*, (Maxwell AFB, Alabama: Air University Press, 1956).
8. Of course, in reality it is all more complicated than explained here. Several web sites attempt to explain it in more detail. In particular, Andreas Parsch maintains an excellent site at http://www.designation-systems.net that contains a great deal more detail on designation systems, and Andrew Chorney also has a site with a good amount of history on designation systems at http://www.driko.org/des.html.
9. http://www.designation-systems.net/usmilav/projects.html#_MX. It is not certain from the available records how many MX numbers were ultimately issued. In an R&D summary published in January 1952, the Air Materiel Command announced its intent to discontinue the MX system as of 1 July 1952, but a cancellation directive has yet to be found, and there is circumstantial evidence showing that MX numbers continued to be used for several years thereafter. The highest number identified by Andreas Parsch thus far is MX-2276; it appears to have been assigned in 1954.
10. The Air Corps became a subordinate element of the Army Air Forces on 20 June 1941, and it continued to exist as a combat arm of the Army (similar to the Infantry) until disestablished by Congress with the creation of the U.S. Air Force in 1947.
11. Raymond Puffer, "First Flights at Edwards AFB," http://www.aerofiles.com/ff-eafb.html, accessed 9 May 2007. Puffer is an Air Force historian stationed at Edwards, and this information was originally on the Edwards website, but has since been removed "for security reasons."

Chapter 1 – Innovative Dead Ends

1. Gerald H. Balzer, "Request for Data R-40C: The Origins of the XP-54, XP-55, and XP-56," *AAHS Journal*, Vol. 40, No. 4, Winter 1995, pp. 247-248.
2. Ibid.
3. Ibid.
4. Draft copy of the "Final Report of the Procurement, Inspection, Testing, and Acceptance of the XP-54 Airplane," January 1944, in the files of the Federal Record Center, St. Louis, 342-69A-449, 08-07-53-3-1.
5. It is important to note the terminology here. A supercharger was a mechanically driven compressor, often integral within the engine block casting. A turbocharger was an exhaust-driven compressor. Prior to the 1970s, turbochargers were frequently called "turbo-superchargers." Many aircraft engines used both, since superchargers tended to work best at low power settings and turbochargers at high power settings.
6. Balzer, "Request for Data R-40C."
7. Draft copy of the "Final Report of the Procurement, Inspection,

Testing, and Acceptance of the XP-54 Airplane," January 1944, in the files of the Federal Record Center, St. Louis, 342-69A-449, 08-07-53-3-1.
8. Ibid.
9. O. B. Thornton, Air Force Technical Report No. 5714, "Final Report of Development, Procurement, and Acceptance of the XP-56 Airplane," 30 July 1948; "Final Report of the Procurement, Inspection, Testing, and Acceptance of the XP-54 Airplane."
10. "Final Report of the Procurement, Inspection, Testing, and Acceptance of the XP-54 Airplane."
11. Paul B. Smith, "Final Report on the XP-68 Airplane," Memorandum Report ENG-50-855, Army Materiel Commend Engineering Division, 17 April 1943, in the files of the Federal Record Center, St. Louis, 342.69-A-449, 08-07-53-3-5.
12. Ibid.
13. Balzer, "Request for Data R-40C," pp. 45-46.
14. Ibid, pp. 48-50.
15. Ibid, pp. 48-50.
16. Ibid, pp. 90-94.
17. Ibid, pp. 93-98.
18. Ibid, pp. 98-103, 164.
19. Ibid, pp. 102-103.
20. Ibid, pp. 163-165.
21. Ibid, pp. 167-168.
22. Ibid, pp. 170-173.
23. Ibid, pp. 173-174; http://home.att.net/~jbaugher1/oldseriesfighters.html
24. Balzer, "Request for Data R-40C," p. 174.
25. http://www.airzoo.org/
26. Ibid, p. 177.
27. O. B. Thornton, Air Force Technical Report No. 5714, "Final Report of Development, Procurement, and Acceptance of the XP-56 Airplane," 30 July 1948.
28. Ibid.
29. Ibid.
30. Ibid.
31. http://www.nasm.si.edu/research/aero/aircraft/northrop_xp56.htm
32. Thornton, "Final Report of Development, Procurement, and Acceptance of the XP-56 Airplane," no page numbers.
33. Ibid.
34. Ibid.
35. Ibid.
36. Historian Gerald H. Balzer notes that although it is usually reported that 3-4 square feet of area was added, this does not agree with photographs of the airplane before and after the modification. Instead, it appears that the stub vertical was raised 3 or 4 feet in height, not in area. See Gerald H. Balzer, "Request for Data R-40C: The Origins of the XP-54, XP-55, and XP-56," *AAHS Journal*, Volume 42, Number 1, Spring 1997, p. 49.
37. O. B. Thornton, Air Force Technical Report No. 5714, "Final Report of Development, Procurement, and Acceptance of the XP-56 Airplane," 30 July 1948.
38. Ibid.
39. Ibid.
40. Ibid.
41. Ibid.
42. Ibid. Historian Gerald H. Balzer, in his 1996 *AAHS Journal* article, points out that there is conflicting data that indicates this flight might have lasted for 10 minutes.
43. Ibid.
44. Ibid.
45. Ibid.
46. http://www.nasm.si.edu/research/aero/aircraft/northrop_xp56.htm
47. John F. Aldridge, Jr., Army Engineering Report 431-25, "Final

Report on the XP-67 Airplane," November 1944.
48. Aldridge, "Final Report on the XP-67 Airplane;" Balzer, "Request for Data R-40C," pp. 256-257.
49. Aldridge, "Final Report on the XP-67 Airplane;" Balzer, "Request for Data R-40C," pp. 256-257.
50. Balzer, "Request for Data R-40C," pp. 256-257.
51. Aldridge, "Final Report on the XP-67 Airplane."
52. Ibid.
53. Ibid.
54. Ibid. Two different dash number engines were used since one rotated clockwise and the other rotated counter-clockwise.
55. Ibid.
56. Ibid.
57. Ibid.
58. Ibid.
59. Ibid.
60. Ibid.
61. Ibid.
62. Ibid.
63. Ibid.
64. Ibid.
65. Paul B. Smith, "Final Report on the XP-68 Airplane," Memorandum Report ENG-50-855, Army Materiel Command Engineering Division, 17 April 1943, in the files of the Federal Record Center, St. Louis, 342.69-A-449, 08-07-53-3-5.
66. Ibid.
67. Joe Baugher's online history located at: http://home.att.net/~jbaugher1/oldseriesfighters.html
68. Smith, "Final Report on the XP-68 Airplane."

Chapter 2 – The First jets

1. Lee Payne, "The Great Jet Engine Race … And How We Lost," *Air Force Magazine*, January 1982.
2. Arnold quote from Thomas J. Goetz, "Birth of the American Jet Age," *Aviation History*, September 2006, p. 24.
3. Army Technical Report 5234 (X-140692-2), "Final Report on Development of XP-59A and YP-59A Model Airplanes," October 1945.
4. "Final Report on Development of XP-59A and YP-59A Model Airplanes;" "Case History of the XP-59, XP-59A, YP-59A, P-59A, P-59B, and XP-59B Airplanes," prepared by the Historical Office, Intelligence Department, Air Materiel Command, December 1947, pp. 2-3. The number behind the "I-" indicated the expected amount of thrust from each engine – the I-16 produced 1,650-lbf, the I-20 produced 2,000-lbf, etc.
5. "Case History of the XP-59, XP-59A, YP-59A, P-59A, P-59B, and XP-59B Airplanes," pp. 2-3.
6. Charles L. Hall, "Final Report on the Bell XP-52 Airplane," Memorandum Report ENG-5M-50-701, Air Corps Materiel Division, 19 June 1942, in the files of the Federal Record Center, St. Louis, 342.69-A-449. Author Graham White has a beautifully restored I-1430 that he has displayed (and run) at the Aircraft Engine Historical Society meetings.
7. Charles L. Hall, "Final Report on the Bell XP-59 Airplane," Memorandum Report ENG-5M-50-838, Air Corps Materiel Division, 31 March 1943, in the files of the Federal Record Center, St. Louis, 342.69-A-449.
8. Ibid.
9. Ibid.
10. "Final Report on Development of XP-59A and YP-59A Model Airplanes."
11. Joe Baugher's online history located at: http://home.att.net/~jbaugher1/oldseriesfighters.html

12. "Final Report on Development of XP-59A and YP-59A Model Airplanes."

13. Ibid.

14. Thomas J. Goetz, "Birth of the American Jet Age," *Aviation History*, September 2006, p. 25

15. "Final Report on Development of XP-59A and YP-59A Model Airplanes." http://www.au.af.mil/au/goe/eaglebios/93bios/craigi93.htm

16. "Final Report on Development of XP-59A and YP-59A Model Airplanes."

17. Ibid.

18. "Case History of the XP-59, XP-59A, YP-59A, P-59A, P-59B, and XP-59B Airplanes," pp. 4-5.

19. "Final Report on Development of XP-59A and YP-59A Model Airplanes."

20. Ibid.

21. http://www.history.navy.mil/avh-1910/APP30.pdf

22. "Final Report on Development of XP-59A and YP-59A Model Airplanes." www.edwards.af.mil/moments/docs_html/42-09-19.html; http://www.hq.nasa.gov/office/pao/History/Timeline/1940-44.html

23. "Final Report on Development of XP-59A and YP-59A Model Airplanes."

24. Army Memorandum Report EBG-47-1739-A, "Official Performance Tests of YP-59A Airplane," 15 April 1944.

25. "Case History of the XP-59, XP-59A, YP-59A, P-59A, P-59B, and XP-59B Airplanes," pp. 1-2; quote is from "Final Report on Development of XP-59A and YP-59A Model Airplanes."

26. "Case History of the XP-59, XP-59A, YP-59A, P-59A, P-59B, and XP-59B Airplanes," p. 5.

27. Ibid, pp. 8-9.

28. Ibid.

29. Capt. Donald T. Tuttle, Army Technical Report 5509, "Final Report on the Development of the Northrop XP-79B Airplane," 11 July 1946.

30. Ibid.

31. Northrop used Harper Dry Lake, California, and Roach Dry Lake, Nevada, as alternate test sites during the early 1940s when Muroc Dry Lake was unavailable, especially during the winter of 1944 when rains flooded Muroc. Aircraft known to have been tested at the alternate lakes include the MX-334 glider, XP-56, and N-9M.

32. Tuttle, "Final Report on the Development of the Northrop XP-79B Airplane."

33. Ibid.

34. Ibid.

35. Ibid.

36. Ibid.

37. Ibid. A second serial number, 43-52438, was also reserved for an XP-79B, which is odd considering only a single aircraft was ordered. It is possible that the two serials were intended for the original rocket-powered XP-79 prototypes, and the first one was reused by the jet-powered XP-79B.

38. Ibid.

39. Engineering Division Memorandum Report ENG-50-897, "Limited Engineering Inspection of the XP-79 Airplane," 5 July 1943.

40. Ibid.

41. Tuttle, "Final Report on the Development of the Northrop XP-79B Airplane."

42. Ibid.

43. Ibid.

44. Ibid.

45. Ibid.

46. Ibid.

47. Bastian Hello, Air Corps Technical Report No. 5235, "Final Report on the Development, Procurement, Performance, and Acceptance of the XP-80 Airplane," 28 June 1945.

48. Clarence L. "Kelly" Johnson with Maggie Smith, *Kelly: More Than My Share of it All*, (Washington: Smithsonian Institution Press, 1985), p, 97.

49. Marcelle Size Knaack, *Post-World War II Fighters, 1945–1973*, (Washington, DC: Office of Air Force History, 1986), pp. 1-2; Hello, "Final Report on the Development, Procurement, Performance, and Acceptance of the XP-80 Airplane." This final cost included somewhat under $40,000 allocated to flight tests of the XP-80As in addition to the XP-80.

50. Ben R. Rich and Leo Janos, *Skunk Works*, (New York: Little, Brown, and Company, 1994), pp. 111-112; http://www.lmaeronautics.com/lmaerostar/pdfs/year03/palm_jun_03.pdf. There are many variations of this story, most told by people who were there, so it is difficult to judge exactly what happened.

51. Engineering Division Memorandum Report No. ENG-50-917, "Mockup Inspection of the XP-80," 30 July 1943.

52. Hello, "Final Report on the Development, Procurement, Performance, and Acceptance of the XP-80 Airplane."

53. "Case History of XP-80, XP-80A, YP-80A, P-80-1, P-80A-5, P-80B-1, P-80B-5, P-80N, and P-80R Airplanes," prepared by the Historical Office, Executive Secretariat, Air Materiel Command, August 1948, pp. 2-3.

54. Hello, "Final Report on the Development, Procurement,

Performance, and Acceptance of the XP-80 Airplane."

55. Engineering Division Memorandum Report ENG-47-1720, "Flight Tests of the XP-80,"13 March 1944.

56. Hello, "Final Report on the Development, Procurement, Performance, and Acceptance of the XP-80 Airplane;" http://www.nasm.si.edu/research/aero/aircraft/lockheed_xp80.htm. The XP-80 was accepted by the Army on 15 November 1944, not 1943 as usually reported (the 1943 date would have been before its first flight and makes no contractual sense).

57. Ibid. The Army needed to ramp up J33 production much quicker than was possible using General Electric facilities so the government licensed J33 production to the Allison Division of General Motors. Notably, Allison would go on to build thousands of the GE-designed engines while General Electric built only 300. A similar process was followed on the J35.

58. "Case History of XP-80, XP-80A, YP-80A, P-80-1, P-80A-5, P-80B-1, P-80B-5, P-80N, and P-80R Airplanes," pp. 3-4.

59. Joe Baugher's online history located at: http://home.att.net/~jbaugher1/oldseriesfighters.html; Rene Francillon and Kevin Keaveney, *Lockheed F-94 Starfire*, (Arlington, Texas: Aerofax, 1986), pp. 1-2

60. "Case History of XP-80, XP-80A, YP-80A, P-80-1, P-80A-5, P-80B-1, P-80B-5, P-80N, and P-80R Airplanes," pp. 4-5.

61. Hello, "Final Report on the Development, Procurement, Performance, and Acceptance of the XP-80 Airplane."

62. Ibid.

63. "Case History of XP-80, XP-80A, YP-80A, P-80-1, P-80A-5, P-80B-1, P-80B-5, P-80N, and P-80R Airplanes," pp. 5-6.

64. Letter, Brig. Gen. Lyman P. Whitten to Brig. Gen. James S. Stowell, 17 October 1946, and the response dated 4 December 1946. In the files of the Air Force Historical Research Agency.

65. Hello, "Final Report on the Development, Procurement, Performance, and Acceptance of the XP-80 Airplane."

66. http://www.edwards.af.mil/gallery/html_pgs/fight2.htm

67. Knaack, *Post-World War II Fighters*, pp. 8-11; Robert F. Dorr, "Lockheed P-80 Shooting Star Variant Briefing," *Wings of Fame*, Volume 11, 1998.

68. "Air Force Developmental Aircraft," a report prepared by the Air Research and Development Command and the Air Materiel Command, April 1957, pp. 9-10.

69. Frank W. Davis (assistant chief engineer), Consolidated Vultee Report ZP-50-0003, "YP-81, History and Current Possibilities," 1 September 1950. This report included a copy of Davis' article "Problems of Gas-Turbine Propeller Combinations," in *Aeronautical Engineering Review*, Vol. 7, No. 4, April 1948.

70. http://www.edwards.af.mil/moments/docs_html/45-02-07.html

71. http://tanks45.tripod.com/Jets45/ListOfEngines/EnginesUSA.htm

72. Convair proposal DEV-368-14, "Model YP-81 Airplane, Long Range Offensive Fighter, Powered by TG-110 Prop-Jet and J33-19 Turbo Jet," no date; "Air Force Developmental Aircraft," pp. 9-10.

73. Davis, "YP-81, History and Current Possibilities;" "Air Force Developmental Aircraft," pp. 9-10.

74. "Air Force Developmental Aircraft," p. 10.

75. Davis, "YP-81, History and Current Possibilities."

76. Ibid.

77. Ibid.

78. Joe Baugher's online history located at: http://home.att.net/~jbaugher1/oldseriesfighters.html

79. Robert E. Bradley, "The Birth of the Delta Wing," *AAHS Journal*, Vol. 48, No. 4, Winter 2003; Davis, "YP-81, History and Current Possibilities;" "Air Force Developmental Aircraft," pp. 10-12.

80. AMC History Report, "Historical Data on Aircraft Designed But Not Produced: 1945-Present – Fighters," March 1957; "Air Force Developmental Aircraft," pp. 10-11.

81. "Air Force Developmental Aircraft," pp. 10-11.

82. http://www.edwards.af.mil/moments/docs_html/45-02-07.html

83. The Double Mamba was also known as the Twin Mamba. It was used on the Fairey Gannet anti-submarine aircraft developed for the Fleet Air Arm of the Royal Navy. The Nene was the third Rolls-Royce jet engine to enter production, designed in an astonishingly short five-month period in 1944, first running on 27 October 1944. The design saw little use in British designs, being passed over in favor of the Avon that followed, and the only significant use of the Nene in Great Britain was in the Hawker Sea Hawk and Supermarine Attacker. However, licensed production was undertaken by Pratt & Whitney as the J42 (JT6B) and it went on to power the Grumman F9F Panther. The Soviets reverse engineered the Nene to develop the Klimov RD-45 and Klimov VK-1, which soon appeared in various Soviet fighters including Mikoyan-Gurevich MiG-15. The Nene was also made under license in Australia for the RAAF deHavilland Vampire fighters.

84. Letter, Lt. Col. J. L. Zoeckler/Acting Chief of the Engineering Division, to Col. Anderson/Air Force Headquarters, subject: Ground Support Version Study of XP-81, 14 September 1950.

85. Ibid.

86. Frank G. Morris, Flight Test Division Memorandum Report TSFER-1949, "Performance Tests on the Bell XP-83 Airplane, AAF No. 44-85990," 28 September 1945; "Air Force Developmental Aircraft," p. 17. This aircraft was later called the Bell Model 40.

87. "Air Force Developmental Aircraft," p. 17.

88. Ibid. The serial numbers were assigned on 12 August 1944.

89. http://www.aircrash.org/burnelli/chg_bio.htm

90. Air Force Technical Report 5536, "Final Report on the Development, Procurement, and Acceptance of the XP-83 Airplane," 6 January 1947; "Air Force Developmental Aircraft," p. 18.

91. "Air Force Developmental Aircraft," p. 18.

92. "Air Force Developmental Aircraft," p. 18.

93. Morris, "Performance Tests on the Bell XP-83 Airplane, AAF No. 44-85990."

94. Ibid.

95. "Air Force Developmental Aircraft," p. 18.

96. http://www.edwards.af.mil/gallery/yeager/docs_html/XP-83.html

97. "Final Report on the Development, Procurement, and Acceptance of the XP-83 Airplane."

98. "Air Force Developmental Aircraft," p. 19.

99. Ibid, pp. 19-20.

100. Werner R. Rankin, Air Force Technical Report 5818, "Final Report on the Procurement, Inspection, Testing, and Acceptance of the Republic Aircraft Corporation XP-84 Airplane," May 1949.

101. Ibid.

102. Ibid; Dorothy L. Miller, "Case History of the F-84 Airplane," Historical Office, Intelligence Department, Air Materiel Command, April 1950, pp. 2-5; Knaack, *Post-World War II Fighters*, p. 24.

103. Rankin, "Final Report on the Procurement, Inspection, Testing, and Acceptance of the Republic Aircraft Corporation XP-84 Airplane."

104. Air Materiel Command Report TSESE-2-1146, "Mockup Inspection of the XP-84 Airplane," 7 March 1945.

105. Rankin, "Final Report on the Procurement, Inspection, Testing, and Acceptance of the Republic Aircraft Corporation XP-84 Airplane;" Air Materiel Command Report TSESE-2-1223, "Engineering Inspection of the XP-84 Airplane," 18 October 1945.

106. Rankin, "Final Report on the Procurement, Inspection, Testing, and Acceptance of the Republic Aircraft Corporation XP-84 Airplane."

107. Air Materiel Command Report TSFTE-2013, "Phase II Performance Tests of the XP-84 Airplane, 6 September 1946.

108. Rankin, Air Force Technical Report 5818, "Final Report on the Procurement, Inspection, Testing, and Acceptance of the Republic Aircraft Corporation XP-84 Airplane."

109. Ibid; Knaack, *Post-World War II Fighters*, p. 25.

110. Rankin, "Final Report on the Procurement, Inspection, Testing, and Acceptance of the Republic Aircraft Corporation XP-84 Airplane."

111. Knaack, *Post-World War II Fighters*, pp. 25-26.

112. Ibid, pp. 26-27.

113. Ibid, pp. 32-33.

114. Ibid, pp. 36-37.

115. Miller, "Case History of the F-84 Airplane," p. 7.

116. Kevin Keaveney, *Republic F-84 (Swept-Wing Variants)*, (Arlington, TX: Aerofax, 1987), p. 1.

117. Miller, "Case History of the F-84 Airplane," pp. 5-11.

118. There seems to be great confusion about this designation. Documentation is very inconsistent – some documents call it an XF-84F, others a YF-84F. Given that the YF-96A had carried the "Y" prefix, that is what will be used here, although logically the first airplane should have been the XF-84F.

119. Knaack, *Post-World War II Fighters*, p. 39; Keaveney, *Republic F-84 (Swept-Wing Variants)*, p. 2. The F-84 series actually had three official names – Thunderjet, Thunderstreak, and Thunderflash – in addition to the unofficial "Thunderscreech" applied to the XF-84H.

120. Dennis R. Jenkins, *Magnesium Overcast: The Story of the Convair B-36*, (North Branch, MN: Specialty Press, 2001), pp. 175-176.

121. Knaack, *Post-World War II Fighters*, p. 39.

122. Ibid, p. 40.

123. Ibid, p. 40.

124. Keaveney, *Republic F-84 (Swept-Wing Variants)*, pp. 1-3.

125. Knaack, *Post-World War II Fighters*, p. 41; Keaveney, *Republic F-84 (Swept-Wing Variants)*, pp. 2-3.

126. Joe Baugher's online history located at: http://home.att.net/~jbaugher1/oldseriesfighters.html

127. Knaack, *Post-World War II Fighters*, p. 49.

128. Ibid, pp. 48-49.

129. Keaveney, *Republic F-84 (Swept-Wing Variants)*, pp. 5-15.

130. http://www.edwards.af.mil/history/html/aircraft/first_flights.html; Knaack, *Post-World War II Fighters*, pp. 48-49.

131. Joe Baugher's online history located at: http://home.att.net/~jbaugher4/a2d.html

132. http://www.edwards.af.mil/moments/docs_html/55-07-22.html

133. Ibid.

134. http://www.nationalmuseum.af.mil/factsheets/factsheet.asp?id=58

135. Ibid.

136. http://www.hill.af.mil/museum/photos/coldwar/j79.htm

137. Knaack, *Post-World War II Fighters*, p. 45.

138. Ibid, pp. 8-9.

139. "Historical Data on Aircraft Designed But Not Produced: 1945-Present – Fighters."

140. "Air Force Developmental Aircraft," a report prepared by the Air Research and Development Command and the Air Materiel Command, April 1957, p. 25.

141. "Historical Data on Aircraft Designed But Not Produced: 1945-Present – Fighters;" "Air Force Developmental Aircraft," p. 25.
142. "Air Force Developmental Aircraft," pp. 26-27.
143. Ibid; *Aviation Week*, 18 October 1948, p. 12; Walton S. Moody, *Building a Strategic Air Force*, (Washington, DC: Air Force History and Museums Program, 1996), p. 238.
144. "Historical Data on Aircraft Designed But Not Produced: 1945-Present – Fighters."
145. Robert Jackson, *Cold War Combat Prototypes*, (Marlborough, Wiltshire: Crowood Press, 2005), pp. 51-52.
146. "Air Force Developmental Aircraft," pp. 25-27; conversation between Scott Crossfield and Dennis R. Jenkins, 12 June 2005.
147. Ibid.
148. "Historical Data on Aircraft Designed But Not Produced: 1945-Present – Fighters."
149. Ibid; Individual Aircraft Record Cards for both airplanes, in the files of the Air Force Historical Research Agency; http://www.sacmuseum.org/collections/F-85.html.
150. http://www.nasm.si.edu/research/aero/aircraft/NA_FJ1.htm. Somewhat embarrassingly, the Navy quickly discovered that the "D" manufacturing designator had already been assigned to Douglas, so the two McDonnell aircraft were redesignated as "H" manufacturer.
151. Ibid.
152. Roy E. Mann, Air Force Technical Report No. 6168, "Final Report on the XF-86 Aircraft," January 1952, no page numbers.
153. Ibid.
154. Ibid.
155. Ibid.
156. Ibid.
157. Ibid.
158. Joe Baugher's online history located at: http://home.att.net/~jbaugher1/oldseriesfighters.html
159. Mann, "Final Report on the XF-86 Aircraft."
160. Ibid.
161. Flight Test Division Memorandum Report, "Performance Flight Tests on XF-86 Airplane, Air Force No. 45-59597," 15 January 1948.
162. Ibid; Knaack, *Post-World War II Fighters*, p. 57.
163. Knaack, *Post-World War II Fighters*, p. 79; http://home.att.net/~jbaugher1/oldseriesfighters.html
164. Joe Baugher's online history located at: http://home.att.net/~jbaugher1/oldseriesfighters.html
165. Knaack, *Post-World War II Fighters*, pp. 69-70.
166. Ibid, p. 70.
167. AFSC Historical Publication 61-51-2, "Development of Airborne Armament, 1910–1961," October 1961, p. III-463.
168. Joe Baugher's online history located at: http://home.att.net/~jbaugher1/oldseriesfighters.html.
169. Knaack, *Post-World War II Fighters*, p. 79.
170. Ibid, p. 76.
171. Ibid, p. 76.
172. Ibid, pp. 77-78.
173. Ibid, p. 78.
174. Ibid, pp. 78-79.
175. http://en.wikipedia.org/wiki/F-86_Sabre
176. Knaack, *Post-World War II Fighters*, p. 79.

Chapter 3 – All-Weather Fighters

1. This was an American derivative of the German MG-151 15.2mm machine gun. Although 300 weapons were manufactured along with more than six million rounds of ammunition, the weapon never worked as expected and the T-17 never saw service.
2. These were developed as part of project MX-2014.
3. Ibid, p. 83; Gerald Balzer and Mike Dario, *Northrop F-89 Scorpion*, (Arlington, TX: Aerofax, 1993), pp. 1-2.
4. O. B. Thornton, Air Force Technical Report No. 5905, "Final Report on the Inspection, Testing, and Acceptance of the Curtiss-Wright Corporation XF-87, XF-87A, XRF-87, and XRF-87C," June 1949.
5. Knaack, *Post-World War II Fighters*, p. 83.
6. Thornton, "Final Report on the Inspection, Testing, and Acceptance of the Curtiss-Wright Corporation XF-87, XF-87A, XRF-87, and XRF-87C."
7. The F-94, ordered in October 1948, and the F-86D, ordered in March 1949, never carried P-for-Pursuit designations.
8. "Historical Data on Aircraft Designed But Not Produced: 1945-Present – Fighters;" Memorandum from Headquarters to Air Materiel Command, Subject: Disposition of Experimental Contract W33-038-ac-19837 and W33-038-ac-6266 (XF-87 Airplanes), 7 December 1948.
9. "Historical Data on Aircraft Designed But Not Produced: 1945-Present – Fighters."
10. Joe Baugher's online history located at: http://home.att.net/~jbaugher1/oldseriesfighters.html
11. Thornton, Air Force Technical Report No. 5905, "Final Report on the Inspection, Testing, and Acceptance of the Curtiss-Wright Corporation XF-87, XF-87A, XRF-87, and XRF-87C."

12. Ibid.
13. Ibid; Wai Yip, "The Curtiss-Wright XA-43 Attack Airplane," *AAHS Journal*, Spring 2007, pp. 68-73.
14. Thornton, "Final Report on the Inspection, Testing, and Acceptance of the Curtiss-Wright Corporation XF-87, XF-87A, XRF-87, and XRF-87C."
15. Ibid.
16. Yip, "The Curtiss-Wright XA-43 Attack Airplane," pp. 68-73; Thornton, "Final Report on the Inspection, Testing, and Acceptance of the Curtiss-Wright Corporation XF-87, XF-87A, XRF-87, and XRF-87C."
17. Thornton, "Final Report on the Inspection, Testing, and Acceptance of the Curtiss-Wright Corporation XF-87, XF-87A, XRF-87, and XRF-87C."
18. Ibid.
19. Ibid.
20. Ibid.
21. Ibid.
22. Ibid.
23. Ibid.
24. Ibid.
25. Ibid.
26. Ibid.
27. "Historical Data on Aircraft Designed But Not Produced: 1945-Present – Fighters."
28. Thornton, "Final Report on the Inspection, Testing, and Acceptance of the Curtiss-Wright Corporation XF-87, XF-87A, XRF-87, and XRF-87C."
29. Ibid.
30. Ibid.
31. Air Materiel Command Memorandum Report MCRFT-2187, "Performance Flight Test on the XF-87 Airplane, Air Force Serial No. 45-59600," 15 February 1949.
32. "Historical Data on Aircraft Designed But Not Produced: 1945-Present – Fighters." Memorandum from Headquarters to Air Materiel Command, Subject: Disposition of Experimental Contract W33-038-ac-19837 and W33-038-ac-6266 (XF-87 Airplanes), 7 December 1948.
33. Knaack, *Post-World War II Fighters*, p. 84.
34. Gerald Balzer and Mike Dario, *Northrop F-89 Scorpion*, (Arlington: Aerofax, 1993), pp. 4-5; Knaack, *Post-World War II Fighters*, p. 84.
35. Balzer *Northrop F-89 Scorpion*, p. 10.
36. Ibid, pp. 10-11.
37. Knaack, *Post-World War II Fighters*, p. 85; http://home.att.net/~jbaugher1/p89.html
38. Balzer, *Northrop F-89 Scorpion*, pp. 13-14.
39. Ibid, p. 15.
40. Ibid, pp. 15 and 25.
41. Knaack, *Post-World War II Fighters*, pp. 85-86.
42. Ibid, pp. 86-87.
43. Ibid, pp. 88-89.
44. Balzer, *Northrop F-89 Scorpion*, pp. 28-31.
45. Knaack, *Post-World War II Fighters*, pp. 91-92.
46. Balzer, *Northrop F-89 Scorpion*, p. 33.
47. Knaack, *Post-World War II Fighters*, p. 97.
48. Ibid, pp. 97-98.
49. Ibid, pp. 100-101.
50. Joe Baugher's online history located at: http://home.att.net/~jbaugher1/oldseriesfighters.html
51. Rene Francillon and Kevin Keaveney, *Lockheed F-94 Starfire*, (Arlington TX: Aerofax, 1986), pp. 1-2. Marcelle Knaack lists these as XTF-80C.
52. Joe Baugher's online history located at: http://home.att.net/~jbaugher1/oldseriesfighters.html; http://www.bookrags.com/wiki/F-94_Starfire
53. Joe Baugher's online history located at: http://home.att.net/~jbaugher1/oldseriesfighters.html
54. http://www.bookrags.com/wiki/F-94_Starfire
55. Joe Baugher's online history located at: http://home.att.net/~jbaugher1/oldseriesfighters.html
56. Francillon, *Lockheed F-94 Starfire*, pp. 3-4.
57. Joe Baugher's online history located at: http://home.att.net/~jbaugher1/oldseriesfighters.html. It appears that this was not truly a fuselage intended for an operational F-94A, but a spare fuselage manufactured using company funds.
58. Francillon, *Lockheed F-94 Starfire*, pp. 1-2.
59. Knaack, *Post-World War II Fighters*, pp. 106-107.
60. Francillon, *Lockheed F-94 Starfire*, pp. 3-4.
61. Knaack, *Post-World War II Fighters*, p. 110.
62. Joe Baugher's online history located at: http://home.att.net/~jbaugher1/oldseriesfighters.html
63. Knaack, *Post-World War II Fighters*, p. 110.

Chapter 4 – Point-Defense Interceptors

1. "Air Force Developmental Aircraft," pp. 53-54; Lecture given by William J. O'Donnell, "History of the XF-91 Development," 6 January 1949.

2. Robert E. Bradley, "The Birth of the Delta Wing," *AAHS Journal*, Volume 48, Number 4, Winter 2003.
3. Lecture given by William J. O'Donnell, "History of the XF-91 Development," 6 January 1949.
4. Ibid. The original proposal actually included a General Electric TG-200 that was never approved for development. After evaluating various versions of the Westinghouse 24C and the Rolls-Royce AJX065, Republic and the Army agreed on using the TG-190.
5. Ibid.
6. Republic Aviation Report EAR-240, "Republic XF-91 No. 2 Airplane Rate of Climb and High Speed Performance," 7 March 1951; Lecture given by William J. O'Donnell, "History of the XF-91 Development," 6 January 1949.
7. "Air Force Developmental Aircraft," pp. 53-54.
8. Familiarization Lecture, William J. O'Donnell, "History of the Design of the XF-91," 1 June 1949; "Background Information on Republic XF-91," 1953.
9. "Air Force Developmental Aircraft," pp. 54-55.
10. "Republic XF-91 No. 2 Airplane Rate of Climb and High Speed Performance."
11. Test Directive No. 5049-EL, "Test of the XF-91 Radar Armament Test Vehicle," 3 July 1952; Air Force Supplementary Progress Report Card, Project MX-809 (R-430-266), 6 September 1953; "Historical Data on Aircraft Designed But Not Produced: 1945-Present – Fighters."
12. Air Force Supplementary Progress Report Card, Project MX-809 (R-430-266), 6 September 1953; "Historical Data on Aircraft Designed But Not Produced: 1945-Present – Fighters;" Charles E. Yeager, *Yeager: An Autobiography*, (New York: Bantam, 1986), pp. 189-190.
13. Republic Aviation Report AP-F-91-900, "Summary of Engineering Data for Republic F-91 Interceptor Aircraft," 31 January 1950, pp. 1-2 and 29.
14. Ibid, pp. 5-9.
15. Ibid, pp. 1-2, 35-36, and 41-42.
16. http://modelingmadness.com/reviews/korean/olssonxf91.htm
17. Air Force Supplementary Progress Report Card, Project MX-809 (R-430-266), 6 September 1953; "Historical Data on Aircraft Designed But Not Produced: 1945-Present – Fighters."
18. "Historical Data on Aircraft Designed But Not Produced: 1945-Present – Fighters;" Bradley, "The Birth of the Delta Wing."
19. Ardath M. Morrow, "Case History of the XF-92," Historical Office, Intelligence Department, Air Materiel Command, June 1949, p. 1, 4-5.
20. Ibid, pp. 7-8.
21. Bradley, "The Birth of the Delta Wing."
22. Ibid.
23. "Historical Data on Aircraft Designed But Not Produced: 1945-Present – Fighters."
24. Bradley, "The Birth of the Delta Wing."
25. Ibid.
26. Ibid.
27. Convair Report ZM-7002-006, "Summary Report, U.S.A.F. XF-92A (Convair Model 7002) Research Airplane," 23 August 1949.
28. Ibid.
29. Ibid.
30. Ibid.
31. Ibid; "Historical Data on Aircraft Designed But Not Produced: 1945-Present – Fighters."
32. "Historical Data on Aircraft Designed But Not Produced: 1945-Present – Fighters."
33. "Summary Report, U.S.A.F. XF-92A (Convair Model 7002) Research Airplane."
34. Ibid.
35. Bradley, "The Birth of the Delta Wing."
36. "Historical Data on Aircraft Designed But Not Produced: 1945-Present – Fighters."
37. Bradley, "The Birth of the Delta Wing."
38. "Air Force Developmental Aircraft," pp. 66-67.

Chapter 5 – Penetration Fighters

1. "Air Force Developmental Aircraft," p. 45.
2. Ibid, p. 45.
3. Ibid, pp. 45-46.
4. Bradley, "The Birth of the Delta Wing."
5. Knaack, *Post-World War II Fighters*, p. 321.
6. "Air Force Developmental Aircraft," p. 45.
7. "Historical Data on Aircraft Designed But Not Produced: 1945-Present – Fighters."
8. Ibid; "Air Force Developmental Aircraft," p. 39.
9. McDonnell Report No. 1951, "Model F-88 Estimated Performance Data," 22 December 1950.
10. Joe Baugher's online history located at: http://home.att.net/~jbaugher1/oldseriesfighters.html
11. "Historical Data on Aircraft Designed But Not Produced: 1945-Present – Fighters."
12. Kendall Perkins and E.M. Flesh, "Design and Development of the McDonnell XF-88," 17 July 1952, pp. 2-4 and Figures 1-3.

13. Ibid; "Model F-88 Estimated Performance Data."
14. "Historical Data on Aircraft Designed But Not Produced: 1945-Present – Fighters;" McDonnell Report No. 1951, "Model F-88 Estimated Performance Data," 22 December 1950.
15. Joe Baugher's online history located at: http://home.att.net/~jbaugher1/oldseriesfighters.html.
16. Ibid.
17. McDonnell Engineering Report 1059, "Interceptor Performance: F-88 Airplane and McDonnell Model 58A Airplane," 14 January 1949.
18. Ibid.
19. "Model F-88 Estimated Performance Data;" Letter, James S. McDonnell to Commanding General/AMC, subject: XF-88 Airplane Serial No. 46-525 (without afterburners) and XF-88A Airplane Serial No. 46-526 (with afterburners) – Proposed Phase III Program, 31 October 1949.
20. "Model F-88 Estimated Performance Data."
21. Ibid.
22. Letter, James S. McDonnell to Commanding General/AMC, subject: XF-88 Airplane Serial No. 46-525 (without afterburners) and XF-88A Airplane Serial No. 46-526 (with afterburners) – Proposed Phase III Program, 31 October 1949.
23. "Model F-88 Estimated Performance Data."
24. Ibid.
25. Ibid.
26. Ibid; Letter, James S. McDonnell to Commanding General/AMC, subject: XF-88 Airplane Serial No. 46-525 (without afterburners) and XF-88A Airplane Serial No. 46-526 (with afterburners) – Proposed Phase III Program, 31 October 1949.
27. "Model F-88 Estimated Performance Data."
28. Memorandum, "Recommended Mobilization Planning Program, Combined Models F2H-2 and F-88, McDonnell and Licensee Plants," 26 October 1949.
29. Ibid.
30. McDonnell Report 3134, "Model XF-88B Propeller Research Vehicle, Preliminary Flight Evaluation & Operating Restrictions," 19 June 1953, pp. 1-3 and 5.
31. Ibid, pp. 15-17.
32. Ibid, pp. 5-6; "Historical Data on Aircraft Designed But Not Produced: 1945-Present – Fighters;" "Air Force Developmental Aircraft," a report prepared by the Air Research and Development Command and the Air Materiel Command, April 1957, p. 39.
33. "Air Force Developmental Aircraft," p. 46.
34. Ibid.
35. Ibid.
36. Ibid, p. 47.
37. "Historical Data on Aircraft Designed But Not Produced: 1945-Present – Fighters;" "Air Force Developmental Aircraft," pp. 40, 46-47.
38. "Historical Data on Aircraft Designed But Not Produced: 1945-Present – Fighters;" "Air Force Developmental Aircraft," pp. 47-48.
39. Ibid. The wing used a larger center section to accommodate the new fuselage, but the outer panels were identical to the P-86A and used the same tooling.
40. "Air Force Developmental Aircraft," p. 70.
41. Ibid, p. 71.
42. Ibid, p. 72.
43. Ibid; Joe Baugher's online history located at: http://home.att.net/~jbaugher1/oldseriesfighters.html; http://www.edwards.af.mil/history/docs_html/aircraft/first_flights.html
44. "Air Force Developmental Aircraft," pp. 72-73.
45. "Historical Data on Aircraft Designed But Not Produced: 1945-Present – Fighters."

Chapter 6 – Missiles ?

1. http://www.designation-systems.net/dusrm/app4/other.html
2. Curtiss-Wright Corporation, Wright Aeronautical Report No. 1786, "Ramjet Rocket for MX-904," 15 December 1953.
3. Ibid.
4. Ibid.
5. Warren K. Kernen, "Historical Report, 6540th Missile Test Wing, Air Force Missile Test Center, Holloman AFB, New Mexico," various dates in 1950 through 1953.
6. Ibid.
7. AFSC Historical Publication 61-51-2, "Development of Airborne Armament, 1910–1961," October 1961, pp. III-551-552.
8. Ibid, p. III-552.
9. Calling the Falcon a rocket disregarded the military custom of calling guided vehicles "missiles" and unguided vehicles "rockets." This oversight was corrected when the Falcon was redesignated as an Air Intercept Missile (AIM-4).
10. http://www.designation-systems.net/dusrm/m-4.html
11. "Development of Airborne Armament, 1910–1961," October 1961, p. II-303.
12. Ibid, p. III-555.
13. Ibid, pp. III-569-571.
14. http://www.hill.af.mil/museum/photos/coldwar/falcon.htm
15. "Development of Airborne Armament, 1910–1961," October 1961, p. IV-664.
16. AAF Cognizance Report, "GAPA – MX-606," July 1946.
17. Ibid.
18. http://www.patrick.af.mil/history/6555th/6555c2-3.htm
19. Robert J. Helberg, "The Bomarc Story: How a Missile Was Born," *The Airman*, March-April 1958, pp. 18-20; http://www.afa.org/magazine/gallery/missiles/cim-10.asp
20. John A. Andrade, *U.S. Military Aircraft Designations and Serials*, (Leicester, UK: Midland Counties Publishing, 1997), p. 106; http://www.boeing.com/companyoffices/history/boeing/bomarc.html
21. http://www.patrick.af.mil/history/6555th/6555c2-3.htm
22. Robert J. Helberg, "The Bomarc Story: How a Missile Was Born," *The Airman*, March-April 1958, pp. 18-20.

Chapter 7 – Century Series Fighters

1. Loss rates provided by the Air Force Safety Center, Kirtland AFB, New Mexico.
2. Frederick A. Alling, "History of the Air Materiel Command, 1 July – 31 December 1956, Volume IV: The F-102A Airplane, 1950-1956," December 1957. Interestingly, Craigie had been the first Army pilot to fly a jet airplane, the XP-59A.
3. Ibid.
4. Ibid.
5. Ibid.
6. Knaack, *Post-World War II Fighters*, pp. 112-113.
7. Joe Baugher's online history located at: http://home.att.net/~jbaugher1/oldseriesfighters.html
8. Knaack, *Post-World War II Fighters*, p. 113.
9. Ibid, pp. 113-114.
10. Ibid, p. 114.
11. Ibid, pp. 114-115.
12. Joe Baugher's online history located at: http://home.att.net/~jbaugher1/oldseriesfighters.html
13. Knaack, *Post-World War II Fighters*, p. 115.
14. See, for example, Leonard Sternfield, Technical Note TN-1193, "Effect of Product of Inertia on Lateral Stability," 1947 and William Phillips, NACA Technical Note TN-1627, "Effect of Steady Rolling on Longitudinal and Directional Stability," 1948.
15. Knaack, *Post-World War II Fighters*, pp. 114-115.
16. Ibid, pp. 134-135.
17. Ibid, p. 136.
18. Ibid, pp. 136-137.
19. Ibid, pp. 136-138.
20. Joe Baugher's online history located at: http://home.att.net/~jbaugher1/oldseriesfighters.html
21. Knaack, *Post-World War II Fighters*, p. 140.
22. Ibid; Kevin Keaveney, *McDonnell F-101B/F*, (Arlington TX: Aerofax, 1984), p. 2.
23. Knaack, *Post-World War II Fighters*, p. 145.
24. Jim Upton, *Lockheed F-104 Starfighter*, Volume 38 in the WarbirdTech Series, (North Branch, MN: Specialty Press, 2003), pp. 7-8.
25. Ibid, pp. 8-11.
26. Knaack, *Post-World War II Fighters*, pp. 174-175; Upton, *Lockheed F-104 Starfighter*, p. 12. Not having this clause in the contract eventually worked to Lockheed's favor when the F-104 was licensed for international production.
27. Knaack, *Post-World War II Fighters*, pp. 175-176.
28. Ibid, p. 176.
29. Upton, *Lockheed F-104 Starfighter*, p. 37.
30. Ibid, pp. 37-38.
31. Ibid, p. 38.
32. Ibid, p. 38.
33. Knaack, *Post-World War II Fighters*, pp. 176-178; Upton, *Lockheed F-104 Starfighter*, p. 38. Base drag is a component of aerodynamic drag caused by a partial vacuum in the tail area. The vacuum is the hole created by the passage of the vehicle through the air.
34. Raymond Puffer, "First Flights at Edwards AFB," http://www.aerofiles.com/ff-eafb.html, accessed 9 May 2007.
35. Upton, *Lockheed F-104 Starfighter*, pp. 15 and 41.
36. Ibid, p. 38; "Development of Airborne Armament, 1910–1961," p. III-463.
37. Joe Baugher's online history located at: http://home.att.net/~jbaugher1/oldseriesfighters.html
38. Ibid.
39. Knaack, *Post-World War II Fighters*, pp. 178-182; http://www.aero-news.net/, http://www.i-f-s.nl/index11.htm
40. Knaack, *Post-World War II Fighters*, p. 191.
41. Larry Davis and David Menard, *Republic F-105 Thunderchief*, Volume 18 in the WarbirdTech Series, (North Branch, MN: Specialty Press, 1998).
42. "The F-105: A Chronology (1951-1973)," prepared by the History Office, Mobile Air Materiel Area, Brookley AFB, Alabama, September 1963, p. 4.
43. Ibid, pp. 17-19.
44. It should be noted that until the mid-1970s, the Air Force developed its engines largely separate from its airframes, and there was not the same one-to-one relationship between engines and airframes that is prevalent today.
45. Knaack, *Post-World War II Fighters*, p. 192.
46. The use of the Y (service test) prefix was confusing. The 19 January order used it, but a 16 February 1955 revision to the contract omitted it on the last 13 aircraft. A special contract change notification on 8 March added it back to all 15 aircraft. On 4 November 1955 it was removed again from the last 13 aircraft, leaving only the two YF-105As as service test aircraft.
47. "The F-105: A Chronology," p. 34.
48. Ibid, pp. 53-67.
49. Ibid, pp. 63-65.
50. Knaack, *Post-World War II Fighters*, p. 116.
51. "I" is seldom used in designations to avoid confusion with "1."
52. Knaack, *Post-World War II Fighters*, p. 116.
53. Ibid, p. 329; the "F-107A" designation is confirmed by the flight manual, which is 1F-107A-1, "Interim Flight Handbook for USAF F-107A Series Aircraft," 30 July 1956 (and also 24 January 1958).
54. Ibid, p. 329.
55. "Standard Aircraft Characteristics, McDonnell F-109," in the files at the Air Force Museum.
56. http://www.designation-systems.net/usmilav/missing-mds.html
57. Bell Report 2353-933005, "V/STOL Employing ARL Thrust Augmentation Concepts," Interim Report, Volume 1, 17 May 1968, pp. 27-28.
58. "V/STOL Employing ARL Thrust Augmentation Concepts," pp. 27-28.
59. See, for example, www.ais.org/~schnars/aero/x-planes.htm, home.att.net/~jbaugher1/f109.html, and www.globalsecurity.org/military/systems/aircraft/f-109.htm

Chapter 8 – Century Series Interceptors

1. Frederick A. Alling, "History of the Air Materiel Command, 1 July – 31 December 1956, Volume IV: The F-102A Airplane, 1950-1956."
2. Knaack, *Post-World War II Fighters*, p. 159.
3. "Development of Airborne Armament, 1910–1961," p. III-540. The actual development contract with Hughes was not signed until October 1950.
4. Upton, *Lockheed F-104 Starfighter*, p. 7.
5. Memorandum for the Record, T.L Maloy to Distribution, no subject (but lists milestones for the F-102 and F-106 programs), 1 May 1968; Alling, "The F-102A Airplane, 1950-1956," December 1957.
6. "Development of Airborne Armament, 1910–1961," Volume III, passim and p. IV-591.
7. James W. Cortada, Historical Dictionary of Data Processing, (New York: Greenwood Press, 1987), pp. 333–334; "A Sentry Goes on Guard for America," *Business Machines*, 3 August 1956, pp. 4–5; IBM Press Release, "IBM-Built Computer is Heart of Electronic Air Defense," 30 June 1956; IBM brochure, "The SAGE Computer," undated (but sometime in the late 1950s).
8. http://history.acusd.edu/gen/20th/sage.html, accessed 28 February 2003. Computers before SAGE relied on printed output, not real-time displays.
9. "A Sentry Goes on Guard for America," pp. 4–5; IBM Press Release, "IBM-Built Computer is Heart of Electronic Air Defense," 30 June 1956; IBM brochure, "The SAGE Computer," undated (but sometime in the late 1950s).
10. http://www.mitre.org/pubs/showcase/sage/sage_feature.html, accessed on 28 February 2003.
11. http://history.acusd.edu/gen/20th/sage.html, accessed 28 February 2003.
12. Knaack, *Post-World War II Fighters*, pp. 161-162.
13. Alling, "The F-102A Airplane, 1950-1956."
14. Ibid.
15. Knaack, *Post-World War II Fighters*, pp. 162-163.
16. Ibid, p. 163.
17. Convair Report XC-8-142-19, "Chronology of Significant Events in the YF-102, F-102A, and TF-102A Flight Test Development Program," 1 June 1958.
18. Memorandum for the Record, B. F. Ferguson, subject: Chronological History of the GD/Convair F/TF-102A and F-106A/B Performance Test Programs, no date; "Chronology of Significant Events in the YF-102, F-102A, and TF-102A Flight Test Development Program."
19. Ibid.
20. "Chronology of Significant Events in the YF-102, F-102A, and TF-102A Flight Test Development Program."
21. Knaack, *Post-World War II Fighters*, pp. 163-164.
22. "Chronology of Significant Events in the YF-102, F-102A, and TF-102A Flight Test Development Program."
23. Ibid.
24. "Development of Airborne Armament, 1910–1961," pp. IV-598-600; "Chronology of Significant Events in the YF-102, F-102A, and TF-102A Flight Test Development Program."
25. Alling, "The F-102A Airplane, 1950-1956."

26. Memorandum for the Record, B. F. Ferguson, subject: Chronological History of the GD/Convair F/TF-102A and F-106A/B Performance Test Programs, no date ; Alling, "The F-102A Airplane, 1950-1956."
27. Republic Aviation Report 55RDZ-6387, "System Development Plan for the XF-103 Interceptor."
28. Republic Aviation Report ED-AP57-924, "Detail Design, Tooling, Fabrication, and Ground Testing of Three XF-103 Aircraft," December 1954.
29. Called the "Double Cycle Propulsion System" by Republic.
30. Republic Aviation Report ED-AP57-909, "Descriptive Brochure of the Republic XF-103 Interceptor," 20 June 1952; Republic Aviation Report ED-AP57-921, "XF-103 Descriptive Summary," 15 March 1953.
31. This is different from how the Lockheed Blackbirds handled the problem. The Blackbird partially unloaded the compressor using a bleed-bypass cycle, effectively reducing the compressor exit temperature. The XF-103 completely removed the turbojet engine from the equation.
32. "Descriptive Brochure of the Republic XF-103 Interceptor."
33. Air Force Report 51S-43239-A, "Technical Evaluation – MX-1554, Republic Model AP-57, 27 March 1951, II-19; "Descriptive Brochure of the Republic XF-103 Interceptor," pp. 15-16.
34. "Technical Evaluation - MX-1554, Republic Model AP-57;" "Descriptive Brochure of the Republic XF-103 Interceptor." Things have certainly changed. In 1975, a modified McDonnell Douglas F-15A named Streak Eagle climbed to 65,620 feet (20,000 meters) in 122.94 seconds: a little more than 2 minutes. The airplane eventually went to 98,430 feet (30,000 meters) in 207.80 seconds (3.46 minutes).
35. "Detail Design, Tooling, Fabrication, and Ground Testing of Three XF-103 Aircraft."
36. "Descriptive Brochure of the Republic XF-103 Interceptor." The concept of fly-by-wire had not been conceived of yet, which meant that all of the controls would need to be mechanically or hydraulically linked to the capsule. This would probably have been a maintenance nightmare.
37. This is not completely unreasonable; to withstand the heat, the aluminum aircraft would need to use very thick skins, increasing the weight past that of the relatively thin skins used on the stainless steel aircraft.
38. "Descriptive Brochure of the Republic XF-103 Interceptor."
39. Knaack, Post-World War II Fighters, p. 330.
40. Ibid, p. 329.
41. Ibid, pp. 206-208.
42. Ibid, pp. 208-209.
43. Ibid, p. 209.
44. Memorandum for the Record, B. F. Ferguson, subject: Chronological History of the GD/Convair F/TF-102A and F-106A/B Performance Test Programs, no date.
45. "Development of Airborne Armament, 1910–1961," p. IV-602; Knaack, Post-World War II Fighters, pp. 218-221.

Chapter 9 – Long-Range Interceptors

1. "Development of Airborne Armament, 1910–1961," p. IV-647.
2. Ibid, p. IV-647.
3. Ibid, p. IV-647.
4. Ibid, p. IV-648.
5. Ibid, p. IV-649.
6. The board also included Maj. Gens. James Ferguson, Hugh A. Parker, and Kenneth P. Berquist, Col. J. F. Mocenry, and Dr. C. D. Perkins.
7. "Development of Airborne Armament, 1910–1961," p. IV-651. The radius was further defined in the accompanying documentation, as 350 nautical miles at supersonic speed or 1,000 nautical miles at the optimum subsonic speed.
8. Ibid, p. IV-654.
9. North American Report NA-57-916-9, "Long Range Interceptor, Weapon System 202A, Monthly Status Report for March 1958;" "Development of Airborne Armament, 1910-1961," p. IV-660; interview with Jim Eastham by the authors, 15 May 2004.
10. "Development of Airborne Armament, 1910–1961," p. IV-659.
11. Standard Aircraft Characteristics, "Mockup, North American F-108A," 15 December 1958; North American Report NA-57-916-17, "Long Range Interceptor, Weapon System 202A, Monthly Status Report for November 1958."
12. "Mockup, North American F-108A."
13. "Long Range Interceptor, Weapon System 202A, Monthly Status Report for March 1958;" North American Report NA-57-916-19, "Long Range Interceptor, Weapon System 202A, Monthly Status Report for January 1959;" Knaack, Post-World War II Fighters, p. 330. Various sources, including some Standard Aircraft Characteristics, list thrust reversers on earlier designs, but this was the first engineering model that included them.
14. "Long Range Interceptor, Weapon System 202A, Monthly Status Report for November 1958."
15. "Development of Airborne Armament, 1910–1961," October 1961, p. IV-661; files in the National Archives in College Park showing preliminary I-70 concepts.
16. AFSC Historical Publication 61-51-2, "Development of Airborne Armament, 1910–1961," p. IV-661.
17. Ibid, p. IV-663.
18. Tony R. Landis and Dennis R. Jenkins, Lockheed Blackbirds, Volume 10 in the WarbirdTech Series (North Branch, MN: Specialty Press, 2004), pp. 33-34.
19. Ibid, pp. 35-36.
20. Lyndon B. Johnson, "The President's News Conference of February 29th, 1964," transcript at http://www.presidency.ucsb.edu/ws/print.php?pid=26090
21. Ibid.
22. Landis, Lockheed Blackbirds, p. 41.
23. Ibid, pp. 42-43.
24. Ibid, pp. 44-45.
25. Ibid, pp. 48-50.

Chapter 10 – The End of An Era

1. Joe Baugher's online history located at: http://home.att.net/~jbaugher1/oldseriesfighters.html
2. Ibid.
3. Knaack, Post-World War II Fighters, pp. 264-265.
4. Joe Baugher's online history located at: http://home.att.net/~jbaugher1/oldseriesfighters.html
5. Knaack, Post-World War II Fighters, pp. 265-266.
6. Joe Baugher's online history located at: http://home.att.net/~jbaugher1/oldseriesfighters.html
7. http://www.nationalmuseum.af.mil/factsheet.asp?id=2279
8. Knaack, Post-World War II Fighters, pp. 269-270.
9. Jay Miller, McDonnell RF-4 Variants, (Arlington, TX: Aerofax, 1984), pp. 1-2.
10. Joe Baugher's online history located at: http://home.att.net/~jbaugher1/oldseriesfighters.html
11. Knaack, Post-World War II Fighters, pp. 270-271.
12. http://www.aeromuseum.org/aircraft_mcdonnell.html
13. Tim McGovern, McDonnell F-4E Phantom II, (Arlington, TX: Aerofax, 1987), pp. 2-3.
14. Ibid, pp. 2-3.
15. Miller, McDonnell RF-4 Variants, p. 2.
16. McGovern, McDonnell F-4E Phantom II, pp. 3-5.
17. Knaack, Post-World War II Fighters, pp. 222-226.
18. Ibid, p. 226.
19. Peter E. Davies and Anthony M. Thornborough, F-111 Aardvark, (Wilshire, UK: Crowood, 1997), p. 163. Some sources list these as YF-111Ks.
20. Accident rates provided by the Air Force Safety Center, Kirtland AFB, New Mexico.
21. Joe Baugher's online history located at: http://home.att.net/~jbaugher1/oldseriesfighters.html
22. Frederick A. Johnsen, Northrop F-5/F-20/T-38, Volume 44 in the WarbirdTech Series, (Northop, MN: Specialty Press, 2006), pp. 7-8.
23. Joe Baugher's online history located at: http://home.att.net/~jbaugher1/oldseriesfighters.html
24. Johnsen, Northrop F-5/F-20/T-38, p 8.
25. Ibid, pp. 42-44, -49.
26. Ibid, p 8.
27. http://www.alexstoll.com/AircraftOfTheMonth/8-01.html
28. Johnsen, Northrop F-5/F-20/T-38, p. 62.
29. Knaack, Post-World War II Fighters, pp. 291-292.
30. Johnsen, Northrop F-5/F-20/T-38, pp. 63-72.
31. Knaack, Post-World War II Fighters, p. 292.
32. Johnsen, Northrop F-5/F-20/T-38, pp. 74-75.
33. Ibid, pp. 76-77.
34. Ibid, pp. 74-75.
35. Ibid, pp. 92-93.
36. Ibid, pp. 22-38.
37. Joe Baugher's online history located at: http://home.att.net/~jbaugher1/oldseriesfighters.html
38. Ibid.
39. Johnsen, Northrop F-5/F-20/T-38, pp. 94-95.
40. Ibid, pp. 96-97.
41. Ibid, pp. 97-98; http://www.californiasciencecenter.org/Exhibits/AirAndSpace/AirAndAircraft/AirAndAircraft.php

Chapter 11 – Another Revolution

1. Joe Baugher's online history located at: http://home.att.net/~jbaugher1/oldseriesfighters.html
2. Eric Hehs, "Harry Hillaker – Father of the F-16," Code One Magazine, July 1991.
3. Ibid.
4. Dennis R. Jenkins, McDonnell Douglas F-15 Eagle: Supreme Heavy-Weight Fighter, (Leicester, England: Aerofax, Inc., 1998), pp. 10-11.
5. Ibid, pp. 15-16.

6. Ibid, pp. 17-18.
7. Ibid, pp. 27-28
8. Personal experience by Dennis R. Jenkins.
9. Eric Hehs, "Harry Hillaker – Father of the F-16," Code One Magazine, July 1991.
10. Joe Baugher's online history located at: http://home.att.net/~jbaugher1/oldseriesfighters.html
11. Ibid.
12. Ibid.
13. Ibid.
14. http://home.att.net/~jbaugher/1975.html
15. Eric Hehs, "F-16 Evolution," Code One Magazine, July 1997.
16. Ibid.
17. Ibid.
18. http://www.nasa.gov/centers/dryden/news/FactSheets/FS-023-DFRC.html
19. Laurie A. Marshall, "Boundary-Layer Transition Results From the F-16XL-2 Supersonic Laminar Flow Control Experiment," TM-1999-209013, December 1999.
20. Personal experience, Tony R. Landis, who photographed the taxi test.
21. Jay Miller, McDonnell Douglas F/A-18 Hornet, (Arlington, TX: Aerofax, 1988), p. 4.
22. Brad Elward, Boeing F/A-18 Hornet, Volume 31 in the WarbirdTech Series, (North Branch, MN: Specialty Press, 2001), pp. 14-15.
23. Miller, McDonnell Douglas F/A-18 Hornet, pp. 5-7.
24. Elward, Boeing F/A-18 Hornet, pp. 14-15.

Chapter 12 – The Stealth Generation

1. David C. Aronstein and Albert C. Piccirillo, Have Blue and the F-117A – Evolution of the "Stealth Fighter," American Institute of Aeronautics and Astronautics, Reston, VA, 1997, p 14.
2. There have been reports that XST stood for "Experimental Stealth Testbed," but this is unlikely given the term stealth had not been widely used in relation to aircraft at the time, and would have been too much of a security compromise in any case.
3. Aronstein, HAVE BLUE and the F-117A – Evolution of the "Stealth Fighter."
4. Ibid, p 42.
5. Tony R. Landis and Yancy D. Mailes, F-117 Nighthawk Photo Scrapbook, (North Branch, MN: Specialty Press, 2006).
6. Lockheed Report SP4763F, "Advanced Technology Aircraft (ATA) Budget and Schedule Summary," 27 February 1978.
7. Jon Lake, "Lockheed Martin F-117 – Under the Skin of the Black Jet," AIR International, August 1998.
8. Jay Miller, Lockheed Martin F/A-22 Raptor, (Hinckley, England: Aerofax, 2005), pp. 7-9.
9. Ibid, pp. 9-10.
10. Tony Chong, "The YF-23: A Glorious Moment, A Stunning Defeat," The Leading Edge, July 2004, pp. 4-5.
11. Miller, Lockheed Martin F/A-22 Raptor, pp. 13-14.
12. Ibid, pp. 20-21.
13. Ibid, pp. 19-20.
14. Ibid, pp. 19-20.
15. Ibid, pp. 22-23.
16. Ibid, pp. 31-33.
17. Ibid, pp. 32-33.
18. Joe Baugher's online history located at: http://home.att.net/~jbaugher1/oldseriesfighters.html
19. Ibid.
20. Ibid.
21. Miller, Lockheed Martin F/A-22 Raptor, pp. 42-43.
22. Ibid, pp. 22-23.
23. Tony Chong, "The YF-23: Return to Glory?" The Leading Edge, August 2004, pp. 1-2.
24. Tony Chong, "The YF-23: A Glorious Moment, A Stunning Defeat," The Leading Edge, July 2004, pp. 4-5.
25. Ibid.
26. Miller, Lockheed Martin F/A-22 Raptor, pp. 29-30 and 38-39.
27. Ibid, pp. 29-30 and 38-39.
28. Data from the YF-23 flight logs, courtesy of Tony Chong.
29. Tony Chong, "A Glorious Moment – A Retrospective View of the YF-23," copy supplied by the author.
30. Bill Sweetman, Joint Strike Fighter, (Osceola, WI: MBI, 1999).
31. http://www.jsf.mil/history/his_jsf.htm
32. Ibid.
33. Ibid.
34. http://www.nationalmuseum.af.mil/factsheets/factsheet.8761
35. Ibid.
36. Ibid.
37. Ibid.
38. Ibid

The second McDonnell XF-85 (46-524) in a posed photo from 1 December 1948 in the loading pit at Edwards. The Goblin was the smallest jet fighter ever built for the U.S. Air Force. Note the details of the B-29 trapeze that the nose hook is attached to. (National Archives)

APPENDIX C
INDEX

A-10 (Fairchild-Republic), 233
A-11 (Lockheed), 204
A-12 (Lockheed), 204, 206-207, 231
AAM-A-2 (Hughes), 149
Aerojet, 32, 34-35, 41, 120, 250
AF-12 (Lockheed), 204
AF33, 108, 165, 172, 176, 183, 192, 200
AIM-4 Falcon, 152
AIM-47 Falcon, 152, 202, 205
AIM-54 Phoenix, 153, 214
AIM-7 Sparrow III, 211, 217, 224
AIM-9 Sidewinder, 169, 217, 235
Air Combat Fighter, 222, 224, 228-229
Air Defense Command, 96, 134, 183, 191, 196, 199, 205
Air Force Academy, 171, 226
Air Force Headquarters, 73, 132, 172, 180, 199
Air Force Museum, 18, 51, 71, 78, 85, 116, 121, 128, 213, 236, 238
Air Ministry (British), 19
Air National Guard, 78, 100, 113
Airplane Development Corporation, 245, 250
Allis-Chalmers, 42, 49
Allison, 1, 6-7, 14, 16, 22, 51, 76-77, 93, 98, 102, 107-110, 118, 124, 136-137, 164, 172, 221
Anderson, Neil R., 224
AN/ASG-18, 200, 204
Atwood, Lee, 166, 176
AV-8 (McDonnell Douglas), 249
AVCO Corporation, 245-246, 250
Avion, 32, 41, 245, 247, 249-250

B-29 (Boeing), 67, 80-81, 83-85, 96, 129, 131
B-35 (Northrop), 80-81, 131
B-36 (Consolidated), 34, 71-72, 80-81, 83-85, 96, 131-132, 164
B-45 (North American), 104, 144
B-47 (Boeing), 74, 132, 248
B-52 (Boeing), 132, 149, 157, 164
B-58 (Convair), 157, 199, 202, 236
B-70 (North American), 149, 200, 202
Baker, J. Robert, 91, 177
Bakersfield Municipal Airport, 49-50, 78
Barkley, Herman D., 81
Barnes, David, 219
Beaird, Henry G., 76, 174
Beatle, LT Ralph H., 29
Beesley, Jon, 235
Bell Aircraft, 22, 26-27, 60, 129, 180, 245-246
Bell, Lawrence D., 22, 25, 28, 244-245
Bellinger, Carl, 74, 117-118
Bendix Corporation, 149, 183, 188, 247
Boeing, 14, 65, 71, 74, 96, 104, 117, 129, 131, 148, 153, 155, 157-158, 164, 176, 178-180, 199-200, 222-223, 229-230, 232, 234-235, 240, 246-250
Boeing, William E., 246, 250
Bomarc, 148, 153-155, 180, 184
Borsodi, Frederick, 50
Bowman, R. G., 116
Boyd, Albert, 51, 199
Boyd, John, 222
Bretcher, Fred C., 102
British Air Commission, 22, 46
British Science Museum, 19
Buick Division, 74
Burcham, Milo, 47, 50

Burrows, Irving W., 223
Burstein, Adolph, 122

C-130 (Lockheed), 248
Canadair, 92, 247
Cape Canaveral, 148, 153-155
Capp, Al, 45
Carroll, Franklin O., 44
CCV, 211, 213, 224
Century Series, 147, 157-181, 183-197, 209, 214
Cessna Aircraft, 247
Chance Vought, 246, 248, 250
Chidlaw, Benjamin W., 166
Chouteau, Hank, 215-216, 218, 228
Chrysler, 136
Chuck Yeager, 62, 118, 122, 127, 129, 158
CIA, 204, 206-207, 231
CIM-10 (Boeing), 155
Coleman, R. V., 103
Commonwealth Aircraft Corporation, 92
Consolidated, 52, 95, 124, 245-246, 250; See also Convair
Consolidated-Vultee, 52, 115, 122, 131, 245-247, 250; See also Convair
Continental, 1, 6, 14, 17, 24, 183, 202

Convair, 34, 52-53, 55, 58-59, 71-72, 76, 80, 95, 107, 114-116, 121-126, 128, 131-132, 138, 150-151, 155, 157-159, 164, 166, 172, 183-186, 188-189, 191-192, 197, 199, 202, 209-210, 236, 246-247
Cook, Orval R., 158
Cook-Craigie, 158, 160, 164, 172-173, 185, 191, 214, 222
Cooney, James, 206
Cornell, Darrell, 217, 219
Cox Muni Airport, 128
Craigie, Laurence C., 28-29, 158
Crosby, Harry, 12, 32, 41
Crossfield, A. Scott, 85, 128, 163, 178
Culver City, 149, 200
Curtis, Billy A., 207
Curtiss, 1, 4, 6-7, 9, 17, 52, 80-81, 86, 95-98, 100-102, 137, 245-247
Curtiss-Wright, 6-7, 73, 76, 95-97, 101, 116-117, 120, 131, 246-247
CW24-B, 6

Daniel, Walter, 206
DARPA, 231, 233, 240-241
Davis, David R., 247
Davis, Frank W., 4, 52-53, 122
Dayton-Wright, 246
De Seversky, Alexander P., 250
Department of Defense, 210-211, 214-215, 221, 240, 249

The first F-15A (71-0280) during its maiden flight on 27 July 1972. Although the aircraft was rolled-out wearing an all air-superiority blue paint scheme, orange was added prior to the first flight. Most of the Category I F-15s wore similar paint schemes. Note the early unclipped wingtips and the horizontal stabilizer without the leading edge dogtooth. (AFFTC History Office Collection)

Detroit Aircraft Company, 248
Dobronski, Joe, 212
Douglas, 58, 76, 78, 83, 95-96, 115, 131, 157-158, 163, 173, 183, 199, 209, 217, 219-224, 226-228, 231, 233-234, 237, 240, 246-249
Douglas, Donald, 247, 249
Dyson, Ken, 232-233

Eastham, Jim, 204, 206
Eaton, George, 211
Echols, Oliver P., 3, 14, 44
Eddy, Edwin, 116
Edholm, Robert M., 133
Edwards AFB, 4, 51, 176-177, 225-226, 230, 239
Eglin AFB, 152, 155, 171
Elliott, Everett E., 16-17
Emory, Frank, 163

F-100 (North American), 91, 157-159, 160-161, 163-164, 166, 176, 178, 215
F-100B (North American), 163, 176
F-100BI (North American), 176
F-100I (North American), 176
F-101 (McDonnell), 132, 134-135, 137, 157-159, 164-165, 166, 180, 191, 200
F-102 (Convair), 107, 115, 121, 128, 150-152, 155, 157-159, 166, 172, 183-186, 188-189, 191-192, 197, 199-200, 209
F-103 (Republic), 115, 150, 192, 199
F-104 (Lockheed), 110, 113, 157-158, 166-167, 169-171, 183, 199, 215, 217, 222, 224, 231, 235
F-105 (Republic), 67, 73, 76, 156-158, 172-177, 179, 194, 209-210
F-106 (Convair),107, 157-158, 172, 184-185, 189, 191, 197, 199, 209-210
F-107 (North American), 156-157, 163, 166, 176-179
F-108 (North American), 152-153, 180, 200, 202-204
F-109 (McDonnell, Bell), 180
F-110 (McDonnell), 209-212
F-111 (General Dynamics), 209, 214, 221-222, 226, 234-235
F-117 (Lockheed), 232-233, 235
F-12 (Lockheed), 206-207
F-14 (Grumman), 152-153, 221-222
F-15 (McDonnell Douglas), 158, 209, 219-224, 226-228, 233, 236-237, 249
F-16 (Lockheed Martin),14, 158, 176, 209, 218-222, 224, 226, 229, 233-235
F-19, 219
F-20 (Northrop), 217-219, 239
F-22 (Lockheed Martin), 160, 231
F-24, 240
F-4 (McDonnell Douglas), 157, 210-213, 217, 222-223
F-5 (Northrop), 215-219, 239
F-80 (Lockheed), 51, 108, 130, 189
F-84 (Republic), 64, 68, 70-74, 78, 91, 93, 120, 143, 147, 164, 172, 196
F-86 (North American), 65, 70, 89-93, 96, 100-101, 110, 113, 118, 131-132, 138, 144-145, 147, 151, 160, 164, 176, 188-189
F-88 (McDonnell), 132, 134, 136-137, 143, 147, 164
F-89 (Northrop), 90, 96, 105-107, 110-111, 149-152, 164, 183, 191
F-90 (Lockheed), 130, 143, 164
F-91 (Republic), 117, 120-121, 164
F-93 (North American), 132, 145, 164
F-94 (Lockheed), 50-51, 90, 96, 108-113, 164
F-95 (North American), 90-91
F-96 (Republic), 91, 147
F-97 (Lockheed), 91, 113
F-98 (Hughes), 150, 152
F-99 (Boeing), 153
F-X, 221-223
F/A-18 (McDonnell Douglas), 222, 228-229, 234, 237, 249
F100 (Pratt & Whitney), 221-222, 224, 228, 234
F101 (General Electric), 222, 224
F110 (General Electric), 221-222, 226, 234
F2H (McDonnell), 136
F4H (McDonnell), 209-210
F9C (Curtiss), 81-82
FAI (Fédération Aéronautique Internationale), 163, 206
Fairchild, 71, 117, 223, 231, 245, 249-250
Farver, Lyle, 14
Fausel, Robert W., 9
Fay, Charles, 63
FICON, 71-72, 74, 85
Fitzgerald, Ray, 71
Flesh, Bud, 6, 8, 132, 164
Flight Research Center, 207, 227, 238
Fluid Tech, Inc., 143
Ford, President Gerald R., 223
Fritz, John M., 217
FSQ-7, 184
Fulkerson, Glenn, 110, 112

Gallaudet Aircraft, 246
GAPA, 153
GAR-1, 118, 148, 152, 188, 191, 194, 196
GAR-2, 152
GAR-3, 152
GAR-8, 169
GAR-9, 152-153, 196, 200, 202-204, 206
General Dynamics, 209, 214, 218-219, 222-226, 231, 234-235, 240, 246-249
General Electric, 4, 10, 14, 16, 19-23, 25-26, 28-29, 31, 42, 49-50, 52, 60-61, 64, 78, 86, 89-91, 93, 96-97, 102, 110, 113, 118, 120, 123, 138, 149, 157, 160, 165-166, 170, 172, 180, 183, 200, 204, 209, 211, 215-219, 221-222, 224, 226, 234, 240
General Motors, 74, 136, 246, 248
George AFB, 163
Glascow, William C., 8-9
Good, Clyde E., 71
Goodyear, 95, 131, 136
Goszkowicz, Brian, 243
Goudey, J. Ray, 168
Grand Forks AFB, 223
Gray Ghost, 45, 49, 237
Gray, J. Harvey, 6, 9
Great Engine War, 222, 234
Greene, Laurence P., 86
Griffith, Alan, 19
Groom Lake, 204-205, 232-233
Gross, Robert, 42, 248
Grumman, 77, 110, 153, 199, 221-223, 230-231, 234, 238, 247-250

H-2470 (Lycoming), 4, 17
H-2600 (Pratt & Whitney), 1-2, 10, 14
Hamilton Standard Division, 250
Harper Dry Lake, 32
Harrigan, W. P., 100
Have Blue, 231-233
He-178, 19-20
Heinkel, Ernst, 20
Hibbard, Hall, 42
Hillaker, Harry, 226
Holloman AFB, 153, 211
Horton, Victor W., 207
Hughes Aircraft, 107, 149, 152, 183, 231, 247-248

I-14 (General Electric), 29
I-1430 (Continental), 1, 6, 16-17
I-16 (General Electric), 22-23, 28-29, 31, 61
I-20 (General Electric), 16
I-40 (General Electric), 23, 49, 52-53, 55, 60-61, 93, 97, 123
I-70 (North American), 202
I-A (General Electric), 21-23, 25-26, 28-29, 42
IBM, 184, 209
IM-99, 153, 155, 180
Irwin, Walter W., 170

J31 (General Electric), 21-23, 42
J33 (Allison), 23, 50, 52, 93, 97-99, 101, 108-109, 124
J34 (Westinghouse), 50, 93, 97, 99-100, 130, 133-136, 141, 143
J35 (Allison), 67, 73, 93, 102-103
J36 (Allis-Chalmers), 42, 49
J40 (Westinghouse), 185
J47 (General Electric), 78, 89, 93, 116, 118, 120, 144, 157, 160
J48 (Pratt & Whitney), 110-113, 144
J57 (Pratt & Whitney), 157-158, 160-161, 164, 172, 185-186, 209
J58 (Pratt & Whitney), 204
J65 (Wright), 73-74, 166, 247
J67 (Wright), 156, 185-186, 192, 194, 197, 247
J71 (Allison), 107, 157, 164, 172
J73 (General Electric), 78-79, 91, 172
J75 (Pratt & Whitney), 157, 172, 174, 209
J79 (General Electric), 78, 157, 165-166, 168-170, 200, 209, 211, 226
J93 (General Electric), 204, 209
Johnson, Howard C., 170
Johnson, Clarence L. "Kelly," 18, 42, 44-46, 50, 108, 138-139, 141, 158, 166, 204, 231, 248
Johnson, Richard L., 188, 190, 197, 214
JSF, 240-241
JT3 (Pratt & Whitney), 157; *see also* J57
JT4 (Pratt & Whitney), 157; *see also* J75

Kammerer, Mike, 232
Kartveli, Alexander, 70, 86, 115-117, 120, 133, 158, 172, 184, 192, 194-195, 250
KC-135 (Boeing), 157, 164
Keirn, Donald J., 29
Kennedy, John F., 215
Kenny, George C., 3

Keute, Les, 233
Knox, Fred, 240

L-1000 (Lockheed), xi, 23, 131, 138, 249
L-133 (Lockheed), 6, 42
Lambert Field, 17, 135, 137
Langley AFB, 137, 210
Langley Research Center, 226, 237
Lawson, Clem, 90
Layton, Ronald J., 207
Leach, Everett W., 7
LeVier, Tony, 45, 49-50, 110-112, 138-139, 141, 168
Lien, William A., 65
Lindbergh Field, 188
Lindbergh, Charles, 245
Ling-Temco-Vought, 217, 222, 246, 248
Lippisch, Dr. Alexander, 123
Little, Robert C., 164-165
Lockheed Martin, 18, 42, 44-46, 72, 94, 108-109, 111, 130, 138-139, 141-142, 156, 160, 166-168, 170, 205-206, 218, 221, 232-233, 235-236, 240, 242-243, 247-249
Los Angeles Airport, 160, 178
Luftwaffe, 19-20, 50, 80, 217
Luke AFB, 223
Lycoming, 3-4, 245, 250

Mamlock, Max, 248
March AFB, 89
Martin Marietta Corporation, 247-249
Martin, Glenn, 14, 96-97, 247, 249
Martin, Harry G., 67
McDonnell, 14, 16-18, 24, 80-81, 83, 85-86, 118, 129-138, 143, 157-159, 164-166, 180, 191, 199, 209-213, 215, 217, 219-224, 226-227, 231, 233-234, 237, 240, 246-249
McDonnell Douglas, 158, 209, 217, 219-224, 226-227, 231, 233-234, 237, 240, 246-249
McDonnell, James S. Jr, 249
McGuire AFB, 184
McKinney, James A., 226
McNarney, General Joseph T., 132
Menasco, xi, 249
Metz, Paul, 237-238
MiG-21, 222
MiG-23, 222
MiG-25, 206, 222-223
Miller, Lee, 100
Moore, Paul, 250
Morgenfeld, Tom, 235-236
Morris, Jack D., 171
Morris, Lt. Frank G., 7, 61
Morris, Raymond, 91
Moss, Sanford A., 19, 21
Myers, John, 11, 32

NACA, 2, 6-7, 12, 33, 41, 47, 50, 68, 74, 81-83, 85, 114-115, 118, 120, 122, 124, 127-128, 136-137, 144-147, 161, 163, 171, 174, 178, 182, 185-186, 188-190
NASA, 6, 33, 68, 73-74, 128, 161, 178, 189, 204, 206-207, 226-228, 237-238, 240
National Air Museum, 8, 12, 31, 45
National Air Show, 71, 128
NATO, 74, 91, 171, 215, 224
Navy, 3-4, 6, 19, 24, 29-30, 35, 45-46, 76-77, 80-81, 86, 90, 95-97, 121, 124, 131-132, 134-136, 153, 157, 180, 183, 209-211, 214, 217-218, 221-222, 228, 240-241, 243
Northrop, 1, 10-13, 32-36, 38, 41, 80, 90, 94-96, 101-106, 110-111, 115, 131, 150-152, 164, 166, 183, 191, 199, 215, 217-220, 222-223, 228, 230-232, 234-235, 237-240, 244-245, 247-250
Northrop, Jack, 32, 102, 245, 247-249
Norton AFB, 85, 207

Odlum, Floyd B., 246
Oestricher, Phil, 224
Olds, Robin, 200
Oldsmobile Division, 74

P-38 (Lockheed), 1, 32, 44
P-39 (Bell), 22
P-40 (Curtiss), 1
P-47 (Republic),64, 80
P-51 (North American), 55, 61, 80, 86, 122
P-59A (Bell), 31, 42
P-80 (Lockheed), 18, 45, 50-51, 61-67, 86-87, 102, 108-112, 124, 131
P-82 (North American), 87, 96
P-84 (Republic), 67-68, 86, 102, 116, 131

P-85 (McDonnell), 82
P-86 (North American), 89, 102, 131, 144-145
Pacific Aero Products, 246
Pacific Air Transport, 246
Pacific Missile Range, 235
Packard Commission, 234
Palmer, Don, 44, 138
Pappas, Costas E., 116
Park, Bill, 168, 205, 232
Pavlecka, Vladimir, 10
Perkins, Kendall, 132
Phillips, William, 163
Power, General Thomas S., 131
Pratt & Whitney, 2, 10, 14, 22, 24-25, 52, 110, 144, 157-158, 160-161, 164, 172-174, 176, 185, 204, 209, 221-222, 226, 231, 234, 236, 240-241, 246, 250
Price, George E., 152
Price, Nathan C., xi, 42
Project Quick Draw, 152
Project RAND, 247
Pulver, Dick, 45
Purifoy, Dana D., 227
Putt, Donald L., 166

QB-17 (Boeing), 150-152, 155

R-2160 (Wright), 4, 14, 17
R-2800 (Pratt & Whitney), 10, 12-13, 24-25, 52
R-40C (Request for Data), 1, 6, 10, 14, 24
Ralston, William P., 44, 138, 166
Rankin, Werner, 116
Reaction Motors Incorporated, 116
Reagan, President Ronald, 219
Rentschler, Fred, 250
Republic, 64, 74, 131, 192, 250
Reynolds, Tom, 243
RF-101 (McDonnell), 211
RF-110 (McDonnell), 210-211
RF-4B (McDonnell), 211
RF-84F (Republic), 73-74, 76, 85, 133, 165, 172-173, 175
Rice, Raymond, 160
Rich, Ben, 45
Riddle, John Paul, 245
Roach Lake, 12
Rogers Dry Lake, 28, 48
Rolls-Royce, 16, 50, 52, 58-59, 109-110, 144, 157, 241
Roosevelt, President Franklin D., 10, 30
Rosenmeyer, Ed, 212
Ross, William S., 211
Roth, Rusty, 79, 118, 173
Royal Air Force, 19, 214
Royal Aircraft Establishment, 19
Royal Navy, 19, 241
Ryan Aeronautical, 149, 250

SAGE (Semi-Automatic Ground Environment), 91, 153, 155, 184, 197
Sandberg, Jim, 237
Schmued, Edgar, 86, 160
Schoch, Edwin F., 85
Schwendler, William, 247
Scott, Russell J., 219
Shannon, Sam, 125-126
Shawnee Municipal Airport, 66
Shick, Ralph H., 122
Skonk Works, 45
Skunk Works, 18, 43, 46, 51, 139, 205, 231, 235, 243
Smith, Paul B., 17
Smithsonian Institution, 48, 242
Sprey, Pierre M., 222
SR-71 (Lockheed), 206-207, 227
Stanley, Robert M., 25, 28
Stephens, Robert, 206
Sternfield, Leonard, 163
Streak Eagle, 220, 223
Strike Eagle, 223, 226
Stucky, Mark P., 227
Sweeney, Joe, 242
Swofford, Ralph P. Jr., 29, 46

T-131 (rocket), 95, 118, 121
T-171 (cannon), 110, 113, 166-167, 169
T-31 (General Electric), 95-96, 103, 105
T-33 (Lockheed), 51, 109
T-38 (Northrop), 78, 215, 218
Thigpen, David J., 224

Thomas, Dick, 218
Thompson, D. J., 237-238
Torres, Peter A., 242
Trapnell, Frederick M., 29
Truman, President Harry S., 132
Tucker, Charles, 103
Tulsa Municipal Airport, 100
Turkey, 171, 211, 218
Turton, Arthur, 103

University of Göttingen, 20
USS *Akron*, 80
USS *Macon*, 80
USS *Titania*, 124

War Department, 17, 24-25
Warner, Noel, 206
Wayne, John, 103
Welch, George S., 90, 161, 163
Whitcomb, Richard, 144, 174, 189
Whittle, Frank, 19-23, 26, 28, 31
Wild Weasel, 175, 226
Wolf, Alex, 226
Woods, Robert J., 22, 25, 28, 245
Woolams, Jack, 60
Wright-Patterson AFB, 18, 78, 101, 121, 166, 197, 224
WS-105L, 165
WS-201A, 183, 192
WS-204A, 192
WS-303A, 166
WS-306A, 172
WS-306L, 172-173

X-1 (Bell), 117, 122, 129, 158
X-13 (Ryan), 180
X-32 (Boeing), 230, 240-241
X-33 (Lockheed), 240
X-35 (Lockheed Martin), 240, 242-243
XA-43 (Curtiss), 95-97, 101
XB-35 (Northrop), 10, 12, 102
XB-36 (Convair), 34
XB-46 (Convair), 58
XB-70 (North American), 195, 198, 200, 204
XC-113 (Curtiss), 52
XCALR-200 (Aerojet), 32
XF-100 (North American), 160
XF-101 (McDonnell), 164
XF-103 (Republic), 121, 158, 182, 184, 192-196
XF-104 (Lockheed), 110, 113, 149, 156, 159, 166-171
XF-107 (North American), 177
XF-108 (North American), 198, 200, 202
XF-109 (McDonnell; Bell), 180
XF-110 (McDonnell), 210
XF-111 (General Dynamics), 214
XF-117 (Lockheed), 232
XF-14 (Lockheed), 48, 50-51
XF-15 (McDonnell Douglas), 223
XF-24, 240
XF-25, 240
XF-5 (Northrop), 215, 219
XF-84F (Republic), 147
XF-84H (Republic), 73, 76-79, 137, 164
XF-85 (McDonnell), 18, 83, 85, 93, 129, 131
XF-86 (North American), 89, 93
XF-87 (Curtiss), 96-97, 101-102
XF-88 (McDonnell), 118, 130, 132-137, 143, 164
XF-89 (Northrop), 96, 102-103, 105
XF-90 (Lockheed), 50, 130, 132, 136, 138-139, 141-143
XF-91 (Republic), 69, 114-121, 166
XF-92 (Convair), 114, 122, 124-128, 185-186
XF-98 (Hughes), 149-152, 192, 194
XF-99 (Boeing), 153-154
XF119 (Pratt & Whitney), 234
XF2H (McDonnell), 86, 132
XF3D (Douglas), 95-96, 102
XF4D (Douglas), 163
XFH (McDonnell), 86
XFJ (North American), 86-87
XGAR-1 (Hughes), 152
XH-2470 (Lycoming), 3-4
XI-1430 Continental), 14, 24
XIM-99 (Boeing), 153, 155
XJ30 (Westinghouse), 35-36, 122
XJ31 (General Electric), 28-29
XJ33 (Allison), 49, 52, 60-61, 97, 123
XJ34 (Westinghouse), 81-82, 97, 131-132, 138-139, 141

XJ35 (General Electric), 64, 86, 96, 102, 131
XJ37 (Lockheed),131, 249
XJ39 (General Electric), 16
XLR11 (Reaction Motors), 117-119, 129
XLR25 (Aerojet), 116-117
XP-52 (Bell), 1, 24
XP-54 (Vultee), 2, 5, 17
XP-55 (Curtiss), 1, 6-9, 86
XP-56 (Northrop), 1, 10-13, 32, 34, 39
XP-58 (Lockheed), 3
XP-59 (Bell), 1, 24-25
XP-59A (Bell), 21, 24-31, 42, 46, 48, 60-61, 244
XP-59B (Bell), 31
XP-67 (McDonnell), 14-17, 24
XP-68 (Vultee), 4, 17
XP-79 (Northrop), 32, 34-36, 39, 41, 102, 245
XP-79B (Northrop), 32, 34, 36-41, 95
XP-80 (Lockheed), 18, 31, 42-51, 61, 93, 109, 138-139
XP-80R (Lockheed), 51
XP-81 (Convair), 52-60, 93, 124
XP-83 (Bell), 60-63, 93
XP-84 (Republic), 64-67, 79, 86, 115
XP-85 (McDonnell), 80-85, 132
XP-86 (North American), 86-89
XP-87 (Curtiss), 96-102
XP-88 (McDonnell), 96, 131-133
XP-89 (Northrop), 94, 96, 101-102, 104-107
XP-90 (Lockheed), 131, 138-139
XP-91 (Republic), 115-117, 131, 133
XP-92 (Convair), 115-117, 122-123, 128, 138
XP-92A (Convair), 123-124
XRF-87C (Curtiss), 101
XRJ55 (Wright), 192, 194
XRP-87 (Curtiss), 97-98
XS-1 (Bell), 129
XST (Northrop), 231-232
XT31 (General Electric), 52
XT38 (Allison), 76, 136-137

Yeager, Charles E., 126
YF-100 (North American), 160-163
YF-101 (McDonnell), 164
YF-102 (Convair), 128, 182, 185-191
YF-104 (Lockheed), 167-171
YF-105 (Republic), 159, 172-175
YF-106C (Convair), 197
YF-111 (General Dynamics), 214
YF-12A (Lockheed), 152-153, 198, 202-207, 234
YF-12C, 206-207
YF-15 (McDonnell), 223
YF-16 (General Dynamics), 222, 224-226, 228-229, 234
YF-16/CCV, 224
YF-17 (Northrop), 220, 222, 224, 226, 228-229, 234, 236, 239
YF-22 (Lockheed), 158, 234-238
YF-23 (Northrop), 234-235, 237-239
YF-5 (Northrop), 215-216, 218
YF-84 (Republic), 70-75, 147
YF-86C (North American), 132
YF-86D (North American), 90-91, 113, 144, 160
YF-86K (North American), 91
YF-89 Northrop), 103, 105-107
YF-93 (North American), 89, 132, 136, 143-147
YF-94 (Lockheed), 94, 108-113
YF-96 (Republic), 70-71, 147
YF-97 (Lockheed), 111
YF-98 (Hughes), 151-152
YF-99 (Boeing), 153
YFM-1 (Bell), 22
YGAR-1 (Hughes), 152
YIM-99 (Boeing), 153, 155
YP-59A (Bell), 25, 28-31
YP-80A (Lockheed), 47-50
YP-81 (Convair), 52, 59
YP-86 (North American), 87, 89
YP-86C (North American), 131
YRF-101 (McDonnell), 165
YRF-105 (Republic), 172
YRF-4 (McDonnell Douglas), 211, 213
YRF-84 (Republic), 71-72, 74-75, 79, 120

(National Archives)

THE END